Palgrave Studies in the History of the Media

Series Editors
Bill Bell
Cardiff University
Cardiff, UK

Chandrika Kaul
University of St Andrews
St Andrews, UK

Alexander S. Wilkinson
University College Dublin
Dublin, Ireland

Palgrave Studies in the History of the Media publishes original, high quality research into the cultures of communication from the middle ages to the present day. The series explores the variety of subjects and disciplinary approaches that characterize this vibrant field of enquiry. The series will help shape current interpretations not only of the media, in all its forms, but also of the powerful relationship between the media and politics, society, and the economy.

Advisory Board:
Professor Peter Burke (Emmanuel College, Cambridge)
Professor Nicholas Cull (University of Southern California)
Professor Bridget Griffen-Foley (Macquarie University)
Professor Monica Juneja (Heidelberg University)
Professor Tom O'Malley (Aberystwyth University)

More information about this series at
http://www.palgrave.com/gp/series/14578

Catherine Dewhirst • Richard Scully
Editors

Voices of Challenge in Australia's Migrant and Minority Press

palgrave
macmillan

Editors
Catherine Dewhirst
University of Southern Queensland
Toowoomba, QLD, Australia

Richard Scully
University of New England
Armidale, NSW, Australia

ISSN 2634-6575   ISSN 2634-6583   (electronic)
Palgrave Studies in the History of the Media
ISBN 978-3-030-67329-1   ISBN 978-3-030-67330-7   (eBook)
https://doi.org/10.1007/978-3-030-67330-7

This Palgrave Macmillan imprint is published by the registered company Springer Nature Switzerland AG.
The registered company address is: Gewerbestrasse 11, 6330 Cham, Switzerland

PREFACE

Like its counterpart volume (*The Transnational Voices of Australia's Migrant and Minority Press*), this book is the result of an interdisciplinary conference held at the University of Southern Queensland, Toowoomba, in 2017: "Voices of the Australian Migrant and Minority Press: Intercultural, Transnational and Diasporic Contexts". The aim of the conference was to share the most recent research on minority-community print culture in Australia, 50 years on from its foundation as a field of study through the seminal publication of Miriam Gilson and Jerzy Zubrzycki's *The Foreign-Language Press in Australia, 1848–1964*. In drawing together a diversity of historical and extant community newspapers, printed between the 1840s and 1960s—from the Albanian community to the Welsh and others largely marginalised from history—their work is recognised by scholars and students working on Australia's migrant and minority cultures as central to the historiography of minority communities. The publications and presses which Gilson and Zubrzycki identified, as well as the subsequent rediscovery of countless other newspapers and periodicals, reveal a burgeoning resource for multi- and cross-disciplinary collaborations today. By implication, the conference presenters engaged with specific community newspapers—created by Indigenous Australian, migrant and other minority group efforts—for exploring the implications of their transnational and global networks and examining questions about community-building, inter-communal relations and the national ideal.

The overall aim of this book and its companion is to present a concerted picture of the dynamism of minority community newspapers and other news periodicals from a historical perspective. While our first volume dealt with the transnational connections so evident in much of Australia's migrant and minority press—defying cultural stereotypes to address community needs and to assert a presence in the public eye—this one extends the discussion on the way that the periodical press unsettled and challenged the predominant narratives of colonial, national and cultural homogeneity. Again, using the lens of "voices" as our analytical frame, the chapters in this collection bring to light the predominantly concealed activities, experiences and narratives of minority groups from colonial and national history. They not only build on knowledge about the pluralism of Australia's cultural, social and political past but also contribute a more inclusive dimension addressing the lesser-known interchanges within and beyond local communities. Here we bring together the latest scholarship on how such print enterprises have responded to the pressures of minority status and shaped their communities' place and sense of wellbeing within an often-hostile landscape. As well as focusing on their individual case-studies, each chapter asks the question: what do the business initiatives of these presses—launched by individuals on the periphery of mainstream society—tell us about the influence and limitations of imperial and transnational connections, intercultural relations and the national narrative, and how these were contested by a register of still small yet influential "voices" of multicultural Australia?

We wish to thank our respective universities, the School of Humanities and Communication at the University of Southern Queensland, and the School of Humanities, Arts and Social Sciences at the University of New England, without whose support this book would not have been possible. We express sincere thanks to the Ian Potter Foundation for a grant funding the original conference and the University of Southern Queensland's Office of Research for further funding, both of which supported the conference keynote speakers, Professor Simon J. Potter and Associate Professor Richard Scully, respectively. We also acknowledge the generous support of the National Archives of Australia for the use of several images in promoting the conference, Dr Jayne Persian and Dr Mark Emmerson, and John Zubrzycki for contributing to the conference opening with his and his family's memories of his father's vision, research and achievements, over Australia's multicultural era. Further we are grateful for the work and support of Emily Russell, Joseph Johnson, Ruby Panigrahi, Hemalatha Arumugam and G. Nirmal Kumar and teams, and the Series Editors. Thanks are also due to the rights-holders of the various images used herein, as we often forget how much of a *visual* (not merely textual) experience connecting with the press has been, historically.

To our families and friends—especially Maureen O'Hara, Raphaela Dewhirst, Helena Menih, Patrick and Arthur Scully—we also owe a great debt of gratitude.

Toowoomba, QLD, Australia   Catherine Dewhirst
Armidale, NSW, Australia   Richard Scully

CONTENTS

NOTES ON CONTRIBUTORS

Angela A. Alessi completed a Bachelor of Arts with First Class Honours in 2016 at the University of Adelaide, Australia. Her Honours dissertation examined the development of the Italian migrant community in Adelaide, South Australia, after the Second World War. She recently completed a Masters of Teaching at the University of Adelaide in 2018, and now works within the University to facilitate quality assurance and enhancement processes.

Simone Battiston is Senior Lecturer in History and Politics at the Swinburne University of Technology, Australia. His research examines different aspects of postwar Italian emigration, with a particular attention to the Australian experience: external voting behaviour, history and memory of migrant radicals, media history and history of workers and entrepreneurs in the building and construction workers, especially terrazzo and mosaic artisans. His publications include the monograph, *Immigrants Turned Activists* (2012) and the edited books *Il Globo* (with Bruno Mascitelli, Connon Court Publishing, 2009) and *Autopsia di un diritto politico* (with Stefano Luconi, Accademia University Press, 2018).

Alexis Bergantz is Lecturer in Global and Language Studies at RMIT University, Australia. He completed his PhD from the Australian National University in 2016, for which he was awarded the John Molony Prize for best thesis in History, and the ANU J. G. Crawford Prize for Academic Excellence. His research focuses on the French Pacific, New Caledonia and Franco-Australian history. His first book, *French Connection: Australia's Cosmopolitan Ambitions*, was published by NewSouth in 2021.

Andrew G. Bonnell is Associate Professor of History at University of Queensland, Australia. His publications include *The People's Stage in Imperial Germany: Social Democracy and Culture, 1890–1914* (2005), *Shylock in Germany: Antisemitism and the German Theatre from the Enlightenment to the Nazis* (2008) and *Red Banners, Books and Beer Mugs. The Mental World of German Social Democrats, 1863–1914* (2021).

John Budarick is a senior lecturer in the Department of Media at the University of Adelaide, Australia. He is a media sociologist who works in the areas of journalism, ethnic media, race, migration and theory. He is the author of *Ethnic Media and Democracy: From Liberalism to Agonism*, published by Palgrave Macmillan. His research has appeared in journals such as *Communication Theory, Media, Culture and Society* and the *International Journal of Communication*.

Caryn Coatney is Lecturer in Journalism at the University of Southern Queensland, Australia, and has received global awards for her research on Australian World War II Prime Minister John Curtin's secret media talks with journalists. She holds a PhD in Journalism and History, an MA in Research/Coursework—Journalism and a BA in Double Honours, Literature and History; her latest book is *John Curtin: How He Won Over the Media*. Coatney has been an investigative news journalist in Australia and internationally and worked in many fields of communication since 1990. She completed a Fellowship at the Australian Prime Ministers Centre in the Museum of Australian Democracy (2011), Old Parliament House, Canberra.

Catherine Dewhirst is Senior Lecturer in History at the University of Southern Queensland, Australia. Her publications on Italian migrant history appear in the *Australian Journal of Politics and History, Journal of Imperial and Commonwealth History, Studi Emigrazione, Queensland History Journal, Spunti e Ricerche* and *Journal of Australian Studies*. She is co-editor (with Richard Scully) of *The Transnational Voices of Australia's Migrant and Minority Press* (Palgrave Macmillan, 2020).

Jeremy Fisher is Adjunct Senior Lecturer in Writing at the University of New England, Australia, and formerly Executive Director of the Australian Society of Authors. He was awarded a Medal in the Order of Australia (OAM) in 2017 for services to literature, education and professional organisations. In addition to many papers on writing and publishing in Australia, his publications include *Perfect Timing* (1993), a children's novel, since translated into Vietnamese, *Music from Another Country* (2009), *How to Tell Your Father to Drop Dead* (2013), *The Dirty Little Dog* (2015) and *Faith Hope and Stubborn Pride* (2016).

Mei-fen Kuo is a lecturer in the Department of Media, Communications, Creative Arts, Language and Literature at the Macquarie University, Australia, where she teaches and researches in the area of modern Chinese history with a focus on diaspora identity and transnational mobility. Her books include *Making Chinese Australia: Urban Elites, Newspapers, and the Formation of Chinese Australian Identity, 1892–1912* (2013) and *Unlocking the History of the Australasian Kuo Min Tang 1911–2013* (2013) with Judith Brett.

Bruno Mascitelli is an Adjunct Professor at Swinburne University of Technology, based in Melbourne. He was previously a Jean Monnet Chair and previously taught European Studies at Swinburne University. He was president of the European Studies Association and has undertaken research in European and Italian Studies. He has edited or authored 24 books and continues to take an interest in European affairs today. His latest book is entitled *Italy and the European Union: A Rollercoaster Journey*, published in 2021.

Lara Palombo teaches cultural studies at Macquarie University, Australia, and her work has been published in the *Journal of Global Indigeneity*, *Globalization*, *Journal of Intercultural Studies* and *Continuum*. Her current research is on settler colonialism and intersectional penal violence, carceral mechanisms and abolitionist feminist politics. This work expands her doctoral research on racial camps in Australia.

Richard Scully is Associate Professor in Modern History at the University of New England, Australia. He is the author of *Eminent Victorian Cartoonists* (3 volumes, London, 2018) and *British Images of Germany: Admiration, Antagonism & Ambivalence, 1860–1914* (2012), and the co-editor of *Comic Empires: Imperialism in Cartoons, Caricature, and Satirical Art* (2020) and *Drawing the Line: Using Cartoons as Historical Evidence* (2009).

Natasha Walker is a PhD candidate at the University of Southern Queensland, Australia. Her research focus is on the transnational influence of the first-wave feminist press, which she explored from an Australian perspective in the Honours dissertation, "Vida Goldstein: The Transnational Web of a Twentieth Century Suffragist". She plans to further investigate how women communicated their aims for equality and world peace on a transnational scale through feminist print media during her candidature.

ABBREVIATIONS

AAPA	Australian Aboriginal Progressive Association
ABC	Australian Broadcasting Commission
ACMA	Australian Communications and Media Authority
ADV	Allgemeiner Deutscher Verein
AIRE	Registry of Italians Resident Abroad
ALP	Australian Labor Party
AMPCo	Australasian Medical Publishing Company
ANU	The Australian National University
APA	Australian Progressive Association
ARU	Australian Railways Union
ASIO	Australian Security Intelligence Organisation
ASNC	Australian Steam Navigation Company
AUSNC	Australasian United Steam Navigation Company
BIPR	Bureau of Immigration and Population Research
CATU	Clothing and Allied Trade Unions
CBD	Central Business District
CIA	Central Intelligence Agency
CPA	Communist Party of Australia
DLP	Democratic Labor Party
FEC	Fitzroy Ecumenical Centre
FILEF	Italian Federation of Migrant Workers and their Families
FMWU	Federated Miscellaneous Workers' Union
JCPML	John Curtin Prime Ministerial Library
MAE	Ministère des Affaires Etrangères
MJA	*Medical Journal of Australia*
NAA	National Archives of Australia
NFSA	National Film and Sound Archives

NITV	National Indigenous Television
PCI	Italian Communist Party
RCIDIC	Royal Commission into Aboriginal Deaths in Custody Report
SBS	Special Broadcasting Service
SDV	Social Democratic Vanguard
SI	Système Internationale (SI) [Units]
STM	Scientific, technical and medical [publishing]
WCTU	Women's Christian Temperance Union
WPA	Women's Federal Political Association

LIST OF FIGURES

LIST OF TABLES

Australia's Migrant and Minority Community Press and Cultural Heritage: An Introduction

Catherine Dewhirst and Richard Scully

It has now been more than 50 years since the publication of Miriam Gilson and Jerzy Zubrzycki's *The Foreign-language Press in Australia, 1848–1964*: the seminal modern text for assessing the impact and importance of minority and migrant press culture in Australia's history. Published at a key moment in Australia's move towards multiculturalism, prior to Gilson and Zubrzycki only Rudolf Lowenthal's *The Chinese Press in Australia* (1937), Derek van Abbé's study of the German press in South Australia (1958), and Desmond O'Grady's work on Italian-migrant newspapers (1960) covered non-Anglophone newspapers in any detail.[1] Minority newspapers have much more disparate histories along the lines of local-community, provincial, political, and women's presses and frequently focussing on

C. Dewhirst (✉)
University of Southern Queensland, Toowoomba, QLD, Australia
e-mail: catherine.dewhirst@usq.edu.au

R. Scully
University of New England, Armidale, NSW, Australia
e-mail: rscully@une.edu.au

© The Author(s), under exclusive license to Springer Nature
Switzerland AG 2021
C. Dewhirst, R. Scully (eds.), *Voices of Challenge in Australia's Migrant and Minority Press*, Palgrave Studies in the History of the Media, https://doi.org/10.1007/978-3-030-67330-7_1

1

biographies.[2] Mainstream press history tended to avoid any sideways glances in relating the advance of Australian journalism, with only James Bonwick's *Early Struggles of the Australian Press* (1890) making much mention of foreign-language periodicals (*Die Deutsche Post*, of 1848, and even then referring only to one extant copy). W. Macmahon Ball's edited *Radio Press and World Affairs: Australia's Outlook* (1938), W. S. Holden's *Australia Goes to Press* (1961), and Henry Mayer's *The Press in Australia* (1964), all are "definitely histories of the Anglophone mainstream".[3] Since Gilson and Zubrzycki's epoch-making book, historians, sociologists, and other scholars have delved freely—if haphazardly—into aspects of non-mainstream press culture, and those cultures have increasingly found their way into important works, such as Bridget Griffen-Foley's *A Companion to the Australian Media*.[4] More deliberately, however, this present volume is one of a pair of similar such works that have built upon the Gilson and Zubrzycki legacy and sought to take the study of migrant and minority presses in new and exciting directions, situating their significance within Australia's cultural heritage.

Although mostly worldwide today (the periodical press having been retrieved and archived onwards from the sixteenth century, when this innovative style of print culture began growing in England and other European countries), access to such material culture has generally proven one of the major obstacles for researchers. For one thing, much of the monthly, weekly, and daily printed news has historically met with an early death, particularly since so many publications were short-lived, as is shown by the case of Australia's non-English language newspapers.[5] To be sure, physical copies kept by owners and editors, or readers who held a keen interest in a newspaper's aims and purpose—or even through haphazard hoarding—helped to secure the ongoing life of a paper for posterity and enabled the rescue of others from perishing altogether. However, with a major focus on information important for "today's news", to be traded, bought, consumed, and disposed of (as "yesterday's news"), the loss of much printed media of earlier eras has detracted from interpreting unique layers within past societies and their politics to a deeper level, including gleaning insights from popular imagination and evidence that defies stereotypes. The periodical press was "a creature of the day", wrote E. S. Dallas in Britain's *Blackwood's Magazine* in 1859, and, at the very least, as Benedict Anderson remarks, it is this "obsolescence" that produced an "extraordinary mass ceremony", which in turn reinforced the sense of being part of an extensive community, though one experienced through imagination on the whole.[6] Researchers, however, face a second problem through the costs and the time it traditionally takes to access these sources, including those only archived abroad. The digital revolution has contributed to overcoming the restrictions of travel and time but, more importantly, also aided in the transformation of this field of study, prompting new questions and reframing discussions about the printed press' history.

This has become evident through the establishment of the National Library of Australia's online research discovery site, Trove. Since 2009, a collaborative "mass digitisation" process has been underway, facilitating the capacity for anyone with access to the internet to encounter and discover previously "hidden histories and stories" for themselves, as Hilary Berthon explains in our first volume.[7] Researchers have begun taking full advantage of the site, including its crowdsourcing participatory tool. Of significance, as Berthon notes, are the works of scholars now using Trove to reconstruct the histories of both minority migrant communities and families, via local and metropolitan newspapers. Importantly, nine per cent of the total of Trove's digitised collection accounts for migrant-community newspapers, which includes more than 200 in languages other than English.[8] In many cases, what this infers is the need for specialist language skills, yet it also marks a more clearly-defined shift in using print media sources; that is, from employing them as subsidiary sources only (to document factual information in mere footnotes) to acknowledging their centrality as part of periodical press culture for recovering histories of minority groups and their interconnections within wider colonial, national, and transnational spheres.

The history of newspapers and other periodicals sits largely within studies of the history of the book and of globalising movements, as we discuss elsewhere.[9] Taking this further from the perspective of the histories *created* by migrant and minority communities, a multitude of lesser-known, contemporary, not-always-especially literary, and seldom-remembered presses represents a means for conceptualising them as part of Australia's cultural heritage. In describing the workings of heritage from the position of major historical transformations, Alexandra Dellios and Eureka Henrich argue that:

> Heritage is a stage for the negotiation of shifting identities and the legacies of race and racism; for the rewriting of traditions and historical narratives of belonging and becoming; ... a tool for legitimising and contesting political visions for the future.[10]

They approach heritage—defined as "migrant", "diasporic", and "multicultural"—from the perspective of migrants as "instigators and makers, as well as subjects of the heritage processes under study".[11] There has in recent years been some acknowledgement of newspapers as part of the cultural heritage of our collective past as a result of the digitisation processes, but the emphasis we place on minority group presses as remnants of material culture aims more in recovering the voices and histories of their past.[12] Analysing the periodical presses, their makers and/or readers, builds on a series of stories and narratives, which adds to understanding the multicultural dimensions of past lives.

Historically, a shared—if also transient—sense of community from broadsheets and tabloids galvanised concepts of class consciousness, activism, and the people's voice when they converged with ideas of popular sovereignty and democracy from the eighteenth century onwards. Anderson suggests that newspapers—as a product of printing-press inventions and their secularising and nationalising nature, including the growth of vernacular languages—contributed to a readership's conceptualisation of being part of a wider community (specifically the nation) in two ways: first, by creating a means for identifying with such a community through the regularity and continuity of a paper's appearance, produced through its "novelistic format"; and, second, by participating in the mass popularity of a paper's commodification within the market, creating an imagined collective.[13] As tempting as it is to appreciate the "imagined community" of a newspaper as qualified by a unified outlook and allegiance between editor and reader, the context of the long nineteenth century's revolutionary era and transformations reveals it was anything but. In other words, at the same time newspapers brought to the people hopes of transforming their societies and lives during the age of reason and revolution, the perceived power of the press to influence the public caused alarm in elite and bourgeois circles.[14]

In interrogating assumptions about the Habermasian public sphere through an analysis of the colonial press in North America and its postrevolutionary period, Michael Schudson highlights the dichotomy between the models of "an early press devoted to political controversy and a later, commercial press that pursues the commodification of news"; the former being participatory, the latter focused on ideological control which gained traction over the nineteenth century.[15] Even before the rise of the commercial agenda, he argues, "political conversation" rarely occurred in colonial newspapers and usually only at times of high political drama.[16]

The shift occurred "somewhere between the world of conversation and the world of information", as he describes the politicisation of the printed press for cultivating reader loyalty for political purposes.[17] The result was an increasingly partisan and manipulative printed press. Yet, this is not to say that a discerning public remained silent. Within this atmosphere editors and readers—conservative, socially-conscious, and from the working classes—took advantage of the medium of the press and were often forthright in voicing their views. A good example comes from Lowell, Massachusetts, where the town's young factory-working women launched *Voices of Industry*. "Harken to me, I also, will show mine opinion" was written under the masthead from its first edition on 29 May 1845. And, they went on:

> we have very little sympathy with the wholesale system of slavish pledging, which is carried on to so great an extent at the present day by a large portion of our political, sectarian and party presses; the influence of which is making dupes of the mass, keeps them ignorant of their true natures and interests, and fills the community with dogmatical errors and contracted tenets—while the leaders and advocates of these various sects and parties are as jealous of their preservation as the apple of their eye—growing out of a long train of bigoted, hereditary results, a vicious education, ambitious aspirancy, love of social aristocracy, or that dearest god of the age, "yellow gold".[18]

The increasing popularity of newspapers and other periodicals was aided by the adoption of steam presses from 1814 in Britain, with the growth of their specialisation and volume of production by the mid-nineteenth century.[19] The daily news captivated the public and grew rapidly across imperial and transnational channels with the result that, by the 1880s, Britain, its empire, Europe, and the United States can be said to have become enmeshed through this new sense of global connection via a mass market.[20] Inherent in the "commodification of news", which was global as well, was a great fear of the emergence of socialism as a threat to the nation-building enterprise. Well before the influence of Friedrich Engels, Karl Marx, and others, governmental controls, through restrictive regulations, began affecting newspaper directors and editors across all societies. This was certainly the case in colonial Australia where two unique newspapers made their appearance: in the colony of New South Wales, *The Sydney Gazette, and the New South Wales Advertiser* (1803–1842), and in Van Diemen's Land, the first Indigenous Australian journal, *The Aboriginal and Flinders Island Chronicle under the Sanction of the Commandant* (1836–1837). While we discuss the former briefly in our first volume, focusing on its colourful convict founder, George Howe, the latter is more controversial. Scholars are divided on the authenticity of the Aboriginal editors' contributions to the *Flinders Island Chronicle* and have frequently dismissed its value. This is worth exploring briefly in relation to the cultural heritage of the journal's history and for establishing one approach for recapturing the editors' authentic voices.

In the transferral of First Nations peoples from Van Diemen's Land to the Wybalenna settlement on Flinders Island over the 1830s and 1840s, the appointed superintendent George Robinson established the *Flinders Island Chronicle* and engaged two teenage Aboriginal writers, Thomas Brune (c. 1822–1841) and Walter George Arthur (c. 1820–1861), to compose it.[21] Leonie Stevens' recent history of the Aboriginal people at Wybalenna points to the general lack of scholarly attention that this hand-written journal has received over the past 150 years, and the divided interpretations of its value and credibility, particularly in light of Robinson's supervisory role and censorship, and its official aim "to Christianise and civilize" the Aboriginal peoples.[22] There is no question that the *Flinders Island Chronicle* goes to the heart of settler colonialism, which Patrick Wolfe describes as the "logic of elimination": a concept that amounts to colonisers superimposing a structure through dispossession of the land and relocating or murdering the original land-owners while also implementing a number of strategies to reinforce a comfortable narrative of "settler discourse" for justifying such action and maintaining the new system.[23]

Keeping this context at the forefront, as well as being aware of the likely conditioning of the two boy authors from very young ages (4 and 3 years old, respectively, when taken to an orphanage), Stevens argues that the *Flinders Island Chronicle* itself cannot be dismissed as pure propaganda; instead, it opens "a window into everyday life on the island" of the diverse Indigenous peoples and how they managed under the gaze and rule of the colonial settlers.[24] She is not alone in considering the great value of the journal: "[T]he Aboriginal peeps through occasionally"; there are "many very valuable and revealing elements in the straightforward reportage"; there are "revelations of the determination of the adult exiles to retain culture"; and the editors' "self-censorship, suggest[s] this may be an act of resistance": here she quotes and paraphrases the reflections of other historians on the 29 volumes.[25] However, Stevens contests the "credibility" question by taking one of Walter George Arthur's statements—"I am a man and I am a free man too"—which has nevertheless been challenged in recent times.[26] She does this by adopting "an inversion model" to shift the emphasis back onto a lens through which one might understand Walter George Arthur's reality:

> If Walter Arthur says, repeatedly, that he is a free man, the inversion model demands that we enter history through his world: his story, worldview, community and options. When he writes those words, he is a free man, and fighting to stay that way.[27]

The idea of "enter[ing] history through his world" resonates with post-colonial approaches to history. In adopting the inversion model, Stevens also contradicts the view of the passivity of the Aboriginal women in Wybalenna, exploring their political agency from the archived sermons of Thomas Brune, Walter George Arthur, and other Aboriginal men, as well as Robinson himself, and retrieving the occasional recording of women's voices. They were constantly surveilled for their resistance against conforming to white social, cultural, and "Christian" ways:

> Underlying the discussions on morality and female sexuality was European frustration at continuity of culture: ochre was still getting to Wybalenna, and practices such as the 'obscene dance', invented years earlier by Mother Brown, were still conducted. The 'wickedness' of the women, and their determination to control their own affairs are a constant [in the records] at Wybalenna.[28]

Stevens engages further with authenticating the Aboriginal community's views and actions when a new superintendent was appointed, the controversial Doctor Henry Jeanneret, whose conduct was debated at the time and after he left the island, and subsequently by scholars. Jeanneret's abusive behaviour towards the Aboriginal islanders led to a judicial inquiry, prompted by Walter George Arthur, as well as their petition to Queen Victoria. Some historians have interpreted this action as being orchestrated by sympathetic colonisers. Of course, they played a role. Yet the petitioners were not "puppets of interfering Europeans", as Stevens argues, and in fact had been pursuing a "goal of self-sufficiency and self-determination" for some time.[29] While legal and administrative advice and support were needed, the "Humble Petition" articulated a clear statement that they were petitioning as the Queen's "Free Children" for her "not [to] let Doctor Jeanneret come to Flinders Island again to be our Superintendent", listing 22 abuses he had committed against the Aborigines, including those who signed; Walter G. Arthur, David Bruny (Thomas' brother), Washington (Big River warrior Maccamee), and Mary Ann Arthur (Walter's wife).[30] The model of inversion that Stevens applies suggests one workable approach for retrieving voices and community perspectives from the periodical press of the past.

As this example indicates, of course, the usual contrast between a migrant/minority press and a "settled" mainstream of Anglo-Celtic press culture ignores the fact that the latter is itself a migrant (if not a minority) enterprise, perhaps even more heavily contrasted when one considers the Indigenous cultures it sought to deny and supplant. But as Lara Palombo (Chap. 2) shows, the importation of western press culture to Australia was not only yet another aspect of colonialism, designed to privilege the voice of the coloniser, but an opportunity for Indigenous Australians to adopt and subvert this mode of communication in order to challenge the implied colonial hierarchy, and the explicit narrative of (supposedly) inevitable Aboriginal and Torres Strait-Islander decline. Focusing on *The Australian Abo Call*, Palombo also addresses how more recent Indigenous media reorientates Indigenous sovereign knowledges and struggles.

One of the most effective forms of challenge was not simply to rebut or deny the relevance of established imperial or national narratives but to substitute alternatives in a constructive fashion. As Alexis Bergantz (Chap. 3) shows, in its first five years of print from 1892 *Le Courrier Australien* substituted an imagined space (*Australasie*) for the British Australasia, taking in the Coral Sea from the Australian colonies to the Francophone New Caledonia and New Hebrides (the latter governed by joint Franco-British regimes for nearly a century, from the late 1880s to independence as Vanuatu in 1980). Insisting on an alternative sense of belonging and ownership was a strategy underpinned by a cosmopolitan, pan-European, settler colonial approach to expansion and sovereignty, often neglected in exclusionary histories of nations and empires.

In an atmosphere charged by ideas of race, such positive alternative narratives were not always possible for non-white migrants in Australia. This volume continues to focus on the Chinese experience in particular, as the largest and most visible non-white component of society for much of the nation's history, via chapters by Mei-fen Kuo and Caryn Coatney. The efforts to sustain Sydney's Chinese press at the time of Federation (a political movement inspired in part by hostility to Chinese immigration) are framed as a combined struggle for voice, for community and diasporic solidarity, and—fundamentally—for survival. As Kuo (Chap. 4) shows, it was through the three earliest Sydney-based papers—the *Chinese Australian Herald*, *Tung Wah News* (*Tung Wah Times*), and *Chinese Republic News*—that an authentic voice of Chinese Australia was able to be heard, and make comment on local as well as international affairs, at a time of resurgent Chinese national feeling. However, the rise and fall of a key commercial venture, the Chinese Australian Steamship Corporation (1916–1924), is taken as an indicator of the immense challenges facing an often-divided Chinese community. Conversely, Coatney's (Chap. 5) tracing of the untold story of 1920s–1940s Chinese-Australian journalism is a more positive one, in which the changing international political climate enabled Chinese Australians to subvert ideas of race. In the face of increasing Japanese aggression, China was reimagined (not unproblematically) as a key ally, and an outspoken Chinese-Australian journalism engaged with mainstream politics and the press—via professional and informal networks—to boost their community's status. Coatney's chapter highlights the importance of drawing not only on the published press itself but also on archival materials (such as personal correspondence and classified surveillance reports).

The other ethnic community to have dominated assessments of the migrant experience in Australia—the Italian—is also well-represented here. In three separate chapters, Angela A. Alessi, Bruno Mascitelli, and Simone Battiston explore the way an historical reimagining of key Italian-Australian papers and periodicals exposes tensions, both spatial and temporal. The absolutely crucial role of Sydney's *La Fiamma* in shaping South Australia's post-war Italian community is explored anew by Alessi (Chap. 6). Here she demonstrates how the paper created a unique Italian geography that overlaid and made sense of the new homeland. This is an extension of international understandings of the "Little Italy" phenomenon, but emphasises not only the way internalised place-making promoted the formation of a distinct and homogenous Italian community but also the way this facilitated inter-communal relationships with mainstream Anglo-Celtic society. Shifting the focus from Adelaide to Melbourne, Mascitelli (Chap. 7) explores the fluctuating fortunes of Italian media over time, with an eye to the larger context of Italian media across the continent, but concentrated on *Il Globo*. This is an inter-generational story, as the longevity of a migrant press itself becomes a source of challenges unanticipated by the earlier, founding generations, as readerships decline owing to demographic as well as cultural factors. In this biography of a newspaper, Mascitelli traces the transformations of *Il Globo*'s life history, reflecting changes in Australia's social and political landscape, and transnational influences from Italy.

Simone Battiston's (Chap. 8) analysis of the early years of *Nuovo Paese* (New Country) invites the reader to reconsider the very notion of a community defined primarily on lines of ethnicity and observe the way a community of socio-economic class has played just as essential a role as national origin. *Nuovo Paese* was a newspaper launched by the Italian Federation of Migrant Workers and their Families (FILEF) in Melbourne in 1974 which, in its first decade or so of existence, was defined by a commitment to political activism that embraced as well as transcended local concerns. Using oral history, Battiston contextualises these concerns in terms of wider issues and globalising forces. The peripatetic nature of the paper in its early years (moving headquarters five times before relocating from Melbourne to Sydney in 1984, and then to Adelaide in 1989) also underscores the importance of wider contexts in informing *Nuovo Paese*'s approach.

The class-based concerns of *Nuovo Paese* find an intriguing counterpart in Andrew G. Bonnell's (Chap. 9) examination of Hugo Kunze (1867–1934), and the socialist propaganda press of Queensland. While concentrating on a very different context (Kunze and his associates worked in pre-1914 Brisbane), the prominent role played by socialist activists from non-English-speaking backgrounds is evident here also. Indeed, Kunze used the worker-oriented press in Queensland to keep the reading public informed of socialist literature. Bonnell emphasises the way preexisting print cultures imported by those from German backgrounds merged with the transnational socialist tradition, and the literal *world* view (as opposed to a circumscribed, parochial view) that this helped convey to Australian-based readerships, just as the Italians of *Nuovo Paese* were able, decades later.

Whilst class presents a significant lens for interpreting and reinterpreting the experience of those producing migrant and minority newspapers, so too does gender. Natasha Walker and Catherine Dewhirst (Chap. 10) take a forensic look at the press surrounding Vida Goldstein's 1903 candidature for the Senate in Victoria during the Federal election. Women had little representation within the public sphere, which places Goldstein's newspaper, *The Australian Women's Sphere*, in a minority situation, especially since the suffrage movement marked the embryonic presence of women's political participation. Promoting the idea of women in politics and how women could embrace their democratic rights to cast their vote for the first time, her campaign attracted criticism from the major daily newspapers. Focusing on the gendered subtext through the exchange between Goldstein's newspaper and *The Age* and *The Argus*, Walker and Dewhirst explore the debates and tactics aimed at discrediting her in the public eye, as well as Goldstein's interpretations and women's voices.

A further example of Australia's minority press considers a journal whose readers were and are defined as a "privileged minority". Jeremy Fisher's (Chap. 11) discussion presents the first history of the *Medical Journal of Australia* (MJA) to appear. In focusing on the journal of an elite minority—one well-practised at challenging aspects of government policy as well as social and cultural practices—the *MJA*'s changing fortunes over time are well-represented by someone who worked as an editor on that magazine, and who weaves into this history narrative elements of autobiography and personal recollection, akin to the oral history approaches of other chapters. In an example of the reach of the minority press beyond its immediate, assumed constituency and readership, Fisher shows how the *MJA* has contributed much more than medical research to Australia. In fact, it has provided a basis for the development of Australian editorial standards across the board.

Rounding-out the collection is a return to a defined ethnic category of migrant and minority press experience, but one with broader applicability. As John Budarick (Chap. 12) argues—using the African-Australian media as a case study—the nature of liberal democracies has long been scrutinized by ethnic media, which have questioned issues impacting on migrant and refugee integration and cultural identity, as well as relationships between different kinds of social and political groups. He engages in particular with Chantal Mouffe's theory of agonistic pluralism, which rejects the consensus politics associated with liberal universalism, and puts forward a more workable alternative through the re-articulation of "ineradicable differences" between political identities: a thesis of challenge if ever there was one. Budarick examines the contested terrain of journalistic professionalism by exposing how ethnic minority voices are marginalised in public discourse through a rationalist strategy.

So pervasive has an assimilationist white-Anglo culture been throughout Australia's modern history that there is general consensus that minority migrant voices were only officially "heard" after the Whitlam government inaugurated a culturally pluralist approach through multiculturalism and legislation on anti-discrimination (and then again only after the backlash from reversals after Whitlam's dismissal).[31] Citizenship and therefore "belonging" have been major themes since the 1970s. Yet, for communities historically not represented within the power structures of Australian society, the newspaper endeavours of not only migrants but also Australia's First Nations peoples, women and even an elite group offering professional services suggest a much longer history of struggle for such themes. Examining their experiences and narratives allows us to uncover their contributions to the development of Australia as a nation and to its history.

From the discussions encompassed in this book, and the previous volume, more histories of the migrant and minority press are beginning to emerge from the shadows of time to reshape how we view and approach researching minority community periodical presses and their communities and cultures today. The more specific experiences and narratives from within their pages, as well as other sources, contribute complex understandings of the issues such communities faced locally. Yet they also go beyond the local to demonstrate how these communities were not only intricately part of Australia's colonial and national discourses, but also interconnected beyond to the homeland, wider region, or international groups of people and transnational activities. Neglecting the significance of these newspapers, journals, magazines, and other forms of minority media risks overlooking the deeper significance of how the encapsulated image of such print culture unsettled and challenged the predominant narratives of colonial, national, and cultural homogeneity within Australia. The field of the foreign-language and minority community press forms part of Australia's cultural heritage and, we hope, continues to attract ongoing attention, perspectives, and contributions.

Notes

1. Catherine Dewhirst and Richard Scully, "Australia's Minority Community Printed Press History in Global Context: An Introduction", in *The Transnational Voices of Australia's Migrant and Minority Press*, Palgrave Studies in the History of the Media, ed. Catherine Dewhirst and Richard Scully (Cham, Switzerland: Palgrave Macmillan, 2020), 4.
2. See, for instance: John Russell, Rod Kirkpatrick and Victor Isaacs, *Australian Newspaper History: A Biography* (Andergrove, Qld: Australian Newspaper History Group, 2009).

3. Dewhirst and Scully, "Australia's Minority Community Printed Press History in Global Context", 3.
4. Bridget Griffen-Foley, ed., *A Companion to the Australian Media* (North Melbourne: Australian Scholarly Publishing, 2014).
5. See, for example, Miriam Gilson and Jerzy Zubrzycki, *The Foreign-Language Press in Australia, 1848–1964* (Canberra: ANU Press, 1967), 179–223.
6. E. S. Dallas, cited in Joanne Shattock, ed. *Journalism and the Periodical Press in Nineteenth-Century Britain* (Cambridge: Cambridge University Press, 2017), 2; Benedict Anderson, *Imagined Communities* (London & New York: Verso, 1991), 35.
7. Hilary Berthon, "A Treasure Trove of Community Language Newspapers", in *The Transnational Voices of Australia's Migrant and Minority Press*, Palgrave Studies of the Media History, ed. Catherine Dewhirst and Richard Scully (Cham, Switzerland: Palgrave Macmillan, 2020), 211.
8. Berthon, "A Treasure Trove of Community Language Newspapers", 213–214. Notably, Gilson and Zubrzycki list 432 "foreign-language" newspapers, which have increased as others have been discovered and subsequent migrants, refugees, asylum seekers have formed new communities and newspaper initiatives, including online: Gilson and Zubrzycki, *The Foreign-Language Press in Australia*, 179–233.
9. Dewhirst and Scully, "Australia's Minority Community Printed Press History in Global Context", 5–6.
10. Alexandra Dellios and Eureka Henrich, "Migratory Pasts and Heritage-Making Presents: Theory and Practice", in *Migrant, Multicultural and Diasporic Heritage: Beyond and Between Borders*, ed. Alexandra Dellios and Eureka Henrich (London: Routledge, 2020), 3.
11. Dellios and Henrich, "Migratory Pasts and Heritage-Making Presents".
12. See, for example: Johan Jarlbrink and Pelle Snickars, "Cultural heritage as digital noise: nineteenth century newspapers in the digital archive", *Journal of Documentation* 73, no. 6 (2017): 1228–1243; Paul Gooding, *Historic Newspapers in the Digital Age: Search All About It!* (London: Routledge, 2017).
13. Anderson, *Imagined Communities*, 33–36.
14. Uriel Heyd, *Reading Newspapers: Press and Public in Eighteenth-century Britain and America*, Oxford University Studies in the Enlightenment Series (Oxford: Voltaire Foundation, 2012); Colin Heywood, "Society", in *The Nineteenth Century*, ed. T. C. W. Blanning (Oxford: Oxford University Press, 2000), 61–62.
15. Michael Schudson, "Was There Ever a Public Sphere? If So, When? Reflections on the American Case", in *Habermas and the Public Sphere*, ed. Craig J. Calhoun (Cambridge, MA, and London: The MIT Press, 1992), 152.

16. Schudson, "Was There Ever a Public Sphere? If So, When?", 154.
17. Schudson, "Was There Ever a Public Sphere? If So, When?", 155–156.
18. *Voices of Industry*, May 29, 1845, p. 2.
19. Joanne Shattock, Introduction", in *Journalism and the Periodical Press in Nineteenth-Century Britain*, ed. Joanne Shattock (Cambridge: Cambridge University Press, 2017), xvii, 3.
20. See Shattock, "Introduction", 5–6.
21. Both boys were aged 14 and 13, respectively, having been orphaned— Thomas Brune of the Nuenonne nation on Bruny Island at the age of 4, and Walter George Arthur of the Ben Lomard (*turapina*) nation at 3—and taken to Newtown's Kings Orphan School before being exiled to Wybalenna in 1835: Leonie Stevens, '*Me Write Myself*': *The Free Aboriginal Inhabitants of Van Diemen's Land at Wybalenna, 1832–47* (Clayton, Vic.: Monash University Press, 2017), xiv, xxxv.
22. Stevens, '*Me Write Myself*', xxxv, 147.
23. Patrick Wolfe, "Structure and Event: Settler Colonialism, Time, and the Question of Genocide", in A. Dirk Moses, ed., *Empire, Colony, Genocide: Conquest, Occupation, and Subaltern Resistance in World History* (New York: Berghahn Books, 2008), 103.
24. Stevens, '*Me Write Myself*', xxxv, 147–149.
25. Stevens cites and paraphrases N. J. B. Plombley, Michael Rose, Lyndall Ryan and Elizabeth Burrows: Stevens, '*Me Write Myself*', 147.
26. Stevens, '*Me Write Myself*', xxiii.
27. Stevens, '*Me Write Myself*', xxv, xxx.
28. Stevens, '*Me Write Myself*', 156.
29. Stevens, '*Me Write Myself*', xl–lii.
30. Stevens, '*Me Write Myself*', 260–172.
31. Alistair Davidson, *From Subject to Citizen: Australian Citizenship in the Twentieth Century* (Cambridge: Cambridge University Press, 1997), 167.

CHAPTER 2

Indigenous Media and the Countering of the Racial Insular Imaginary in Settler-Colonial Australia

Lara Palombo

In the settler colony of Australia the racial "insular imaginary" of the state, law and mainstream media has been constantly challenged by Indigenous media.[1] This imaginary, as discussed by Perera, is understood here as part of processes of western territorial ordering that envision Australia as an insular Island nation that continues to produce a geo-body of "shifting coastlines and watery foundations" that displace existing geographies, configure and shape an(ideological) insularity and the sense of a compact, singular, white Australian nationalist imaginary.[2] Within a settler-colonial insularity the autonomy and control of media representation become part of assertions and negotiations over Indigenous sovereign struggles.[3] This chapter provides an overview of how the settler state and law configure a racial insular imaginary that works to deny Indigenous sovereign

L. Palombo (✉)
Media Music Communication and Cultural Studies, Macquarie University, Sydney, NSW, Australia
e-mail: Lara.Palombo@mq.edu.au

© The Author(s), under exclusive license to Springer Nature Switzerland AG 2021
C. Dewhirst, R. Scully (eds.), *Voices of Challenge in Australia's Migrant and Minority Press*, Palgrave Studies in the History of the Media, https://doi.org/10.1007/978-3-030-67330-7_2

knowledges and imagine Australia as a white possession.[4] It demonstrates how mainstream white media historically has participated in the circulation of an insular imaginary of the state and law with grave consequences at policy, practical and everyday level. The second part of the chapter examines the ongoing circulation of Indigenous media and its assertion of autonomous Indigenous knowledges and sovereign struggles and the ways more recent media productions reterritorialise and create dissent and opposition to the reconfigurations of a racial insular imaginary. Aboriginal and Torres Strait Islander peoples should be aware that the following chapter contains names of deceased persons.

As part of a critical historical analysis of Indigenous media, in particular, the chapter examines the six editions of *The Australian Abo Call* (also known as the *Abo Call*), a 3d. tabloid published monthly between April and August in 1938 and edited by John Thomas (Jack) Patten (1905–1957), a Yorta Yorta activist and President of the Australian Progressive Association (APA) in New South Wales.[5] This analysis demonstrates how the newspaper was the voice of the APA and part of a broader Indigenous network that demanded the eradication of the insular imaginary, which had been reconfigured in racial policies, and created a vision for citizenship rights rooted in collectivised Indigenous knowledges and sovereign struggles. It shows how the settler state and law reconfigures the possessiveness of patriarchal white sovereignty by enacting the insular imaginary of the *Newspaper Act of 1898* (NSW) that shut down the newspaper. This Act normalised the ways the circulation of Indigenous media in a liberal democracy was in the past and still today tied to the white possession of capital that denied Indigenous people's control and sovereign ownership of lands and resources. The analysis of this chapter also positions the closure of the newspaper within the context of the liberal state and the law banning the circulation of marginal radical imaginaries that questioned the sovereignty of state as, for example, circulating in the transnational anarchist newspaper, Il Risveglio (*The Re-Awakening*), in 1927 whilst demonstrating ongoing support for the Italian fascist newspaper, *Il Giornale Italiano* (*Italian Newspaper*) (1932–1940). Finally, the chapter introduces the ways in which diverse Indigenous media fulfils a range of roles and has expanded and intensified the countering of the racial insular imaginaries and demonstrates the ways current media productions reterritorialise Indigenous sovereign knowledges and struggles.

In this chapter whenever possible, when referring to or quoting Aboriginal and Torres Strait Islander peoples, I use their nation or clan affiliation. I use the terms "Indigenous", "Aboriginal" and "Aboriginal and Torres Strait Islander" and "First Nations" here and as appropriate. I acknowledge that the very usage of these identifications is bound up with the struggle for Indigenous sovereignties. I also want to note that some of the terms referenced in the *Australian Abo Call* newspaper responded to racist colonial language and policies of its time and that these terms are considered offensive.

The settler-colonial terrain of Australia has been constituted by monitoring and securitising the circulation of Indigenous sovereignties. A central concern of the settler-colonial state has been that of securitising against pre-existing and ongoing Indigenous sovereign struggles. Settler state-based technologies—including protectionist policies and related state and federal mechanisms and the law—have been reconfigured over time as part of a deployment of a European onto-epistemology of raciality that re-imagines and territorialises Australia as a white possession. Such onto-epistemology consists of political-symbolic strategies grounding settler-colonialism that carve out racial difference and cultural difference as human (moral) attributes.[6] Media and the settler state in the settler-colonial terrain deploy these political strategies by partly mobilising the insular imaginary, which is a "form, image, idiom, ideology that territorializes an order and emplacement as it secures the settler-colonial order".[7] This is an order that claims "a racial-geographical exceptionalism" which reinforces exclusionary borders and settler-colonial occupation and, in Perera's words, "is premised on a subject that is racialised as white and imperial".[8] This insular imaginary securitises the denial of Australian Indigenous sovereign ontologies and epistemologies, and their struggles to assert them, and normalises what Goenpul woman and Distinguished Professor of Indigenous Research Aileen Moreton-Robinson calls a possessive logic that maintains Australia as a white possession:

> the concept "possessive logics" ... denote a mode of rationalization, rather than a set of positions that produce an inevitable answer, that is underpinned by an excessive desire to invest in reproducing and reaffirming the nation-state's ownership, control, and domination. As such, white possessive logics are operationalized within discourses to circulate sets of meanings about ownership of the nation, as part of common-sense knowledge, decision making, and socially produced conventions.[9]

The territorialisation of the white possessive logic through insular imaginaries of the state and media has long been countered by Indigenous media produced across the platforms of print, radio, television, digital and social media. The complex, multifaceted roles and varied views circulating in Indigenous media are also partaking in Indigenous sovereign struggles that counter this insular imaginary and assert sovereign ontologies and epistemologies.

Insular Imaginary and Indigenous Media

As part of the arsenal of raciality, the insular imaginary securitises the sovereignty of the settler-colonial state. It territorialises Australia as an insular "Island nation", that is, in Perera's words, "with no pre-existing geopolitical social-cultural relations", or formally as *Terra Nullius* that is a "nobody's land, or un-owned, vacant land".[10] For Moreton-Robinson settler-colonial sovereignty is "white and patriarchal" and a constraining and enabling power that defines Australia as a white possession.[11] Fundamentally, the insular imaginary is part of the political-symbolic strategies of raciality that define Australia as a white possession as it informs *Terra Nullius* and the protectionist mechanisms, including Chief protectors, protection boards and Native Affairs departments that have segregated and imposed settler-state intervention over the everyday relations of Aboriginal and Torres Strait Islander communities, families and peoples. More recently, Irene Watson, a woman from the Tanganekald, Meintangk and Boandik First Nations peoples and Professor of Law, points out that the reversal of the legal fiction of *Terra Nullius* has been followed by the introduction of *Mabo No.2* (Mabo v Queensland No. 2) 1992 (Commonwealth) and the *Native Titles Act 1993* (Commonwealth).[12] These laws enable the extinguishment of the connection of Aboriginal and Torres Strait Islander people to land, and by so doing deny the sovereignty of Indigenous laws that make this pre-colonial and ongoing connection unbreakable. These and other laws and actions, such as the Northern Territory Intervention (2007), continue to give the settler-colonial state the power to determine Indigenous peoples' futures, based on the negation of Indigenous sovereignties, and territorialise Australia as a white possession.[13]

Since the eighteenth century, mainstream white media has been part of the configuration of an insular imaginary that gives primacy to a white possessiveness. The research on mainstream white media, especially since the 1970s, has repeatedly identified racialised and racist discourses, stereotypes and negative representations as having contributed to the ongoing negation of Indigenous ontologies and epistemologies and suspicion towards Aboriginal and Torres Strait Islander people. From continual associations with crime and criminality to stories of crisis, policy failure, individual failure and depravity, such discourses have supported further state surveillance and maintained Aboriginal people exclusion from debates.[14] Lack of concern for Aboriginal and Torres Strait Islanders' knowledge/s on Indigenous and non-Indigenous issues has amplified an insular racial imaginary that has denied self-representation and posited media as a white possession. [15] In 1991 the Royal Commission into Aboriginal Deaths in Custody Report (RCIDIC) which was set up to investigate the causes for the high number of deaths of Aboriginal people in custody and how to prevent them reported on the ways (white) media used a western framework that had a negative impact upon the everyday living of Aboriginal and Torres Strait Islander people, their welfare, relations to the criminal legal system and rights:

> The media is also another place where Aboriginal people experience discrimination in access and presentation. There is a different historical role of the media, one that has relegated Aboriginal people to the fringes of society ....
>
> A second, and perhaps more widespread, approach to Aboriginal issues in the media is the construction of Aboriginal people as a 'problem' ... [in] matters of welfare such as health, education, housing, and employment. [and] law & order issues, including those relating to deaths in custody—the representation, that is, of Aboriginal people as a dissident, disruptive, or criminal element.[16]

Media's western framework and discrimination are also contrasted in the RCIDIC report to the self-representation produced in the Indigenous media of the late 1980s that provided "Aboriginal people legitimacy in the world that is taken for granted by non-Aboriginal people. It also makes them actors, not victims, in this world, an interest group which is at last gaining a voice in the public arena."[17]

In 2005, however, Wendy Bacon demonstrates that despite the Royal Commission intervention the role of mainstream media has continued to give little coverage to deaths in custody. Bacon argues that Australian journalists "have not sustained a 'vigilant scrutiny' of government, let alone protected more disadvantaged group".[18] Despite some feature articles, there have been little attempts to investigate the growth in the incarceration rates of Aboriginal and Torres Strait Islander people and how this links to the continuation of deaths in custody. Mostly, the state failure to implement the recommendations from the Royal Commission has not been scrutinised by the media with grave consequences. Bacon argues that this "failure in accountability does not mean that [mainstream] media are mainly responsible for the deaths but that journalists have contributed by failing to keep the issue in the public sphere by scrutinising those with political, judicial or coercive power".[19] It has been more recently that *The Guardian* has responded to the failure of mainstream media by collecting and analysing all available coronial data and other sources to build a searchable database of deaths in custody from 2008 to 2019.[20]

In the analysis of the media's response to the 2007 Northern Territory Intervention, Moreton-Robinson argues that this participates in a race war.[21] In brief, the Intervention was set up by the Howard government after a report on the high rates of child sexual abuse and family violence in Aboriginal communities in the Northern Territory was released. Without direct consultations with Aboriginal communities, the government suspended the Racial Discrimination Act and sent the armies into specific Aboriginal communities. It enacted a range of harsh penalties, demonstrating the prohibition of recognition of customary laws within the criminal legal system, and enforced leasing of land and a range of welfare, employment and health restrictions.[22] White media overall supported the Intervention. Moreton-Robinson's argument about a race war asserted a white patriarchal sovereignty by reconfiguring an insular racial imaginary of an Indigenous "pathology" that had been actively promoted since the late 1880s and took a different form in the negative headlines and stories of the 1970s, shifted after 1991 to negative stories about Indigenous people's "demands" and "dysfunctional behaviour" in the press.[23] So rather than investigating the settler-state denial of delivering relevant services in Indigenous communities, reported by Indigenous women since the 1980s, and its "disavowal of Indigenous sovereign resources rights", the mainstream media with the state pathologises Indigenous people. This denial legitimised patriarchal white sovereignty as it denies colonialisation and the ongoing "race war against Indigenous people". [24] Since 2007 mainstream media have also rarely scrutinised the link between the Intervention and the rise in the number of Aboriginal and Torres Strait Islander women and children incarcerated in the Northern Territory since the Intervention.

This settler-colonial insular imaginary has been countered by the persistent circulation of Indigenous sovereign knowledges and struggles including by way of media productions. In his powerful critique of white histories, Indigenous author Tony Birch observes that sovereignties are embodied in daily struggles and not reliant on white recognition:

Sovereignty within Indigenous communities, themselves is not reliant on either European law or occasional state paternalism. ... It is both actual and spiritual (within a coexisting framework). It is also enacted in daily struggles of Indigenous people striving to retain autonomous lifestyle.[25]

It is not the intention of this chapter to articulate a unifying definition of Indigenous sovereignty or to reduce it to a western understanding of state sovereignty. Natalie Cromb, a Gamilaraay woman and writer for the Twitter publication of Indigenous X, alerts us that "Indigenous Sovereignty is vastly different to the notion of State sovereignty. To associate the two undermines the notion of Indigenous Sovereignty".[26]

Within the settler-colonial insularity, control over media representation becomes part of asserting and negotiating Indigenous sovereignties.[27] These media have been ongoing and persistently present alongside, and in struggles with, the denial posed by the insular racial imaginaries of the settler state and media. In fact, the presence of Aboriginal and Torres Strait Islander voices through print media has been dated to 1837, when the *Flinders Chronicle* was being edited by the two Indigenous editors, Walter George Arthur and Thomas Bruny, within the confines of an indefinite imprisonment at the Wybalenna Camp in Tasmania, after the so-called Black War (1828–1832).[28] Despite the heavy editorial interference with its content by white colonial authorities, this newspaper embodies traces of the Indigenous struggles operating within the camp itself and within the newspaper itself as Thomas Bruny openly critiqued the deaths in the camp.[29]

It was not until 1930s, however, in the realm of the modern, liberal settler state, that as Elizabeth Burrows argues, the production of Indigenous newspapers was linked to the struggles of organisations advocating for Aboriginal peoples' human rights and social changes. These newspapers struggled against the denial of Indigenous knowledges by giving "higher priority to Indigenous ... voices and allow[ing] the community to drive their own public sphere communication processes and empower the community".[30] For newspapers, such as the *Abo Call* (as I demonstrate here), these not only provided a space for Indigenous people to be heard but also to counter the insularity of the racial settler-colonial state's policies and practices and propose alternative policy solutions. As the history of the national Indigenous TV broadcaster (NITV) notes: "from the first-time [mainstream] media impacted on Indigenous people, they sought to get some control over how they were portrayed".[31] The struggles for self representation with the visibilisation of autonomous

Indigenous media productions and knowledges across community radio and TV broadcasting have made Indigenous media important cultural resources controlled and managed by communities that "own them".[32] In this sense, this ownership and autonomy are part of Indigenous self-determination and autonomy and have driven the cultivation of Indigenous media across print, radio, TV and digital platforms, including on social media, to fulfil a number of critical roles "as conduits of community information; in Indigenous activism; as mechanisms for debate and development of public opinion; in language-sharing; as tools of resilience and education" and to shape and affect political and policy reponses.[33] Indigenous media has become multifaceted and diverse, and fulfils varied roles, including the countering of the insular imaginary by opening up the circulation of Indigenous sovereign knowledges and struggles.

More recently, social media have been harnessed to expand the existing circulation of diverse and dissenting voices, and engage with institutional media, and perform protest, as part of social movement and a growing global sphere of Indigenous media activism.[34] First Nations scholars Alex Wilson, Bronwyn Carlson and Acushla Sciascia, in "Reterritorializing Social Media: Indigenous People Rise Up", argue that social media is reterritorialised to create the promotion of Indigenous activism on a global level, including around cultural and political issues. These authors state that:

> Mainstream media cannot necessarily be counted upon to take interest in issues specific to or of concern to Indigenous peoples. Social media … is providing the means whereby Indigenous people can "reterritorialize" and "Indigenise" the information and communication space. The ability to create international solidarity as well as elevating Indigenous issues to a global platform remain key strengths for Indigenous activism. The level of visibility social media has given Indigenous issues is unprecedented.[35]

The reterritorialisation and Indigenisation of this space enables the creation of dissent and opposition to the reconfigurations of a racial insular imaginary. It creates cultural and political interactions and networks that as the authors argue "reaffirm Indigenous sovereignty and connections to ancestral homelands".[36] These responses to mainstream media, as also argued in Bronwyn Carlson et al.'s "Shared Recognition and Indigenous Resistance on Social Media", do not mean that Indigenous people on social media are not free from racism and trauma. On the contrary, as

Carlson et al. advocate, "online hate and harassment are very real issues for Indigenous people and constitute a form of "shared recognition" whereby trauma is understood as a consequence of colonialism and the continued subjugation and vilification of Indigenous people".[37] The reterritorialisation and Indigenisation of social media, then, is a viable response to "shared recognition" and evidence of Indigenous people "understanding of the codes of racial vilification, but also, our resistance to it", as this becomes a tool for dissent and opposition.[38]

So, the production of Indigenous media is part of a first line for responding to an insular imaginary and asserting sovereignty struggles. This is evident when one brings into focus the historical imaginaries circulating in the Indigenous newspaper the *Australian Abo Call* (1938). This analysis focuses on its grounding as an independent and autonomous imaginary that questioned the racial insularity of the settler state of the time. It is part of the argument that the newspaper was still subjected to a range of micro-interventions that reconfigure a racial insular imaginary that is already and always tied to the negation of Indigenous sovereign ontologies and epistemologies and that eventually lead to its closure.

THE AUSTRALIAN ABO CALL

The newspaper, *The Australian Abo Call*, continued as well as created an independent political imaginary. The newspaper under the Chief Editor Patten as it was argued in an article called 'New Hope for Old Australians' was part of the APA "propaganda" for equal rights".[39] Via the newspaper, the APA was critical of the governmental technologies controlling Indigenous life and death through a range of protectionist laws especially the Protection Boards that were invested in a white possessive logic. They also called for the abolition of these laws, the introduction of full citizenship rights and a Royal Commission into the management of reserves.[40] In few words, it questioned and demonstrated the way the white possessive logic racially distinguished Aboriginal people and communities as non-sovereign subjects: with no citizens' rights, property right and capital, in ways that impoverished and limited every aspect of their living conditions.[41] As Burrows painstakingly details, its politics was inspired by, as well as continuing the work of, the Australian Aboriginal Progressive Association (AAPA):

In late 1923, AAPA founders Charles Frederick (Fred) Maynard and Thomas Lacey's actions created a blueprint for the future Aboriginal rights protest movement. They travelled to Aboriginal reserves and communities, chaired meetings and developed formal AAPA resolutions ('Young Australia, My dear young friends', 1925; 'Racial equality', 1927). They formed alliances with non-Indigenous Aboriginal rights campaigners, such as Elizabeth McKenzie Hatton, who promoted the AAPA's work (Goodall, 1996). Maynard and Lacey were influenced by American Marcus Garvey's Universal Negro Independence Association (Maynard, 2007). In turn, Maynard and Lacey inspired future Aboriginal leaders such as William Cooper, who in 1936 formed the Australian Aborigines League (AAL) in Victoria, and William Ferguson and John T. Patten, who launched the Aborigines Progressive Association (APA) in New South Wales in June 1937.[42]

As part of current and earlier work of these organisations, this newspaper in 1938 visibilised Indigenous struggles across country and firmed a social movement. It called for the abolition and repealing of protectionist policies and practices as racial governmental technologies and demanded the introduction of equal citizen rights.

The newspaper was published within a few months after the National Day of Mourning held on 28 January 1937. This was organised by Patten with William (Bill) Ferguson (1882–1950), the Indigenous co-founder and Secretary of the APA and William Cooper, a Yorta Yorta man and activist from the Australian Aborigines League. This was also attended by Indigenous activists from around the country to mourn the 150th anniversary of the occupation and launch the 10-point plan part of the National Policy for Aborigines.[43] Patten, as the President of the APA, opened the proceedings by addressing the effects of the white possessiveness by way of the negation of pre-existing sovereignties and racial protectionist policies that had created "frightful" living conditions for Indigenous people across Australia. [44] In the speech Patten demanded that the state introduce a National Policy for Aborigines as envisioned by Indigenous struggles across Australia and the abolition of racial protectionist practices and citizenship rights:

On this day, the white people are rejoicing, but we, as Aborigines, have no reason to rejoice on Australia's 150th birthday. Our purpose in meeting today is to bring home to the white people of Australia the frightful conditions in which the native Aborigines of this continent live. This land belonged to our forefathers 150 years ago, but today we are pushed further and further into the background. ... We have decided to make ourselves heard. ... We have had 150 years of white men looking after us, and the result is, our people are being exterminated. ... We ask for ordinary citizen rights, and full equality with white Australians.[45]

This refusal to rejoice at the arrival of settler-colonialism, but rather to mourn its effects, articulates an anti-colonial national imaginary grounded upon and defining Indigenous struggles from across Australia, something which was continued in the *Abo Call*. The speeches and the policy launched on the Day of Mourning were all republished in the newspaper's first edition to encourage the forming of what Ferguson called a "movement for great progress" and the abolition of racial governmentality by demanding full citizenship rights.[46]

The *Abo Call* claimed it drew a readership of 80,000 Indigenous readers from around Australia, with 100 copies distributed by Patten personally to Aboriginal communities in New South Wales, and a subscription rate of 848, including an influential white readership made up of white politicians and journalists.[47] Burrows suggests that Patten wanted to expand the newspapers' reach to include a white audience that could shape public opinion and harness it to pressure the government for change.[48] Ferguson, however, fought for the newspaper to remain driven by and for the Aboriginal community so they could connect and view it as their own.[49] These differences by May of 1938 partly contributed to Ferguson's move away from the branch of the APA.

In its first edition, the newspaper set the space for grounding an anti-colonial and autonomous political imaginary. This is introducing a self-determined imaginary for Aboriginal affairs based on distinguished and varied Indigenous struggles from around the country. Published in the first edition and referenced in subsequent issues, its broad scope of demands and powerful overall proposal drew from these varied and distinguished struggles. These were collectivised into a broad vision for Indigenous people in Australia that questioned what Moreton-Robinson defines as "the excessive desire to control"[50] of the white possessive logic and securitise against Indigenous sovereignties:

1. We respectfully request that there should be a *National Policy for Aborigines*. We advocate Commonwealth Government control of all Aboriginal affairs.
2. We suggest the appointment of a Commonwealth Ministry for Aboriginal Affairs; the Minister to have full Cabinet rank.

3. We suggest the appointment of an Administrative Head of the proposed Department of Aboriginal Affairs, the Administrator to be advised by an Advisory Board, consisting of six persons, three of whom at least should be ... Aboriginal ..., to be nominated by the Aborigines Progressive Association.

4. The aim of the Department of Aboriginal Affairs should be to raise all Aborigines throughout the Commonwealth to full Citizen Status and civil equality with the whites in Australia. In particular, and without delay, all Aborigines should be entitled:

   (a) To receive the same educational opportunities as white people.
   (b) To receive the benefits of labor legislation, including Arbitration Court Awards, on an equality with white workers.
   (c) To receive the full benefits of workers' compensation and insurance.
   (d) To receive the benefits of old-age and invalid pensions, whether living in Aboriginal settlements or not.
   (e) To own land and property, and to be allowed to save money in personal banking accounts, and to come under the same laws regarding intestacy and transmission of property as the white population.
   (f) To receive wages in cash, and not by orders, issue of rations, or apprenticeship systems.[51]

The 10 points list includes also demands for equal rights to marry anyone irrespective of colour, maternity and free hospital treatment for women, land settlement with financial support, Commonwealth training for Aboriginal people and more. It covers multiple needs as linked to questions of national and local self-representation in government bodies/ boards; citizenship rights; equal entitlements to industrial, social, financial and health benefits; the introduction of provisions for land tenure; and management of people living in reserves. As published, this plan stood to voice a broad range of Indigenous struggles effectively across Australia— each countering the insular imaginary of the settler state and its mechanisms by seeking to abolish racial governmental technologies and foster the introduction of equal rights.[52]

The first edition grounds the newspaper as an independent and autonomous Indigenous publication open to, and based upon, varied and distinguishable struggles. In this edition its imaginary is defined by the editor's description of the newspaper as "The Voice of the Aborigines" and by direct interpellation of Indigenous readers through the headlines, "To All Aborigines" and "Our Ten Points Plan". Its content signifies a commitment to voicing Indigenous struggles involved in the undoing of the insular imaginary of settler-colonialism and its racial onto-epistemologies. As it is boldly argued in the article, "To All Aborigines", this newspaper is to be from "the point of view of the Aborigines themselves" and have "nothing to do with missionaries, or anthropologists, or with anybody who looks down at Aborigines as an inferior race".[53]

This notion of independence connects with a call for cultural autonomy. Dharawal Elder and scholar Dr Shayne Thomas Williams has argued that independence was central to discussions by Aboriginal activists. Williams discusses how his Indigenous grandfather Hugh Anderson had always discussed independence with other activists at gatherings on his land at Salt Creek in the 1920s. These gatherings were also attended by Patten and other activists.[54] For Williams this independence is linked to a call for cultural autonomy, a core value of Indigenous sovereignties and interlocks with two other core values of "collectivism and spirituality":

> Autonomy is the collective and spiritual expression of our right to cultural sovereignty, land rights and native title, social justice, and treaty. It engenders our social/collective and cultural/spiritual pride. Most often our autonomy is expressed through the assertion of self-determination, but also self-management, empowerment, sovereignty, independence and so on. These are not catchy cause phrases; they exemplify the subsidiary values we hold regarding autonomy.[55]

In this sense, the *Abo Call* creates an independent space engendering the circulation of distinguished and autonomous Indigenous sovereign ontologies and epistemologies. Distinguished and varied Indigenous voices circulating within the newspaper are collectivised and shown to undo an insular national imaginary and participate in an independent vision that asserted Indigenous knowledge/s of racial governmental regulations and used a right-based politics to demand the re-framing of the settler-colonial state by its abolition of racial governance. As it writes "we are not an inferior race, we have merely been refused the chance of an education that whites receive and we raise our voice to ask for education, equal opportunity, and full citizens' rights".[56]

The newspaper's valuing of independence is further asserted by the circulation of varied autonomous struggles from across country. The reporting of varied local news asserted a political imaginary that visibilised diverse and distinguished Indigenous knowledge/s of sovereign struggles partly based on the recognition that the territorialisation of settler-colonialism produced diverse effects across the country. Subscribers from across the country would raise news with Patten during his travels to different locations or send letters to the editor.[57] Heather Goodall also argues that the newspaper:

> was an extremely important vehicle for the movement, distributed far more widely than its organizers could travel and enable contact with Aboriginal people in the Northern Territory and remote areas of Queensland.[58]

In the second edition, there is an exchange of news regarding distinguished Indigenous struggles across country. Under the heading of "News from The Reserves" a range of letters from Lismore, Clarence River, Deniliquin and Baryugil are featured.[59] They provide diverse local news that reports on attempts to organise meetings with Indigenous people, local discussions on the overcrowding, and poor housing and living conditions in reserves, the wanting of a Royal Commission into the management of Reserves, the discrimination against Aboriginal Returned Soldiers and their families unable to access welfare services, and the voicing of support for the ongoing work of the APA and the newspaper. This news presented local struggles that asked to "fight for our justice and freedom" in "Letter from Cherbourg" and the "smashing up" of the Protection Board in "Letter from Lismore".[60] Additional news also featured under the headings of "News from" Melbourne, Darwin and Queensland. This news, overall, was based on exchanges that exposed the multiple and varied contexts of settler-colonial territorialisation and tapped into the local struggles that were shaping Indigenous lives. In this way—to borrow from Fiona Nicoll's words—this tapping enabled the fortification of existing "networks of exchanges", which connected Indigenous people across the continent.[61]

Anti-colonial imaginaries of Indigenous struggles extend to the recounted histories of "massacres" conducted by white settlers. Despite the massacres being denied and silenced by mainstream media, the newspaper exposed records of killings. The newspaper produced a series of articles drawing attention to the ways Indigenous epistemological and ontological sovereignties were violently negated by the colonial territorialisation of the white possessive through evidenced killings and annihilation from justice. The newspaper in this sense responds directly to the insular imaginary of the *Sydney Morning Herald* that had "attempted to deny" that massacres had occurred against Aboriginal people.[62] Following from this, the April, May, June and September editions published a series of histories of massacres, based on extracts from Judge Terry's book "Reminiscences of Thirty Years Residence in New South Wales and

Victoria" (1863); Member of Parliament William Henry Suttor's book "Australian Stories Re-told, and Sketches of Country Life" (1877); and inspector of schools and historian James Bonwick's "The White Wild Man & the Blacks of Victoria (1863).[63] Under the incisive headings of "Massacre at Myall Creek, The Massacres at Bathurst and Massacres in Victoria", the extracts from white authorities produced counter-evidence to the insular imaginary of the media and settler-colonial state that negated any massacres and, in contrast, demanded justice.[64] The first article, entitled "Massacres", posited that these were racial killings by "white people" against "blacks" that occurred regularly and were widespread across Australia:

> We have definite evidence, which will be published in future numbers of *The Abo Call*, that massacres occurred in almost every district and that the blacks were shot down and poisoned like dingoes. Why are white people such hypocrites as to deny they have treated us badly? We ask them to face up to the truth and to give us a fair deal now, to make up for past atrocities.[65]

Evidence of massacres in conjunction with extracts from white authorities effectively works to undo the insular imaginary negating justice for Indigenous people. In this sense, the *Abo Call* participated in asserting Indigenous struggles for sovereign ontologies and epistemologies by calling into account the killings of Indigenous peoples in the territorialisation of the settler-colonialism.

LOSS OF POLITICAL AUTONOMY

It is because the juridical was part of a racial arsenal which legitimated the regulation of Aboriginal lives (through *Terra Nullius*, Protection Acts, and Protection Boards and more) that the newspaper would have quickly and always received legal and state scrutiny. The *Abo Call* was both visited by the police within three months of its inception and by June 1938, as it reported in its article, "The Abo Call: Difficulties Overcome", it received a letter from the Registrar General calling Patten to register and pay a fee "to enter into recognizances", the "amount of recognizances being $300 pounds together with two or three sureties for like amount".[66] This recognisances law had been enacted under the state-based *Newspaper Act, 1898* (NSW), a colonial act that controlled the printing and publishing of any newspapers in NSW and carried the authority to fine and disallow their circulation. According to the *Newspaper Act, 1898* (NSW):

(1) No person shall print or publish for sale any newspaper until he [*sic*] had entered into a recognizance before the persons hereinafter mentioned, together with two or three sufficient sureties, to the satisfaction of the person taking such recognizance (every editor, printer, or publisher of any such newspaper in the sum of three hundred pounds and his sureties in a like sum in the whole), conditioned that such editor, printer, or publisher shall pay to Her Majesty every such fine or penalty as may at any time be imposed upon or adjudged against him by reason of any conviction for printing or publishing any blasphemous or seditious libel at any time after entering into such recognizance.

(2) Every such recognizance entered into in respect of a newspaper to be printed and published in the city or district of Sydney shall be taken before one of the Judges of the Supreme Court.

(3) Every such recognizance entered into in respect of a newspaper to be printed and published in any part of New South Wales other than the city or district of Sydney shall be entered into before the police magistrate of the district in which such newspaper is to be printed and published, and shall be forthwith transmitted by such police magistrate to the prothonotary of the Supreme Court or to one of the Clerks in the said Court authorised in that behalf by the said prothonotary that the same may be duly registered and recorded in the said Court.

(4) Whosoever prints or publishes any newspaper without having first entered into such recognizance with such sureties shall for every such offence forfeit the sum of twenty pounds.[67]

So the *Abo Call* is targeted for printing and publishing without entering "into a recognizance ... together with two or three sufficient sureties".[68] The insularity of this law disallows the existence of the newspaper unless its publisher and editor pay the fee and record their obligations (i.e. entered recognisance) before the Supreme Court.

Whilst this law applies to all newspapers in NSW its insularity is not neutral as it stands upon a European onto-epistemology of raciality that distinctively negates Indigenous sovereign rights to sovereign resources and impoverishes communities and individuals. So, this act participates in a liberal democracy that ties newspapers to the possession of capital and ignores the ongoing denial of Indigenous people's sovereign resources. By enforcing the registration, the Act effectively renders Indigenous media accountable to a white, patriarchal sovereignty that deters its circulation.

Drawing from Denise da Silva's and Moreton-Robinson conceptual work, this settler-colonial law is grounded upon the onto-epistemology of raciality that it is already and always invested in the recuperation the insular imaginary of the nation as a white possession.[69] This recuperation by law in Moreton-Robinsons' words enables the securitisation of the settler-state sovereignty as it controls the production and circulation of Indigenous struggles for sovereignties in media by:

> disavow[ing] and dispossess[ing] the Indigenous subject of an ontology that exist outside of capital, by demanding our inclusion within modernity on terms that it defines. ... The possessive logics of patriarchal white sovereignty require the constructions of Indigeneity to be validated and measured through different regulatory mechanisms and disciplinary knowledges within modernity.[70]

The terms defined by settler-colonial law imagine the newspaper as breaking settler-colonial law and reinforcing the pathologising of Indigenous people as criminal. It denies the Indigenous ontologies and epistemologies circulating in the paper by asserting the insular possessive logic that internalises the existence of the newspaper within the occurrence of a financial exchange that measures its legal viability. The workings of raciality enmesh with questions of financial capability and class that negate the dispossession and impoverishment of Indigenous Australians and distinguish the Indigenous editor and the readers of the newspaper as without capital in order to curtail the circulation of the *Abo Call* as an autonomous Indigenous newspaper.[71] By not having the funds to pay these fees, the newspaper was considered as not financially or commercially viable and, consequently, forced to shut down.

This law operates as a micro-security liberal governmental mechanism that securitises the white possessiveness tied to settler-colonial sovereignty. The scrutiny of the circulation of the *Abo Call* exercised by the visit of the police and the enforcement of the *Newspaper Act* extend the insular imaginary posed by technologies of control enforced over Indigenous populations. It partakes in the ongoing scrutiny also given to publications holding radical marginal imaginaries and/or written in a foreign language that were monitored after the First World War configured by the liberal state "drive to expel socialism and communism from Australia' and to eliminate radical socialists, Bolshevists, Wobblies, pacifists, trade unionists, Sinn Feiners and anarchists".[72] For example in 1927 the Italian-migrant

Anarchist newspaper, Il Risveglio (*The Re-Awakening*), was closed down within a few months from its inception after the Italian fascist Consular-General Grossardi complained to the authorities that it was subversive, violent and criminal in nature. Edited by communist Giovanni Terribile Antico, in collaboration with anarchists Francesco Carmagnola and Isidor Bertazzon, this proposed a transnational anarchist politics that rejected state sovereignty and its relation to capitalism and proposed creating a united white working class.[73] The editors, however, were formally accused by authorities of not registering the newspaper as demanded by the *Publication of Newspapers in Foreign Languages Regulations, 1921*.[74] It is worthwhile noting how the treatment of these two newspapers is in contrast to the response to the fascist newspaper Il Giornale Italiano (The Italian Newspaper) which was supported by the fascist Italian state and expressed approval of the imperial and racial imaginary of the Australian settler state. Even when *Il Giornale Italiano* supported the colonial occupation of Abyssinia under Mussolini and the League of Nations posed sanctions against Italy, the Department of Foreign Affairs ignored the call issued by the Investigation Branch to enact the *Publication of Newspapers in Foreign Languages Regulations* after it investigated the newspaper.[75] Although the *Abo Call* and Il Risveglio did not share the same political project, they were both part of marginal and critical media opposing the sovereignty of the settler state and laws (unlike Il Giornale Italiano). They both came under the scrutiny of the authorities and were very quickly shut down by liberal laws that demanded a registration fee for local newspapers and in foreign languages.

Crucially, the *Abo Call* served Indigenous readers who were often unable to pay for copies of the newspaper's edition, thus making it impossible for the editor to pay the "recognizance" fee. When informing the readers, the editor compared the forcefulness of the *Newspaper Act, 1898* (NSW) to a "knockout blow" used against the poor or, as in this case, against Aboriginal people:

> This [demand] was almost a knock-out blow for The Abo Call and shows that, under our existing Australian press laws, since the year 1898, the poor man has no hope of starting a newspaper or practicing 'freedom of the press'. The Aborigines of Australia certainly are unable to put up £300 recognizance for a newspaper.[76]

To resist this forceful and violent juridical "blow", the newspaper at first relinquished its publishing autonomy by negotiating for the fee to be paid by the Publicist Publishing Company and for this company to become the legal publisher of the paper. This company, controlled by J. Miles, became the legal publisher.

Historians make the point that the relationship between journalist P. R. Stephenson and J. B. Miles had started from the National Day of Mourning. They were involved in the publishing and editing of the paper since April of 1938.[77] Moreover, this partnership was partly responsible for the split between Ferguson and Patten, as the former was concerned over political interference and questioned the interests of the publishing company. Ferguson was primarily concerned with the publishing house's direct association with the right-wing organisation Australia First Movement, founded by W. J. Miles.[78] In practical terms, however, the relinquishing of publishing rights, or its interventions in the publication of its editions, did not mean that the editor allowed political interference in its content. The content of the newspaper promoted and valued Indigenous independence and autonomy throughout its editions, and despite the split with Ferguson and attempts from Patten to expand its readership and support from a white readership, there is no relenting on these values.

What must be noted is that this new formal arrangement did not clear the *Abo Call*'s debts. Irrespective of the relationship with the Publicist Publishing Company, within a few months the newspaper closed. Patten wrote in the final September edition of 1938 that its closure was due to financial and membership-based pressures:

> Until the Aborigines Progressive Association is on a stronger footing, numerically and financially, it will not be possible to conduct our propaganda ... [using] a monthly newspaper. It is intended, however, to continue the propaganda ... [using] a series of pamphlets and booklets, the first of which, to be entitled THE CASE FOR THE ABORIGINES, by J. T. Patten, is now in preparation and will be published shortly.[79]

Although Patten claimed that this closure was temporary, *Abo Call* was not re-opened. The newspaper itself was subjected to a forceful unitary power of the settler-colonialism, via the exercise of the state's judicial apparatus; this colonial sovereign power intervened in the *Abo Call*'s political determination by barring its capacity to circulate in the social.

CONCLUSION

The circulation of the *Australian Abo Call* in 1938 was part of an ongoing and urgent move to creating an independent autonomous space that engendered the collectivisation and promotion of distinguished Indigenous struggles grounded on sovereign ontologies and epistemologies. It exists in a continuum with continuing moves today. Distinguished and varied Indigenous voices are collectivised as part of an independent vision that asserts Indigenous anti-colonial knowledge/s and used a right-based politics to demand the re-framing of settler-colonialism. This assertion of autonomy, however, was negated by settler-colonial law. The intervention of such law securitised the circulation of a racial "insular imaginary" that reinforces a white possessive logic of the nation that is grounded on the denial of Indigenous sovereignties and struggles including Indigenous media.

Today, insular settler-colonial relations still work to reconfigure white possessive control over Indigenous issues. This is demonstrated by actions launched by various ministers against recent attempts to scrap altogether the celebration and/or change the date of Australia Day.[80] Whilst some of the mainstream white media altogether ignored the opposition to the celebration of Australia Day, others framed this as an issue open for debate by non-Indigenous people. Natalie Cromb counters and exposes the current racial insular imaginary of white mainstream media that reconfigure a white nation by denying Indigenous media, voices and knowledges:

> We have all seen the panels where a bunch of white 'personalities' debate something so far outside the realm of their understanding that it is laughable and yet, it continues, it influences and it pays them to continue saying what they want without basis, without evidence and without any real challenge. They are—after all—on mainstream media platforms voicing their ignorance as though they have some sort of authority to speak on issues.[81]

In particular Cromb is critiquing the investigation run by the Australian Communications and Media Authority (ACMA) on the racial commentaries made against Indigenous peoples during a panel discussion on the 2019 march on Invasion Day. ACMA argued that these were "suggestions" that "could provoke negative feelings in a reasonable person" and did not consider the racist insular logic of these suggestions. Its finding rests on a white possession of the "reasonable person" imagined by ACMA, as it denies that Indigenous peoples and communities are the "reasonable person/s" provoked by the panellists' comments:

> While the ACMA is not authority on what is racist, they are making a strong suggestion that the comments by Kennerley would be received as such 'to the ordinary person' but what about our communities? With the exception of known right wing darling, the Indigenous communities throughout Australia have condemned Kennerly's comments as racist.[82]

The countering of this racial insularity by Cromb forms part of the reterritorialisation of Indigenous knowledges in some digital media platforms. On the eve of Australia Day in 2018, Indigenous X had also published a series of articles on the Day of Mourning, including one by Irene Watson who poignantly asked in the title of her paper: "Why celebrate on the day that marks crimes of colonialism and genocide?" This article evokes and expands the concern posed in 1938 by the organisers of the Day of Mourning over the devastation brought by colonisation. She territorialises Indigenous knowledge/s by directing readers to the survival of "Aboriginal people and Nation" and their ongoing unbreakable relations to "laws and lands".[83] Mostly, Watson asserts the sovereignty of Indigenous laws:

> Since the invasion of our lands by the British Empire, the First Nations of Australia have asked the question: "by what lawful authority do you come to our lands? What authorises your efforts to dispossess us of our ancient connections to them?[84]

The territorialising of First Nations sovereign laws and the struggles to assert them point to the illegitimacy of a white possessiveness of sovereignty. It rejects and counters the denial of Indigenous sovereignty. Most potently, this evokes a "we" and "our" that calls out Indigenous readers in the assertion of sovereignty and distinguishes the non-sovereign settlers. In this context, Indigenous sovereign ontologies and epistemologies embodied in the laws are asserted and reterritorialised alongside, and in struggle with, western and colonial onto-epistemologies of raciality that work to deny or transform the significance of their existence.

Acknowledgement I would like to thank Stefania Capogreco and Dr Jenny Jones for reading an earlier draft of the chapter and the editors of this book for the constructive feedback.

NOTES

1. Suvendrini Perera, *Australia and the Insular Imagination: Beaches, Borders, Boats and Bodies* (New York: Palgrave Macmillan, 2009), 8.
2. Perera, *Australia and the Insular Imagination*, 22.
3. Michelle Wilson and Pamela Wilson, "Introduction: Indigeneity and Indigenous Media on the Global Stage", *Global Indigenous Media: Cultures, Poetics, and Politics*, ed. Pamela Wilson and Michelle Stewart (London: Duke University Press, 2018), 5.
4. Aileen Moreton-Robinson, *The White Possessiveness, Property, Power and Indigenous Sovereignty* (Minneapolis: Minnesota Press, 2015).
5. 'Remembering Jack Patten (1905–1957)', *KooriHistory.com*, February 29, 2016, http://koorihistory.com/jack-patten/ (accessed June 29, 2014).
6. Denise F. da Silva, *Toward a Global Idea of Race* (Minneapolis: University of Minnesota Press, 2007).
7. Perera, *Australia and the Insular Imagination: Beaches, Borders, Boats and Bodies*, 10.
8. Perera, *Australia and the Insular Imagination*, 163.
9. Moreton-Robinson, *The White Possessiveness*, xi–xii.
10. Perera, *Australia and the insular imagination*, 1–10.
11. Moreton-Robinson, *The White Possessiveness*, 139.
12. Irene Watson, *Aboriginal peoples: Colonialism and international law* (New York: Routledge, 2014).
13. Watson, *Aboriginal peoples: Colonialism and international law*, 8.
14. Kerry McCallum and Lisa Waller, *The Dynamics of News and Indigenous Policy in Australia* (Bristol, UK: Intellect Books, 2017).
15. See Wendy Bacon, "A case study of ethical failure: twenty years of media coverage of Aboriginal deaths in custody", *Pacific Journalism Review* 11, no. 2 (2005): 17–41; Elizabeth Burrows, "Writing to be Heard: The Indigenous Print Media's Role in Establishing and Developing an Indigenous Public Sphere", Doctor of Philosophy thesis, Griffith University, 2009; Clemence Due and Damien W. Riggs, Representations of Indigenous Australians in the Mainstream News Media (Teneriffe, Queensland: Post Pressed, 2011); Greg Gardiner, "Running for Country: Australian Print Media Representation of Indigenous Athletes at the 27th Olympiad", *Journal of Sport and Social Issues* 27, no. 3 (2003): 233–260; Heather Goodall, "Constructing a Riot Television News and Aborigines", *Media International Australia*, 68, no. 1 (1993): 70; Heather Goodall, *Invasion to embassy: Land in Aboriginal politics in New South Wales, 1770–1972* (Sydney: Allen & Unwin, 1996); Kerry McCallum and Lisa Waller, *The Dynamics of News and Indigenous Policy in Australia* (Bristol, UK: Intellect Books, 2017).

16. Elliott Johnston, Royal Commission into Aboriginal Deaths in Custody National Report, Volume 2, Chapter 12.6. http://www.austlii.edu.au/au/other/IndigLRes/rciadic/ (accessed February 20, 2020).
17. Johnston, Royal Commission into Aboriginal Deaths in Custody National Report, Para 13.
18. Wendy Bacon, "A case study of ethical failure: twenty years of media coverage of Aboriginal deaths in custody", *Pacific Journalism Review*, 18.
19. Bacon, "A case study of ethical failure", 36.
20. "Deaths Inside: Indigenous Australian Deaths in Custody 2019", *The Guardian*, Database, https://www.theguardian.com/australia-news/ng-interactive/2018/aug/28/deaths-inside-indigenous-australian-deaths-in-custody (accessed February 19, 2020)
21. Moreton-Robinson, *The White Possessiveness, Property, Power and Indigenous Sovereignty*, 164–165.
22. The Northern Territory Intervention was a Government response to reports about child sexual abuse in Aboriginal communities in the northern Territory. The Government declared a 'national emergency' and suspended the Racial Discrimination Act 1975 (RDA). Over 600 military personnel was deployed, Federal Australian Police and the Australian Crime Commission (ACC) Investigators into 73 targeted Aboriginal communities across Northern and Central Australia. As a result, these communities saw alcohol and pornography banned, mandatory income quarantining regimes introduced, community assets seized and the Government compulsorily reacquiring Aboriginal land on five-year leases. See also: Jillian, Kramer, "'Legitimating Fictions': The Rule of Law, the Northern Territory Intervention and the War on Terror", *Law Text Culture* 19 (2015): 12–153.
23. Moreton-Robinson, *The White Possessiveness, Property, Power and Indigenous Sovereignty*, 164–165.
24. Moreton-Robinson, *The White Possessiveness, Property, Power and Indigenous Sovereignty*, 165.
25. Tony Birch, ""The invisible fire": sovereignty, history and responsibility", in *Sovereign subjects: Indigenous sovereignty matters*, ed. Aileen Moreton-Robinson (Crows Nest, NSW: Allen & Unwin, 2007), 107.
26. Natalie Cromb, "How White Privilege Imposes on Sovereignty", *NITV*, June 8, 2017, https://www.sbs.com.au/nitv/article/2017/05/18/how-white-privilege-imposes-sovereignty (accessed 17 February, 2020).
27. Wilson and Wilson, "Introduction: Indigeneity and Indigenous Media on the Global Stage", 5.

28. Note here that I am using the European names because their birth names are unknown. The Editor Walter George Arthur was the son of Rolepa, a senior man of the Ben Lomond people in north-eastern Tasmania; Arthur shared the job with Thomas Brune (or Bruny), the youth editor of the Flinders Island Chronicle and the copy clerk of the Commandant. His place of birth is unknown. See also Leonie Stevens, *Me write myself: The free Aboriginal inhabitants of Van Dieman's Land at Wybalenna 1832–47* (Clayton, Vic.: Monash University Publishing, 2017).

29. Lara Palombo, "Racial penal governance in Australia and moments of appearance: disrupting disappearance and visibilizing women on the inside", *Globalizations:* (12 December, 2019). https://doi.org/10.108 0/14747731.2019.1700047.

30. Elizabeth Burrows, "Writing to be Heard: The Indigenous Print Media's Role in Establishing and Developing an Indigenous", Doctor of Philosophy, Griffith University, 2009, 263.

31. National Indigenous Television, "History of NITV", 2015, https://www.sbs.com.au/nitv/article/2015/06/25/history-nitv (accessed January 28, 2020).

32. Susan Forde, Kerrie Foxwell and Michael Meadows, *Developing Dialogues, Indigenous and Ethnic Community Broadcasting in Australia* (Bristol UK: University of Chicago Press, 2013) 18.

33. Lisa Waller, Tanja Dreher and Kerry McCallum, "The listening key: unlocking the democratic potential of indigenous participatory media", *Media International Australia* 154, Issue 1 (2015): 60.

34. Kerry McCallum, Lisa Waller and Dreher Tanja, "Mediatisation, Marginalisation and Disruption in Australian Indigenous Affairs" *Media and Communication* 4, Issue 4 (2016): 36.

35. Alex Wilson, Bronwyn Carlson and Acushla Sciascia, "Reterritorializing Social Media: Indigenous People Rise Up", *Australasian Journal of Information Systems* 21 (2017): 2.

36. Wilson, Carlson and Sciascia, "Reterritorializing Social Media: Indigenous People Rise Up", 1.

37. Bronwyn Lee Carlson, Lani V. Jones, Michelle Harris, Nelia Quezada and Ryan Frazer, "Trauma, Shared Recognition and Indigenous Resistance on Social Media", *Australasian Journal of Information Systems* 21 (2017): 5.

38. Carlson et al., "Trauma, Shared Recognition and Indigenous Resistance on Social Media", 14.

39. John T. Patten "New Hope for Old Australians", *The Australian Abo Call*, May, 1938, https://trove.nla.gov.au/newspaper/title/51 (accessed January 28, 2020).

40. Anita Heiss, *Dhuuluu-Yala: To Talk Straight—Publishing Indigenous Literature* (Canberra: Aboriginal Studies Press 2003), 48.

41. Moreton-Robinson, *The White Possessiveness, Property, Power and Indigenous Sovereignty*, 66.

42. Elizabeth Burrows, "Interrogating and interpreting the mediation of an emerging Australian Aboriginal social movement between 1923 and 1940", *Social Movement Studies* 15, no. 5 (2016): 474.

43. This event has been described as the first national Indigenous gathering and protest that culminated after years of organizing on local and national Indigenous related issues. See: "Jack Patten, Remembering Jack Patten 1905–1957", KooriHistory.com, http://koorihistory.com/jack-patten/ (accessed January 30, 2020); John Maynard, *Fight for Liberty and Freedom* (Canberra: Aboriginal Studies Press 2007); Heather Goodall, *Invasion to Embassy: Land in Aboriginal Politics in New South Wales, 1770–1972* (Sydney: Sydney University Press, 2008); Jack Horner, *Seeking Racial Justice* (Canberra: Aboriginal Australian Press 2004).

44. "Jack Patten, Remembering Jack Patten 1905–1957)".

45. "Jack Patten, Remembering Jack Patten 1905–1957)".

46. William Ferguson, "Our Historic Day Of Mourning and Protest", *The Australian Abo Call*, April 1938, https://trove.nla.gov.au/newspaper/title/51 (accessed January 28, 2020).

47. Burrows, "Interrogating and interpreting the mediation of an emerging Australian Aboriginal social movement": 478; Burrows, "Writing to be Heard", 107–108.

48. Burrows, "Interrogating and interpreting the mediation of an emerging Australian Aboriginal social movement": 477–479.

49. Burrows, "Writing to be Heard", 103–104.

50. Moreton-Robinson, *The White Possessiveness, Property, Power and Indigenous Sovereignty*, 67.

51. Please note that the language and terms used here were part of racist colonial language of the settler colonial state. This chapter does not imply that the Editors of the newspaper or the 10 Points Plan endorsed these terms. John T. Patten, "Our Ten Points Plan", *The Australian Abo Call*, April, 1938, https://trove.nla.gov.au/newspaper/title/51 (accessed 28 January, 2020).

52. John T. Patten, "Calling all Aborigines Straight Talk", *The Australian Abo Call*, June, 1938, https://trove.nla.gov.au/newspaper/title/51 (accessed 28 January, 2020).

53. John T. Patten, "To All Aborigines", *The Australian Abo Call*, April, 1938, https://trove.nla.gov.au/newspaper/title/51 (accessed January 28, 2020).

54. Hugh Anderson who was born at Rushworth Diggings which lies on the border of the traditional lands of the Ngurelban (Ngooraialum) and the Bangerang peoples of mid-west Victoria, and Ellen Anderson born at Five

Islands, Wollongong, NSW, which is located on the traditional lands of the Dharawal, had bought and owned land at Salt Creek in NSW. This site became a meeting place for various Indigenous and non-local Indigenous families and individuals at times escaping from reserves and the control of the Protection Board. This was a space where Indigenous politics would be discussed "all the time" thus in effect becoming a productive political space. See Shayne T. Williams, "Indigenous values informing curriculum and pedagogical praxis", Doctor of Philosophy thesis, Deakin University, 2007, pp. 46–47, 40. http://dro.deakin.edu.au/eserv/DU:30023289/williams-indigenousvalues-2007.pdf (accessed January 30, 2020); Heather Goodall and Allison Cadzow, *Rivers and Resilience: Aboriginal People on Sydney's Georges River* (Sydney: UNSW Press, 2009), 193.

55. Williams, "Indigenous values informing curriculum and pedagogical praxis", 40.
56. Patten, "To All Aborigines".
57. "Jack Patten, Remembering Jack Patten 1905–1957".
58. Goodall, *Invasion to Embassy*, 289.
59. John T. Patten, "News from The Reserves", *The Australian Abo Call*, May 1938, https://trove.nla.gov.au/newspaper/title/51 (accessed January 28, 2020).
60. Patten, "News from The Reserves".
61. Fiona Nicoll, "De-facing Terra Nullius and Facing the Public Secret of Indigenous Sovereignty in Australia", *Borderlands*, 1, no. 2 (2002): par. 3.
62. John T. Patten, "Australian Abo Call, Massacres", *Australian Abo Call*, April 1938, 4. https://trove.nla.gov.au/newspaper/title/51 (accessed January 28, 2020).
63. Roger Therry, *Reminiscences of thirty years residence in New South Wales and Victoria* (London: Sampson Low, Son & Co, 1863); William H. Suttor, *Australian Stories Re-told, and Sketches of Country Life, Australian stories retold, and, sketches of country life* (Bathurst, NSW: Glyndwr Whalan 1877); James Bonwick, *The White Wild Man & the Blacks of Victoria*, 2nd edn (Melbourne: Fergusson & Moore, 1863).
64. John, T. Patten, "Massacre at Myall Creek", *Australian Abo Call*, May, 1938, 3 https://trove.nla.gov.au/newspaper/title/51 (accessed February 18, 2020); John, T. Patten, "The Massacres at Bathurst", *Australian Abo Call*, June 1938, 3 https://trove.nla.gov.au/newspaper/title/51 (accessed 18 February 18, 2020). Jack, T. Patten, "Massacres in Victoria", *Australian Abo Call*, September 1938, 3 https://trove.nla.gov.au/newspaper/title/51 (accessed February 18, 2020).
65. Patten, "Australian Abo Call, Massacres".

66. John, T. Patten, "The Abo Call: Difficulties Overcome", *Australian Abo Call*, June 1938, 2. https://trove.nla.gov.au/newspaper/title/51 (accessed 18 February 18, 2020).
67. Act no. 23, Newspaper Act 1898 (NSW), https://jade.io/article/442225 (accessed February 16, 2020).
68. Act no. 23, Newspaper Act 1898 (NSW).
69. See: Da Silva, *Toward a global idea of race*; Moreton-Robinson; Moreton-Robinson, *The White Possessiveness, Property, Power and Indigenous Sovereignty*.
70. Moreton-Robinson, *The White Possessiveness*, 191.
71. Moreton-Robinson, *The White Possessiveness*, 31.
72. See David Dutton, *One of Us?: A century of Australian citizenship* (Sydney: University of New South Wales Press, 2002), 106; Nick Fischer, "Lacking the will to power? Australian anti-communists 1917–1935", *Journal of Australian Studies* 26, no. 72 (2003): 224–225; Joan Beaumont, *Broken nation: Australians in the Great War* (Crow Nest, NSW: Allen & Unwin, 2013), 550.
73. See Gianfranco Cresciani, "The proletarian migrants: Fascism and Italian Anarchists in Australia", *Radical Tradition: An Australasian History Page*, http://www.takver.com/history/italian.htm (accessed January 18, 2020); David Faber, "The Italian Anarchist press in Australia between the wars", *Italian Historical Society Journal*, 17 (2009): 5–6.
74. Deana Heath, "Literary censorship, imperialism and the White Australia Policy', in *A History of the Book in Australia: A Nationalised Culture in a Colonised Market*, ed. Martyn Lyons and John Arnold (St Lucia, Qld: University of Queensland Press, 2002), 69–70.
75. Lara Palombo, "The Racial Camp and the Production of the Political Citizen", Doctor of Philosophy thesis, Macquarie University, 2015, pp. 267–168.
76. John T. Patten, "The Abo Call Difficulties Overcome", *Australian Abo Call*, June 1938, 2. https://trove.nla.gov.au/newspaper/title/51 (accessed January 28, 2020).
77. Anita Heiss and Peter Minter, ed , *Macquarie PEN Anthology of Australian Aboriginal literature* (Crows Nest, NSW: Allen & Unwin, 2008), 49; Penny Van Toorn, "Indigenous Texts and Narratives", in *The Cambridge Companion to Australian literature*, edited by Elizabeth Webby, Melbourne: Cambridge University Press, 2000.
78. Goodall, *Invasion to Embassy: land in Aboriginal politics in New South Wales*, 288.
79. John, T. Patten, "The Abo Call an important announcement", *Australia Abo Call*, September, 1938, 4 https://trove.nla.gov.au/newspaper/title/51 (accessed January 28, 2020).

80. See: SBS News, "Dutton threatens councils over Australia Day date change", November 8, 2018. https://www.sbs.com.au/news/dutton-threatens-councils-over-australia-day-date-change (accessed January 20, 2020); Paul Carp "Australia Day's date will not change while I'm Prime Minister, Turnbull says", *The Guardian*, January 28, 2018. https://www.theguardian.com/australia-news/2018/jan/29/australia-days-date-will-not-change-while-im-prime-minister-turnbull-says (accessed January 20, 2020).

81. Natalie Cromb, "Was KAK really cleared of racism?", *Indigenous X*, October 9, 2019, https://indigenousx.com.au/was-kak-really-cleared-of-racism/ (accessed January 20, 2020).

82. Cromb, "Was KAK really cleared of racism?".

83. Irene Watson, "Why celebrate on the day that marks crimes of colonialism and genocide?", *Indigenous X*, 25 January (2018). https://indigenousx.com.au/irene-watson-why-celebrate-on-the-day-that-marks-crimes-of-colonialism-and-genocide/ (accessed January 20, 2020).

84. Watson, "Why celebrate on the day that marks crimes of colonialism and genocide?".

CHAPTER 3

Remembering *Australasie*: European Settlers and Trans-imperial Thinking in the Cosmopolitan *Le Courrier Australien* (1892–1896)

Alexis Bergantz

Le Courrier Australien (or the *Courrier*) was long celebrated as the oldest surviving foreign-language newspaper in print in Australia. It enjoyed an uninterrupted 119-year run, from 1892 until 2011, gradually changing from a weekly publication with global ambitions to a niche monthly local periodical focused on French affairs for French expatriates.[1] It was revived in 2016 as an online bi-lingual edition once again with eyes turned to the world.[2] The Sydney-based publication was launched by a Polish man, Charles Wroblewski (c. 1855–1936), and one of its first managers and long-serving editors, Leon Magrin, was a Mauritian; its brief was local and international, conciliatory and pluralistic. It was subtitled "Journal cosmopolitain du samedi" though the word "cosmopolitan" was dropped

A. Bergantz (✉)
Global & Language Studies, RMIT University, Melbourne, VIC, Australia
e-mail: alexis.bergantz@rmit.edu.au

© The Author(s), under exclusive license to Springer Nature
Switzerland AG 2021
C. Dewhirst, R. Scully (eds.), *Voices of Challenge in Australia's Migrant and Minority Press*, Palgrave Studies in the History of the Media, https://doi.org/10.1007/978-3-030-67330-7_3

43

during 1896, and the scarcity of surviving issues makes it impossible to know exactly when and why.[3] The newspaper had been in financial difficulties from the start, and 1896 coincided with Wroblewski's move to Melbourne.[4] In 1898 it was bought by a group of Sydney-based French notables who turned the periodical into a more utilitarian publication serving the interests of their community.[5]

Wroblewski's early *Courrier*, by contrast, had a "dual purpose".[6] It was addressed to French and Francophone migrants and also sought a broader audience. Who that broader audience was imagined to be, and what ambitions were contained within the cosmopolitan epithet, has not been explored. This chapter thus first takes a step back from the link between the *Courrier* and the French and Francophone community to flesh out the deployment of the ideal of cosmopolitanism under the directorship of the newspaper's creator. I start by examining cosmopolitanism in the *Courrier* as a form of liberal universalism that sought to collapse differences between the British and French empires in the Pacific through the articulation of a shared goal of extending "European" civilisation to the region. From there I build and expand on Donald Denoon's injunction for historians to "remember" the idea of Australasia, "a significant political and cultural entity until the end of the nineteenth century".[7] As Denoon suggests, remembering Australasia allows us to think of the late nineteenth-century Pacific outside a neatly teleological story of political and cultural progress towards separate nationhood. Thinking of *Australasie* through the *Courrier*, therefore, allows us to remember an even larger world, both real and imagined, at the nexus of two empires, the French and British, and their respective local—and shared (in the case of the New Hebrides—present-day Vanuatu)—outposts in the Pacific. The early *Courrier* gives us a glimpse of a world stretched across two empires across the Coral Sea and is a reminder of some of the trans-imperial connections that national and imperial historiographies have tended to obscure. While Empire studies in the Pacific have recently made strides in shifting their focus away from the classic metropole/colony axiom to more nuanced trans-imperial and less colonial-nation-bound geographies, it remains generally confined within the British empire.[8] The early years of the *Courrier* help us retrace some of the hazy contours of Australasia but also to start moving beyond the one empire.

The idea of Australasia had acquired "a British pedigree" at least since Captain Cook's first voyage in 1768–1771, but in the *Courrier* the idea takes on a broader pan-European dimension that could comprise non-British societies, including French New Caledonia. This was the third settler society of the Pacific with Australia and New Zealand. New Caledonia has been, until very recently, often left out of the equation by English-language scholars; and French-language scholars seldom conceptualise of it as a settler society at all.[9] Underpinning this broader—if vague—pan-European idea of *Australasie* we find an equally pan-European settler colonial logic of expansion and sovereignty at play in the late nineteenth-century Pacific, one that is often obscured by a focus on national as well as (discrete) imperial formations.[10]

Reading the *Courrier* through this settler colonial lens ties it back to its other intended readership: migrants. By deploying ideas about land cultivation, labour and race, the *Courrier* put in place a strategy of belonging that served to justify the presence of European migrants in British Australian colonies. This strategy of belonging was premised on the dispossession of the indigenous populations of the Pacific and the imagining of a shared oceanic frontier in the New Hebrides. The unclaimed and uncertain status of the New Hebrides, until the establishment of a condominium in 1906, made the group of islands the ideal site onto which to project settler-migrant anxieties about belonging and the forward march of civilisation. Remembering this often-neglected pan-European dimension of the migrant and colonial past opens our thinking of the region to a more fluid and subtle configuration that is suggestive of some of the trans-local and trans-imperial connections that are yet to be fully explored, particularly beyond the English-speaking world.[11]

COSMOPOLITANISM IN FRENCH

The predecessors of the *Courrier* were all short-lived. *Le Journal de Melbourne* (1858) only lasted three issues. *The Revue Australienne* (1873–1874) and L'Océanien (1874) lasted only a few months each, for lack of a paying readership.[12] On the other hand, the *Courrier* was launched at a juncture in time that helped sustain it. At the peak of the French presence in Australia in 1891 there were some 4500 migrants from France itself and its overseas territories.[13] More specifically, by the 1890s a more defined Francophone community had emerged around Franco-Australian trade in wool, first in Melbourne and then in Sydney during the economic depression. Many of the permanent migrants from northern France and Belgium attached to that trade, along with interested diplomats, helped set up various societies around which the French and Francophone communities coalesced, such as the Comptoir National d'Escompte de Paris in

1881, the Société de Bienfaisance in 1891, the Alliance Française de Sydney and a French Chamber of Commerce, both in 1899.[14] The French Ministry of Foreign Affairs provided the *Courrier* with some 3000 francs of start-up money and continued to provide regular funding until 1908–1909.[15] Since its launch, large French companies also ensured an income through regular front-page advertising, notably the Banque Nationale de Paris, the state-sponsored steamship company Messageries Maritimes and the Neo-Caledonian Ballande society. Following Wroblewski's departure in June 1896, the *Courrier*'s offices moved to the "Bond Street Chambers" (2 Bond Street), joining the French Consulate-General, the French Société de Bienfaisance, the Alliance Française Library and, from 1899, the newly created Alliance Française of Sydney and the French Chamber of Commerce. In 1899, a year after it was sold to the French notables, it styled itself as the "Organe de la Chambre de commerce et du Comité de l'Alliance française de Sydney".[16] But Wroblewski had wanted his French-language cosmopolitan *Courrier* to look out to the world, rather than inward.

That a "cosmopolitan" newspaper should be published in French in an English-speaking British colony makes sense when we consider Wroblewski's own background. He was a Francophile Polish migrant whose name is sometimes preceded by the French nobiliary particle "de", or the title of Count (he had a filiation to the nobility of the court of the last King of Poland, Stanisław II Augustus (1764–1795), through his maternal grandmother). He had spent two decades in France before coming to Australia and working as an analytical chemist for the royal commission on water conservation in New South Wales.[17] The year before the publication of the *Courrier* he married Daisy Serisier, the daughter of a French pioneer of the region of Dubbo, Jean-Emile de Bouillon-Serisier, himself allegedly a descendant of the Comte de Bouillon, guillotined in the 1789 French Revolution.[18]

In the late nineteenth century French was still considered by many to be a global lingua franca, spoken by a mobile cultivated elite, and conferring through its practice but also in itself, it was believed, particularly edifying and civilising properties. In fact "French" and "Cosmopolitan" could often be amalgamated: the Sydney "French Club" (or the "Cercle Français"), an association created in 1885 as a port-of-call for French residents and travellers in New South Wales, morphed into the Cosmopolitan Club as it gradually attracted people of other nationalities and became increasingly focused on the arts.[19]

The first edition of the *Courrier* was addressed to "*la jeunesse Australienne et à tous ceux qui veulent apprendre cette belle langue française*" [the youth of Australia and all those who wish to learn the beautiful French language] which was the language of diplomacy and was destined, so it was thought, to be that of commerce.[20] Expanding the point and the geographical scope, the second editorial talked (in English this time) to "the intelligent public of Australasia". It noted the usefulness of French as an instrument of social mobility and personal improvement: "no education is considered complete *anywhere* which does not include French as one of its principal elements" and is needed outside the English-speaking world to secure "entry into cultivated society". As such the *Courrier* promised to provide French lessons in its forthcoming issues to fulfil its promise to both educate and enlighten its readership.[21]

The French language was seen as a tool for self-edification and would help the development of commerce in Australia, and commerce would help the progress of Australia.[22] The *Courrier* thus espoused a form of liberal universalism that laid emphasis on the primacy of the individual and their responsibility for self and collective moral and material improvement. With such lofty aims it purported to be detached from the politics of any one nation, and while not anti-nationalist (it supported greater political unity in Federation) it denounced chauvinistic patriotism as the cause of war and death. It stressed the redemptive properties of science and industry in resolving conflict and cementing the universal goals of civilisation (epitomised in Universal Exhibitions).[23] It was an idealist publication, but it met with resistance from the start.

The Sydney tabloid *Truth* showed characteristic condescension towards what it called a "quaint little journalistic venture".[24] And it castigated the *Courrier*'s editors as either uninformed or naïve. Following an interview with "Max O'Rell", the world-renowned writer and conferencier, at the Australia Hotel, the *Courrier* reported as an "exclusive" the already well-known familial origin of the celebrity's stage name.[25] In a similar fashion, references to "Jacques Bonhomme" (a dated reference to the *Jacquerie* peasant uprising in the north of France, near Beauvais, in the fourteenth century) as a metonym for the tax-payer—rather than the more fin-de-siècle "proletariat"—were picked up on by readers as being old-fashioned.[26] More importantly, the *Courrier*'s purported political neutrality did not sit well with its readers. After sitting on the fence for about six months it eventually had to declare in favour of New South Wales' free-trade policies.[27] It is also worth noting that the idea of teaching French through the pages of the *Courrier* was idealist at best. Language in fact was a problem and a barrier from the beginning. The second editorial clarifying the civilisational and cultural importance of the French language was written in English. The same issue asked for volunteers to translate future editorials into English, so the publication could reach more readers.[28]

AUSTRALASIE ACROSS THE CORAL SEA

As Donald Denoon and Philippa Mein Smith have pointed out, historians often think of Australasia as a "transitional concept" used by settlers to demarcate themselves from Asia—Australasia meaning the lands south of Asia.[29] It was interchangeably used with the name Australia in the early drafts of a federal constitution until New Zealand pulled out of the process from 1897.[30] Australasia is certainly difficult to define. It is a "fuzzy" concept and a space that changed over time, but it does not make it any less "real", as James Belich puts it, even if it was "very loose, vague and semi-tangible".[31] Following Denoon and Smith, I suggest that by simply relegating the idea of Australasia to an intermediary space between settlement and formal nationhood we not only verge on anachronism and teleology but we also lose something of the world some people inhabited in the late nineteenth century, how they made sense of it and imagined its future.

The word *Australasie* was first coined by the French writer Charles de Brosses in 1756. His *Histoire des navigations aux terres australes* would later influence Cook's voyages.[32] Australasia then quickly became a British idea, designating a British community created through the expanding settlements moving outward from the "mother colony" of New South Wales. It always had Australia as its centre and New Zealand as its Pacific frontier, but its contours changed over time, sometimes including Australia's adjacent isles, but eventually divesting itself of Papua New Guinea in the 1860s, making Australasia not solely British but specifically white.[33] In the late 1890s, the Victorian parliament defined it legally as comprising the Australian mainland—New Zealand, Tasmania, Fiji "and any other British Colonies or possessions in Australasia now existing or hereafter to be created".[34] And while the historiographies of Australia and New Zealand split after 1901 and made the idea of Australasia gradually outmoded, the lived reality of exchanges of people and ideas through well-established maritime networks across the Tasman Sea did not come to a standstill (in fact they only increased).[35]

For the *Courrier*, *Australasie* was broader and crossed formal empires. Buoyed by its universalist liberal ideology of improvement, it imagined Australasia as a shared European, or at least "British plus" (i.e. plus the French), space where the goal was the development of European civilisation in the Pacific region. This is evident in the layout of the publication which, until 1896, had a regular column on colonial affairs (*Revue Coloniale*—although the title changed often), which included the Australian colonies, New Zealand as well as New Caledonia. Where it could, the *Courrier* toned down reports of international conflict between the French and British empires. On the matter of French transportation to New Caledonia—a point of ongoing tension between France, Great Britain and the Australian colonies—the *Courrier* discursively displaced the problem to frame it as a shared burden.[36] It nebulously talked about *"tous les convicts des colonies australasiennes"* [all the convicts of the Australasian colonies] when referring to French convicts. And it further tied French transportation to the unresolved status of the New Hebrides by suggesting that French convicts could be used to transform the islands into arable lands to make way for "European" and "white" colonisation (two terms I problematise below).[37]

Historians have recently shone a light on the importance of both material and mental trans-imperial connections on the shaping of colonial thinking about racial and class hierarchies, as well as subaltern resistance.[38] There is momentum to continue re-writing the histories of discrete empires as interconnected and mutually defining spaces.[39] But more can be done to challenge the idea that larger imperial formations, particularly ones that did not share the same language, were culturally, politically and socially sealed off. As Briony Neilson has recently noted in a study of the dialectic constitution of settler colonial legitimacy between the Australian colonies and New Caledonia, scholars are yet to contemplate fully the implications of movement, and indeed the implications of *thinking*, across empires.[40] In this regard the *Australasie* described and imagined in the pages of the *Courrier* can serve as a point of entry. It depicts a mental as well as a material world that is obscured by English-language, British world historiography. It opens the door to a French-speaking world balanced, at times precariously, between but also dependent upon two empires that it brings into contact in its weekly four pages.

As Frances Steel has shown for the Anglo Pacific, imaginative geographies change in tandem with the rise and fall of technologies and communication networks.[41] The *Australasie* of the *Courrier* partly hinged on the real, imaginary and hoped for commercial, technological and cultural connections that tied New Caledonia to the Australian colonies, particularly New South Wales. Since French annexation in 1853 and until the end of the nineteenth century, New Caledonia was dependent on the Australian colonies for the most basic necessities, including capital, free settlers and food.[42] The French opened a penal colony in New Caledonia in 1864, sending approximately 30,000 convicts to the island prison until 1897. Thousands of convicts represented as many mouths to feed and an important market for Australian food.[43] The French island could "be fairly described as a French penal colony", wrote travel writer George Griffith in 1901, "and a commercial dependency of Australia".[44]

Trade came hand-in-hand with increased transport and communication and, for a time, traffic between the French and British colonies looked set to bring them in an ever-closer embrace. From 1876 the Australian Steam Navigation Company (ASNC) provided a monthly (and at times twice monthly) service to New Caledonia as part of its Fiji route.[45] In 1882 the French government-subsidised steamship company, the Messageries Maritimes, opened a monthly service linking Marseilles to Noumea via Sydney, in effect making the NSW capital New Caledonia's gateway to France.[46] In 1893 a submarine cable linked Bundaberg in Queensland to Gomen in New Caledonia, subsidised by France, New South Wales and Queensland.[47] Leafing through the pages of the *Courrier*, readers could follow the movement of ships and the passengers of note they carried back and forth across the two regional centres of Sydney and Noumea. These included the celebrated pianist of le-tout-Sydney, Henri Kowalski and colonial officials from both empires: the Governors of New Caledonia, Emile Laffon and Paul Feuillet, and their counterpart in New South Wales, Lord Jersey. Accompanying her husband in 1892 on the first official visit by an Australian colonial governor to Noumea, Lady Jersey, like many English travellers, remarked on the "motley elements constituting a Noumean crowd—French, Australians, Kanakas" and "Arabs wrapped in white bornouses [sic]" and further noted the Australian provenance of horses and cattle.[48]

However, by the late nineteenth century capital came increasingly from European sources (including Rothschild investments in the growing mining industry).[49] Restrictive French policies, such as heavy duties, gradually discouraged foreign ships from trading along the New Caledonian coast and, from 1892, protective French tariffs further hindered trade so that

Australia ceased being the largest supplier of goods and settlers.[50] New Caledonia was made to look to France and Australia moved on.

The *Australasie* of the *Courrier* was a project-in-the-making also frustrated by a lagging infrastructure that fell short of its denizens' dreams. There was little coordination between the different steamship companies operating in and out of New Caledonia and their boats often followed one another by only a few days. Australasian United Steam Navigation Company (AUSNC) ships stopped by New Caledonia and the New Hebrides on their way to Fiji, but ignored Noumea on their way back, leaving local produce of coffee, corn, bananas, coco and minerals stranded for several weeks. The *Courrier* petitioned the NSW government to subsidise the AUSNC line to stop by Noumea on its return voyage seemingly unaware of the heavy fees the French government levied on non-French or non-French run vessels operating in New Caledonian waters.[51]

The contours of the *Courrier*'s contemporary *Australasie* were also defined by bringing together disparate pieces of the French imperial present, cemented with a certain form of nostalgia for the glories of the lost First Empire. If there was, perhaps briefly, a French-speaking *Australasie* before Federation that extended across French and British colonies, if it was indeed "real", the *Courrier* was not just a reflection of it but also a constitutive medium.[52] Reports of the visit in Sydney of Comoros Island Prince Jaffar (then in exile in New Caledonia for rebelling against the French protectorate over the island of Anjouan) or the stopover of the Count of Keroman, the Resident of Wallis and Futuna, in the pages of the weekly newspaper, give the deceptive impression of a coherent mass centred upon the New South Wales capital.[53] When a cyclone devastated then-British Mauritius in 1892, the expatriate polymath Marin la Meslée published a call for financial aid by underscoring the island's connection to France, dubbing it one of the jewels of the French empire "*d'autrefois*" [of days gone by].[54] The *Australasie* of the *Courrier* partly took shape through a nostalgic imaginary anchored in references to the past which served to compensate for a future that seemed to take time to materialise.

Pan-European Settler Colonialism

While on the surface the cosmopolitanism embraced by the early *Courrier* can appear perhaps naïve, even old-fashioned to some of its readers, it is a concept and an ideology deeply anchored in European thinking about universalism and, as a corollary, colonial expansion.[55] As a migrant newspaper with such universal aspirations, the *Courrier* reconciled its "double purpose" through the deployment of a settler colonial logic of sovereignty and expansion conceived through a pan-European lens which allowed not only for a vision of a shared Pacific between Europeans and their hosts but also justified their presence within predominantly English-speaking Australian colonies. This implicit strategy of belonging, which hinged on the imperative of land development, is most evident in the *Courrier*'s obtuse treatment of convict transportation as a civilising force (in spite of vociferous Australian criticism) and, as the remainder of this chapter shows, in its paternalist racism towards non-white migration and the strength of its disavowal and embrace of frontier violence against the native populations of Australia, New Caledonia and the New Hebrides.

Much of the vast and multidirectional British world depicted by "British world" history and the New Imperial history was underpinned by the idea of British race patriotism, which also gave the idea of Australasia more currency in the late nineteenth century, particularly during the various conferences to discuss Federation.[56] At the same time, other modes of identification and connections also gave meaning to people's lives. Across the Atlantic the promise of an Anglo-Saxon brotherhood beckoned.[57] Yet, as Yves Rees has recently shown, the "Anglospheric" kinship networks that tied Anglo-Saxons and Britons loosely together were disrupted in the 1920s by the development of normative migratory regimes and migration quotas that laid emphasis on differences of national origin rather than racial sameness.[58] As these studies remind us, the invented categories of "Briton" and "Anglo-Saxon" were contextual and served specific purposes. Ideas about race are essentially ideas about belonging and exclusion.[59] The term "European" in the *Courrier* is just as problematic and contingent, contextually moving along an axis where outward appearance meets culture and geography. Here "European" refers to people coming from the European continent (Italians, French, Poles) but also Mauritians (of a European culture). It can also refer to physical whiteness (shared by Europeans, Anglo-Saxons and Britons) in *comparison* to the native populations of the Pacific. But whiteness did not of necessity mean white skin.[60]

At the core of the settler colonial process is the impetus of land development. As Lorenzo Veracini further explains, the settler colonial situation on that land is itself shaped by the triangular relationship between the settlers, the indigenous populations who are colonised and various "exogenous alterities"—such as new migrants.[61] To counter recurring and vexing nationalist demands in the Australian press of "Australia for the

Australians", the *Courrier* harnessed the toil, labour and hardship on the land endured by European migrants, such as the Germans or the Italians, as proof of their right to ownership. Through their labour, these migrants had demonstrably contributed to the creation of new wealth and so were recast as productive settlers with a symbiotic relationship to the land. Going further, the *Courrier* made their presence a moral imperative for the advancement of civilisation. It thus called for more *"cultivateurs"* (or labourers, literally those who cultivate the land) whether *"anglais"* or *"Européen"* to contribute *"à l'amélioration de la production et à la richesse du pays"* [to the increase of production and to the wealth of the country].[62] In contrast to the straightforward case of European migration, the *Courrier* adopted a somewhat nuanced view of non-white migration, less clear cut than some of the shifts taking place at the time in the Australian colonies building up to Federation and the White Australia policy, but nonetheless still dictated by a logic of development that posits some (i.e. the Chinese) as assimilable and others (i.e. Indigenous peoples) as not.

From the first issue the *Courrier* declared in favour of migration restrictions on racial grounds, repeating the well-trodden dogma of fin-de-siècle Australia that the attainment of self-government in the Australian colonies was proof of the success of colonisation by a homogenous white population.[63] As Marilyn Lake and Henry Reynolds have shown, the development of a binary thinking between white/non-white hardened in the final years of the nineteenth century that led to the establishment of the White Australia policy; and English-speaking countries were "pace-setters" in lumping together in the one category of non-white "the previous multiplicity of nations, races and religions".[64] In the *Courrier*, ideas about the advancement of civilisation still trumped that binary thinking. Geographic and ancestral origin could count for more than external appearance so that race was not always conflated with skin colour. When the "Colored Races Restriction Bill" was introduced in the Legislative Assembly of New South Wales in 1896, the newspaper supported Syrian migrants' claims to whiteness on the grounds of geographic origin and descent. It argued that *"les Syriens étaient caucasiens et que par droit de conquête ils descendaient en ligne droite des Macédoniens, des Grecs et des Romains"* [Syrians were Caucasians, and that by right of conquest they were direct descendants of the Macedonians, the Greeks and the Romans]. Whiteness did not necessarily mean white skin as *"ils sont de race caucasienne, de race blanche, aussi blanche assurément que les peaux brunes qui ont vu le jour en Italie, en Espagne, en Grèce et en général dans la plupart des régions méditerranéennes*" [they are of Caucasian race, of white race, certainly as white as the people with brown skins born in Italy, in Spain, in Greece and generally in most Mediterranean regions].[65] In a different way, restricting the mobility of British Indians on racial grounds went against British imperial citizenship, an idea pregnant with the promise of belonging to something greater than the nation.[66]

Mainly, the *Courrier* saw migration restriction as a way to curb new Chinese arrivals. Here as well, it tended towards a more paternalist form of racism. It suggested that industrious Chinese already in the colonies ought to be treated with (condescending) kindness rather than be ungraciously deported: "*Certes nous n'aimons pas les Chinois et nous voudrions les voir ailleurs ... mais il y a aussi une question d'humanité qui s'impose et une sorte de compensation que l'on doit*" [Certainly we do not like the Chinese and we would like to see them elsewhere ... but there is an obligation to treat the question with humanity and a certain compensation is due].[67] Even seen as a labour problem the newspaper tried to be accommodating, thinking of ways to cordon off the Chinese and making them work to help develop commerce but on the margins of white labour, by creating parallel industries, "*pourquoi ne pas proposer aux chinois la culture de la soie?*" [Why not suggest to the Chinese to cultivate silk?].[68] Ultimately, in the early *Courrier Australien* the Chinese were subjected to the same logic of settler colonial legitimacy as industrious Germans or Italians. But there were good Chinese migrants and bad Chinese migrants. Bad Chinese were opium-den dwellers who lived in insalubrious conditions; good Chinese (already in the colonies) spoke of social mobility from vegetable vendors to the public service—a level of European achievement, the *Courrier* mused, not attained by some Europeans.[69] Germans or Italians were discussed as homogenous peoples where each individual could be said to be imbued with the qualities of the group whereas the Chinese remained "probationary settlers" judged individually depending on their morality and contribution.[70]

If, in the early *Courrier*, European migrants could claim settler status by virtue of their proven ability to develop the land, and some non-white migrants were at least given the chance to become settlers, Indigenous peoples were, unsurprisingly, either cast as beyond the pale of civilisation, or simply ignored. Looking at the Pacific, the *Courrier* sought to legitimise a pan-European presence in the region by pushing the oceanic frontier of development away from Australia to the New Hebrides. It did so by ignoring the strength of colonial violence in Australia, and by focusing its attention on the necessity to extend that same violence to the last frontier of the New Hebrides. The *Courrier*'s settler colonial denial of land usurpation and Indigenous peoples' sovereignty was not uniformly applied to the Pacific but weakens the further we move away from the Australian colonies. Indigenous Australians warrant almost no mention at all. Kanaks in New Caledonia are portrayed as repulsive and impulsive savages. When the native police ("police indigène") is disbanded the *Courrier* rejoices that they will be put back in their rightful subordinate place and that the humiliating practice of having these "*affreux canaques capables de tous les excés et de toutes les turpitudes*" [hideous Kanaks capable of all excesses and all depravity] protect white settlers will come to an end.[71] But most coverage to do with indigenous populations focuses on the New Hebrides.

The New Hebrides remained unclaimed by European powers until the establishment of a joint Anglo-French condominium in 1906, and until then both the French and British governments dragged their feet. For the *Courrier*, the undefined status of the New Hebrides made those islands an ideal site to project anxieties about the forward march of civilisation. Numerous articles emphasised the brutality with which New Hebrideans killed white Europeans (French, British or Australian) and supported and encouraged the banality of retribution. When one Father Suaz Ambryn was killed in 1896, the *Courrier* noted in passing that a few "cannibal" chiefs were exterminated to avenge him—before commenting on the progress of coffee and banana plantations on the islands, a development precisely premised on the decimation of a native population whose presence was seen as a hindrance. The *Courrier* denounced Blackbirding in Australia for the threat of miscegenation, but saw it, as with convictism, as a useful practice to develop the New Hebrides. When another white man was killed while recruiting workers "*pour les braves colons de l'île*" [for the brave colonists of the island] the *Courrier* called for brute force to colonise and finally "pacify" the islands. Significantly, in this still contested territory, it demanded action be taken by either the French or the British, or jointly, as long as it be decisive: "*attendront-ils que les sauvages aient massacrés le dernier des hardis pionniers européens qui consentent à vivre abandonnés sur ces îles de pestilence et de meurtre?*" [will they wait for the savages to have massacred the last of the adventurous European pioneers who have accepted to live, left to their own device, on these islands of pestilence and murder?].[72]

CONCLUSION

From 1870 a certain unease had developed in Australia about New Caledonia and many expressed regret that the island had been allowed to fall into French hands in the first place. Calls for a British or Australian take-over of the New Hebrides thus became even stronger.[73] The *Courrier Australien*'s idea of a pan-European civilisation elicited many vexed responses. The editors received "*plusieurs longues lettres de correspondants anonymes preconisant comme nous l'annexation*" [several long letters from anonymous readers who, like us, recommend annexation] but arguing strongly for British annexation. These letters repeated the widely held view that France was not an effective coloniser and that Britain would develop the infrastructure of the islands much faster, which would then pave the way for Australian colonists. British colonisation would bring "*tout ce qui constitue la civilisation anglaise, y compris le refoulement lent et progressif, et même l'anéantissement de la race indigene*" [everything that is part of English civilisation, including the slow and progressive confinement of the native race, even its annihilation].[74]

The *Courrier* had been in financial difficulty since its launch and was steadily losing readers when it changed hands in 1896.[75] This can certainly be attributed, in part, to the difficulty of selling a foreign-language paper in English-speaking British colonies. But clear fault lines also appear between the universalist pan-European idea of civilisation of the *Courrier*, with its appended colonial impetus, and an Australian population which increasingly saw the isles of the Pacific as its own domain and migrant populations with suspicion. Yet, despite this rift, the early years of the *Courrier* also show us something of a mental world and a—perhaps at times precarious—material world that expanded beyond Sydney across the Coral Sea to New Caledonia and the New Hebrides. It serves as a reminder and as an invitation to continue exploring the dynamic connections that crossed formal empires and gave shape and meaning to the Pacific world.

We find some echoes of the early cosmopolitan *Courrier Australien* in the online version revived in 2016. After being sold to the French notables in 1898 it gradually became narrower in scope, focusing on the French community in Australia and the commercial interests between France and Australia. The new edition is once again opened to the world, seeking to address the French in Australia while trying to reach a broader readership. Articles cover local and international affairs, and are written in both French and English, perhaps somewhat conceding the limited scope of French as an international language in Australia, in a way Wroblewski did not in the late nineteenth century.

NOTES

1. I wish to thank Alessandro Antonnello, Louis-José Barbançon, Ruth Gamble, Kyle Harvey, Benjamin Huf, Briony Neilson, Yves Rees and Alexandra Roginski for reading a draft of this paper and for helpful comments and suggestions.
2. Miriam Gilson and Jerzy Zubrzycki, *The Foreign-Language Press in Australia, 1848–1964* (Canberra: ANU Press, 1967), 14–17; Lech Paszkowski, *Poles in Australia and Oceania 1790–1940* (Canberra: Australian National University Press, 1987), 295; Ivan Barko, "The Courrier Australien and French-Australian Relations during the Biard d'Aunet Years (1892–1905)", in *The Culture of the Book: Essays from Two Hemispheres in Honour of Wallace Kirsop*, ed. David Garrioch (Melbourne: Bibliographical Society of Australia and New Zealand, 1999), 432; Bogumila Zongollowicz, "Wroblewski, Charles Adam Marie (1855–1936)", in *Australian Dictionary of Biography* (Canberra: National Centre of Biography, Australian National University), http://adb.anu.edu.au/biography/wroblewski-charles-adam-marie-13258 (accessed December 6, 2018); "Le Courrier Australien: le plus ancien journal de langue étrangère en Australie!", *Courrier Australien* (blog), October 24, 2016, https://www.lecourrieraustralien.com/le-courrier-australien-le-plus-ancien-des-journaux-franco-australien/.
3. There are large gaps in the record. For 1893 only January issues could be found and nothing seems to have survived from then until 28 March 1896.
4. Déjardin to Hanotaux, April 20, 1896; Consul General to Ministry of Foreign Affairs, February 25, 1913, Ministère des Affaires Etrangères (MAE), Correspondance Politique et Commerciale, Nouvelle Série (CPC-NS), box 21.
5. Barko, "The Courrier Australien", 432–33; Zongollowicz, "Wroblewski, Charles Adam Marie (1855–1936)"; Edward Duyker, *Of the Star and the Key: Mauritius, Mauritians and Australia* (Sylvania, N.S.W: Australian Mauritian Research Group, 1988), 99–100.
6. Naomi Forwood, "Les Français en Australie à travers *Le Courrier Australien* 1892–1901. Analyse Sociologique." Bachelor of Arts Honours Thesis (University of Sydney, 1983); Barko, "The Courrier Australien".

7. Donald Denoon, "Remembering Australasia: 2002 Eldershaw Memorial Lecture", *Tasmanian Historical Research Association* 49, no. 4 (December 2002): 225.

8. Ann Laura Stoler and Frederick Cooper, "Between Metropole and Colony: Rethinking a Research Agenda", in *Tensions of Empire: Colonial Cultures in a Bourgeois World*, ed. Ann Laura Stoler and Frederick Cooper (Berkeley: University of California Press, 1997); Frances Steel, "Anglo-Worlds in Transit: Connections and Frictions across the Pacific*", *Journal of Global History* 11, no. 2 (July 2016): 251–70; Julia Martinez, Claire Lowrie, Frances Steel and Victoria Haskins, *Colonialism and Male Domestic Service across the Asia Pacific* (London: Bloomsbury Academic, 2019).

9. Donald Denoon and Philippa Mein Smith, *A History of Australia, New Zealand, and the Pacific* (Malden, MA: Blackwell Publishers, 2000), 5; For recent work breaking new ground in this area see Briony Neilson, "Settling Scores in New Caledonia and Australia: French Convictism and Settler Legitimacy", *Australian Journal of Politics and History* 64, no. 3 (2018): 391–406.

10. Lorenzo Veracini, *Settler Colonialism: A Theoretical Overview* (Basingstoke: Palgrave Macmillan, 2010), 2.

11. Antoinette Burton, *After the Imperial Turn: Thinking with and through the Nation* (Durham, NC: Duke University Press, 2003).

12. *Le Courrier Australien*, April 30, 1892, 1.

13. Anny Stuer, *The French in Australia* (Canberra: Australian National University), 110.

14. Alexis Bergantz, "French Connection: The Culture and Politics of Frenchness in Australia, 1890–1914", Doctor of Philosophy thesis, The Australian National University, 2016, 116.

15. Déjardin to Hanotaux, April 20, 1896; Consul General to Ministry of Foreign Affairs, February 25, 1913, MAE, CPC-NS, 21.

16. Barko, "The Courrier Australien", 333–434.

17. Zongollowicz, "Wroblewski, Charles Adam Marie (1855–1936)".

18. Forwood, "Les Français en Australie", 12; Zongollowicz, "Wroblewski, Charles Adam Marie (1855–1936)".

19. Les Hetherington, "The Sydney French Club, 1885–1893", *The French Australian Review*, no. 58 (Australian Winter 2015): 32, 43.

20. *Le Courrier Australien*, April 30, 1892, 1. All translations unless otherwise indicated are my own.

21. *Le Courrier Australien*, May 7, 1892, 1.

22. Brett Bowden, *The Empire of Civilization: The Evolution of an Imperial Idea* (Chicago: University of Chicago Press, 2009), 90.

23. *Le Courrier Australien*, July 9, 1892, 1.

24. *Truth*, 8 May 1892, 6.

25. *Le Courrier Australien*, May 14, 1892, 2.
26. *Le Courrier Australien*, May 21, 1892, 1; May 28, 1892, 1.
27. *Le Courrier Australien*, May 14, 1892, 1; November 19, 1892, 1.
28. *Le Courrier Australien*, May 7, 1892, 1.
29. Denoon and Mein Smith, *A History of Australia, New Zealand, and the Pacific*, 30;
30. Philippa Mein Smith, "Retracing Australasia: The History of a British Idea", in *Body and Mind: Historical Essays in Honour of F. B. Smith* (Melbourne: Melbourne University Press, 2009), 156.
31. Cited in Philippa Mein Smith, "Mapping Australasia", *History Compass 7*, no. 4 (2009): 1102.
32. Charles de Brosses, *Histoire des navigations aux terres australes* (Paris: Durand, 1756).
33. Smith, "Retracing Australasia", 157–58; Smith, "Mapping Australasia", 1102, 1108.
34. Cited in Denoon, "Remembering Australasia", 226.
35. Smith, "Retracing Australasia", 160; see Philippa Mein Smith et al., *Remaking the Tasman World*, ed. Tanya Tremewan (Christchurch, N.Z.: Canterbury University Press, 2008); Frances Steel, *Oceania Under Steam: Sea Transport and the Cultures of Colonialism, c. 1870–1914* (Manchester: Manchester University Press, 2011); Catherine Bishop, 'Women on the Move Gender, Money-Making and Mobility in Mid-Nineteenth-Century Australasia', *History Australia* 11, no. 2 (2014): 38–59; Helen Bones, *The Expatriate Myth: New Zealand Writers and the Colonial World* (Dunedin, New-Zealand: Otago University Press, 2018).
36. Alexis Bergantz, '"The Scum of France": Australian Anxieties towards French Convicts in the Nineteenth Century', *Australian Historical Studies* 49, no. 2 (2018): 150–66.
37. *Le Courrier Australien*, July 16, 1892, 1.
38. Tracey Banivanua Mar, *Decolonisation and the Pacific: Indigenous Globalisation and the Ends of Empire* (Cambridge: Cambridge University Press, 2016); Sophie Loy-Wilson, *Australians in Shanghai: Race, Rights and Nation in Treaty Port China* (London: Routledge, 2017); Julie McIntyre, "'Trans-'Imperial Eyes' in the Atlantic on the British Imperial Voyage to Australia, 1787–1791", *History Australia* 15, no. 4 (2018): 1–19; Nadia Rhook, "Affective Counter Networks: Healing, Trade, and Indian Strategies of In/Dependence in Early 'White Melbourne'", *Journal of Colonialism and Colonial History* 19, no. 2 (2018); Julia Martinez, Claire Lowrie, Frances Steel and Victoria Haskins, *Colonialism and Male Domestic Service*.
39. Paul A Kramer, "Empires, Exceptions, and Anglo-Saxons: Race and Rule between the British and United States Empires, 1880–1910", *The Journal*

of American History 88, no. 4 (2002): 1315–53; Jane Carey and Frances Steel, "Introduction: On the Critical Importance of Colonial Formations", *History Australia* 15, no. 3 (2018): 399–412.

40. Neilson, "Settling Scores", 402; see also McIntyre, "Trans-'imperial-Eyes'".

41. Frances Steel, "Re-Routing Empire? Steam-Age Circulations and the Making of an Anglo Pacific, c.1850–90", *Australian Historical Studies* 46, no. 3 (2015): 356–73.

42. John Connell, *New Caledonia or Kanaky?: The Political History of a French Colony* (Canberra: The Australian National University, 1987), 40–52.

43. Neilson, "Settling Scores", 397–98; *Le Courrier Australien*, October 22, 1892, 1.

44. George Griffith, *In an Unknown Prison Land: An Account of Convicts and Colonists in New Caledonia with Jottings out and Home* (London: Hutchinson & Co, 1901), 95.

45. Margot Simington, "Australia's Political and Economic Relations with New Caledonia, 1853–1945", Doctor of Philosophy thesis, University of New South Wales, 1978, 77.

46. Martin Lyons, *The Totem and the Tricolour* (Kensington, N.S.W: New South Wales University Press, 1986), 80.

47. *Le Courrier Australien*, April 30, 1892, 3; December 12, 1896, 3; Louis José Barbançon, *Gomen à l'ombre du Kaala* (Kaala-Gomen: Mairie de Kaala-Gomen, 1992)

48. Lady Jersey, "A French Colony", in *The Nineteenth Century: A Monthly Review*, vol. 22 (London: Sampson Low, Marston & Co, 1892), 527–28; *Le Courrier Australien*, July 12, 1892, 1; July 23, 1892, 1; October 22, 1892, 1; November 26, 1892, 2; January 28, 1893, 1; June 13, 1896.

49. Simington, *Australia's Political and Economic Relations with New Caledonia*, 74–85

50. Connell, *New Caledonia or Kanaky?*, 57; Simington, *Australia's Political and Economic Relations with New Caledonia*, 74–85.

51. *Le Courrier Australien*, September 10, 1892, 3; September 17, 1892, 2; September 24, 1892, 2; October 22, 1892, 1; Simington, *Australia's Political and Economic Relations with New Caledonia*, 83.

52. Benedict Anderson, *Imagined Communities: Reflections on the Origin and Spread of Nationalism* (London: Verso, 2006).

53. *Le Courrier Australien*, July 16, 1892, 1; September 17, 1892, 1; October 22, 1892, 1; August 8, 1896, 3; Jean Martin, "Les débuts du protectorat et la révolte servile de 1891 dans l'île d'Anjouan", *Outre-Mers* 60, no. 218 (1973): 53, 74; Jersey, "A French Colony", 528.

54. *Le Courrier Australien*, June 11, 1892, 1.

55. Bowden, *The Empire of Civilization*, 94.

56. Stoler and Cooper, "Between Metropole and Colony"; Carl Bridge and Kent Fedorowich, *The British World: Disapora, Culture and Identity* (London: Frank Cass Publishers, 2003); Kate Darian-Smith, Patrica Grimshaw, and Stuart Macintyre. ed., *Britishness Abroad: Transnational Movements and Imperial Cultures* (Melbourne: Melbourne University Press, 2007); Graeme Davison, John Hirst, and Stuart Macintyre, ed., *The Oxford Companion to Australian History* (Oxford University Press, 1999), 466.

57. Marilyn Lake, "British World or New World? Anglo-Saxonism and Australian Engagement with America", *History Australia* 10, no. 3 (2013): 36–50; Marilyn Lake, *Progressive New World: How Settler Colonialism and Transpacific Exchange Shaped American Reform* (Cambridge, Mass: Harvard University Press, 2019).

58. Anne Rees, "'Treated like Chinamen': United States Immigration Restriction and White British Subjects", *Journal of Global History* 14, no. 2 (2019): 239–60.

59. Matthew Frye Jacobson, *Whiteness of a Different Color: European Immigrants and the Alchemy of Race* (Cambridge, MA: Harvard University Press, 1998), 6.

60. Kramer, "Empires, Exceptions, and Anglo-Saxons: Race and Rule between the British and United States Empires, 1880–1910"; Jacobson, *Whiteness of a Different Color.*

61. Veracini, *Settler Colonialism*, 16.

62. *Le Courrier Australien*, January 28, 1893, 1.

63. *Le Courrier Australien*, May 7, 1892, 3.

64. Marilyn Lake and Henry Reynolds, *Drawing the Global Colour Line. White Men's Countries and the International Challenge of Racial Equality* (Cambridge: Cambridge University Press, 2008), 6, 9.

65. *Le Courrier Australien*, October 24, 1896, 3

66. *Le Courrier Australien*, May 30, 1896, 3.

67. *Le Courrier Australien*, July 2, 1892, 1.

68. *Le Courrier Australien*, July 2, 1892, 1; January 21, 1892, 2; August 18, 1892, 1; May 30, 1896, 3; October 24, 1896, 3.

69. *Le Courrier Australien*, August 22, 1896, 2; August 29, 1896, 3.

70. Veracini, *Settler Colonialism*, 26.

71. *Le Courrier Australien*, September 24, 1892, 2.

72. *Le Courrier Australien*, June 13, 1896, 3; July 16, 1892, 4; December 31, 1892, 1; November 26, 1892, 1.

73. Connell, *New Caledonia or Kanaky?*, 38.

74. *Le Courrier Australien*, December 3, 1892, 1.

75. Déjardin to Hanotaux, April 20, 1896; Consul General to Ministry of Foreign Affairs, February 25, 1913, MAE, CPC-NS, 21.

CHAPTER 4

Publishing Sydney's Chinese Newspapers in the Australian Federation Era: Struggle for a Voice, Community and Diaspora Solidarity

Mei-fen Kuo

The Immigration Restriction Act of 1901 imposed limitations by introducing a dictation test to screen non-European applicants for entry to Australia and by assessing an extensive system of Certificates of Domicile and Certificates of Exemption from the Dictation Test, which proscribed the rights of travel and mobility of the Chinese who were residents in Australia at that time. This pattern of systemic discrimination isolated many Chinese Australians, codifying them as an "other" in contrast to British and European Australians.[1] Chinese newspapers provide a window through which to see Chinese Australians in their struggle against racial

M.-f. Kuo (✉)
Department of Media, Communications, Creative Arts, Language and Literature, Macquarie University, Sydney, NSW, Australia
e-mail: mei-fen.kuo@mq.edu.au

© The Author(s), under exclusive license to Springer Nature Switzerland AG 2021
C. Dewhirst, R. Scully (eds.), *Voices of Challenge in Australia's Migrant and Minority Press*, Palgrave Studies in the History of the Media, https://doi.org/10.1007/978-3-030-67330-7_4

63

discrimination. They also recorded the transformation of the Chinese community into a modern civic and transnational one.

Yet in the twenty-first century Beijing has enjoyed a "controlling" interest in Chinese-language media in Australia that has triggered Australia's concern about this as a threat to democratic politics and multiculturalism.[2] At the turn of the twentieth century, Australia's Chinese-language newspapers played a significant role in community building, transnational networking and the formation of associated narratives of belonging in the broader Chinese diasporic community.[3] This chapter does not aim to explore Beijing's control over the current Australian Chinese media. Instead it advances the debate around the shifting role of Chinese newspapers in Australia by examining the early twentieth-century history of voices from the margin. They created a new social space that aimed to strengthen solidarity and create an imagined diasporic community as part of the fight against discrimination and inequality.

Sydney was the main home of early Chinese Australian newspapers and, by 1923, there were five Chinese weeklies: the *Chinese Australian Herald* (1894–1923), *Tung Wah News* (1898–1902) which continued as the *Tung Wah Times* (1902–1936), the *Chinese Times* (1902–1922 in Melbourne, 1922–1949 in Sydney), the *Chinese Republic News* (1914–1937) and the *Chinese World News* (1922–1950s). The circulation of the newspaper had grown in the early twentieth century from hundreds to thousands.[4] Before establishing these five newspapers, there was the *Chinese Advertiser* (later *English and Chinese Advertiser*), published on the Victorian goldfields in the 1850s. It was the earliest bilingual Chinese–English-language newspaper in Australia but short-lived.[5]

Sydney's Chinese publishers and editors experienced difficulties common to all minority migration press enterprises, including a shortage of investment and limited readership. This is clear from Sydney's first three Chinese newspapers' strategies employed to extend their social capital to survive. They established joint-stock limited liability corporation for capital, collaboration with European and Chinese journalists, and themselves as profit-trading companies to the strengthened readership in the name of diaspora solidarity. These newspapers were distributed in Australia and across New Zealand and the South Pacific Islands through Chinese Australian commercial and social ties. Consequently, the Chinese-language press was the most significant and only foreign-language press to publish without interruption over three decades from the 1890s to the 1920s in Sydney.[6] In the 1930s Sydney, the Chinese also published two short-lived

English weekly newspapers, such as the *Sino-Australasian Times Newspaper* (1930–1931) and *Eastern Commercial Press* (1931–1932?), in order to foster trade between Australia and the East.[7]

By examining the ownership, corporate structure and commercial strategies of the first three of Sydney's Chinese newspapers—the *Chinese Australian Herald*, the *Tung Wah News* (*Tung Wah Times*) and the *Chinese Republic News*, this chapter argues that Chinese newspapers in Sydney had demonstrated a minority "print capitalism". Christopher Reed defines print capitalism in modern China as "best understood to mean the social, economic, and political system that resulted from the reciprocal influences of the mental realm of literati print culture and the material world of industrialized mechanical duplication of printed commodities for privatized profit".[8] Sydney Chinese publishers had established their journalist business in "White Australia" by mobilising their ethnic resources to respond to social inequality and limited financial opportunity.

It has been well documented that new Chinese migrants have built a strong presence in migrant media because of their mature ethnic enclave economy and the growing economic power of China.[9] However, in the early twentieth century, Chinese newspapers operating under racial discrimination have been little acknowledged in current Chinese diaspora media studies because they do not explain the phenomenon of Chinese new media aboard. Scholars have highlighted the differences between old and new Chinese migrants.[10] While this chapter acknowledges that the "Chinese community" is diverse rather than a homogenous ethnic group, it is also essential to recognise the Chinese diasporic community's diversified voices, which are not always beholden to their motherland. Chinese Australian newspapers in Sydney offer a case study that helps us to revise our historical understanding of the strategies used by Chinese migrant presses throughout the Chinese diaspora at a time when China had not yet become a global power.

The development of Chinese newspapers in the Australian Federation era will also revise our understanding of how Chinese minority migrant newspapers survived despite their small capital, limited advertising market, the impact of racial discrimination and keen competition. According to Donald R. Browne and Enrique Uribe-Jongbloed, newspapers produced by and for minority, migrant groups were not financially rewarding due to the difficulty of attracting a large enough readership.[11] Alicia Ferrández Ferrer's current research claims that commercial pressure to maintain advertisers and investors pushed minority media to adapt to commercial demands.[12] Consequently, minority media engaged less and less with the political and social needs or interests of their public.

In contrast, this chapter argues that commercial pressure did not weaken the voice of Sydney's early Chinese newspapers' engagements with political and social interests. The *Chinese Australian Herald, Tung Wah Times* and *Chinese Republic News* had formed alternative patterns of commercial cooperation and social networking through various bilingual partnerships, merchant associations and republican political alliances, in order to ensure their survival and speaking out about facilitating community building. Their voices towards civil rights and universal values were not dampened by commercial pressure. In response to competition, inequality and discrimination Chinese newspapers highlighted solidarity to enhance commercial cooperation and community building. According to Lyn Spillman, the concept of solidarity needs to be understood as the root of modern economic power because merchants made sense of their commercial actions through disinterested commitments rather than profit-seeking orientation. [13] In the Australian Federation era, Sydney Chinese had asserted their diaspora solidarity which aimed to promote "public interests" such as civil rights economic equality rather than privatised profit.

Publishing the First Two Chinese Australian Newspapers in Sydney

In the wake of Australia's gold rush and mining boom, the predominantly male Chinese population shrank from 38,077 in 1891 to 33,165 in 1901, and again to 25,772 in 1911.[14] The Chinese moved into market gardening and other occupations in the gold rush towns.[15] As Sydney developed into an international trading centre by the late nineteenth century, it became a hub for mobile Chinese traders and labourers.[16] Yet at the turn of the twentieth century, Sydney's Chinese community was still the largest in Australia, with about 4000 living in the metropolitan area.[17]

Meanwhile, increasing anti-Chinese prejudice and the 1901 Immigration Restriction Act had restricted Chinese rights in Australia. At the same time it is noted that Chinese-Australian working-class collaboration increasingly occurred not only among the Chinese community but also in partnership with Anglo-Celtic communities in efforts to establish new enterprises. On such enterprise was the establishment of the first Chinese newspaper with a national Australian circulation, the *Chinese Australian*

Herald (*Guangyi huabao*). It was founded on a collaboration between European proprietors: James Alexander Philp (c. 1860–1935) and George Arthur Down and the Chinese bilingual editors, Lee Caizhang (?–1896) and Sun Johnson (c. 1865–1925). It was Sydney's first Chinese-language newspaper and was launched on 1 September 1894. It promoted itself as an informative agency for up-to-date world affairs and commercial intelligence.

The *Chinese Australian Herald* reported on the market price of fruits and vegetables. This service was an important incentive for Chinese market gardeners, hawkers and fruit storekeepers to become a significant part of the newspaper's readership in the 1890s. However, the newspaper's publishing success lay in the financial support it received from Australian advertisers, through Philp's entrepreneurial endeavours.[18] Even though most of the readership of the *Chinese Australian Herald* was ethnic Chinese, the advertisements placed by non-Chinese advertisers within its pages indicate that the Chinese were considered valuable customers and partners.[19]

The newspaper also entered into an arrangement with the booksellers, Gordon and Gotch, in order to enlarge its commercial network and circulation.[20] Once Gordon and Gotch had taken on the *Chinese Australian Herald*'s distribution the newspaper became available in Melbourne, Brisbane and London; it became a newspaper for the Chinese not only in New South Wales but also in Victoria, Queensland and overseas, and its commercial and circulation potential was greatly enhanced. In 1897, the *Chinese Australian Herald* had a good circulation of 800 copies per issue, distributed through Chinese storekeepers around Australia and New Zealand.[21]

Sun Johnson, the *Chinese Australian Herald*'s proprietor, credited the Australian firms with providing a very substantial amount of advertising revenue for the newspaper, although he also noted that the newspaper was often obliged to buy goods from their major Australian advertisers in exchange for annual advertising contracts.[22] A further dimension to the *Chinese Australian Herald*'s financial dealings was its role as a source of retail advertisements of patent medicines, groceries and Chinese imports.[23] The network of Chinese storekeepers in the newspaper's local circulation and promotion also played a significant role in its success. By 1900 its circulation had expanded further to New Caledonia, Samoa, Fiji, Tahiti, Rarotonga, Java, the Philippines and China itself.[24]

At this time, the number and influence of Chinese fruit traders in particular had risen within these communities, and they were searching for a new paradigm to enhance their commercial dynamic and looking for alternative ways of expanding their enterprises. In 1898, in order to promote their interests, aspirations and values, Sydney's Chinese merchants founded the *Tung Wah News* which would be continued as the *Tung Wah Times* (1902–1936). Unlike the *Chinese Australian Herald*, the proprietors of *Tung Wah News* were all ethnic Chinese, holding joint-stock options. The start-up capital holdings totalled £1000, divided into 5000 shares of four shillings each.[25] In addition to the more prominent traders, many of the smaller shareholders were market gardeners. The *Tung Wah News* formed on 10 June 1898 and was registered on 21 June as a limited company.[26] Its first issue was published on 29 June 1898, and the newspaper was printed every Wednesday and Saturday by Geo. Murray and Co. Ltd.[27] Its financial support came principally from subscriptions and advertising placed by Australian and Chinese companies.[28]

The *Tung Wah News'* management style reflected its diverse ownership and corporate structure which can be understood as a Chinese model of print capitalism in Australia. Each year, the company elected six managers to oversee the running of the newspaper. They were required to attend meetings on the first day of every month. A number of rules and procedures were laid down regarding the shareholders, managers, editors and those in charge of printing, to ensure that the *Tung Wah News* was run as efficiently as possible and in keeping with modern business practices.[29]

The make-up of its shareholders and financial sources reflected the *Tung Wah News'* aims and commercial interests. Aside from local advertising and business information concerning the Chinese community, it also reported more generally on Sydney and provided business information and news of Chinese communities in Hong Kong, Macao, Singapore and Honolulu by printing excerpts from various overseas newspapers. It also started to report regularly on the gold exchange rate in Hong Kong and the volume of gold exports from Australia to Hong Kong and that big profits could be made on Hong Kong's exchange market. *Tung Wah News* became the critical institute of remittance trade advertisements to Chinese Australians at the turn of the twentieth century.[30]

In Chinese remittance networks, local Chinese merchants, clan associations, mobile brokers, bankers, postmasters and interpreters collaborated through various channels. Print culture in particular played an essential role in building the Chinese diaspora network.[31] In Australia, Chinese newspapers did not simply enhance remittance trade by circulating remittance advertisements and news but also through orientating their readers to take advantage of the emergence of Australian economic power through the process of remittance exchange. From 1898 through to the late 1910s, the scale and network of the Chinese Australian remittance trade included Chinese stores in Australian towns and cities as well as Chinese firms in New Zealand, Annam, Hong Kong and San Francisco that carried out remittance business. In this process of building Chinese enterprises, newspapers did not just function as an informative tool for merchants but also as a social association of commercialisation. Growing commercial profits strengthened levels of confidence amongst Sydney's Chinese merchants, who came to extol and embrace modern capitalism as a dynamic force of community solidarity and cooperation.

Emerging Diaspora Solidarity after 1904 and Publishing the Third Chinese Newspaper

While both the *Chinese Australian Herald* and *Tung Wah News* benefited Australia's growing economic power, they also experienced challenges in terms of increasingly discriminatory sentiment and legislation directed at the Chinese community. Chinese merchants, in particular, mobilised resources to counter the ill effects of White Australian nationalism and fought to maintain their position in the face of the crude Social Darwinism that prevailed at the time.[32] In this circumstance, the *Tung Wah News* became a space for Chinese merchants to enhance their leadership through their struggle against White Australia.

The *Tung Wah News* changed its name to the *Tung Wah Times* in August 1902. From 1904, it became the official newspaper of the first Chinese-Australian merchant association in the country: The New South Wales Chinese Chamber of Commerce.[33] Reflected in its regulations, the purpose of the new society was the promotion of economic mobilisation, and it was explicitly approved of the Western economic system and Western society. Emerging Chinese-Australian merchants shifted their organisational patterns from guild formation to modern associational forms. They developed new styles of business and community leadership in an environment where new kinds of social alliances yielded new forms of mobilisation and new types of political ideology.[34] Though in 1904 the Anti-Chinese and Asiatic League was formed through a union of the Liberal and Reform

Association, the Shop Assistants' Union, the Sydney Labour Council, the United Furniture Traders' Association and the NSW Retail Grocers' Association. The League's work damaged the businesses of Chinese fruit traders and storekeepers based at the Belmore Market severely.[35]

While the Chamber of Commerce was an association with a positive mission, concern over the declining value of their businesses prompted leading Chinese merchants to propose a new association expressly for the purpose of defending their rights and securing positions more directly: the New South Wales Chinese Merchants' Defence Association. The narratives within the Chinese newspapers indicate that they believed they were becoming the victims of the anti-Chinese movement and they proclaimed their intention to work towards achieving a better atmosphere for stable commercial activity.[36] Meanwhile, Sydney's Chinese merchants began adopting the term, "Social Darwinism", to encourage Chinese merchants and traders to fight for their rights and prospects in the face of the anti-Chinese movement.[37] The *Tung Wah Times* also introduced the notion of a trade war (*shangzhan*) in association with the concept of Social Darwinism in order to struggle for further commercial peace, business stability and ethnic equality.[38]

While Chinese newspapers strengthened notions of a trade war and Western practices of commercial association, there was not, however, universal solidarity within the Chinese community on the issue. There were differences between the stance the *Tung Wah Times* and that of the *Chinese Australian Herald*. While the *Tung Wah Times* insisted on the urgent need for some form of protection against the Anti-Chinese and Asiatic League and tried to provide some, the *Chinese Australian Herald* disagreed that the situation was quite so pressing and showed less concern about the White Australia policy overall.[39]

Furthermore, the social and economic circumstances of the Chinese community in Sydney and Melbourne widened the gap between the elite and the working class. In 1902, Thomas Chang Luke, as the editor of *Tung Wah News*, moved to Melbourne to publish the *Chinese Times* to promote his opinions regarding Chinese nationalism, White Australia and community politics. The newspaper editors aimed to draw support from lower-class Chinese by taking a stand against imperialism and highlighting barbaric unfairness. Moreover, the *Chinese Times* encouraged its readership to see exclusion laws as a national humiliation rather than just unequal treatment directed at a particular class.[40]

The widespread participation by Chinese Australians in the anti-American boycott of 1905, which condemned the discriminatory immigration policy of the United States and proposed a boycott in Shanghai,[41] explicitly demonstrated how they had begun to see themselves as part of a larger international community, which resulted in the development of an alternative form of community politics in Australia. Although awareness of anti-Chinese sentiment towards the Chinese diaspora around the globe was growing in Australia, Sydney Chinese merchants and Melbourne pro-labour groups developed different agendas in response to this. From 1905 the *Chinese Times* began to emphasise the emotional suffering and sense of isolation and dispossession experienced by Chinese overseas who were also targeted as a "coolie race".[42]

In Sydney Chinese merchants began enhancing their connection with the Shanghai Chinese Chamber of Commerce during the anti-American boycott. Consequently, the debate over a solution to the increasing exclusion of the Chinese from full participation in Australian life widened the gap between the Sydney elite and Melbourne's pro-labour groups within Chinese communities. In the following years, when the Sydney Chinese merchants proposed sending a petition to the Australian authorities, calling for the relaxation of entry restrictions on the five categories of Chinese exclusion, this was not, on the whole, accepted by the Chinese-Australian community.[43] The community was divided after 1905. As a result, newspapers created a space which allowed negotiation and debate between Chinese Australians. The specific problem for many was that the proposal ignored the rights and interests of the labouring classes. The *Chinese Times* expressed suspicions that Sydney Chinese merchants were acting in their own interest.[44] The *Tung Wah Times* responded in mid-1906 with an article encouraging Chinese Australians to unite in the struggle against the Immigration Restriction Act,[45] which immediately drew a response arguing that the Sydney merchants' proposal was no more than a self serving strategic move. In the first decade of the twentieth century, these debates also helped to craft a Chinese Australian sense of ethnicity, nationalism and modernity through public narratives and cultural rhetoric.[46]

In 1914, the third Sydney Chinese newspaper, *Chinese Republic News* (*Minguobao*, 1914–1937) was published and represented another alternative voice for the community. The establishment of the Republic of China in 1912 inspired Sydney's Chinese merchants to establish new activities and organisations in support of the new republican government. They believed that their own position and that of other Chinese Australians could be substantially improved through mobilisation on behalf of the new republic, because China now had the potential to become a state with values and institutions similar to those of Australia, the United States and other Western countries.

Developments in China naturally affected the beliefs about the Chinese community in Australia after 1912. There was an increasing conflict in China between republicans' party, known as Kuo Min Tang, and the autocratic new President, Yuen Shih-Kai. In short order, Yuen staged a military coup and ordered the dissolution of Kuo Min Tang.[47] Kuo Ming Tang members were evicted from the national parliament while Yuen consolidated power in the President's office and began to develop imperial dynastic ambitions. The Kuo Min Tang became an illegal organisation in China and the only republican newspaper in Oceania, the *Chinese Times*, collapsed in 1914. The *Chinese Republic News* was designed to take over the role of the *Chinese Times*, and the centre of the Chinese republican movement moved to Sydney.

Early in 1914, in a show of solidarity with the defeated republicans, that leading Australian Chinese merchants in Sydney, representing quite diverse interests, came together to publish the *Chinese Republic News*. Notable participants were George Kwok Bew of the Wing On Company, the Rev John Young Wai of the Chinese Presbyterian Church of NSW and James Ah Chuey, Grand Master of the Chinese Masonic Society. The newspaper was first published on 21 February 1914 and stated that profit-making is its primary goal.[48] This joint effort also laid the later foundations for the establishment of the Kuo Min Tang in Australia. The *Chinese Republic News* emerged in the following years as the instrument through which the Republican Party was founded and became a voice of commercial interests of Chinese republicans.

At the same time, Sydney's Chinese merchants extended the republican network in Australia and to New Zealand, Fiji, Tahiti and other Pacific Islands via their commercial ties. In 1915, Kuo Min Tang's first convention was held in San Francisco and Yee Wing from Sydney was appointed as the Australian delegate.[49] One year later, the first convention of Chinese republicans in Australia was duly held in Sydney in 1916. From early 1916, Sydney members of the "Chinese Nationalist League" sent donations from Australia, New Zealand and Fiji Island to Dr Sun Yat-Sen and the Kuo Min Tang in Tokyo to support the revolutionary army. Yuen Shih-Kai died of blood poisoning in June 1916, and with the collapse of his attempt to claim the imperial title for himself, the League formally changed its

Chinese name back to Kuo Min Tang. Increasing numbers of new branches and members demonstrated the power of Sydney's Chinese republican merchants, and in the process the Sydney branch became the Kuo Min Tang's leading Australasian office.

SOLIDARY FOR BUILDING THE FIRST CHINESE AUSTRALIAN STEAMSHIP CORPORATION

The *Chinese Republic News* regularly reported, not just on the Chinese republican movement but also on commercial news in China, Southeast, Asia and the Pacific Rim. One document notes that the *Chinese Republic News* was registered as a trading company for a large merchandise business with a significant merchandise and import and export trade.[50] In 1916, Percy Lee (1877–?), the new editor of the *Chinese Republic News*, raised the idea of forming a Chinese Australian steamship corporation to enhance Chinese Australian mobility, guaranteeing their ability to cross oceans in the Pacific Rim.[51] Born in 1877 Lee migrated to Australia in 1898. He was a storekeeper before he became the editor of the *Chinese Republic News* in 1916.[52] His idea was inspired by the Chinese Mail Steamship Company launched by Chinese merchants in San Francisco in 1915 for cross-Pacific trade.[53] He had been appointed as a promoter for that company in Australia.[54] Rather than simply investing in the Chinese Mail Steamship Company himself, Lee called on Chinese in Australia and South Pacific Islands to work together for this undertaking. His idea attracted attention from both Sydney Chinese merchants and general readers in Australasia.[55] According to C. F. Yong, the lack of shipping space and increase in freight and passengers' rates by the Japanese shipping companies were two of the main factors driving the Chinese in Australasia to form their own shipping line.[56]

The *Chinese Republic News* reported the success of the Chinese Mail Steamship Company in order to attract more interest and investment in steamship entrepreneurship in early 1917.[57] Both the *Chinese Republic News* and then the *Tung Wah Times* began to emphasise the need to break up the Japanese shipping dominance and to extend the Sino-Australian import and export trade. In June 1917, the Chinese Consul-General, T. K. Tseng, advised the New South Wales Chinese Chamber of Commerce to form the shipping line.[58] Meanwhile Chinese republican merchant George Bew, who was also the President of Sydney's Kuo Min Tang branch, presented a comprehensive report on the shipping trade between Hong Kong and Australia, which strengthened Chinese merchants' confidence in Sydney to form their own shipping line.[59] On 8 September 1917, Sydney's Chinese merchants gathered together to discuss whether they should accept a joint-shares proposal from the Sino-American Steamship or whether to establish the first Chinese Australian Steamship under their direct ownership. George Bew (1868–1932) was appointed as the chair of the meeting. After discussion, leading Sydney Chinese merchants including Bew agreed with Lee on the decision to form their own company.[60]

Bew arranged more meetings to make this corporation possible.[61] Historians have overlooked his leadership in forming the steamship corporation from the beginning. Bew's service for the commercial groups had strengthened his reputation.[62] After 1906 he was in charge of various collective donations and fundraising schemes by Chinese Australians. From that time, Bew's Wing Sang and Co. was the leading representative for quite a few fundraising campaigns and commercial investments in Australia, Hong Kong, Shanghai and other ports in the Pacific Rim. In late 1916, he was appointed as the Managing Director of Wing Ong Department Store, so he left Sydney. But it was mainly as a result of Bew's efforts that the paid-up capital from Australia deposited in Shanghai's Wing On was HK$500,000.[25] Launching the committee for the steamship was his last task before he left Sydney. The *Chinese Republic News* also noted that he arranged a meeting to call for shareholders in Hong Kong on his trip from Sydney to Shanghai.[63]

Sydney's three Chinese newspapers emphasised the notion of solidarity when promoting commercial interests such as those related to the steamship company. The *Tung Wah Times* stated that "the steamship corporation would strengthen the solidarity of ethnic Chinese and enhance the community's status against unfair competition, social inequity, and racial discrimination".[64] It was believed that the success of the steamship corporation would benefit the whole Chinese community in Australasia for by improving their mobility, prosperity and respectability. The Chinese Chamber of Commerce campaign culminated in forming the China-Australia Mail Steamship Company Ltd in November 1917, and eight representative stores also established a committee.[65] The proposal received £108,000 from Sydney, Melbourne, Hong Kong, New Zealand and Fiji. Shareholders with over 100 shares were eligible to be elected as a member of the board committee.[66] In November 1918, board members were elected.[67]

In just a few weeks, in December 1917, the SS *Gabo* was purchased in the name of William Liu of Wing Sang and Co. in December 1917. By January 1918 another cargo ship, SS *Victoria*, was added to the shipping line. However, in April and July 1918, the Federal government requisitioned the *Gabo* and the *Victoria* for war service under the War Precautions Act.[68] Even though the Armistice was signed on 11 November 1918, the two ships were not returned until October 1919. In April 1920 a passenger ship—*Hwah Ping*—was chartered from the Chinese government in Peking.[69] By April 1920 the Line was running all three vessels on the China-Australia run. Still, formidable competition from the old-established Japanese and British shipping companies caused immediate difficulty when the Line started to carry trade. Chinese newspapers and associations urged solidarity by asking Chinese merchants to refuse the discount offers from Japanese and British shipping companies and use the China-Australia Mail Steamship Company's services instead.

The letters of an Australian-born Chinese student—Joe Tong—offer a perspective based on his reading of the local Chinese press on this issue. In his view the creation of the steamship corporation reflected a dream of sustained diaspora connectivity and mobility.[70] His father and uncles purchased shares in the company and, while it turned out to be a poor investment due to wartime delays in bringing the ships into service, Joe Tong's letter nonetheless highlights his own and his family's support for the steamship company (not least because of anti-Japanese sentiment among patriotic Chinese in the wake of the Paris Peace treaties of 1919, which granted Japan Treaty rights in China's Shandong Province). The same merchants and newspapers promoted the Australia-China Steamship Company as a vehicle for saving China, deploying a new style of patriotic rhetoric to win shareholders among Chinese community members with little commercial interest in the venture. The Chinese press in Australia presented the Shandong concession as an act of national humiliation heralding China's "national extinction".[71] Joe Tong's letters home repeated the use of the phrase "national humiliation" as part of his arguments in support of boycott:

By reading the newspaper I learnt of a movement of resistance of Japanese goods in Shanghai, Hong Kong and Beijing. In this movement, if the Chinese could be able to hold on until the end without forgetting potential national humiliation, the movement would reach its aim that was to promote Chinese national products over international products. As [a] result,

the Chinese national industry would be able to achieve significant development. It was everyone's responsibility, in China, to not purchase Japanese
seafood and other goods, regardless of its relative affordability.[72]

Joe Tong offered his opinion about the anti-Japanese boycott and the
"marketing" of the Australia-China Steamship Company as a patriotic gesture.[73] His letters demonstrated the role of *Tung Wah Times* and *Chinese
Republic News* in shaping the connection between personal consumption
and national humiliation. The concept of solidarity in the face of national
humiliation had strengthened a nationalist alliance and community building in Australia in 1920 and 1921. In late 1920 and early 1921, Kuo Min
Tang constructed two buildings in Sydney and Melbourne while other
new associations were formed to seek justice and public good for the community. However, the concept of solidarity did not secure commercial
interests and cooperation. In 1921, Yee Wing of Kuo Ming Tang replaced
Liu as the manager of the steamship company and sought more capital
from Chinese Australians as well as from Hong Kong, in an attempt to
save it. But support failed to materialise, and the steamship company collapsed in 1924 (one year before, the Chinese Mail Steamship Company in
the United States had also collapsed). Historian Yong claimed that Chinese
merchants were able to collect capital and drive the start of a new enterprise, but lacked sufficient knowledge and experience to maintain it. This
and the emergence of several unexpected disasters caused the failure of the
steamship company.[74]

CONCLUSION

In an interview in 1978, William Liu recalled that forming the steamship
company from 1917 to 1921 showcased the best of the Chinese community because Chinese Australians demonstrated they had an interest in
something of mutual concern and hope. But that hope was not realised,
and the community split.[75] His words revealed the driving force behind
the first Chinese Australian Steamship was its meaning as a symbol of diaspora solidarity. It showed how Chinese in Australia sought to fulfil for
their interests, dreams and hopes with the establishment of multiple cor-
porations. However, seeking diaspora solidarity did not guarantee a
homogenous voice of the community. Sydney's Chinese newspapers demonstrated that minority groups were able to express their diversified opinions even within a society that discriminated against them.

By discussing the development of Sydney's first Chinese newspapers through a bilingual archive, family records and reports published by the *Chinese Australian Herald*, the *Tung Wah News* and the *Chinese Republic News*, this chapter has argued that there was an emerging sense of community and diasporic solidarity within a developing political consciousness. Those new commercial practices, which were embedded, in turn, in broader processes of social transformation affected the Sydney Chinese commercial groups and Chinese-Australian communities. The anti-Chinese racism of White Australia converged with partisan Chinese politics to evoke a shared vision for members of a transnational community that pined for a homeland and yet lay rooted in Australian soil.

The development of three Australian Chinese-language newspapers in Sydney is significant. It reflects the fact that commercial pressure did not reduce the voices speaking out about political and social engagements of all minority migrants. Sydney Chinese newspapers sought bilingual partnership, associational support and nationalist alliance in their struggle for survival. These newspapers also extended their links at the commercial level, involving transnational groups and mobility, which indicates that non-economic, social conditions and international politics were also crucial for the minority migrant press in the Australian Federation era. Publishing Chinese newspapers in Sydney during Australia's Federation era demonstrates that minority group presses strengthened the connection between personal consumption and diaspora identity. They showed dreams, hopes and political aspirations as crucial points of innovation in the transition and formation of not only the minority migrant printing industry and diaspora identity.

Notes

1. Myra Willard, *History of the White Australia Policy to 1920* (Melbourne: Melbourne University Press, 1978); C. Y. Choi, *Chinese migration and settlement in Australia* (Sydney: Sydney University Press, 1975).
2. John Fitzgerald, "Chinese Australians and the public diplomacy challenge for Australia in the 21st century", in *Chinese Australians: Politics, engagement and resistance*, ed. S. Couchman and K. Bagnall (Leiden, Netherlands: Brill, 2015), 267–289; Wanning Sun, John Fitzgerald and Jia Gao, "From multicultural ethnic migrants to the new players of China's public diplomacy: The Chinese in Australia", in *China's Rise and the Chinese Overseas*, ed. B. Wong and C. B. Tan (New York: Routledge, 2018), 55–74.

3. C. F. Yong, *The New Gold Mountain: the Chinese in Australia, 1901–1921* (Adelaide: Raphael Arts, 1997); Mei-fen Kuo, *Making Chinese Australia: Urban Elites, Newspapers and the Formation of Chinese Australian Identity, 1892–1912* (Melbourne: Monash University Publishing, 2013).

4. The statistics are based on the author's research. In 1897, the *Chinese Australian Herald* stated its circulation of 800 copies per issue; see a letter from *Chinese Australian Herald* to Colonial Secretary, Colonial Secretary's correspondence, State Records Authority of New South Wales (SRNSW), 5/6363 dated on 15 July 1897. In 1925, according to the boarder officer to the Secretary of Home and Territories Department, the average circulation of the *Chinese Republic News* was stated to be 5000 copies weekly. "Chinese Republican [Republic] News—Exemption for staff", National Archives of Australia (NAA), A433, 1947/2/6297, PART 2.

5. The Chinese Advertiser was published by Robert Bell in Ballarat from 1856 to 1858(?). It was published every Saturday and had a circulation of 400 copies. Its primary aim was to carry advertisements and inform the Chinese community in the goldfields about government regulations.

6. German newspapers made up the largest foreign-press group in Australia as a whole because of the growth of the German immigrant population during the last decades of the nineteenth century, chiefly in South Australia, Queensland and Melbourne, but less so in Sydney. See Miriam Gilson and Jerzy Zubrzycki, *The Foreign-language Press in Australia, 1848–1964* (Canberra: Australian National University Press, 1967), 10–13, 209. The Scandinavian foreign-language press, *Norden*, was published in Australia from the 1890s to the 1940s, which played an important role in reshaping the ethnic identity of Scandinavian in Australia. See Mark Jospeh Emmerson, "'Vi er alle Australiere': The Migrant Newspaper Norden and its Promotion of Pan-Scandinavian Unity within Australia, 1896–1940", Doctor of Philosophy thesis, University of Southern Queensland, 2015.

7. Mei-fen Kuo, "Sydney Chinese press, diaspora capitalism and the White Australia Policy: the case of Percy Lee", in "Voices of the Australian Migrant and Minority Press: Intercultural, Transnational and Diasporic Contexts" Conference, University of Southern Queensland, Toowoomba, 22–23 November 2017. Emmerson, "'*Vi er alle Australiere*'".

8. Christopher A. Reed, *Gutenberg in Shanghai: Chinese Print Capitalism, 1876–1937* (Vancouver: UBC Press, 2004), 258.

9. Wanning Sun and John Sinclair, *Media and Communication in the Chinese Diaspora: Rethinking Transnationalism* (London: Routledge, 2006); Min Zhou, *Contemporary Chinese America* (Philadelphia, PA: Temple University Press, 2009).

10. Min Zhou and Gregor Benton, "Intra-Asian Chinese Migrations: A Historical Overview", in *Contemporary Chinese Diasporas*, ed. Min Zhou (Singapore: Palgrave, 2017), 1–25.
11. D. Browne and E. Uribe-Jongbloed, "Introduction: ethnic/linguistic minority media-what their history reveals, how scholars have studies them and what might ask next", in *Minority Languages and Social Media: Participation, Policy and Perspectives*, ed. E. Haf Jones and E. Urine-Jongbloed (Bristol: Multilingual Matters, 2013), 1–28.
12. Alicia Ferrández Ferrer, "Towards a democratization of the public space? Challenges for the 21st century", in *The Handbook on Diasporas, Media, Culture*, ed. J. Retis and R. Tsagarousianou (Hoboken: Wiley, 2019), pp. 255–268.
13. Lyn Spillman, *Solidarity in Strategy: Making Business Meaningful in American Trade Association* (Chicago: The University of Chicago Press, 2012).
14. H. A. Smith F.S.S., *The Official Year Book of N.S.W. 1920* (Sydney: W. A. Gullick, Govt. Printer, 1921), 66.
15. Ann Curthoys, "Men of All Nations, Except Chinamen: Chinese on the New South Wales Goldfields", in *Gold Forgotten Histories and Lost Objects of Australia*, ed. Andrew Reeves, Iain McCalman and Alexander Cook (Cambridge: Cambridge University Press, 2001), 115–116.
16. T. A. Coghlan, *General Report on the Eleventh Census of New South Wales* (Sydney: Government Printer 1894), 127; T. A. Coghlan and T. T. Ewing, *The Progress of Australia in the Century* (London: Chambers, 1903), 137.
17. Yong, *The New Gold Mountain*, 261.
18. Philp, the Scottish-born author, printer and columnist, had not been long in Australia, having arrived from New Zealand in 1889 and joined *The Bulletin* in Sydney. See Matthew J. Fox, *The history of Queensland: its people and industries: an historical and commercial review descriptive and bio-graphical facts, figures and illustrations: an epitome of progress* (Brisbane: States Publishing Company, 1923), 805. He was also a member of the Dawn and Dusk Club, which included many of Sydney's avant-garde artists and intellectuals. See George A. Taylor, *Those were the days: being reminiscences of Australian artists and writers* (Sydney: Tyrell's Limited, 1918), 11.
19. According to Browne and Uribe-Jongbloed, only when a minority becomes "economically attractive" could advertisers be interested in supporting a minority group: Browne and Uribe-Jongbloed, "Introduction".
20. *Chinese Australian Herald,* January 26, 1897, p. 4. Although the *Chinese Australian Herald* had a Melbourne agent (H. Scott in Queen Street, from May 1895 to March 1896), the number of Chinese readers in

Melbourne before 1896 is unclear. Chinese Australian Herald, May 10, 1895, pp. 7, 20; *Chinese Australian Herald*, March 1896, p. 1.

21. See a letterhead from *Chinese Australian Herald* in 1897 to the Colonial Secretary, SRNSW, Colonial Secretary's correspondence, item 5/6363, 15 July 1897.

22. Bankruptcy files 1888–1929: Sun Johnson, SRNSW, 23567.

23. *Chinese Australian Herald*, November 30, 1894, p. 7, January 5, 1895, p. 8, January 18, 1895 (calendar poster), May 24, 1895, p. 1, August 21, 1896, p. 6.

24. *Chinese Australian Herald*, January 27, 1900.

25. 'Defunct Company packet for *Tung Wah News*', SRNSW, no. 3/5733 in 1723. See also *Chinese Australian Herald*, April 5, 1902, p. 4 and April 12, 1902, p. 5. Yong (1977:117) claims that the £1000 capital was divided into 4000 shares, but this appears to be an error. *Chinese Australian Herald*, April 26, 1902, p. 3.

26. *Chinese Australian Herald*, April 5, 1902, p. 4.

27. *Tung Wah News*, August 10, 1898, p. 4.

28. From 1898 to 1900, *Tung Wah News* earned around £240 per year from subscriptions and advertising, but in 1901 it was involved a court case which reduced its earnings to around £114 (*Chinese Australian Herald*, April 5, 1902). Advertisements in the *Tung Wah News* and other newspapers are an important resource for understanding the development of Sydney Chinese firms and businesses and their location in the social network.

29. For records on managing *Tung Wah News* see its various news reports and later Minutes of NSW Chinese Chamber of Commerce: Noel Butlin Archives Centre, The Australian National University, NBAC 111-4-1.

30. Mei-fen Kuo, "Jinxin: the remittance trade and enterprising Chinese Australians, 1850–1916", in *Qiaopi Trade and Transnational Networks in the Chinese Diaspora*, ed. Gregor Benton, Hong Liu and Huimei Zhang (Abingdon, Oxon, UK: Routledge, 2018), 160–178.

31. Hong Liu and Gregor Benton, "The Qiaopi Trade and Its Role in Modern China and the Chinese Diaspora: Toward an Alternative Explanation of "Transnational Capitalism"", *Journal of Asian Studies* 75, no. 3 (2016): 575–594.

32. *Sydney Morning Herald*, August 22, 1904, p. 5.

33. "Chinese Chamber of Commerce of New South Wales, Records of meetings, 1903–1904", ANU NBAC, 111/2/1, 111/4/1; "Correspondence of NSW Chinese Chamber of Commerce of New South Wales, 1913–1917", ANU NBAC, 111/2/1.

34. Mei-fen Kuo, "The making of a diasporic identity: the case of the Sydney Chinese commercial elite, 1890s–1900s", *Journal of Chinese Overseas* 5, no. 2 (2009), 336–363.
35. For example, George Bew claimed that the value of his business, Wing Sang and Co., fell from £4000 in 1903 to £1000 in 1905, 'George Bew, Leon Bew, Pearl Bew, Percy Bew, Daisy Alma Bew, George Noel Bew, Walter Bew, Elsie Bew, Edith Bew, Darling Bew', NAA, SP244/2, N1950/2/3885.
36. *Tune Wah Times*, July 16, 1904, supplement; *Chinese Australian Herald*, November 19, 1904, p. 5.
37. Kuo, *The making of a diasporic identity*.
38. On the concept of trade war, see Min Ma, *Shangren jingshen de shanbian: jindai Zhongguo shangren guannian yanjiu* [Transformation of the Chinese merchant spirit: studies on modern Chinese merchant concepts] (Wuhan: Huazhong shifan dzxue chubanshe, 2001), 80–83; Erh Min Wang, 'Shangzhan guannian yu zhongshang sixiang' [The concept of trade war and mercantilist thought]) in *Zhongguo jindai sixiang shiliun* [History of modern Chinese thought]) (Taipei: Hua shi chu ban she, 1977), 233–279. For en example of Sydney Chinese understandings of trade war, see *Tune Wah Times*, July 16, 1904, supplement.
39. *Tung Wah Times*, July 2, 1904, supplement.
40. Mei-fen Kuo, "Reframing Chinese labour rights: Chinese unionists, pro-labour societies and the nationalist movement in Melbourne, 1900–10", *Labour History* 113 (2017): 133–155.
41. The Shanghai boycott soon received supports from Chinese overseas.
42. *Chinese Times*, May 18, 1904, p. 2; October 21 1905, p. 2.
43. The proposal suggested to allow five categories of Chinese temporarily exemption for entry into Australia, such as merchants, students, officials, visitors and missionaries.
44. *Chinese Times*, March 10, 1906, supplement.
45. *Chinese Times*, July 14, 1906, p. 2.
46. Mei-fen Kuo, "Confucian heritage, public narratives and community politics of Chinese Australians at the beginning of the 20th century", in *Chinese Australians: politics, engagement and resistance,* ed. Sophie Couchman and Kate Bagnall (Boston: Brill, 2015), 137–173.
47. Jonathan Fenby, *History of Modern China* (3rd edn, London: Penguin Books, 2019), 133–138.
48. *Chinese Republic News*, February 21, 1914, p. 2.
49. Mei-fen Kuo and Judith Brett, *Unlocking the History of the Australasian Kuo Min Tang, 1911–2013* (North Melbourne: Australian Scholarly Publishing, 2013), 17.

50. National Archive of Australia, "Chinese Republican [Republic] News—Exemption for staff", A433 1947/2/6297 PART 1.
51. *Chinese Republic News*, September 23, 1916, p. 2.
52. "Percy Lee [also known as Bert Hee Lowe]", NAA, SP42/1, C1941/1585.
53. On the history of the Chinese Mail Steamship Company, see Shehong Chen, *Being Chinese, Becoming Chinese American* (Urbana & Chicago, University of Illinois Press, 2002), 106–111.
54. Zhongguo you chuan gong si and Zhuojing He, *China Mail Steamship Co. ltd.; report, 1915–1919* (San Francisco: Shi jie ri boa she, 1919).
55. *Chinese Republic News*, October 7, 1916, p. 3 and November 4, 1916, p. 2.
56. Yong, *The Gold Mountain*, 98.
57. *Chinese Republic News*, January 13, 1917, p. 7.
58. Minutes of NSW Chinese Chamber of Commerce, dated on 10 June 1917 in Noel Butlin Archives, The Australian National University, NBAC 111.
59. *Chinese Republic News*, August 11, 1917, p. 7.
60. *Chinese Republic News*, September 15, 1917, p. 6.
61. *Tung Wah Times*, October 13, 1917, p. 7; *Chinese Australia Herald*, October 20, 1917, p. 1.
62. *Tung Wah Times*, September 29, 1906, p. 6.
63. *Chinese Republic News*, January 12, 1918, p. 5.
64. *Tung Wah Times*, July 7, 1917, p. 7.
65. *Tung Wah Times*, December 8, 1917, p. 8.
66. *Chinese Republic, News*, July 27, 1918, p, 6.
67. *Chinese Australian Herald*, November 2, 1918, p. 2.
68. Yong, *The New Gold Mountain*, 102.
69. Yong, *The New Gold Mountain*, 106.
70. Joe Tong's letter to mother, 28 February 1919 in "Papers of the Chau family", National Library of Australia, MS10030.
71. Mei-fen Kuo and John Fitzgerald, "Chinese students in White Australia: state, community, and individual responses to the student visa program, 1920–1925", *Australian Historical Studies* 47, no. 2 (2016): 259–277.
72. Joe Tong's letter to mother, July 5, 1919. Joe Tong's letter also repeated the term as "cold animal" which was appeared widely printed in Chinese Australian newspapers. The term was produced by Chinese newspapers since 1900s to promote Chinese national products over foreign products.
73. Joe Tong's letter to parents, November 24, 1921.
74. Yong, *The Gold Mountain*, 109.
75. William Liu and Hazel de Berg, "William Liu interviewed by Hazel de Berg, 1978", National Library of Australia.

CHAPTER 5

Recovering an Optimistic Era: Chinese-Australian Journalism from the 1920s to the 1940s

Caryn Coatney

On the eve of the Pacific war, Australian Prime Minister John Curtin initiated an ambitious media campaign to promote China and strengthen ties with the Chinese-Australian community in late 1941. As a former labour-oriented journalist, Curtin announced to a close circle of reporters that he would consider changing Australia's settled policy for Chinese migrants.[1] Consequently, *The Canberra Times* reported: "Until strong racial barriers between the two countries were broken down, the two nations could not become friendly."[2] In one of his lesser-known achievements, Curtin praised China's gallantry and supported an extraordinary upsurge of Chinese arrivals, from refugees to journalists, into Australia during the wartime media campaign.[3] The campaign also overlooked the migrant journalists' own longstanding struggle for equality in Australia. The rarely

C. Coatney (✉)
School of Humanities and Communication, University of Southern Queensland, Springfield Central, QLD, Australia
e-mail: Caryn.Coatney@usq.edu.au

© The Author(s), under exclusive license to Springer Nature Switzerland AG 2021
C. Dewhirst, R. Scully (eds.), *Voices of Challenge in Australia's Migrant and Minority Press*, Palgrave Studies in the History of the Media, https://doi.org/10.1007/978-3-030-67330-7_5

explored news ventures contradict the early notion of a disengaged press. In fact, more recent scholarship has found that migrant journalists were deeply involved in being a voice for their communities.[4]

This chapter examines the changing status of the Chinese-Australian news ventures in Australia during the escalating Pacific crises leading to the Second World War. China's defiant battles against the ascending Japanese forces in the 1930s became the most high-profile conflict of the era. News correspondents lauded the spirit of Chinese resistance to Japan's assault on Manchuria in 1931. The journalists' reports of escalating atrocities, including the Rape of Nanking in 1937, swayed their readers' opinions in favour of China.[5] Japan had already emerged as a major, modern power with its humiliating ousting of China from the Korean Peninsula in 1895. The unexpected Japanese conquests and the nation's continued military expansion unsettled Western nations and as William Sima has commented: "The greatest security concern for Australia in the years following Federation in 1901 was the rise of the Empire of Japan and its regional ambitions."[6] The growing danger of the Pacific war was also the main focus of Australia's international diplomacy, spy surveillance and news headlines.[7] Notwithstanding, the prospect of multitudes of Chinese refugees fleeing war zones had similarly alarmed previous Australian governments, which mainly used the discriminatory *Immigration Restriction Act 1901*—or White Australia Policy—to curb the flow of China's migration.[8] By this time, Chinese newspapers were the largest foreign-language press group in Sydney despite the settlement ban. They also held the national record in continuous publication.[9] This chapter reveals fresh insights into how the news groups recast their community identity from a former threat to that of a loyal patriot. Their associations with political and press leaders elicited more support for their communities.

Australia's wartime administration persuaded Chinese migrant journalists to promote Chinese-Australian citizens while suppressing their opponents, the fascist, pro-Japanese members of the "Australia First" movement that had formed in 1936. However, Curtin's media campaign marked a high point in Australia-China relations and the media portrayed many Chinese reporters as celebrities. These popular images also masked Chinese-Australian journalists' initiatives to improve their communities' status.[10] They used editorial protests to destabilise the White Australia Policy and also challenged the interwar appeasement of Japan's military government.[11] In short, the newspaper ventures disrupted race barriers. These ventures included Sydney's democratic *Chinese Republic News*

(1914–1937), the business-owned Chinese World's News (1921–1951) and the constitutionalist *Tung Wah Times* (1902–c. 1941). The newspapers circulated widely within Australia and the Asia-Pacific region.[12] Not surprisingly, their independent stance increasingly clashed with China's officialdom, including the Kuomintang newspaper, the *Chinese Times* (1902–1949). The battling editorialists countered impressions that they shared a singular identity.[13] By uncovering rare news sources, personal correspondence and top-secret surveillance reports this chapter explores how the three Chinese-Australian press ventures established their independence from the Kuomintang's influence and elicited more support for what effectively was assertive patriotism.[14]

This study contributes to the scholarship on Chinese migrant journalism of the Pacific war and the impact of secret surveillance, censorship and immigration policies on Allied relations with China. Significant research on the press attitudes of Chinese-Australian communities includes the works of Ann Curthoys, Sophie Loy-Wilson and Mei-fen Kuo. Curthoys and Loy-Wilson found that racial anxieties dominated the news portrayal of Chinese migrants at the turn of the twentieth century.[15] Kuo notes that some prominent commentators praised the cosmopolitanism of Australia's Chinese communities by the 1930s. According to Kuo: "Australia's urbanising Chinese communities certainly brought a spirit of adventure and a boldness of vision to their Australian dreams."[16] The stance/focus I take in this chapter is to reveal that the government developed an increasingly tolerant approach towards Chinese-language journalism.

Other studies have focused on the interactions within the migrant news groups themselves. China's journalists often valued the ethos of press responsibility to help society.[17] Hongy Bai has observed: "This includes a sense of being part of the world, patriotism and even heroism."[18] Independent working-class newspapers had emerged in local Chinatowns with affiliations to labour movements in Great Britain and the United States by the late nineteenth century.[19] In Australia, the Chinese-language press often represented a business elite that formed in transient communities. Rivalries intensified as the independent migrant journalists began to publish moderate criticisms of the Kuomintang-led *Chinese Times* in both San Francisco and Sydney while some press ventures also played out homeland politics by generating goodwill for China in the Sino-Japanese conflict.[20]

Scholars have also analysed the era as a triumph of the Chinese government's media diplomacy. China's Generalissimo Chiang Kai-Shek permitted more press freedom and hired trained journalists to sway public sympathies for his country's fight.[21] In a pragmatic gesture, Curtin cooperated with Kai-Shek to publicise their alliance.[22] After the war, critics dismissed some Allied correspondents as Chinese propagandists.[23] Even so, a group of Australian public figures and newspaper editors hoped the alliance would forge closer relations with post-war China.[24] Whereas scholars have examined the impact of Kai-Shek's propaganda techniques on the Allied media, few studies have delved into the journalists' relations with Japan in the interwar years. One aspect of this history is that Australian officials detained two high-profile Australian commentators accused in the mainstream press of collaborating with Japan in the era of wartime spy mania.[25] The commentators were Curtin's former friend, Adela Pankhurst-Walsh, who was the daughter of the celebrated British suffragette, Emmaline Pankhurst, and the influential writer P. R. Stephensen. This study shows that the media blitz bolstered Chinese news ventures by marginalising anti-China attitudes.

This chapter is the first to demonstrate that the Chinese-Australian press ventures actively raised awareness of their communities. Successive Australian governments developed an increasingly tolerant approach towards Chinese-language journalism. Indeed, as analysis will show, the newspaper editors' efforts contributed to the growing inclusion of their ventures and communities in wider societies. The approach taken in this chapter is to examine the migration of Chinese journalists not only as a spatial network but also as an evolving process to gain official recognition.[26] This study analyses the journalists' immigration records and their related correspondence, as well as the secret government surveillance of their newspapers.[27] These sources are compared with the journalists' commentaries in the Chinese-language newspapers and Sydney's *Daily Telegraph* and *Evening News* from 1920 to 1945. The Chinese migrant newspapers include the *Chinese Republic News, Chinese Times*, the *Chinese World's News* and the *Tung Wah Times*, whose issues have been lodged at the National Archives and the digitised collection at the National Library of Australia.[28] Moreover, by evaluating the mainstream and labour-oriented news coverage of the migrant journalists and the editorial debates that they initiated, and by drawing from 25 urban and regional newspapers, this study aims to capture the media portrayal of the Chinese minority print ventures.[29]

This chapter also ascertains the growing enthusiasm for Chinese journalists and the corresponding repression of anti-China commentaries. For this purpose, the chapter investigates the secret enquiries into enemy spy networks through a rare analysis of government intelligence reports and Allied correspondence, including the diary of General Lewis Brereton.[30] Moreover, this study compares Curtin's secret news briefings to journalists about China with his administration's public and private communication about China.[31] The use of neglected accounts as sources helps to ascertain the changing status of the minority newspaper ventures and their communities. Such analysis aims to identify how the minority press ventures contributed to destabilising anti-Chinese sentiments.

Underground Resistance: Interwar Chinese-Australian Journalism

Chinese journalists formed a literate, mobile elite in Australia who defied the immigration ban and its intention to exclude China's professional classes along with Chinese wives and children. Before the White Australia policy, fortune-seeking Chinese migrants flocked to the nation in the 1850s and their communities numbered some 35,000 residents in the gold rush era; however, the migrant population swiftly declined after 1901.[32] In a rare exception, Curtin's government accepted the arrival of new Chinese migrants and refugees, whose numbers peaked at some 3000 people during the Pacific war. According to Paul Jones, they added to Australia's longer-term population of 14,000 people of Chinese backgrounds.[33] The size of this figure has given no indication of the vital role of the Chinese-language press in contributing to the communities' survival. In 1902, a Melbourne-based journalist reported on the independent *Chinese Times* founder, Zheng Lu (Thomas Chang Luke), who advised that his news columns were "principally about Chinese subjects, but, he added, his readers like to know what is going on outside their own sphere, and he also gave reports of all kinds of sensations."[34] The migrant journalists had established some six newspapers prior to the 1920s, cultivating a new sense of Chinese-Australianness.

While publicising a peaceful image, the owners of the Chinese-Australian migrant news disrupted immigration policies to bolster their communities' status over the 1920s and 1930s. They did so by obtaining exemptions from the government to employ more Chinese editors and hired migrant students to hand-set the Chinese characters in the newsprint.[35] The independent Chinese-Australian newspapers began cooperating with the *Chinese Times* to persuade Australian officials of the need to recruit skilled compatriots.[36] For example, the *Chinese Times* tried to bring over an editor-in-chief from China by asserting: "There are certainly very few men in Australia who have a proper knowledge and practical experience in editorial work such as is required to conduct a Chinese newspaper in a journalistic manner."[37] Other journalists welcomed the newspapers for aiming to foster international friendship by the 1920s.[38] Indeed, the Chinese-language editors generated more support because their specialised newsrooms would "not keep a local man out of employment," as it was said.[39]

Another example was the strategy to target the Australian government directly. The *Chinese World's News* increasingly protested against the White Australia Policy. For instance, the *Sydney Morning Herald* circulated a scathing critique by the Chinese World's News managing director and editor, Sidney Hing Lowe (1882–1959): "We believe that every country has a right to protect itself against the alien, but are certainly opposed to any country singling one or two races as aliens, without any excuse beyond that they have a tint in their skin, and on the other hand permitting the riff-raff of any other country to land here without question."[40]

The government reluctantly permitted a group of Sydney-based storekeepers and merchants, known as the Chinese Masonic Society, to establish the newspaper in 1921 on the basis that they did not discuss politics.[41] During the same year, the Chinese-Australian press was required to provide English translations of the newspapers for the government censors. Officials soon abandoned the practice of censoring each issue due to the *Chinese World News'* objection to paying for a Chinese translator.[42] This unexpected liberty allowed the Society to cultivate an activist editorial stance.[43] In contrast to the ghettos of the Chinese-American press, Chinese-Australian newspaper founders thus interacted with the political establishment. For example, one of the newspaper's representatives, Sydney millionaire William Yinson Lee (1884–1965), managed to have the threatened deportation of his wife and daughter to China overturned by appealing to the customs comptroller-general, with whom he had been friends at a selective school. Lee asserted he was "quite shocked" at the proposed separation of his family. [44] Officials removed the immigration ban because Lee was "held in high esteem by the commercial community, and is one who is foremost in any charitable movement."[45] Newspaper columnists had already publicised "Mr and Mrs W. Yinson Lee" as socialites among the Chinese-Australian community by 1916 (see Fig. 5.1).[46]

Fig. 5.1 Mr and Mrs William Yinson Lee in 1916. National Archives of Australia, A1, 1916/31599. (Courtesy of the National Archives of Australia)

The *Chinese World's News* proprietors cultivated mainstream journalists to improve the news coverage of their community. Sydney's Chinese Masonic Society representative and popular newspaper identity, William Gockson, published a leading commentary in Sydney's *Evening News* and *Truth* in 1922. The *Evening News* reported Gockson urging:

the local Press to encourage, rather than rupture, that sense of our dependence upon local journalists to do the right thing towards us, which is of such vital importance in the matter of framing and shaping public opinion for or against our Chinese abroad here.[47]

He had won fame for his migrant story of success by using his business networks in the *Chinese Republic News* and *Tung Wah Times* to help establish the China-Australia Mail Steamship Line. A journalist opined: "The China-Australia line has been wonderfully successful since its inception, and the story of how it came into being is a standing advertisement for the foresight and business acumen of the Chinese."[48]

Soon afterwards, the *Chinese World's News* managing director, Sidney Hing Lowe, wrote a bluntly worded commentary for the *Daily Telegraph* and *Sydney Morning Herald* to criticise the White Australia Policy. Lowe opined:

> We are anxious to build a trade between Australia and China, but are hampered considerably by your Alien Restriction Act, and so long as it is specifically directed against the Chinese, so long is there a chance of Australia losing markets right at its very door. [49]

The commentary caused one reader to complain to the government that Lowe was "a most bitter advocator."[50] Privately, the investigation branch director dismissed the reader's objection as "peculiarly phrased for an English-born writer, and it might be a good thing to ascertain who he [the complainant] is and whether he has any particular axe to grind."[51] The correspondence suggested that the government supported the *Chinese World's News*.

Likewise, a customs detective-inspector investigated another *Daily Telegraph* commentary, believed to have been written by *Chinese Times* editor, Mu Hang Su,[52] in 1925. Other news outlets reproduced the sharply worded commentary on the White Australia policy. The article was published under the byline of "Mai Tien Hua," reportedly Su's alias. He wrote: "When I find, in a country like Australia, profit ever being put before righteousness, it is as difficult for me to converse coherently, as it would be to split kindling under a bench. I am oppressed. I am smothered."[53] The government did not repress the manifestations of protest.[54] The newspaper proprietors were gaining more press empathy for their communities by 1927; and Curtin, then a labour-oriented journalist, published an editorial to assert: "Australia not only has no quarrel with Chinese

Nationalism, but, indeed, should have a profound sympathy with it."[55] The ventures were overcoming their threatening image among Australia's surveillance agencies.

CHANGING ALLEGIANCES: THE CRACKDOWN ON THE ANTI-CHINA PRESS

The Pacific crisis impacted on how Chinese-Australian journalists with allegiances to either China or Japan were treated in Australia. In a confidential report, the government initially characterised the *Chinese Republic News* as "cautious and timid" while the *Tung Wah Times* was considered to "not express any strong views on political subjects."[56] In fact, both news groups were deeply involved in raising awareness of their industry across the broader society. Their commentaries recommended bolstering the status of the Australian Chinese character newspaper and battling the rise of Japanese propaganda (*xuanchan*) in the nation.[57] Reflecting China's journalistic tradition, the *Tung Wah Times* closely aligned the newspaper to the intellectual values of the homeland by reporting: "The nation's intellectuals know how to go in a difficult way."[58] The *Chinese Republic News* affirmed the need for patriotic education and bold nationalism in the homeland: "The nation's greatest task is to deepen its moral and academic responsibilities, and its greatest obligation."[59] Both weeklies reflected the Western-inspired professionalisation of Chinese journalism (*zhiyehua*), combining news summaries with specialised opinion that criticised Kai-Shek for his policy of appeasement of Japan until 1937.[60] As the *Chinese Republic News* predicted: "Terror is unavoidable, and the mentality of self-confidence has now been determined."[61] The *Tung Wah Times* appealed to China's nationalistic student movements: "It is the call to resist and save the country."[62] Both newspapers also encouraged readers to resist the so-called soft traitors (*hanjian*), a frequently used term in the Chinese popular press to describe Japanese collaborators.[63] The newspapers accentuated a desire for independence, equality and peace.[64]

By 1935, Australian journalists began increasingly portraying a thriving Chinese press industry. Journalists quoted China's visiting quarantine director at a news conference:

We have many Chinese-born Australians, many of whom received their education in Sydney and Melbourne, and have become most successful journalists, authors, merchants and—most difficult of all—good hosts and hostesses. It was always harder to move a big, old, and cultured land, but it would get there all right in the end.[65]

Australian reporters praised Chinese journalists for fighting fascism. For instance, Melbourne radio station 3DB-3LK publicised a Chinese-Australian co-host Mrs Fabian Chow as a celebrity journalist. Listeners could tune to the Heckle Hour radio show to hear Chow arguing the case against the Nazi tenet restricting women's roles to the "Three K's" of "*Kinder, Küche, Kirche*" (children, kitchen and church).[66] Another mainstream correspondent advised readers that the migrant Chinese press was pro-Australian.[67] The Chinese-Australian migrant journalists persuaded other reporters to accept them as colleagues.

In contrast, in the early 1940s, Curtin's government launched a media blitz to expose the commentators involved in an underground anti-China movement. They included Adela Pankhurst-Walsh, regarded as one of Australia's most colourful female figures, and well-known writer P. R. Stephensen. According to the *Sunday Telegraph*, such commentators represented an "aid-the-enemy conspiracy" threatening Australia's alliance with China.[68] Government informants began spying on Pankhurst-Walsh and alleged that she had privately asserted that "China is done, that the British Empire is going" and that "Australia should belong to Japan."[69] Furthermore, Attorney-General Herbert Vere Evatt dismissed an enquiry into jailing suspected Chinese dissidents in 1941: "I see little or no evidence to warrant internment. The submission rather suggested old or ageing or eccentric persons with a zest for taking the unpopular side in discussions."[70] The next year, official attitudes hardened towards alleged turncoats and the government confined Pankhurst-Walsh and Stephensen in detention camps.

Curtin's administration went further by punishing the anti-China press for causing Allied distrust of Australia.[71] Investigators charged that Pankhurst-Walsh had passed military secrets to Japan's wealthiest family, the Mitsui industrialists, in 1941. Mitsui had used Chinese workers and, later, Allied prisoners of war as slave labour in its factories.[72] It was at this point that police questioned Pankhurst-Walsh about confidential correspondence in the Mitsui manager's possession. She replied: "I can't remember but I must have given it to some one there. ... It must have been of some interest to him or he would not have got it."[73] Later, she explained that the secret correspondence was carelessly wrapped in her newspaper edition delivered to Mitsui's office.[74]

The secret documents included a censored news report on United States General Lewis Brereton's trip from the Philippines to Australia a month before the outbreak of the Pacific war. Brereton recalled the challenge of preventing publicity of his trip to place the air force on a war footing. His team tried to operate incognito, but he confided in his diary: "we did not succeed in fooling anybody. A Tokyo broadcast reported my presence in Australia and most of the details of our business."[75] He concluded: "They had agents everywhere."[76]

The press later characterised the antipathy towards China as at variance with the war effort. During a highly publicised trial, news reports focused on Stephensen's admission of promoting an Australian alliance with Japan in a "campaign against banditry" in China.[77] The press emphasised the accusations that Stephensen's editorials were an "attempt to stir up hostilities between Britain and Australia and America and Australia."[78] Journalists also circulated courtroom allegations that Japan's government paid Pankhurst-Walsh for her columns and the crackdown repressed the anti-China commentaries.[79]

Diversifying Chinese News and Views in the Media

Against a carefully constructed Allied backdrop of solidarity, the Australian political and media establishment appeared to concede to Chinese journalists' demands for equality. Upon King George VI agreeing to appoint China's first ambassador to Australia, Dr Hsu Mo, Chinese President Lin Sen remarked to His Majesty on "the sincere desire of this Government to cultivate to the fullest extent the friendship which has so long subsisted between the two countries."[80] Curtin's government focused on a media campaign that generated personality profiles of Kai-Shek and more newsreels of Hsu Mo.[81] Kai-Shek generated widespread coverage of his exclusive interview with *Sydney Morning Herald* war correspondent R. K. Macdonald, defying the official prediction of a tepid response.[82] Hsu Mo was known for his showmanship at public events and his reputation was well-established when he posed for a painting by Australia's portraitist of powerful leaders, Charles Wheeler (see Fig. 5.2).[83]

This media campaign, involving the Australian mainstream and regional press, was not only the result of Curtin's publicised appeal to support the Chinese communities.[84] He was countering Japanese-oriented propaganda about the White Australia Policy that aimed to turn Chinese people against the Allies.[85] Furthermore, Winston Churchill raised this priority at

Fig. 5.2 Portrait of Dr Hsu Mo, 1943. National Library of Australia, file number 3262388. (Courtesy of the National Library of Australia)

a meeting with Curtin by emphasising "the importance that must be given to the strong and real sentiment for China in the United States."[86] Curtin indicated he would consider the Chinese ambassador Hsu Mo's proposal to allow more refugees into Australia, but he did not make a commitment. Confidentially, Curtin insisted to a close-knit group of reporters, who dubbed themselves "Curtin's Circus," that they should avoid mentioning the immigration barriers because of the impact on Chinese readers (see Fig. 5.3). Journalist F. T. Smith noted: "Curtin is anxious that Australian papers should avoid raising the White Australia issue or even referring to the term 'White Australia.'"[87] Curtin's media campaign aimed to abolish the racist term, but overlooked the fact that the Chinese-Australian migrant news ventures had championed this initiative.[88]

Before the campaign, mainstream journalists were already turning to Chinese sources for leading news. Reporters commented on an upsurge of Chinese patriotism and unity as the soldiers rose to a heroic status.[89] A community newspaper portrayed Chinese residents as eagerly following

Fig. 5.3 John Curtin Prime Ministerial Library. Records of the Curtin Family. Former journalist John Curtin meets the Canberra Press Gallery (known as the Circus), 1942–1945. JCPML00376/2

the war reports in the migrant press. A reporter profiled a loyal *Tung Wah Times* subscriber who received detailed war updates about his home country; the reporter concluded that "family ties among the Chinese are great."[90] Another editorial writer complained about the limited range of Chinese-sourced war news in 1940. The commentator opined: "we are indebted almost exclusively to American newspaper correspondents for information concerning what is happening in the Far East." The editorial advocated publishing more dispatches on "the spirit of China's resistance."[91] Established newspapers increasingly sourced Sydney's *Chinese Times*.[92] Reflecting the press optimism, *Sydney Morning Herald* correspondent Selwyn Speight remarked on the liberalised era of Chinese journalism and reported: "censorship has been considerably relaxed."[93]

Furthermore, even journalists of the populist *Smith's Weekly* portrayed *Chinese Times* manager and chief editor George (Georgie) Nock as a

friendly patriot, accentuating his view that "China can never be conquered."[94] In so doing, they reinforced the Kuomintang's pretence that
the bureau was under the direction of a qualified journalist. Reporters
suggested that Nock was a colleague of the highest calibre, repeating his
claim that he never made a mistake in his shorthand.[95] As a journalist
described Nock's office: "The entrance-way is no marble-buttressed and
opulent splendour like the 'Sydney Morning Herald.' But it is more
human."[96] While these journalists were naive in their praise, their continued coverage of the Chinese-language newspapers contributed to images
of inclusion of the migrant community.

During the rise of China's official news bureau, the Australian government instead supported independent Chinese journalists. Publicly, successive Australian administrations tolerated the Kuomintang press, but they
were reluctant to extend any favours that might have disadvantaged its
newspaper competitors. For example, Prime Minister Joseph Lyons's government (1932–1939) refused to intervene in a dispute between the
Chinese Consul-General, Dr W. P. Chen, and the *Chinese World's News* in
1936. The *Chinese World's News* editor, Quan Mane, had joined a chorus
of criticisms against Kai-Shek's appeasement policy before the Sino-
Japanese conflict.[97] The Chinese Consul-General sought Lyons's assistance in revoking the *Chinese World's News* licence for Mane's series of
editorials, branding Kai-Shek as a traitor. One of the editorials also mocked
the resolve of Kai-Shek's armies: "when they have wives and concubines
with them and plenty of money, they will throw brickbats at the frogs" (an
idiom meaning that nothing matters).[98]

Chen argued: "The loyal Chinese are deeply incensed at the objection-
able statements and their anger could well be a breach of the peace with
the supporters of the disloyal press."[99] However, Australian officials
refused to censor the newspaper. They advised Chen:

> the Commonwealth Government takes the view that the issues raised, not
> only in this but in other Chinese newspapers published in Australia, are such
> as to amount to differences purely of political opinion which cannot be
> regarded as constituting an infringement.[100]

Privately, an official warned Mane that his editorial series was offensive.
Mane explained that he modelled his editorials on those of Australian
journalists: "we have followed in their footsteps and written on behalf of
our own beloved country." He added that his community was made up of

"Chinese patriots in the truest sense of the word, and we oppose the Kuomintang bitterly, as we are of the opinion that it is deliberately 'selling' our Mother Country to the Japanese."[101] What is important here is that Lyons's administration allowed the debates between the news rivals.

With Australia's entry into the Pacific war, the government continued to back independent Chinese press workers. By the early 1940s, the *Chinese Republic News* and *Tung Wah Times* were closed, while the Chinese Consul-General advised that the *Chinese World's News* was temporarily halted in 1942 due to the challenge of obtaining news from China, as well as printing shortages. Nonetheless, Quan Mane indicated to the government that he would continue production during the war. [102] The news workers received exemptions to stay in Australia and some compositors retrained for military work.[103] Curtin's administration took up the cause of a former *Chinese World's News* employee, who was receiving about a third of the standard wage. An official noted: "As usual the Con Gen. [Chinese Consul-General] ignored the matter … it seems that there has been laxity on the part of manpower authorities."[104] The government recommended further action for equitable payment. The solution was consistent with Curtin's announcement to allow temporary Chinese workers to remain in Australia, receiving equal pay and working conditions during the war.[105]

More journalists challenged the Chinese immigration barriers, ignoring Curtin's request to avoid the controversial issue.[106] Within his administration, high-profile commentators argued for a fresh approach. *Argus* editor and Australian public relations director-general, Errol Knox, wryly noted in his newspaper: "Perhaps Australia did not have a policy in relation to the Far East other than the White Australia policy."[107] The *Australian Worker* quoted another official public relations director who suggested "the White Australia policy should be restated in such a way that it was not an insult to the rest of the world."[108] And, the popular press promoted readers' debates on removing the laws.[109] Letters to the editor acknowledged a debt to Australia's Chinese allies, with one contributor remarking: "Undoubtedly we owe more to suffering China than is generally realised."[110] *Herald* owner, Sir Keith Murdoch, published letters disputing immigration barriers and led this news section with a correspondent's view: "If colored people are good enough to fight by our side are they not good enough to share the things for which they and we fight?"[111]

Confidentially, Curtin questioned Murdoch's campaign for full citizenship rights for all Australian allies. In a private news conference, Curtin hinted that Murdoch's approach would raise Chinese expectations. According to journalist F. T. Smith, Curtin cautiously received Chinese ambassador Hsu Mo's demands for freer migration. Smith noted: "At the present moment he [Curtin] is engaged in what he describes as a 'tulip dance' with Dr Hsu Mo on the rights of the Chinese in Australia."[112] Faced with fierce political opposition, Curtin did not overturn the unequal laws as did Roosevelt, who repealed the *Chinese Exclusion Act* in the United States in 1943. Yet the newspaper debates showed that the White Australia protests were popularised in the media.

Established Chinese-Australian journalists increasingly challenged China's official news bureau. Mainstream newspapers circulated stories of *Life* correspondent Theodore White's reporting experience in China: "The press lives in a shadow world of gossip, hand-outs and agency despatches. None of the great problems of China—famine, inflation, blockade, foreign relations, or public personalities—can be honestly discussed in public."[113] More Australian journalists quoted China's main opposition daily, the popular *Ta Kung Pao* (Big Public Paper), for leading opinions.[114]

Journalists from the *Argus* and the *Daily Telegraph* depicted *Ta Kung Pao* correspondent, Daniel Lee, as a media personality during his visit to Australia.[115] The press emphasised Lee's affirmation of the Chinese journalists' demands for equality: "I'm your true friend all right. But, how could I convince my people at home that you feel a great friendship for them, while the White Australia policy stands in the way?"[116] Such journalists also underscored Lee's assertion that Chinese journalists shared patriotic values, as printed in the *Mercury*: "The Chinese journalistic world is convinced that international understanding is the first thing to achieve. ... China and Australia are closer together than ever before."[117] In fact, Australia was credited for strengthening the nation's relations with the Chinese communities. According to administration insiders, Roosevelt recognised Australia's value in alliance-building with China. Australia's Minister to China, Sir Frederic Eggleston, advised:

> The President said he wanted to keep China as a friend because in 40 or 50 years China might easily become a very powerful military nation. Continuing, the President said that he thought the Americans and the Australians could work together on a liberal policy on these matters.[118]

In this light, Chinese journalists helped to usher in an enthusiastic era for the post-war relations.

After the war, the *Chinese World's News* owners resumed publishing forthright commentaries about their democratic values. According to *The Sydney Morning Herald*, they were prominent in opposing China's Communist Revolution. On one occasion, an eye-catching headline was portrayed as an important notice: "China is not a Communist country. It is the People's Republic of China!"[119] The newspaper's bitter rival, the *Chinese Times*, was closed in 1949 with the Communist ousting of the Kuomintang.[120] The *Chinese World's News* was shut two years later, presumably due to financial hardship, although the management resisted a relatively new government requirement to print English-language editorials.[121] The newspaper contributed to a legacy of independent Chinese journalism that would re-emerge with the easing of Cold War tensions several decades later.

To conclude, evading the censors, the interwar Chinese-Australian journalists developed a flair for assertive commentaries that protested against national and global injustices. They heralded an era of editorial morale building to encourage readers' unity with China and their participation in Australian society. The news groups quickly recognised their need to elicit support in the corridors of power. Extending the traditional boundaries, they recruited influential allies in their journalistic crusade for equality, professional recognition and the establishment of enduring communities.

Chinese-Australian news ventures were ground-breaking in initiating controversial debates to elicit government and press support. The minority ventures also benefited from the Australian wartime government's media campaign that publicised Chinese news and denounced anti-China sentiments. Curtin ushered in a new era of inclusion for the migrant communities. Before him, Lyons's government supported the independent migrant press to develop a particularly irreverent editorial approach towards the Kuomintang. In turn, Australian reporters increasingly rejected the Kuomintang news services and supported independent Chinese journalism. The media showed that Chinese-Australian journalists' patriotism merged successfully with shared democratic ideals. The news groups contributed to wider discussions on the value of their communities, laying the groundwork for future generations of journalists. Their modern style of journalism suggests the possibilities for today's migrant press to mobilise action for social change by giving voice to their communities.

NOTES

1. John Curtin, "Australian Relations", *Digest of Decisions and Announcements and Important Speeches by the Prime Minister* 7 (November 17, 1941), 6; Clem Lloyd and Richard Hall, ed., *Backroom Briefings: John Curtin's War* (Canberra: National Library of Australia, 1997).
2. "Racial barriers", *The Canberre Times,* November 18, 1941, p. 2.
3. John Curtin, "National Day", *Digest* 45 (8 October 1942): 7–8: *The Mercury,* "Chinese War Correspondent Visits Australia", June 6, 1945, p. 16; "Chinese Refugees for Australia", *The Sydney Morning Herald,* January 15, 1942, p. 6.
4. Catherine Dewhirst, "Collaborating on Whiteness: Representing Italians in Early White Australia", *Journal of Australian Studies* 32, no. 1 (2008): 33–49; Mei-fen Kuo, *Making Chinese Australia: Urban Elites, Identities and the Formation of Chinese-Australian Identity, 1892–1912* (Clayton: Monash University Publishing, 2013); Jayne Persian, "Bonegilla: A Failed Narrative", *History Australia* 9, no. 1 (2012): 64–83; Wanning Sun, ed., *Media and the Chinese Diaspora: Community, Communications and Commerce* (London: Routledge, 2006).
5. Rana Mitter, *Forgotten Ally: China's World War II, 1937–1945* (New York: Houghton Mifflin Harcourt Publishing Company, 2013).
6. Stewart Lone, *Japan's First Modern War: Army and Society in the Conflict with China, 1894–95* (Houndmills: The Macmillan Press, 1994); William Sima, *China & the ANU: Diplomats, Adventurers, Scholars* (Acton: The Australian National University Press, 2015), 2.
7. Thomas Stuart Clyne, *Report of Commissioner,* National Archives of Australia (NAA), 1945, A374.
8. Mobo Gao, "Early Chinese Migrants to Australia: a Critique of the Sojourner Narrative on Nineteenth-century Chinese Migration to British Colonies", *Asian Studies Review* 41, no. 3 (2017): 389–404.
9. Kuo, *Making Chinese Australia.*
10. Curtin, "Australian Relations", *Digest of Decisions and Announcements and Important Speeches by the Prime Minister* 7 (November 17, 1941), 6; *Daily Telegraph,* June 25, 1945.
11. Commonwealth of Australia, *Chinese World's News,* Canberra: National Archives of Australia, Canberra, 1922–1955, A445, 232/4/18; W. M. Gockson, "Chinese Community", *Truth,* January 22, 1922, p. 2; William Gockson, "Chinese Community", *Evening News,* January 21, 1922, p. 4; Mai Tien Hua, "China's Case", *The Daily Telegraph,* August 29, 1925, p. 10; Hua, "China's Case", *The Nambucca and Bellinger News,* September 4, 1925, p. 6; Sidney Hing Lowe, "To The Editor", *The Daily*

Telegraph, November 14, 1922, p. 4; A. Rivett, "A Propagandist of 'Empire'", *The Australian Worker*, September 16, 1925, p. 15.

12. Commonwealth, *Chinese World's News*, Home Affairs Department, Chinese Times Limited, NAA, 1924–1933, A1, 1933/307.

13. Paul Jones, "The View from the Edge: Chinese Australians and China, 1890 to 1949", in *East by South: China in the Australasian Imagination*, ed. Charles Ferrall, Paul Millar and Keren Smith (Wellington: Victoria University Press, 2005), 46–69.

14. Commonwealth, *Chinese World's News*, *Daily Telegraph*, November 14, 1922, August 29, 1925; Department of External Affairs, *William Yinson Lee* [hereafter *Lee*], NAA, 1916, A1, 1916/31599; *Evening News*, January 21, 1922; Home Affairs, *Chinese Times*, Home and Territories Department, *W Howe: Chinese Newspapers and the 'White Australia Policy'* [hereafter *Howe*], NAA, 1922–1923, A1, 1923/1089; *Truth*, January 22, 1922.

15. Ann Curthoys, "'Men of all Nations, except Chinamen': Europeans and Chinese on the Goldfields of New South Wales", in *Gold: Forgotten Histories and Lost Objects of Australia*, ed. Ian McCalman, Alexander Cook and Andrew Reeves (Cambridge: Cambridge University Press, 2001), 103–123; Sophie Loy-Wilson, *Australians in Shanghai: Race, Rights and Nation in Treaty Port China* (London: Routledge, 2017).

16. Kuo, *Making Chinese Australia*.

17. Stephen R. MacKinnon, "Toward a History of the Chinese Press in the Republican Period", *Modern China* 23, no. 1 (1997): 3–32; Marina Svensson, Elin Sæther, Zhi'an Zhang, ed., *Chinese Investigative Journalists' Dreams: Autonomy, Agency and Voice* (Lanham: Lexington Books, 2014).

18. Hongy Bai, "Between Advocacy and Objectivity", in *Chinese Investigative Journalists' Dreams: Autonomy, Agency and Voice*, ed. Marina Svensson, Elin Sæther, Zhi'an Zhang (Lanham: Lexington Books, 2014), 79.

19. Benton, "Chinese Transnationalism in Britain: A Longer History", *Identities* 10, no. 3 (2003): 347–375; Sun, *Media and the Chinese Diaspora*.

20. Kate Bagnall, "Early Chinese Newspapers", 2015, https://www.nla.gov.au/blogs/trove/2015/02/19/early-chinese-newspapers; Jones, "View;" Frederic Wakeman Jnr, "*Hanjian* (Traitor)! Collaboration and Retribution in Wartime Shanghai" in *Becoming Chinese: Passages to Modernity and Beyond*, ed. Wen-hsin Yeh (Berkeley: University of California Press, 2000), 298–341; Michael Williams, "Wading 10,000 li to seek their fortune: *Tung Wah News* selections 1898–1901", 2003, https://arrow.latrobe.edu.au/store/3/4/5/5/1/public/tungwah_article.htm.

21. Parks M. Coble, *China's War Reporters: The Legacy of Resistance Against Japan* (Cambridge: Harvard University Press, 2015); Mitter, *Forgotten.*
22. E. M. Andrews, *Australia and China: The Ambiguous Relationship* (Carlton, Vic.: Melbourne University Press, 1985).
23. Ray Moseley, *Reporting War: How Foreign Correspondents Risked Capture, Torture and Death to Cover World War II* (New Haven: Yale University Press, 2017).
24. Lachlan Strahan, *Australia's China: Changing Perceptions from the 1930s to the 1990s* (Cambridge, Cambridge University Press, 1996).
25. Bob Wurth, *Saving Australia: Curtin's Secret Peace with Japan* (South Melbourne: Lothian Books, 2006).
26. Sun, *Diaspora.*
27. Commonwealth, *Chinese World's News*; External Affairs, *Lee*; Home Affairs, *Chinese Times*; Home and Territories, *Howe.*
28. Commonwealth, *Chinese World's News*; Home Affairs, *Chinese Times*, 1927.
29. The newspapers are *The Advertiser, The Age, The Argus, The Armidale Express and New England General Advertiser* [hereafter *Armidale*], *Army News, The Australian Worker, The Canberra Times, The Courier-Mail, The Daily News, The Daily Telegraph, Evening News, Examiner, Kalgoorlie Miner, The Herald, The Mercury, The Nambucca and Bellinger News, The Newcastle Sun, News, Smith's Weekly, The Sun, The Sunday Telegraph, The Sydney Morning Herald, Truth, West Gippsland Gazette* and *Westralian Worker.*
30. Lewis H. Brereton, *The Brereton Diaries* (New York: William Morrow and Company, 1946); Commonwealth of Australia, *Percy Reginald Stephensen*, NAA, 1943, A373, 4522B; Commonwealth of Australia, *Thomas Walsh*, NAA, 1939, A367, C64736.
31. Cinesound Productions, *First Chinese Minister Arrives* (newsreel), 1941, National Film and Sound Archives (NFSA), Canberra, f72226; John Curtin Prime Ministerial Library (JCPML), *Index to John Curtin's speeches in the Digest of Decisions and Announcements and Important Speeches by the Prime Minister, 1941–1945*, 2007, JCPML01148/1, Bentley; Lloyd and Hall, *Briefings*; Movietone, *Names in the News* (newsreel), 1941, NFSA, 126160; Movietone, *Personalities Living at the Federal Capital* (newsreel), 1941, NFSA, 89268.
32. Curthoys, "'Men of all Nations, except Chinamen'".
33. Paul Jones, "'A Consequent Gain in the Tempo of Effort': Chinese labour and Chinese industrial activism in Australia, 1941–1945", in *The Past is Before Us*, ed. Greg Patmore, John Shields, and Nikola Balnave (The University of Sydney: Australian Society for the Study of Labour History, 2005), http://asslh.econ.usyd.edu.au.

34. "The Chinese Times", *Bendigo Advertiser,* February 14, 1902, 3.
35. Department of Immigration, *Chinese World's News,* NAA, 1933, A2998, 1952/253.
36. Commonwealth, *Chinese World's News;* Home Affairs, *Chinese Times;* Home and Territories, "Howe."
37. Home Affairs, *Chinese Times,* 1928–1929, 60.
38. "Chinese Times", *The Sun,* August 27, 1922, 2; "Interesting Items", *West Gippsland Gazette,* January 25, 1927, 4.
39. Department of Immigration, *Chinese World's News.*
40. Sidney Hing Lowe, "White Australia Policy", *The Sydney Morning Herald,* October 30, 1922, p. 6.
41. Commonwealth, *Chinese World's News,* 1921; Home and Territories, *Howe.*
42. Commonwealth, *Chinese World's News.*
43. Home and Territories, *Howe.*
44. External Affairs, Lee, 24; Home and Territories Department, *'The Chinese World's News' Publication in Australia,* NAA, 1921, A1, 1921/16152.
45. External Affairs, Lee, 27.
46. "Weddings", *The Daily Telegraph,* February 14, 1916, p. 3; "Chinese Weddings", *The Sun,* February 13, 1916, p. 10.
47. Gockson, *Evening News,* 4, *Truth,* 2.
48. "The Luck of Lumb Liu", *Smith's Weekly,* June 12, 1920, p. 3.
49. Lowe, "Editor" p. 4; Lowe, "White Australia Policy", p. 6.
50. Attorney-General's Department, *Chinese Newspapers Australia,* NAA, 1923, A367, 1923/1824, 8.
51. Attorney-General's Department, *Chinese Newspapers,* 9.
52. The available rare records do not confirm the exact details of Ma Hang Su's birth and death.
53. Hua, "Case", *The Daily Telegraph,* p. 10, *The Nambucca and Bellinger News,* 6; Rivett, "Empire", p. 15.
54. Home Affairs, *Chinese Times,* 1927.
55. John Curtin, "The Question of Mr Angwin's Politics", *Westralian Worker,* February 4, 1927, JCPML.
56. Commonwealth, *Chinese World's News,* 1923.
57. *Chinese Republic News,* January 9, 1937; *Tung Wah Times,* January 18, 1936.
58. "本帝堪卜學校教職" ["Dedicated to the School"], *Tung Wah Times,* February 15, 1936, p. 6.
59. "國雛中之教育及教育業者办" ["Education and Management in the Country"], *Chinese Republic News,* January 30, 1937, p. 7.
60. *Chinese Republic News,* January 16, 30 1937; MacKinnon, "Press", *Tung Wah Times,* January 11, 25, February 15, March 7, 1936.

61. "英 法 進 行" [British and French], *Chinese Republic News*, January 9, 1937, p 6.

62. "本 帝 堪 卜 學 校 教 職", *Tung Wah Times*.

63. *Chinese Republic News*, January 2, 1937; *Tung Wah Times*, February 15, 1936; Wakeman, "Traitor".

64. *Chinese Republic News*, January 9, 16, 30 1937; *Tung Wah Times*, January 11, 18, 25; February 1, 8, 15, 22, 29; March 7, 14 1936.

65. "Australian-born Chinese praised", *The Advertiser*, September 3, 1935, p. 20; "China's Debt to Australia", *The Courier-Mail*, September 3, 1935, p. 17.

66. *The Herald*, March 4, 1938.

67. *The Newcastle Sun*, April 25, 1938.

68. "Dramas", *The Sunday Telegraph*, May 17, 1942, p. 24.

69. Commonwealth, "Walsh", 1942.

70. Commonwealth, "Walsh", 1941, 233.

71. Brereton, *Diaries*, December 17, 1941; Clyne, "Report."

72. Christian Caryl, "Unfinished Business", *Foreign Policy*, June 28, 2010, https://foreignpolicy.com/2010/06/28/unfinished-business-2.

73. Commonwealth, "Walsh", 1942, 124.

74. Commonwealth, "Walsh", 1942.

75. Brereton, *Diaries*, November 25, 1941.

76. Brereton, *Diaries*, December 12, 1941.

77. "Additional Revelations Made at Australia First Enquiry", *Army News*, October 7, 1944, p. 4; "Stephenson Tells of 'Arms Agents' Scare'", *The Herald*, October 5, 1944, p. 6.

78. "Admiration for Japan", *The Age*, October 6, 1944, p. 5.

79. *The Canberra Times*, June 20, 1944; *The Sydney Morning Herald*, August 25, 1944.

80. Commonwealth of Australia, *Arrival of Chinese Minister to Australia*, NAA, 1941–1942, A2880, 6/19/3, 13.

81. British Pathé, *Australia 1942* (newsreel), 1942; Cinesound, *Minister*; Curtin, "Australian Relations"; Movietone, *Names*; Movietone, *Personalities*.

82. *The Advertiser*, March 24, 1942; *The Age*, March 26, 1942; Department of External Affairs, *China—Relations with Australia, 1941–1942*, NAA, A981, Chin 94 Part 3; *Examiner*, March 26, 1942; *The Mercury*, March 28, 1942; *The Sun*, April 1, 1942; *The Sydney Morning Herald*, March 24, 1942.

83. "Modern Trends in Art", *The Age*, October 14, 1941, p. 6; "Charles Wheeler's Serene Landscapes", *The Herald*, October 19, 1942, p. 7.

84. Curtin, "Question."

85. Curtin, "Prisoners of War", *Digest* 28 (May 7, 1942): 14; F. T. Smith, cited in Lloyd and Hall, *Briefings*.
86. JCPML, "Australia Visit of Mr. Curtin to USA & UK in connection with Prime Ministers' Conference London", 1944, JCPML00768/3.
87. Smith, *Briefings*, 175.
88. Commonwealth, *Chinese World's News*.
89. *The Canberra Times*, July 10, 1939; *The Daily News*, February 4, 1939; *The Sydney Morning Herald*, May 4, 1939.
90. "Only One War Interests Chinese Resident", *Armidale*, March 13, 1940, p. 4.
91. "The China War", *Kalgoorlie Miner*, June 10, 1940, p. 4.
92. *The Canberra Times*, March 25, 1941; *The Daily Telegraph*, October 10, 1942; *Evening News*, March 25, 1941; *Smith's Weekly*, October 12, 1940, February 28, 1942.
93. Selwyn Speight, "Truth about the Chinese Crisis", *The Sydney Morning Herald*, December 13, 1944, p. 2.
94. "China Can Never Be Conquered", *Smith's Weekly*, October 12, 1940, pp. 1, 5; "Georgie Nock", *Smith's Weekly*, February 28, 1942, p. 13.
95. *The Daily Telegraph*, January 9, 1940, October 10, 1942; Home Affairs, *Chinese Times*, 1929; *Smith's Weekly*, October 12, 1940, February 28, 1942.
96. "Conquered", *Smith's Weekly*, October 12, 1940, p. 5.
97. Commonwealth, *Chinese World's News*, 1935.
98. Commonwealth, *Chinese World's News*, 1936.
99. Commonwealth, *Chinese World's News*, 1936, 45.
100. Commonwealth, *Chinese World's News*, 46.
101. Commonwealth, *Chinese World's News*, 47.
102. Department of Immigration, *Chinese World's News*, 1942.
103. Department of Immigration, *Chinese World's News*, 1922–1946.
104. Department of Immigration, *Chinese World's News*, 1943, 8.
105. Curtin, "Nationals in Australia", *Digest* 23 (March 24, 1942): 11.
106. Smith, *Briefings*.
107. Errol G. Knox, "A Welcome is Ready for Mr Curtin", *The Argus*, December 16, 1943, p. 2.
108. "Australia in a New World", *The Sydney Morning Herald*, November 19, 1943, p. 7.
109. *The Age*, January 5, 1944; *Argus*, January 3, 1944; *The Herald*, May 3, 1944.
110. T. Churchward Kelly, "Suffering China", *The Examiner*, September 1, 1943, p. 4.
111. W. Stewart, "Migration Policy", *The Herald*, May 3, 1944, p. 6.
112. Smith, cited in Lloyd and Hall, *Briefings*, 53.

113. "Background to the World's News", *The Argus*, December 1, 1945, p. 13; "Time Book of the Week", *The Daily Telegraph*, October 27, 1946, p. 30; Theodore White, "Chinese Fight Japs, Inflation—and Other Chinese", *News*, August 5, 1944, p. 2.

114. *The Age*, April 20, 1943, October 17, 1944; *The Canberra Times* January 16, December 21, 1942; *The Sydney Morning Herald*, October 8, 1940, December 25, 1941, August 31, 1943, September 1, 1945.

115. "Chinese Reporter to Join British Pacific Fleet", *The Argus*, June 1, 1945, 3; Lee, "At Last."

116. "Chinese Tells Us Why He Likes Us, But ...", *The Advertiser*, July 9, 1945, p. 2.

117. "Chinese War Correspondent Visits Australia", *The Mercury*, June 6, 1945, p. 16.

118. F. W. Eggleston to H.V. Evatt, *Documents on Australian Foreign Policy 7* (November 21, 1944).

119. Robert McOrland, "What are their readers told in Australia's foreign language newspapers?", *The Sydney Morning Herald*, May 25, 1950, p. 3.

120. Jones, "View."

121. Commonwealth, *Chinese World's News*, 1950, 1952.

CHAPTER 6

Reimagining Italian Spaces: *La Fiamma* as a Lens to Explore the Development of the Italian Community in Adelaide, South Australia, Between 1947 and 1963

Angela A. Alessi

When observing Italian diasporas (large-scale emigration of Italians), it is not uncommon to see residential and commercial concentrations of Italian immigrants, many which are known as "Little Italies". The concept of "Little Italies" relates to the clustering of Italian communities in urban neighbourhoods. Historically, Little Italies can be traced to periods of mass immigration to countries, such as America, Canada and Australia, during the late nineteenth and twentieth centuries. Cultural understandings of their significance have evolved over time—from urban ethnic enclaves in North America during the nineteenth century to more contemporary representations of neighbourhoods dominated by Italian culture and commerce.

A. A. Alessi (✉)
University of Adelaide, Adelaide, SA, Australia
e-mail: angela.alessi@adelaide.edu.au

© The Author(s), under exclusive license to Springer Nature   107
Switzerland AG 2021
C. Dewhirst, R. Scully (eds.), *Voices of Challenge in Australia's Migrant and Minority Press*, Palgrave Studies in the History of the Media, https://doi.org/10.1007/978-3-030-67330-7_6

Scholars have approached the concept of "Little 'Italy'" from diverse sociological, anthropological and historical perspectives. An important historical focus concerns how mainly English-speaking host societies have interpreted these clusters of Italian migrants, usually in the context of apprehension towards Italians (and other migrants perceived to be different to the host nation). Early uses of the term are located in the Australian print press from the beginning of the twentieth century. These examples, as analysed by William Douglass and Catherine Dewhirst, are seen to be framed within fears of potential Italian ghettoisation in the Australian community. For instance, the yellow print *Smith's Weekly* in 1925 claimed that the "Little Italy" in Innisfail, a town far north of Queensland, was swiftly becoming a "Big Italy" where an Italian connection was crucial in gaining employment and "dago" bosses were exploitative.[1] Dewhirst's examination of a cartoon by Oswald Paul (published in *The Worker* in 1907) depicts a "Little Italy" likened to a circus and site of immoral and criminal activity.[2] Perspectives such as those above form the basis of Donna Gabaccia's argument which claims Little Italies arose in English-speaking countries where Italians were considered racially inferior.[3] Italian settlements were much more visible because of "Italophobia"; rarely were such Italian neighbourhoods called "Little Italy" in places such as Germany, France, Switzerland or Latin America.[4] While Gabaccia's ethnocentric approach resonates with anthropologists, such as Nicholas Harney and Loretta Baldassar, the latter are more concerned with perspectives within Italian neighbourhoods and communities more than how non-Italian communities perceived Little Italies. These scholars have examined how the identity of Italian migrants and their descendants is shaped within multiethnic and multiracial societies, and how migrants claim and use space to express identity and belonging in place (in Italian neighbourhoods).[5] Alternatively, historians, such as Robert Pascoe, emphasise a geographical understanding of the concept. In Pascoe's view, a Little Italy is an area in a country other than Italy where there is a strong concentration of Italian residential and commercial activities.[6]

Research in this field is predominately from North American scholarship with a burgeoning of literature during the 1970s and 1980s.[7] Australian Italian neighbourhoods are noted to have been smaller and less cohesive than those found in North America.[8] Studies of Italian settlement in Australia have tended to adopt regional, provincial or national frames of analysis—for instance South Australia, Queensland and so on—although some analyses of Italians in Australian urban neighbourhood settings exist.[9] More recent literature on Australian Italian neighbourhoods is grounded in a contemporary context, tending to explore either how Italian culture is manifested and interpreted in the landscape or how Italian neighbourhoods and/or institutions support language and cultural maintenance.[10]

This chapter presents an analysis of the Adelaide Italian "community" from the Little Italy perspective to seek a better understanding of Italian settlement and how identity was evoked in space and place. Pascoe's definition is employed to determine whether a Little Italy emerged in Adelaide given that this definition provides a more tangible framework for the physical boundaries of an ethnic neighbourhood. Influence is drawn from Gabaccia when considering the relationship between Italian migrants and the wider Australian community. Theories of place-making are adopted from Harney and Pascoe. It is argued that Adelaide did not develop a "Little Italy" to the same extent as those overseas and in other Australian states. Instead, the Adelaide Italian "community" created cohesive and identifiably "Italian" social, religious and economic spaces, which were dispersed across Adelaide rather than contained within a single neighbourhood or district. While broad trends in Italian settlement are visible across various Italian diasporas and more notably in settler colonies such as America, Canada and Australia, a closer examination of Little Italies in various socio-political contexts helps to demonstrate the complexity of migrant settlement patterns. In the Adelaide case it appears that village or regional connections were crucial, suggesting that these transnational links were pertinent to negotiating life in Australia, at least initially. Previous descriptions concerning Italians in South Australia focus on the extent to which they integrated into Australia society—an approach which has the tendency to represent a singular aspect of the migrant experience, often with a normative approach that can homogenise the experience of migrants. This case study of an Italian community in South Australia presents its members as agents through their practices of place-making.

To identify and explore the significance of Italian spaces, this chapter draws on original research based on close readings of the Sydney-based Italian newspaper, *La Fiamma*, between 1947 and 1963. This timeframe spans a period from the newspaper's inception leading up to its release of a South Australian supplement.[11] Initially, *La Fiamma* was religiously orientated, but the newspaper's brief shifted in 1951 under the editorship of qualified journalist Evasio Costanzo (1921–1993). Under Costanzo, the newspaper became secularised and in the late 1960s had begun to identify with the Australian Labor Party.[12] During Costanzo's editorship, the newspaper became a source of advice and support for its readers on issues of migration, assisted passage and the daily challenges of settlement. *La Fiamma* also served as a link between Australia and Italy in various ways during a period of mass migration following the Second World War, including reporting on news in both Australia and Italy; supporting the development of Italian literacy in migrants; and allowing Italian language and culture to be maintained in Australia.[13]

While advertisements are useful in mapping Italian commercial activity, articles featured in weekly South Australian segments of *La Fiamma* reveal the social significance of Italian spaces. Beginning in 1952, these segments reported on religious, social, sporting and political affairs in Adelaide and in the industrial city of Port Pirie, located north of Adelaide. The social impact of Italian businesses is evident in a 60-page supplement, published in 1963. This supplement features Italian "pioneers", or those individuals (mainly businessmen), who were acknowledged for their contributions to the development of the Adelaide Italian community in areas of commerce, sport, religion and community support. While strictly not a migrant newspaper, an Italian-language section, "L'angolo degli italiani" or "The Italian Corner", in *The Southern Cross* also remains a useful source in understanding the religious dimension of Italian experiences and relations between the Catholic Church and the Adelaide Italian community. "The Italian Corner" featured in this newspaper and was published by the Catholic Archdiocese of Adelaide between 1952 and 1954.

This chapter takes two approaches in its examination of "*italianità*" (Italianess), in the landscape. Firstly, Italian neighbourhoods in South Australia are shown to be significantly less developed than the Little Italies in North America, as consistent with the historiography. However, the characteristics of a Little Italy could still be located in Adelaide, indicating that Italians still expressed identity in space and created places of belonging as evident in place-making practices.

The Little Italy Framework: Comparisons Between Australia and North American Little Italies

In nineteenth-century America, Little Italies first developed as self-contained communities. George Pozzetta's study of Italian migrants in the Mulberry District in New York demonstrated that given the large scope of Italian-specific services and institutions, there was little incentive for Italians to venture out of the district, and indeed numerous residents had not.[14] Furthermore, Italian migrants were able to define and negotiate life through the "aspects of their old world culture".[15] The existence of the *"padroni"* (boss) system is notable in American Little Italies. The *"padroni"* often sponsored Italian male sojourners and acted as employment agents, bankers, landlords, interpreters, legal advisors and bosses.[16] The *padroni* system consolidated power over migration networks, employment avenues and commercial enterprises in the Little Italy. Overall, services within these segregated communities could accommodate virtually every necessity and supplemented a need for Italian migrants to integrate with wider society.

Other Little Italies in North America were also initially self-contained but became less segregated from the 1920s onwards. While the *"padroni"* system emerged in South Philadelphia between 1890 and 1920, familial forms of chain migration would become the main means of migration to the area.[17] This shift encouraged greater integration of immigrants into the wider society and brought more women and children into these communities, changing the nature and structure of the Italian community in Philadelphia.[18] Italians also increasingly integrated into mainstream American society through their participation in Roman Catholic worship and education.[19] As such, the Italian community in Philadelphia remained distinct, although not as segregated as the Mulberry District in the nineteenth century.

Neighbourhoods with high proportions of Italian commerce and residency emerged in Australia although they were smaller and less segregated compared to ethnic enclaves in America. The development of ethnic enclaves in Australia was mitigated through government policies which placed restrictions on sponsorship and controlled movement of migrants.[20] Carlton, a small inner-city suburb of Melbourne, provides a good example of an Italian-Australian neighbourhood of the post-war period. By 1960, the population of Italian-born individuals in Carlton was estimated at over 7000, with approximately 47 Italian businesses operating in the area.[21] These three examples of Little Italies—Mulberry District, South Philadelphia and Carlton—neatly align with Pascoe's concept in that Italian residency and commercial activity simultaneously existed within a defined area. In his study of Italians in the sugarcane town of Ingham, North Queensland, Douglass reflects that some districts could have well developed a "Little Italy".[22] He considers there was a strong representation of Italian surnames in shopfronts and the influence of Italian culture on hospitality in the region.[23]

There was no Adelaide suburb that mirrored Carlton, Ingham or the even larger districts in North America, in either the density of Italian commerce or residential occupation. A 1961 census recorded that a total of 6936 Italians lived in the inner-eastern municipals including Payneham, Kensington and Norwood, St Peters and Campbelltown.[24] Other settlements in the west of Adelaide (West Torrens and Woodville) had a smaller, but still sizeable, population of 4918 Italians. The City of Adelaide itself had around 1194 Italian residents. As discussed below, an Italian commercial centre developed within the City of Adelaide's Central Business District (CBD) with greater levels of Italian residency outside of this municipality. With the dispersion of Italian settlement and commercial activity, it appears that Italians did not have one geographical point of reference for their material and/or social needs.

The dispersion between these concentrated Italian residential and commercial areas in Adelaide could have been the result of Italian settlement patterns. In the 1920s, the west end of the Adelaide CBD became a popular first point of reference for recently arrived migrants.[25] The west end, particularly Hindley Street, contained Italian-managed boarding houses and many prospective migrants recorded this area as their intended address when embarking for Australia.[26] However, this focus of initial settlement would eventually shift towards the inner-city eastern and western suburbs where Italian migrants were predominately occupied in market gardening activities.[27] Despite a move away from market gardening during the postwar period, Italian migrants continued to have a growing presence in the eastern and western suburbs.[28] While Pascoe argues it is not unusual for smaller, secondary settlements to develop from a primary settlement (in this case the west end of the Adelaide CBD), the primary settlement should continue to grow and diversify.[29] Although the west end in Adelaide flourished commercially (as discussed further below), this growth did not correspond with greater Italian residential settlement. A reading of *La Fiamma* supports this claim, demonstrating that the west end in the CBD did not have the same level or range of Italian services available compared to other Little Italies, despite the high rates of Italian residential settlement. During the 1950s and 1960s, there was no area that had the same level of Italian residency and commercial services, which encouraged Italian migrants to remain within such defined areas.

The Development of an Italian Community in South Australia

The development of the Adelaide Italian "community" did not entirely align with Pascoe's concept of a Little Italy.[30] While comprising the characteristics of a Little Italy, Italian residential and economic hubs in South Australia were dispersed (though still largely centred in Adelaide and its surrounding suburbs), rather than being grouped together in a single location. Though different to other Little Italies, the reason for the emergence of neighbourhoods with a strong Italian presence was similar: a variety of migratory factors, including the rate and scale of migration; the economic and regional structure of the host country; transnational networks; and wider relations between Italians and the broader community.[31] Although Australia's economic and regional structures were influential in determining where Italians settled (with migration patterns following employment opportunities), the migration processes and anti-Italian attitudes encouraged Italian migrants to settle close together.

It is important to note that chain migration and the high rate of migration in the post-war period encouraged the growth of neighbourhoods with strong Italian presence, many of which were also associated with a region of Italy. South Australia had a relatively insignificant Italian population until an influx of Italian migrants immigrated shortly after the Second World War. The last pre-war census, held in 1933, reported that there were approximately 1489 Italian-born people living in South Australia.[32] This figure rose exponentially, and by 1971, which was the peak of Italian migration to South Australia, there were 32,428 Italian-born residents.[33] A sizeable community, then, did not emerge in South Australia until after 1945. Yet, distinct patterns of Italian residential settlement occurred even before this mass migration. For instance, high proportions of Italian migrants from Molfetta, Apulia, initially settled in Port Pirie and Port Adelaide during the 1930s. These port areas were attractive given fishing activities were a traditional trade of the Molfettesi community.[34] As previously mentioned, larger numbers of Italians also settled in the western and eastern suburbs where "pockets" of Italian settlement with very strong regional affiliations are noted. A high proportion of Calabrese migrants settled in the west of Adelaide and the Adelaide Hills, whereas migrants from the Campagna region established themselves in the east of Adelaide.[35]

Chain migration thus often facilitated this regional clustering. This pattern of regional settlement was not unique to South Australia and can be seen in other Italian diasporas.[36] Overall, approximately 80 per cent of Italian migrants to Australia relied on chain migration, with the remainder entering via assisted passage.[37] Chain migration refers to the process whereby family, friends and townspeople (*"paesani"*) join a migrant who has established himself in a host country. [38] Sponsors and other migrants within the village network would arrange transport, employment and host new migrants until they either bought or rented their own homes.[39] Most sponsored migrants wished to remain close to their support networks and would settle near to *"paesani"*.[40] The processes of chain migration thus encouraged Italian migrants to maintain strong community bonds, which were reflected in the residential patterns of Italians. By facilitating and maintaining community and family links, these networks were important for adjusting to a new life in Australia.

Societal racism also shaped the experiences of Italians and the nature of the places they created. Discrimination, hostility and racism against Italian migrants have been a prominent part of the Italian narrative in Australia. Under the White Australia Policy (1901–1966)—the informal name for Australia's national immigration legislation of 1901—migrants who conformed to certain ideas of a "white" race were prioritised.[41] Accordingly, preference was given to British and certain European migrants who visually and/or culturally conformed to the imagined ideal of a White, Anglo-Celtic nation.[42] Italian migrants, especially southern Italians, were considered an inferior "white race" and therefore a less desirable type of migrant.[43] These beliefs were reinforced by fears from some members of the Australian community that an influx of Italians would reduce the proportion of British and northern Europeans, affecting the ethnic composition (and purity) of the Australian population.[44] Italian migrants were often targets for criticism, hostility and overt racism, the extent of which varied according to place and time.[45]

An Italian commercial hub also developed in the post-war era. During the early stages of migration and the interwar period, Italian-owned businesses were associated with traditional craft skills and reflected the socio-economic backgrounds of migrants. Accordingly, many businesses centred around fishing, construction or agriculture. Opportunities for a diversified market to meet the needs of the Italian community only emerged in the post-1945 period, as there was now a large enough clientele to support this market.[46] This trend was reflected in the South Australian supplement of *La Fiamma*, where most featured businesses were established after 1945. Many of these businesses were located in the CBD, particularly along Hindley and Gouger Streets. Businesses included retail, electrical, travel, pharmaceutical, hairdressing and clothing stores. Although Italian-owned businesses were also located outside of the CBD, these were often dispersed and smaller. Yet some suburbs, such as Campbelltown, Glynde, Hectorville, Stepney and Norwood Parade, had a sizable presence of Italian-owned businesses. Despite a strong commercial presence in the CBD and eastern suburbs, in this period there is no evidence in *La Fiamma* to support the development of a commercial centre elsewhere.

Although not a "Little Italy" by Pascoe's definition, the emergence of vibrant residential and commercial Italian hubs in Adelaide demonstrates how migrants established their own physical spaces.

PLACE-MAKING STRATEGIES

Applying the concepts of Harney's and Pascoe's "place-making" to an analysis of Adelaide's Italian communities helps to identify the place-making activities of Italian migrants.[47] Pascoe argues that Italian migrants attempted to recreate the ambience of the "*paese*" (village) in their new host countries, and in doing so used three strategies to create a place that was their own. One of these strategies is "renaming", where the community rename physical spaces that signify a unique Italo-Australian community. The second strategy is "ritualisation", where physical space is overhauled to celebrate traditional activities. Lastly, "institutionalisation" describes the process where dedicated spaces for Italian-specific activities are established. Harney also considers three forms of place-making: the "quotidian" form, where individual routinised behaviours collectively make assertions of Italian presence in particular spaces; the "calendrical form", where an ethnic presence in an urban space is manifested in a ritual event, like a religious procession; and, "monumentalism", which refers to the establishment of physical places, such as institutions or monuments.[48] A close reading of *La Fiamma* reveals similar strategies of place-making. Indeed, the newspaper highlights three main examples of renaming practices: "*Piccola Molfetta*" (Little Molfetta); the Italian Corner; and the Italian Street. These examples mainly reflect Pascoe's "renaming" strategy.

The regional city of Port Pirie was referred to as "*Piccola Molfetta*" (Little Molfetta) in *La Fiamma*.[49] It is estimated that some 3000 migrants arrived in Australia from Molfetta, a coastal town in Puglia, with 57 per cent of that total settling in South Australia.[50] There has been a strong association between Port Pirie and Molfetta with a large community having settled in the suburb of Solomontown.[51] Celebration and event notices, as reported in *La Fiamma*, suggest that Solomontown was a site of major social and religious activity for the Molfettesi. Marriages and baptisms were reported to be held in the Church of St Anthony in Solomontown. Social events were also hosted in local halls, such as the Solomontown Football Club or at houses of *"paesani"* (townspeople). The importance of village identity is reflected in the ways in which the Molfettesi continued to engage with their language and culture during the post-war period. For instance, two Italian missionaries described the prominence of the village dialect in an article of *La Fiamma* (1950), "In some parts of town they have even formed localities where you hear only Molfettese spoken".[52] The annual festival of Our Lady of Martyrs, in celebration of Molfetta's patron saint "Madonna dei Martiri", is considered by the community, even in recent times, as an important way to connect with their traditional fishing origins.[53] Use of the term, *"Piccola Molfetta"*, to describe Port Pirie informs how Italians identified and distinguished themselves *within* the community, and indicates that Italians did not assume a uniform national identity. Further, the diminutive adjective, "little", is telling in how individuals or groups located the boundaries of Italian migrants and identified their spaces of social interaction and economic activity.[54]

Another example of renaming is seen in *La Fiamma* where specific commercial precincts in Adelaide were claimed as "Italian". For instance, a weekly advertisement between August 1958 and 1959 claimed Gouger Street as "La Via degli Italiani" or "The Street of Italians".[55] A 1963 full-page advertisement referred to Gouger Street as "Centro Commerciale" (Commercial Centre) featuring a range of Italian-owned businesses including "Farmacia italiana Ravesi" (Ravesi's Italian pharmacy), "Dominic" hairdresser, "Agenzia Viaggi Lamberto" (Lamberto's travel agency) and Olympic Coffee Bar and Restaurant.[56] While Hindley Street did not have its own dedicated section, it was periodically called "L'angolo italiano" (the Italian Corner) in both general issues of *La Fiamma* and the South Australian supplement.

The Catholic Church was one institution that enabled Italians to transfer specific rituals, traditions and celebrations from Italy to Australia, reflecting Pascoe's strategy of "ritualisation" and Harney's "calendrical" form of place-making. Although relations between Italian migrants and the Church in Australia were not always harmonious—due to the tensions between Irish Catholicism and the perception of anti-clerical, "pagan" forms of worshipping by working-class migrants—the arrival of Italian priests played an increasingly important role in facilitating the integration of Italians.[57] The transfer of religious figures and rituals to Adelaide provided familiar places and points of assistance and guidance, and enabled an environment where rituals and social links were maintained.[58] Italian-language Sunday masses were celebrated in areas with large Italian populations, such as the Adelaide CBD, Campbelltown, Flinders Park, Port Adelaide and Port Pirie.[59] The Church also created a social meeting place for migrants, holding dances and other community events.[60] Another form of institutionalism within the Church is seen in the construction of the Church of St Francis of Assisi in Newton (eastern suburbs), which the Italian community called "Piccola Assisi" (Little Assisi). The significance of this church to the community was evident in articles of *La Fiamma* and the *Southern Cross*. The *Southern Cross* reported lists of migrants who had donated to its construction.[61] *La Fiamma* regularly announced *feste* (patron saint days), and between August 1957 and February 1958 it was common to see lists of "*martrimoni alla piccola assisi*" (marriages) and "*battesimi*" (baptisms) that were taking place in "Piccola Assisi".[62]

The Church further provided a means for the community to express identities and partake in rituals, which were regional in nature, predominately through "*feste*". Feste were celebrated in Italian neighbourhoods corresponding to the regional affiliations of that area. For instance, celebrations in honour of patron saints from "*paesi*" in Campagna, such as Saint Rocco and "Madonna di Montevergine", were celebrated in "Piccola Assisi". The celebration of *feste* was one way in which migrants used existing structures, such as the Church, to claim an Italian space. The habituality of the "*feste*" was also an assertion of ethnic presence on the street, both for other Italian migrants and the wider community.[63] Some articles in *La Fiamma* described how religious processions were received by the wider Adelaide community. For instance, in 1958 the "Sant'Ilario" (Saint Hilarion) procession "had aroused curiosity, positive comments and admiration from thousands of citizens of diverse nationalities" when travelling through the city centre.[64]

The third form of place-making is institutionalism/monumentalism, or the creation of specific institutions. Generally, there was a proliferation of Italian social clubs, sporting and religious associations during the 1950s and 1960s in Australia.[65] This uptake of institutions and associations was slower in Adelaide, mainly occurring during the 1970s.[66] Many clubs were regional in nature, although religious and sporting affiliations were also common. According to renowned South Australian Italian Antonio Cocchiaro, these institutions were initially established as a "first act of defence for many lonely and lost migrants" and acted as a "community support structure".[67] Accordingly, these institutions were important in providing an "alternative society" in response to anti-Italian hostility.[68] However, it should also be noted that these institutions did not function solely to escape anti-Italian hostility but were important for hosting celebrations and creating opportunities for regular socialisation. The establishment of these physical spaces enabled Italians to assert their "putative permanence" outwardly to the wider community while providing a more durable, regular and longer-lasting sense of Italian-Australian identity than calendrical events such as the *feste*.[69] *La Fiamma* itself could be considered another example of institutionalism which may have served to reinforce Italian identity. While scholars such as Francesco Ricatti question the success to which *La Fiamma* could be representative of a diverse Italian migrant community, the newspaper was seen to support language and cultural maintenance.[70]

By employing several place-making strategies to create sites of significance to the community, Italian migrants contributed to the development of the Italian commercial centre, which provides an example of a larger structure and more complex forms of place-making. Such a centre emerged in west end of the Adelaide CBD, and it was documented across general issues of *La Fiamma* and its supplement "La comunità italiana di Adelaide". Most of the businesses featured in the supplement were located in the west end of the CBD, with concentrations along Hindley and Gouger Streets. There were diverse types of Italian businesses across these retail strips, including cafes, barbers, pharmacies, travel agencies, tailors, hairdressers, land agents, a car dealership and emporium. Italian social life was not necessarily confined to retail spaces. The west end was also frequented by Italians for entertainment, including operas and films, as well as dining. A regular meeting space in Hindley Street, called the Italian Circle, was also formed for sport enthusiasts in 1953. This "circle" was advertised as "strictly Italian", a place where Italians could catch up over beverages and read newspapers.[71] The west end provided a place in which Italians could catch up socially and find Italian-specific services and goods.

Interestingly, non-Italian-owned businesses in the Adelaide CBD tapped into the Italian market using *La Fiamma* to advertise their services. Businesses such as G. W. Cox Jewellers, Miller Anderson fashion store and the Savings Bank of SA (now BankSA) promoted themselves using

Italian-language advertisements.[72] From their first advertisement, published in 1953, department store John Martin promoted the availability of Italian-language services in its store.[73] These initiatives indicate that the Italian community had a presence in the west end which was acknowledged and promoted by the Italian and non-Italian communities.

The Italian business community was not only crucial for the provision of tailored goods and services but also shaped community development. Several "pioneers" featured in "La comunità italiana di Adelaide" were known for their efforts in organising community and social events, providing employment opportunities, and voluntary social support to the community. Bailetti and Sons, commonly known as the Italian Emporium, sold a variety of domestic whitegoods. The influence of the Bailetti family reached beyond their store; Mario Bailetti's influence in the community extended to the sporting and social spheres. Bailetti was known for providing a "different type of work" in the Italian Emporium. Here, Italian clients would call upon Bailetti for "social services", including tax assistance, writing letters and contacting lawyers and/or doctors.[74] Albert Del Fabbro, known as the Father of Terrazzo, was another key figure in the Italian community represented in the supplement. Del Fabbro sponsored and assisted new migrants, particularly those from his home region of Friuli in the north of Italy. As part of this support, he guaranteed employment and provided loans to new migrants for housing and travel expenses. He was actively involved in institutions such as Fogolar Furlan, a regional club established for migrants from Friuli in 1958, and helped found the Italian Club.[75]

Although Italians created their own cultural, commercial and social spaces, they appeared to be active in the non-Italian community. Articles in *La Fiamma*, particularly in relation to the activities of the Good Neighbourhood Council, suggest that migrants were encouraged to participate in activities that assisted the settlement of migrants. The Good Neighbourhood Council sought to assist with the "assimilation" of migrants and would socialise Australian laws, customs, histories as well as support development of English. A 1957 article outlined a "very successful" conference on traffic rules and safety organised by Good Neighbourhood representative Mr Caruzzi, which included a Sergeant Bougham.[76] The article describes how "everyone remained satisfied, including the cordial sergeant who did not need an interpreter to be understood" and "the Italians had in fact, demonstrated a good knowledge of English". Some Italians were engaged in newspaper activities which demonstrated an interest in adapting to Australian life. The Italian section of the "L'angolo degli italiani" held English translation competitions between August and September 1952, where participants could submit their translations of the text. The *Southern Cross* initiated this competition in response to requests by Italian migrants who had been inspired by a German-English version.[77]

Yet articles in *La Fiamma* also indicate that Italians were differentiating themselves from the wider Australian community. Language was important in identifying who frequented Italian spaces and community events. For instance, "La comunità italiana di Adelaide" describes the changing clientele in Italian businesses in the west end, "today the Italian Corner has become a centre frequented not only by compatriots but by many Australians".[78] While "Australians" were also reported as having attended Italian community events and celebrations, such as Italian beauty pageants and debutant balls, the language used to describe these different communities is reflective of trends that occurred in other Italian diasporas.[79] Just as Gabaccia argues, Italian migrants tended "to homogenise the rest of the world, while, at the same time, gradually recognising that those outside of their migrant circles were doing the same thing to them".[80] While further primary sources would be useful to assess this argument in the context of Adelaide, a reading of *La Fiamma* points towards this trend.

CONCLUSION

Italian spaces developed in Adelaide despite the fact that a "Little Italy" in its traditional sense did not form—rather distinct and separate commercial and residential clusters emerged. The importance of transnational links is evident in the settlement pattern of Italian migrants; there was a tendency of establishing "pockets" of settlement along regional lines. Although this pattern of settlement is not necessarily unique to Adelaide, it aligns to perspectives that Italian migrants were heterogeneous communities during these large waves of migration. While *La Fiamma* is seen to distinguish groups both within and outside of Italian communities, it still served as a platform for bringing together Italians. In a sense, this is reflected within the "La comunità italiana di Adelaide", which discusses diversity within the South Australian Italian community but considers it as a whole. Place-making and the case of Adelaide is reflective of how migrants were able to maintain transnational bonds and influence their environment in a host country.

NOTES

1. William Douglass, *From Italy to Ingham: Italians in North Queensland* (St Lucia, Queensland: University of Queensland Press, 1995), 131.
2. Catherine Dewhirst, "Colonising Italians: Italian Imperialism and Agricultural 'Colonies' in Australia, 1881–1914", *The Journal of Imperial and Commonwealth History* 44, no.1 (2016): 23–25.
3. Donna Gabaccia, "Global Geography of 'Little Italy': Italian Neighbourhoods in Comparative Perspective", *Modern Italy* 11, no.1 (2006): 10.
4. Gabaccia, "Global Geography of 'Little Italy'", 10.
5. For a summary on the intersection between Gabaccia, Harney and Baldassar, see further Nicholas Harney, "Italian Diasporas Share the Neighbourhood (in the English-speaking World)", *Modern Italy* 11, no.1 (2006): 5.
6. Robert Pascoe, "Place and Community: Construction of Place and Community of Italo-Australian Space", in *Australia's Italians: Culture and Community in a Changing Society*, ed. Stephen Castles, Caroline Alcorso, Gaetano Rando and Ellie Vasta (North Sydney: Allen & Unwin, 1992), 93.
7. Susanna Iuliano and Loretta Baldassar, "Deprovincialising Italian Migration Studies: An overview of Australian and Canadian Research", *Flinders University Languages Group Online Review* 3, no.3 (2008): 5; John Zucchi, "Ethnicity and Neighbourhoods: Looking Backward, Facing Forward", *Urban History Review* 39, no.1 (2010): 73.
8. Iuliano and Baldassar, "Deprovincialising Italian Migration Studies", 5.
9. For instance, see: Lancaster Jones, "Italians in the Carlton Area: The Growth of an Ethnic Concentration", *Australian Journal of Politics and History* 10, no.1 (1961): 83–95; Gioconda Di Lorenzo, *Solid Brick Homes and Vegie Patches: A History of Italian Migration to Moonee Ponds* (Parkville, Victoria: Department of History, University of Melbourne, 2001).
10. For instance, Kirrily Jordan, Branka Krivokapic-Skoko and Jock Collins, "Immigration and Multicultural Place-Making in Rural and Regional Australia", in *Demographic Change in Australia's Rural Landscapes: Implications for Society and the Environment* ed. Gary Luck, Rosemary Black and Digby Race (Dordrect; New York: Springer, 2010): 259–280; Antonia Rubino, "Multilingualism in the Sydney Landscape: the Italian Impact", in *Multicultural Sydney*, ed. Alice Chik, Phil Benson and Robyn Moloney (London & New York: Routledge, 2019).
11. Due to the unavailability of the newspaper, the years of 1955, 1956 and the first half of 1957 have not been examined. Quotations from Italian language newspapers in this chapter are presented in English and translated

by the author. References to the Italian-language sources are contained in the footnotes.

12. Anne Reynolds, "Italian Language Print Media in Sydney: A short history of *La Fiamma* newspaper", *Italian Historical Society Journal* 9, no.2 (2001): 11–12.

13. Francesco Ricatti, *Italians in Australia: History, Memory, Identity* Palgrave Studies in Migration History (Cham: Palgrave Macmillan, 2018): 125.

14. George Pozzetta, "The Mulberry District of New York City: The Years before World War One", in *Little Italies in North America*, ed. Robert Harney and Vincenza Scarpaci (Toronto: Multicultural Society of Ontario, 1981): 27.

15. Pozzetta, "The Mulberry District of New York City", 27.

16. John Macdonald and Leatrice Macdonald, "Italian Migration to Australia: Manifest Functions of Bureaucracy Versus Latent Functions of Informal Networks", *Journal of Social History* 3, no.3 (1970): 257.

17. Richard N. Juliani, "The Italian Community Philadelphia", in *Little Italies in North America*, ed. Robert Harney and Vincenza Scarpaci (Toronto: Multicultural Society of Ontario, 1981): 96.

18. Juliani, "The Italian Community Philadelphia", 96.

19. Juliani, "The Italian Community Philadelphia", 98.

20. Macdonald and Macdonald, "Italian Migration to Australia", *Journal of Social History*, 258.

21. Jones, "Italians in the Carlton Area", *Australian Journal of Politics and History*, 90.

22. Douglass, *From Italy to Ingham*, 301.

23. Douglass, *From Italy to Ingham*, 301–303.

24. Commonwealth Bureau of Census and Statistics, *Part I Analysis of Population in Local Government Areas and in non-Municipal Towns of 1,000 Persons or More, Census of the Commonwealth Australia* (Canberra: Commonwealth Bureau of Census and Statistics, 1963), 22–29.

25. Robert Pascoe, *Buongiorno Australia: Our Heritage* (Richard, Vic.: Greenhouse Publications, 1987), 16.

26. Desmond O'Connor, *No Need to be Afraid: Italian Settlers in South Australia between 1839 and the Second World War* (Adelaide: Wakefield Press, 1996), 113.

27. Graeme Hugo, "Patterns and Processes of Italian Settlement in South Australia", in *Proceedings: The First Conference on the Impact of Italians in South Australia, 16–17 July 1993*, ed. Antonio Comin and Desmond O'Connor (Adelaide: Italian Congress Inc and Flinders University of South Australia, 1993), 50.

28. Desmond O'Connor, "The post-war settlement of Italians in South Australia", in *Memories and Identities. Proceedings of the Second Conference*

on the Impact of Italians in South Australia, ed. Desmond O'Connor (Adelaide: Australian Humanities Press, 2004), 57.

29. Pascoe, *Buongiorno Australia*, 16.
30. A homogeneous Italian "community" is contested given diversity in village or regional links, class, gender, age and time of migration to Australia. Helen Ware argues that regionalism was a stronger identity marker than "Italian", and there was little intermixing between northern and southern Italians see Helen Ware, "Origins of Post-War Immigrants", in *The Australian People: An Encyclopaedia of the Nation, its People and their Origins* ed. James Jupp (North Ryde: Angus and Robertson, 1988): 617.
31. Hugo, "Patterns and Processes", 54–55; Stephen Castles, "Italian Migration and Settlement since 1945", in *Australia's Italians: Culture and Community in a Changing Society*, ed. Stephen Castles, Caroline Alcorso, Gaetano Rando and Ellie Vasta (North Sydney: Allen & Unwin, 1992), 44.
32. O'Connor, "The post-war settlement", 57.
33. O'Connor, "The post-war settlement".
34. O'Connor, *No Need to be Afraid*, 69, 79.
35. O'Connor, *No Need to be Afraid*, 116.
36. Ware, "Origins of Post-War Immigrants", 618.
37. Nino Randazzo and Michael Ciglar, *The Italians in Australia* (Melbourne: AE Press, 1987), 149–150.
38. Macdonald and Macdonald, "Italian Migration", 249.
39. Macdonald and Macdonald, "Italian Migration".
40. Hugo, "Patterns and Processes", 54.
41. Egon Kunz, *Displaced Persons: Calwell's New Australians* (Sydney: Australian National University Press, 1998), 6.
42. Collins, *Migrant Hands in a Distant Land*, 10.
43. Macdonald and Macdonald, "Italian Migration", *Journal of Social History*, 253.
44. O'Connor, "The Postwar Settlement", 64.
45. Charles Price, *Southern Europeans in Australia* (Melbourne: Oxford University Press, 1963), 35.
46. Jock Collins, "Cappuccino Capitalism: Italian immigrants and Australian business", in *Australia's Italians: Culture and Community in a Changing Society*, ed. Stephen Castles, Caroline Alcorso, Gaetano Rando and Ellie Vasta (North Sydney: Allen & Unwin, 1992), 73, 75.
47. Pascoe, "Place and Community", 85–97; Nicholas Harney, "The Politics of Urban Space: Modes of Place-making by Italians in Toronto's Neighborhoods", *Modern Italy* 11, no.1 (2006): 25–42.
48. Harney, "The Politics of Urban Space", *Modern Italy*, 29, 30, 34.

49. For an example, see *La Fiamma*, "La Voce di Adelaide", May 16, 1958, p. 10.

50. Desmond O'Connor and Daniela Cosmini-Rose, "Pugliesi in Australia: the History and Tradition of the Molfettesi in South Australia", in *Italy's Apulian Migrants in Australia* (Lecce, Associazione Multiculturale Italo-Australiana, 2011), 154.

51. Michael Corrieri, *Italians of Port Pirie: A Social History* (Port Pirie: Our Lady of Martyrs—Port Pirie Italian Community, 1992), 32.

52. O'Connor and Cosmini-Rose, "Pugliese in Australia", 163.

53. O'Connor and Cosmini-Rose, "Pugliese in Australia", 164.

54. Harney, "The Politics of Urban Space", *Modern* Italy, 26.

55. For example, see *La Fiamma*, "Gouger Street—ADELAIDE, La Via degli Italiani", November 12, 1958, p. 16.

56. *La Fiamma*, "Centro Commerciale", January 15, 1963, p. 34.

57. Ricatti, *Italians in Australia*, 107.

58. Ricatti, *Italians in Australia*, 109.

59. *The Southern Cross*, "L'angolo degli italiani", 1952–1954.

60. O'Connor, "The postwar settlement", 58–59.

61. Lists of individual donations are located in issues of *The Southern Cross*, "L'angolo degli italiani", between September and December 1952.

62. One such example is *La Fiamma*, "Alla Piccola Assisi", August 9, 1957, p. 18.

63. Harney, "The Politics of Urban Space", *Modern Italy*, 30.

64. "S. Ilario unisce Reggio Calabria e Campbelltown", *La Fiamma*, November 5, 1958, p. 16.

65. Cresciani, *The Italians in Australia* (Cambridge, Port Adelaide: Cambridge University Press, 2003): 139.

66. Antonio Cocchiaro, "The History and Future of Italo-Australia Associations in South Australia", in *Proceedings: The First Conference on the Impact of Italians in South Australia 16–17 July 1993* ed. Antonio Comin and Desmond O'Connor (Adelaide: Italian Congress Inc, Italian Discipline, Flinders University, 1993), 74–77.

67. Cocchiaro, "The History and Future of Italo-Australian Associations", 67.

68. Cocchiaro, "The History and Future of Italo-Australian Associations".

69. Harney, "The Politics of Urban Space", *Modern Italy*, 34; Pascoe, "Place and Community", 96.

70. Ricatti, *Italians in Australia*, 125.

71. "Circolo Italiano", *La Fiamma*, May 29, 1953, p. 2.

72. Giuseppe Linarello and Giovanni Costa, "La Comunità Italiana di Adelaide. Supplemento di Adelaide", *La Fiamma*, October 1963, pp. 10, 18, 24; "La Voce", *La Fiamma*, January 31, 1958, p. 10.

73. "John Martin", *La Fiamma*, August 28, 1953, p. 7.

74. Linarello and Costa, "La Comunità Italiana", pp. 13–15.
75. Linarello and Costa, "La Comunità Italiana", pp. 16–17.
76. "La Voce di Adelaide", *La Fiamma*, August 16, 1957, p. 11.
77. "L'angolo degli italiani", *The Southern Cross*, August 22, 1952, p. 3; August 29, 1952, p. 3; September 5, 1952, p. 3; September 12, 1952, p. 3.
78. Linarello and Costa, "La Comunità Italiana", p. 41.
79. "Rosa Tarca, Reginetta Italiana", *La Fiamma*, December 17, 1954, p. 8; "Andiamo al ballo bianconero?", *La Fiamma*, May 11, 1958, p. 19.
80. Gabaccia, "Global Geography of 'Little Italy'", *Modern Italy*, 17.

CHAPTER 7

Reflections and Transition of Old and New Italian Media in Australia: The Case of *Il Globo*

Bruno Mascitelli

The Italian language media in one form or another has had a presence in Australia stretching back more than 120 years. Its presence has also included periods when there were few Italians in Australia. In the early days of Australian colonial existence, the Italian media pursued more specific sectoral lines of dissemination, such as Catholicism, or the expression of political ideologies. As the onset of mass Italian migration to Australia became a reality in the 1950s and 1960s, it provided the opportunity for more mainstream media to promote, support and give a "voice" to this migration. *Il Globo* (The Globe), which emerged in Melbourne in the late 1950s, and its sister Italian newspaper *La Fiamma* (The Flame) in Sydney became the most recognisable Italian media in Australia after the 1960s.

B. Mascitelli (✉)
Department of Social Sciences, Swinburne University of Technology,
Hawthorn, VIC, Australia
e-mail: bmascitelli@swin.edu.au

C. Dewhirst, R. Scully (eds.), *Voices of Challenge in Australia's Migrant and Minority Press*, Palgrave Studies in the History of the Media, https://doi.org/10.1007/978-3-030-67330-7_7

127

While *La Fiamma* was established in the 1920s and merged with *Il Globo* in May 1978, since its first edition in November 1959 *Il Globo* became the showpiece of Italian media in Australia, which proposed, stimulated and recorded a substantial slice of Italian migration history to the extent that it is, itself, more than just as an instrument of information and opinion, but an instrumental part of that story.

Italian migration to Australia saw its heyday in the aftermath of the Second World War and especially between 1951 and 1971. Much of this period was covered by the bilateral agreement on migration between Italy and Australia, which accorded rights and protection to the newly arrived from Italy. By 1971 the number of Italy born residents living in Australia had reached 288,000.[1] While there was a significant return migration of Italians back to Italy in the mid-1970s (in part due to better economic circumstances in Italy), the number of Italians—both first and second generations—climbed to almost 800,000 by the turn of the millennium.

It was with irony that one very thorough scholarly overview of the foreign-language press in Australia between 1848 and 1964, when referring to the Southern European press—specifically the Greek and Italian press—noted that "the main difference between the Greek and Italian presses lies in the partisan appeal of the former as compared with the predominantly non-political character of the latter".[2] After explaining the partisan nature of the Greek press in Australia the authors then describe the Italian press:

> By contrast, the Italian press, with one exception, is overwhelmingly non-political. The issues that separate the editors of the principal Italian newspapers concern rather their attitudes to assimilation, the need for retention of certain Italian national features, and the like.[3]

Labelling the politics of *Il Globo* has in part been an exercise in examining the politics of the editor. Pascoe described the view of *Il Globo* as being:

> in the centre right of Australian politics—roughly midway between the Australian labour Party and the Democratic party—in much the same position as *La Fiamma*. Since both papers are now owned by the same men ... this convergence of political orientation is likely to continue.[4]

Gaetano Rando has provided a slight qualifier to this description stating: "centre right in Australian politics and somewhat towards right of centre in Italian politics, *Il Globo* has a similar type of content and readership as *La Fiamma*, but there is no English language content".[5] Curiously however, Rando adds another dimension to *Il Globo* when he states:

> Having begun as a genuine community paper, *Il Globo* has now somewhat fossilized and does not display the innovative tendencies of *La Fiamma*. Nevertheless, it produces some very polemical, sometimes quite lively, editorials and leading articles on issues, such as SBS, the teaching of Italian, the immigration debate, that strike responsive cords in its managing editor Nino Randazzo. [...] The conservative tendencies of the two papers and the consequent selection made of news and information from Italy tend to appeal to the bulk of the older first generation Italian immigrants.[6]

While a number of Italian newspapers paved the way for an Italian media presence in Australia since the 1920s, this chapter focuses primarily on the case of *Il Globo*. The presence of Italian media in Australia has a long history in which *Il Globo* holds a special place (as does its sister newspaper, *La Fiamma*). Central to this chapter is addressing the themes of *Il Globo*'s relevance to giving "voice" to the Italian community as well as providing ways and means for Italian settlement and integration into Australian society. This has, however, come at an expense, which has at times enhanced, troubled and even hurt *Il Globo*'s reputation in the Australian community. The purpose of this chapter is to re-evaluate the continuing role of this newspaper in the changing dynamics of the media and above all Italian migration by engaging with these same challenges and questioning how they have been met by this Italian newspaper. This is undertaken through research initially conducted in 2009 on the 50th anniversary of *Il Globo*.[7] The "new" Italian migration to Australia in the last decade is too strong a word. Small increases through the Italian holiday makers entering Australia since the enactment of the agreement between Italy and Australia in 2004 have accounted for this rise. Yet what was the role for *Il Globo* in this new and much changed context of Italians in Australia? This chapter re-examines the literature and talks to insiders as well as those in *Il Globo*'s management to provide an understanding how a changing community, a changing media industry, changing technology and changing demographics have been and are still being tackled by the newspaper and their response to continue to want to remain relevant to their purpose of being a "voice" for the Italian community in Australia.

Il GLOBO: THE WAY IT WAS

On 4 November 1959 the first weekly issue of *Il Globo* appeared. It was produced as a broad sheet containing approximately 24 pages. The article celebrating the arrival of *Il Globo* was entitled the "Ideal bridge" (*Ponte ideale*). The editors wished to make the link to the 4 November 1918, Italian Victory Day. Without much ado the article posed a question for itself about the formidable task ahead: "We ask ourselves as we begin this task, what should be the function of an overseas Italian weekly newspaper?"[8] The layout of the newspaper in its early days followed a certain pattern with the intention of containing the appropriate headlines (national and international news), editorial commentary and domestic and Italian news. This would also include Italian Community information and news items.[9] In its early days sport, or better still, Italian football news (soccer) was in its infancy although this segment of *Il Globo* would grow over the years. The newspaper was initially produced out of its Sydney Road offices in Italian-dominated suburb of Brunswick and later moved to Peel Street in North Melbourne. But more importantly the emergence of *Il Globo* was largely the inspiration of the entrepreneurial vision of the directors and editors Ubaldo Larobina and Terry (Tarcisio) Valmorbida. Soon after they were joined by Antonino (Nino) Randazzo (born 1932 died 2019), who would take on the role of political interpreter of the news along with editorial commentary of both domestic and international events. This was especially for events occurring in Italy.[10] Nino Randazzo and Michael Cigler describe how *Il Globo* began its rise in the Australian media landscape:

> The youngest, Tarcisio Valmorbida, provided the first [financial] capital for the establishment of *Il Globo* which later, under the editorship of Calabrian born Ubaldo Larobina, was to become the most widely circulated foreign language newspaper in Australia.[11]

In 1961 *Il Globo* covered a scoop with the Bonegilla Riots where Italians (including one Giovanni Sgro) played a leading role. Bonegilla Commonwealth Migrant Reception centre was located in northern Victoria close to Wodonga on the border with New South Wales. It played a key role in housing migrants on their arrival and was also a channel for migrants to then move as unskilled labour to the Snowy Mountains Scheme.[12] Bruce Pennay provides a flavour of the events:

there was a general discontent about not getting jobs among all the resident nationalities, of which Germans, Italians and Yugoslavs (predominantly Croatians) were the most numerous. Unemployed residents had been voicing their discontent for three or four months. Churchmen and consular officials had made representations about the distress of what were becoming long-term unemployed migrants.[13]

These events and Italian government indignation at the causes of this riot caused significant tension between the Italian and Australian governments, ultimately resulting in the Migration Assistance agreement not being renewed. In 1963 the Melbourne Market killings (of four Italians) created a fury of debate about the mafia being present within the Italian community in Melbourne. It was a debate which saw *La Fiamma* and *Il Globo* at war with each other and was one of the more memorable moments of Randazzo's fiery pen at work in Il Globo in protest of ethnic labelling of Italians as "mafia".[14]

In 1967 the Italian President Saragat visited Australia producing a wave of Italian enthusiasm, allowing *Il Globo* to produce important newspaper features and commentary. In the Federal elections of 1969, *Il Globo* through the pen of Randazzo made clear that the Liberal-Country Coalition had lost its right to rule and it was time for a change of government. This was not to be and would only happen three years later. In 1970 Pope Paul also visited Australia, allowing *Il Globo* to provide heavy reporting and commentary, and in 1972 with the victory of the Whitlam Labor government, *Il Globo* despite support for the Labor victory soon made clear its disenchantment with Labor's view of more restrictive immigration.

In the meantime, *Il Globo* moved office again, in 1973, and migrated to its more permanent location and Italian-dominated Faraday Street, Carlton. The 1976 election in Italy was to become a critical one because the Italian Communist Party received 35 per cent of the vote and almost became the largest party, which created great ideological polarisation. *Il Globo* in these elections, and clearly a Randazzo indication, called for the "no vote" to the Italian Communist Party. An important milestone was reached in 1978 when *La Fiamma* in Sydney was on the verge of bankruptcy and was bought out by *Il Globo*, thus creating a single editorial line with two separate community news outlets in the two major cities of Italian presence in Australia.[15] In 1981 *Il Globo* embraced Labor leader and Prime Minister Bob Hawke and engaged in many of the debates of that decade—such as on immigration levels for Australia. The one theme which is close to its heart was that of immigration. In 1994, Italian anti-corruption prosecutor, Antonio Di Pietro visited Australia and was not only embraced by the Italian public but also by *Il Globo*, and in the same year the emergence of Silvio Berlusconi in Italian politics attracted the interest and initially sympathy of *Il Globo*.[16] A major step forward occurred with the establishment of "Rete Italia" (Italian Channel) in 1994, which expanded the umbrella organisation to include *Il Globo* as part of the Italian Media Corporation. In 1998 *Il Globo* became a tabloid paper and in 1999 it went to publishing twice a week (Monday and Friday). It soon moved to three issues per week and in December of 1999 it experimented with including *La Repubblica* (the Italian daily) as an insert into its editions. The substantial leap in *Il Globo*'s approach towards its own positioning as a stable Italian media offering in Australia occurred in September of 2000, which saw it go "daily", publishing each weekday. This was a daring move and possibly one of the directors and editors eventually regretted taking. In 2002 the experiment with *La Repubblica* ceased with *Il Globo* having exhausted its novelty and expertise with a professional Italian daily like *La Repubblica*.

In 2006 Randazzo resigned from *Il Globo* and stood in the Italian elections in the Senate external electoral college—representing Africa, Asia, Oceania and Antarctica for La Margherita Party (the Daisy Flower Party). Some dubbed it "From Editor to Senator".[17] He along with Marco Fedi became two Australian parliamentarians standing in the Italian Parliament. This was certainly the end of an era for *Il Globo* and replacing the driven and outspoken Randazzo would not be easy and would also require significant shifts in the way the editorial culture would work within the newspaper. Dario Nelli became Randazzo's replacement and brought with a different journalistic pedigree.

It is a tragic irony that while preparing this chapter not only had *Il Globo* reached its 60th anniversary, but it marked the passing of *Il Globo*'s first and most prolific editor in Nino Randazzo. As editor of *Il Globo* for almost three decades, he was the pen and the face of the newspaper both inside the newspaper and in the community.

The Italian media in Australia has been surprisingly rich in its activity and presence if only temporary. It also had a tradition of being ideologically aligned, much depending on the global events occurring at the time. Though the large numbers of Italians would only occur in the 1950s and 1960s, Amedeo Tosco has provided a wealth of evidence and literature on the earlier forms of Italian media,[18] despite the fact that large numbers of

Italians arrived much later. One such newspaper which received much attention was *L'Italo-Australiano* which was the first Italo-Australian newspaper, established in 1885 and of socialist persuasion.[19] Equally the varied Italian press during the 1920s through to the 1940s was dominated by the fact that Italy was Fascist and Italians in Australia were essentially the enemy. Much of what the Italian media communicated was very much directed to consolidation of a fascist outcome even for the small numbers of Italians in Australia at that time. Robert Pascoe equally provides us with a broader panorama of the Italian press in Australia stretching back to the early 1900s and how such a phenomenon became critical in identifying ethnic rights.[20]

Ironically, *La Fiamma*, which would become part of the *Il Globo* construction, was launched more than 12 years earlier than *Il Globo* and, while appearing today as a sister newspaper, was the first main Italian newspaper in the post-war period. It was also heavily ideologically oriented against Communism in its early years and a constant voice of both Catholicism and Italian nationalism. Based in Sydney and using a name meaning "a flame", its early days were as a "rabid anti-communist" newspaper especially evident in its earlier editions.[21] It was owned by the Capuchin Order of the Catholic Church under the leadership of Father Anastasio Paoletti and was especially driven to counter the effects and impact of a left-wing Italian newspaper, known as Il Risveglio (Re-awakening), established in 1944, an alliance of anti-fascists led by Omero Schiassi, which lasted until 1956.[22] *La Fiamma* assumed even greater notoriety when it supported the anti-Communist and Catholic Democratic Labor Party (DLP) split of the Australian Labor Party in 1955 and supported the DLP in the 1955 elections in Victoria. *La Fiamma* faced editorial changes in 1951 when Paoletti took a step back from leading the paper allowing Evasio Costanzo to take control in 1951. Its circulation grew, its format expanded and in large part the Italians coming to Australia also grew. Susanna Iuliano describes the change in editorial leadership under Costanzo by stating that "Costanzo steered *La Fiamma* away from obsession with Communism towards a broader expression of spiritual interests".[23] Costanzo maintained a strong religious approach but toned down the anti-communism along with his own "blended Catholicism, nationalism and Italian cultural grandeur".[24] *La Fiamma* reached over 40,000 copies by the mid-1960s after its rival, *Il Risveglio*, disappeared in 1957.[25] In 1997 after it had been bought out by *Il Globo*, *La Fiamma* celebrated its 50th anniversary with a special historical edition of its 50 years in an impressive tabloid format.²⁶ Despite everything it was certainly an achievement.

As an Italian newspaper in Australia, *Il Globo* continues to be the newspaper for all Italians—what some Italian media commentators have called the "omnibus newspaper".²⁷ It continues to produce a paper in Italian with segments on international news, Italian news, local Australian news, almost one quarter of the paper on sport, woman's interests, cooking, pastime activities, death columns and the like. This generic approach was appreciated by the well-known immigration scholar James Jupp when in describing *Il Globo* he observed:

> purely political newspapers rarely do well and *Il Globo* … were wise enough to know that they must cover sport, entertainment, community news and similar topics if they were not to fold like so many other ethnic newspapers.²⁸

Il Globo turned out to be a pillar of strength for Italians in Australia and, in its own way, a voice of policy and politics. With an established Italian community populating large parts of Australia—Melbourne and Sydney primarily—the instrument and voice of *Il Globo* also made Italian views known to mainstream Australian society. *Il Globo* has been adept at adapting to an evolving set of circumstances. In the past it rode the wave of Italian migration and adapted itself to the changing demography as well as the political changes in both Italy and Australia. In the last decades technology has evolved as have media platforms. The first-generation community that gained the most from *Il Globo* is today shrinking. With less immigration from Italy, the cohort of Italian migrants is not growing. Even with the sprinkling of younger Italians temporarily residing in Australia on either working holiday visas of short duration or temporary visas, there is little chance of them becoming permanent. Moreover, the readership of *Il Globo* has changed. The declining first and second generations of Italians in Australia has reduced the newspaper's impact.

The "fathers" of the first editions of *Il Globo*—Larobina, Valmorbida and Randazzo—gave little thought to their future at first. They "rolled with the punches" as the saying goes. Little did they know that in 2019 they would be still in print (albeit twice a week) and in some respects still posing the question of what they should be doing with this newspaper. The fact that they were printing 60 years later might say something about their formula of success, whether conscious of the reasons why or why not.

A COMMUNITY NEWSPAPER FOR A NEW COMMUNITY?

Behind much of what *Il Globo* set out to do in its early days was a sustained arrival of Italians populating the big cities of Australia. The figures at the time evidenced thousands of Italians mostly from the Southern regions of Italy (and the Veneto) seeking new opportunities in a new land. With the Australian Italian Migration Agreement in 1951, the understanding that there would be large numbers of Italians moving to Australia was a reality. The platform for *Il Globo* was that not only was there a role to play in providing news and analysis for this Italian migration but also one in assisting the settlement process. This included providing even mundane exercises such as providing locations for people to meet and become friends. Despite the census indication of around 950,000 people in Australia of Italian descent in 2011, the large arrival numbers from Italy to Australia are no more.[29] Recent data from Australian immigration sources indicate that while numbers spiked from Italy between 2004 and 2015, this was primarily as a result of the 2004 Working Holiday Arrangement between Italy and Australia (see Fig. 11.1). The actual numbers receiving permanent settlement were very small (Table 7.1).[30]

In addition, in examining the top source countries for migrants to Australia, between 2004 and 2015, Italy contributed a total of 1371 against 34,874 Indian, 27,872 Chinese, 21,078 British; and even France and Germany were higher source countries than Italy.[31] Clearly Italian migration to Australia had come to an end.

Acknowledging the growth of the Italian taught in schools, Randazzo observed:

Table 7.1 Italian citizens holding a temporary visa in Australia 2004–2015

Visa holder component	Total 2004–2015	% of Total 2004–2015
Working holiday maker visa holders	51,373	40.7
Visitor visa holders	30,584	24.3
Temporary skilled visa holders	17,682	14.0
Student visa holders	17,024	13.5
Bridging visa holders	5321	4.2
Other temporary visa holders	3984	3.1
Temporary graduate visa holders	265	0.2
Total	126,233	100

Source: Riccardo Armillei and Bruno Mascitelli, *From 2004 to 2016: A new Italian 'exodus' to Australia?* (Melbourne: COMITES, 2016)

> When we started the newspaper 40 years ago in 1959, there were only a handful, I would say only a few hundred, students of Italian at the secondary and tertiary level in this country. Today, we have around (...) 45,000 students of Italian at secondary and tertiary level throughout Australia. They are the type of people who need to keep in touch with the language, which is of course a living language, it evolves continuously, and in order to do this they have to read Italian-Language publications.[32]

While it might be seen as a retrograde step of the first generation of Italians not being fluent with digital technology, this has in a backhanded manner given *Il Globo* a prolonged life and not having to make a decision on placing the newspaper entirely online. The old generation not only like to read a physical newspaper, they are less adept at using online, phone and computer access. Yet incorporating more English into the paper—with the growing difficulty that the second and third generations experience with the Italian language—is a dilemma that is being wrestled with. The previous experience of the four-page insert of English analysis and news was again, according to Nelli, a good idea but needed greater attention and expertise—meaning English-trained journalists. This idea, however, is not off the agenda but will not assume the proportions of the Greek Saturday newspaper, *Neos Kosmos* (New World), which is almost 50 per cent English. On bilingual media—meaning when the newspaper will seek to have segments or whole sections in the language of the country—Randazzo indicates that bilingual examples from overseas are not encouraging. As he explains:

> If one has to produce a bilingual newspaper, one would have to divert sources, the human and financial resources, to production of a newspaper in another language. And the end result would be that both sections, both the Italian language section and the English language section would be impoverished and disappoint readers and lose readers. We have had one particular experience, for example in this area. There used to be an Italian language daily in New York for instance, and the moment that it went bilingual, lost readership. It had to fold.[33]

Randazzo confessed as far back as 1999 that: "I don't think anyone has found any formula to get young readers. The major Australian language newspapers have not found a formula and if they have not found it, with all the resources they have, I don't know what chances a foreign language newspaper in this country would have."[34] New segments of *Il Globo*, like

"Eureka", with creative topics and themes, appear to be making such an attempt. With what success is unclear.

The presence of a large segment of sport in *Il Globo* has from the early days of the paper been an important attraction and created a loyalty base of readers, especially males and those of a certain generation. This strong positioning was largely as a result of the serendipitous fortune of publishing in Australia and being 8 or 10 hours ahead of Italy (and most of the world) to be able to emerge with sports (meaning football) results on a Monday morning before the rest of the world had a chance. Larobina acknowledged this fortuitous occurrence saying: "We were the first in the world to publish the [sports] results, because of the time difference".[35] To this day this serendipity has served *Il Globo* well and the plus 10–12 pages with many photos in colour of the regular newspaper's 44–48 pages is a significant component of the paper. The downside is that the emphasis on sport which is and remains largely male in its focus although female sporting activities are becoming more prominent as they have already become in mainstream Australian society today.

The author of this chapter was also part of an editorial team which in 2009 published an extended researched treatment of *Il Globo*.[36] The study was undertaken as commemoration of *Il Globo*'s 50 years of existence. In conversations with *Il Globo*'s management and staff in preparation for this current study, inevitably the 2009 book on *Il Globo* emerged as conversation and reflection. The study in 2009 became an edited book with book chapters across the history, hurdles and evolution of *Il Globo*. Other chapters also included how *Il Globo* was seen by the left, the use of publicity in the newspaper and of course the personality and literary contributions of Nino Randazzo, its editor. It is interesting to note that in its feedback *Il Globo*'s management said that the book was far too focused on the work and approach of its editor, Randazzo, and not enough about the newspaper more generally. The assertion was that the book had failed to see beyond the Randazzo factor and address the other equally revealing segments of the paper.

Plausible as this concern might be—the study conducted an analysis on what appeared within the Italian newspaper, irrespective of its authorship. In effect, its focus was a critical analysis of this newspaper and its role in the Italian community. The headlines and editorial commentary, generally signed by Randazzo, were to the outside world what they seemed—the views of the editorial group headed by Randazzo from 1978 when he assumed the formal role of editor of the newspaper. When the book was launched in March 2009 this view of excessive emphasis on the role of Randazzo was not shared by the Randazzo family. Nino Randazzo, who was not present for the book launch, provided his own assessment of the book in a written statement read out by his daughter, Carmen Randazzo. The comments were not especially congratulatory of the work and even hinted that we had denigrated his political views. The Randazzo statement made a diplomatic criticism of the work by stating that it was not the history of *Il Globo* but a history of *Il Globo*,[37] alluding to Randazzo's disagreement with our interpretation. On the other hand, as was evidenced in the acknowledgement of the book, the book noted:

> The original idea of writing this anthology [on *Il Globo*] was not that of the editors. It was actually suggested by *Il Globo*'s Director Ubaldo Larobina. As with many other aspects of the strategic direction of this media organization, which will be evident from reading this book, Larobina's ongoing search for the next challenge for his newspaper is a constant.[38]

NEW ITALIAN MIGRATION: NEW DIRECTIONS FOR *IL GLOBO*

When Nino Randazzo was campaigning to become a candidate for the La Margherita Party in the 2006 Italian elections (which for the first time allowed Italians abroad to vote and elect their own parliamentary representatives), it had consequences for *Il Globo*. The newspaper would need to transition to a new style of management and leadership and did so in the guise of Dario Nelli—but under the watchful eye of Ubaldo Larobina. The transition to a post-Randazzo era seemed to occur smoothly without any evident stumbling blocks. Gone were the flamboyancy, loud and outspoken pieces. Randazzo had the ability to impersonate a "shock jock" in one moment and soon after demonstrating acute political perception. Internally within the confines of the working leadership of the newspaper he may have irritated key members of the management with knee-jerk positions not necessarily shared by all.

As Nelli took on the task, it was clear that there would be a new style of leadership. Even ten years ago Carli noted this different style of editing:

> Current editor Dario Nelli continues to write opinion pieces which are published in the Monday paper. They are topical but no longer carry the polemical style nor do they dominate the newspaper as they did in the Randazzo

era. This reflects changes in the style of the paper and a shift that had also been occurring in Italian journalism.[39]

Nelli was firm and clear but not in the style of extravert megaphone politics and more on the task of information provision and neutral reporting and analysis as much as possible. There was a more considered response and analysis to events in Italy and in Australia and the level of political interference from the owners and managers appears to be little to none as the staff know the space they populate and what is expected of them. Nelli was considered a "safe pair of hands" for the after Randazzo period and had the history of working for decades with the previous editor. This has meant more and consistent sales and avoided the collapse of newspapers as many of the English newspapers have felt and continue experiencing.

Indeed, not all changes can be attributed to personnel changes. The end of the Cold War and the move into a lesser-ideological territory produced a less politically divided debate. This was especially noted with the demise of the Communist Party in Italy in 1991, which produced a newspaper and commentary which could be defined as more "centrist". Despite *Il Globo*'s short-lived flirt with Berlusconi and Forza Italia, the late 1990s and into the early twentieth century witnessed some evident toning down of the previous fiery political denunciations. It was the end of the European Cold War and political parties were building around coalitions. This was beginning to blur the divisions and therefore the political commentary was less black and white.

Since then *Il Globo* has been refreshed with new approaches and a greater emphasis on analysis and interpretation of news and facts, and not just the listing of news. This has in part been facilitated by the fact that the paper has steadied as a twice weekly (Monday and Thursday) and has, according to Nelli, sought to ensure that it responded to what was of interest to the Italian community in Australia.[40] Ironically and more recently this newspaper has witnessed an internal revitalisation with the inclusion of younger and more dynamic journalists who have lifted the youth profile and content within *Il Globo* to higher levels of (youth) relevance levels with varying levels of success. The newspaper has become much more national with services on activities across many states of Australia and the incorporation of *La Fiamma*, which after 2000 became increasingly one newspaper with local pages dedicated to local news and publicity related to the community of the different cities, such as Melbourne and Sydney. *Il Globo* continues to maintain many of the categories critical to its survival with a strong Italian news segment, followed by Australian political news, regular columns from informed professionals, a massive sports segment and finally an Australian smaller news segment often divided along state/city lines. The paper is always looking at what can be sustained and done so professionally. From conversations with management, an appreciation of their role as journalists and the seriousness with which they approach their task is quite evident. The discussion on an English language insert was felt beyond the means at this point in time because it "lacked the professional staff to be able to sustain it".[41] This was a refreshing and open admission but not one that was considered illusive for ever. According to the director of the paper appearing twice a week is a neat and proportional balance of circulation.[42] Allowing for the sport features (on the Sunday) and properly spaced out during the week.

Inside *Il Globo* a new layer of younger and more recently arrived Italians have joined the newspaper in the last ten years giving a more vibrant understanding of events in Italy and at the same time providing a political slant with the analysis which is both more topical and reflecting events and political behaviour in Italy. There is little denying that *Il Globo* makes every effort to be relevant, topical and serving the needs of both the past and the current Italian migrants and community. The breakdown of the paper demonstrates this whether this is reflected in extra sales or not.

Financing Italian newspapers abroad, however, is a topic on going relevance and survival. Pascoe noted that in 1989 *Il Globo* was the most financially successful Italo-Australian paper. During the 2000 period Italian government's financial support to Italian media abroad came under scrutiny and typical difficulties of uneven support were the order of the day. The proposal from the government was that the newspaper needed to be a daily and it would then become eligible for financial support in terms of support for the Italians abroad. One of the turning points for *Il Globo* in its drive towards sustainability was when the newspaper decided not to pursue Italian government funding. This was a decision which had its concerns given the need for *Il Globo* to be entirely dependent on its own resources. When quizzed about this decision the response was that Italian government funding was both unreliable and unpredictable, and continuing to rely on this was simply not possible.[43] As precarious and dangerous this move was it was one the newspaper never looked back from and in some respects seemed to make the newspaper stronger and independent.

The pressures on *Il Globo* to survive in Australia are equally as strong on all foreign-language media and certainly all Italian media outside Italy.

Government reports from the Italian Foreign Affairs Department have highlighted how Italian media in countries of the diaspora are in permanent decline.[44] Foreign media are faced not only with the evolving nature and platform of the media which itself is placing all newspapers in danger but also with a dramatic change in the nature of the Italian community in Australia. As the Italian Network, the organisation behind the newspaper, *L'Italiano* (The Italian), which serves the major Italian diaspora of Buenos Aires in Argentina, responded to the possible disappearance of Italian language newspapers:

> Certainly not, there will always be some form of information, possibly less professional. It will be primarily sectoral information, improvised, undertaken by blogs on the web and narrowly defined bulletins with improvised editorial groups often around one person. We will shift from industry professionalism to the good will of individuals.[45]

And there is the financial issue. Producing a paper has a cost—in people and salaries, production, utilities and consultancy and advice. The Italian newspapers abroad have struggled with financial balances from the "get go". As the Buenos Aires editor reminded us: "Editing an Italian daily abroad is not a great business affair. Actually, it is an exercise which is very expensive. Editorial needs, journalists, design and graphics, administration, printing, distribution and publicity marketing." These are the costs involved which need to be met with publicity and advertisement.

In 2016 Italian Network sounded the alarm for Italian newspapers around the world in their quest for survival. It stated:

> The Italian is entering its 10th year of existence, another year of struggle for survival. At this moment only 4 overseas dailies have survived: *La Voce del Popolo* (Croatia), *America Oggi* (New York), *Il Corriere Canadese* (Toronto), *L'Italiano* (Buenos Aires) which has reached its 10th year of existence'. This was noted by Tullio Zembo director of *L'Italiano* from Argentina in his editorial reminding readers that "a few years ago there were exactly double that amount of Italian papers. [...] From 8 to 4 newspapers in a short time is not a picture of success and at this rate it would be easy to expect that we could arrive sooner rather than later at 'total extinction of the species.[46]

The reference to the situation in Australia was to note that the two Italian newspapers *Il Globo* and *La Fiamma*, which were both under the management and ownership of Italian Media Corporation, had reverted to publishing only twice a week.[47] Counterintuitively, however, the number of Italians abroad, of all generations, is not declining, and according to the Registry of Italians Resident Abroad (AIRE), in the 2018 elections the number of Italians that had registered on the elections registry reached more than five million,[48] the highest number since the register was established. Will this translate into helping all Italian newspapers abroad?

Given *Il Globo*'s decision to not seek Italian government aid, its sole funding provider is of course advertising. Most of the advertising is local (Melbourne), while *La Fiamma* also pulls in Sydney advertising and primarily from Italo-Australian organisations. Another important revenue stream for *Il Globo* is from the death columns and to a lesser extent the trade services. The death columns while still lucrative is slightly declining and is set to decline even further as we witness the passing of the first generation of Italians. While it is not possible to speculate on the future of advertising take up, one has to wonder how long this can last. More bad news hit Media Communications when, in August 2019, *Il Globo* announced that "Rete Italia" would be downsized (*"Rete Italia si ridimensiona"*). Effectively, what it announced was that "Rete Italia" was closing down 21 frequencies stations throughout the country leaving radio stations only in Victoria, New South Wales and Queensland.[49] This was not good news at all.

CONCLUSION

Il Globo started as a weekly and progressed into more regular issues which found its way into mostly traditional Italian households, especially in Italian neighbourhoods in Melbourne and beyond. It shaped, informed and formed opinions of Italians living in Australia, at times with their agreement and often not. It provided critical information for a new community seeking to settle and improve their lives in Australia. It was championed by determined individuals like Ubaldo Larobina and the more flamboyant and louder Nino Randazzo until 2006 when he then became a senator in the Italian parliament. Since then it has come under directorship of the more reserved but considered approach of Dario Nelli. This reign too is coming close to its end and, along with the Larobina management, is progressing to the next generation. The survival issues for this newspaper will become their task to address.

Despite all the overarching pressures on *Il Globo*, it remains resilient and constantly in search of avenues to survive and find a purpose to remain relevant to the evolving Italian-speaking community. The broader picture of demographic trends, linguistic patterns, Italian migration to Australia and uptake of the Italian language in Australia along with the financial constraints of running an ethnic newspaper do not provide high levels of encouragement for its survival. Yet this is not the first time *Il Globo* has faced and overcome such hurdles and challenges. It will without doubt adapt to changing circumstances and possibly make significant changes to its model. Onward to its 70th anniversary!

NOTES

1. Italian Historical Society, "Italian migration to Australia" (landing page) (Melbourne: COASIT, 1988) http://coasit.com.au/dbtw-wpd/exec/dbtwpub.dll (accessed June 15, 2016).
2. Miriam Gilson and Jerzy Zubrzycki, *The Foreign language Press in Australia, 1848–1964* (Canberra: Australian National University Press, 1967), 31.
3. Gilson and Zubrzycki, *The Foreign language Press in Australia*, 32.
4. Robert Pascoe, "The Italian Press in Australia", in *The Ethnic Press in Australia*, ed. Abe Wade Ata and Colin Ryan (Melbourne: Academia Press, 1989), 204.
5. Gaetano Rando, "Aspects of the history of the Italian Language press in Australia 1885–1985", in *Italians in Australia Historical and social perspectives*, ed. Gaetano Rando and Michele Arrighi (Wollongong, NSW: Department of Modern Languages, University of Wollongong, 1993), 208.
6. Rando, "Aspects of the history of the Italian Language press in Australia", 209.
7. Bruno Mascitelli, "The first 50 years", in *Il Globo: Fifty Years of an Italian Newspaper in Australia*, ed. Bruno Mascitelli and Simone Battiston (Ballarat Vic.: Connor Court Publishing, 2009), 1.
8. "Il ponte ideale", *Il Globo*, November 4, 1959, 1.
9. Edwards, "1959–1969: An early voice of Italians in Australia", 29.
10. Edwards, "1959–1969: An early voice of Italians in Australia".
11. Nino Randazzo and Michael Cigler, *The Italians in Australia* (Melbourne: AE Press, 1987), 160.
12. Bruce Pennay, "The Bonegilla Riot, July 1961: Maintaining favourable Impressions of the Postwar Immigration Program", November 13, 2017, *Australian Policy and History*, http://aph.org.au/the-bonegilla-riot-july-1961-maintaining-favourable-impressions-of-the-postwar-immigration-program/ (accessed February, 3 2020).
13. Pennay, "The Bonegilla Riot, July 1961".

14. Mascitelli, "The First 150 Years", 32.
15. Virtual tour, Italian Language media in Leichhardt: *La Fiamma* newspaper and Rete Italia, n.d. http://www.virtualtour.com.au/melocco/leichhardt%20-201.6htm (accessed August 22, 2009).
16. Carlo Carli, "A community paper for a changing community", in *Il Globo: Fifty years of an Italian newspaper in Australia*, ed. Bruno Mascitelli and Simone Battiston (Ballarat, Vic.: Connor Court Publishing, 2009), 113.
17. Carli, "A community paper for a changing community", 112.
18. Amedeo Tosco, "Features of early ethnic Italo-Australian newspapers: a case study of *L'Italo-Australiano* (1885)", Doctor of Philosophy thesis, Griffith University, 2005.
19. Rando, "Aspects of the history of the Italian Language press in Australia", 197.
20. Pascoe, "The Italian Press in Australia", 96.
21. Susanna Iuliano, "Constructing Italian ethnicity: A comparative study of two Italian language newspapers in Australia and Canada, 1947–1957", Master of Arts thesis, McGill University, Montreal, Canada, 1994, 58.
22. Iuliano, "Constructing Italian ethnicity", 59.
23. Iuliano, "Constructing Italian ethnicity", 66.
24. Iuliano, "Constructing Italian ethnicity", 83.
25. Pascoe, "The Italian Press in Australia", 204.
26. *La Fiamma, La Fiamma—I primi cinquant'anni* (Sydney: Media Communications, 1997).
27. Carli, "A community paper for a changing community", 99.
28. James Jupp, "Foreword", in *Il Globo: Fifty years of an Italian newspaper in Australia*, ed. Bruno Mascitelli and Simone Battiston (Ballan, Vic.: Connor Court Publishing, 2009), 10.
29. Bruno Mascitelli, "A New Exodus of Italians to Australia?", in *Australia's New Wave of Italian Migration: Paradise or Illusion*, ed. Bruno Mascitelli and Riccardo Armillei (North Melbourne, Vic.: Australian Scholarly Publishing, 2017), 1–13.
30. Mascitelli, "A new exodus of Italians to Australia?".
31. Riccardo Armillei, "A Statistical Analysis of New Italian Migration to Australia: Redressing Recent Overstatements", in *Australia's New Wave of Italian Migration: Paradise or Illusion*, ed. Bruno Mascitelli and Riccardo Armillei (North Melbourne, Vic.: Australian Scholarly Publishing, 2017), 53–78.
32. Interview with Nino Randazzo, May 6, 1999, "Australia's non-English Press", *The Media Report*, Radio National, ABC Melbourne, Melbourne, 1999.
33. Radio National, "Australia's non-English Press".
34. Radio National, "Australia's non-English Press".

35. Andre Jackson, "Keeping Australia's Italians informed", *The Age*, June 9, 2008, 1.
36. Bruno Mascitelli and Simone Battiston, ed., *Il Globo: Fifty Years of an Italian newspaper in Australia* (Ballan, Vic.: Connor Court Publishing, 2009).
37. *Il Globo*, "Un esempio da seguire", March 13, 2009, 33.
38. Mascitelli and Battiston, *Il Globo*, 1.
39. Carli, "A community paper for a changing community", 115.
40. Personal communication with Dario Nelli, April 10, 2018.
41. Personal communication with Julius Larobina, April 24, 2018.
42. Conversation with Director of *Il Globo*, Dario Nelli, April 10, 2018.
43. Noted in a personal conversation in 2018 with Julius Larobina, Director of the Italian media Corporation and son of founder of *Il Globo*, Ubaldo Larobina.
44. Italian Network, "Italiani all'estero—Giornali Italiano all'estero—Dall'Argentina Zembo (Direttore L'Italiano): 'I Quotidiani all'estero stanno scomparendo. La strada della comunicazione globale'", 2016, http://www.italiannetwork.it/news.aspx?id=35888 (accessed September 9, 2019).
45. Italian Network, "Italiani all'estero".
46. Italian Network, "Italiani all'estero".
47. Italian Network, "Italiani all'estero".
48. Ministero Esteri, "Italiani all'estero", 2019, https://www.esteri.it/mae/it/servizi/italiani-all-estero (accessed October 6, 2019).
49. "Rete Italia si ridimensiona", *Il Globo*, August 22, 2019.

CHAPTER 8

Historicising the Early Years of *Nuovo Paese* (1974–1981)

Simone Battiston

In *Nuovo Paese* (New Country) scholars have long viewed a leading alternative voice within the Italian-Australian print press, in spite of the newspaper's limited circulation.[1] Launched by the Italian Federation of Migrant Workers and their Families (FILEF) in 1974, the fortnightly tabloid (later turned monthly magazine) has offered a left-of-centre view to its readers. Issues concerning Italian workers, politics, migration, poverty, the environment and, more recently, climate change have all featured prominently in the newspaper's columns and challenged paternalistic, conservative views of migrant communities in settler societies. *Nuovo Paese* has always strived to promote news and views that are "alternative to those promoted by monopoly-media", even though it no longer republishes selected news items from external sources as *L'Unità*, *The Tribune* or *The Guardian*.[2] Since the late 1980s, the board's commitment to "[…] greater socio-economic equality, respect for individuals and cultures and an

S. Battiston (✉)
Department of Humanities and Social Sciences, Swinburne University of Technology, Hawthorn, VIC, Australia
e-mail: sbattiston@swin.edu.au

© The Author(s), under exclusive license to Springer Nature Switzerland AG 2021
C. Dewhirst, R. Scully (eds.), *Voices of Challenge in Australia's Migrant and Minority Press*, Palgrave Studies in the History of the Media, https://doi.org/10.1007/978-3-030-67330-7_8

environmentally sustainable economy" has reflected the evolution and adjustment of both the magazine and FILEF to the changing needs of Australia's Italians whose upward mobility trajectory has swollen the ranks of the multicultural middle classes.[3]

For the migrant historian, *Nuovo Paese* is more than an alternative voice. It represents a rich site for examining the history and probing the memory of migrant-run print ventures and the politicised environment within them. The newspaper's early period (from its foundation in 1974 to 1981 circa), which was marked by politically charged activism, is one worth exploring. During this period, scholars can find in the lived experience of *Nuovo Paese*'s staff and collaborators, in particular, elements of transcultural activism, political solidarity, electoral ambitions, homeland influences, transnational linkages as well as monitoring activities by intelligence and law enforcement agencies and anti-Communist paranoia. *Nuovo Paese* was shaped by as much local issues and organisational dynamics as wider contexts and globalising forces, which makes it a stimulating case to investigate in the field of migrant and minority press.[4]

Nuovo Paese underwent several changes after 1974. It was initially issued fortnightly and printed on a tabloid format. In 1984, it became a monthly and two years later it adopted a magazine layout. The editorial head office experienced changes too. Between 1974 and 1981, the newspaper, then based in Melbourne, changed address five times before being transferred to Sydney in 1984 and again to Adelaide, its current location, in 1989. Alongside changes in publication frequency, layouts and office addresses, there was a rapid succession of editors and editors-in-chief during the "Melbourne phase" (1974–1984) that reflected the fluidity of the original editorial board. A more stable situation emerged only when the newspaper moved to Sydney and finally to Adelaide.

The first six, seven years of *Nuovo Paese* were arguably the most "political" of the over four decade-long history of the newspaper, and there were political in different ways. It was common for issues demanding political attention, including working conditions and welfare provisions for Italian migrant workers, to feature prominently in the editorials of *Nuovo Paese*. Secondly, local election campaigns, candidate preselections and petitions received prime coverage in the newspaper. Some editorial board members themselves were directly involved in politics (e.g. they stood for preselections, served as elected officials, participated in public debates), whilst others were members of different unions and parties, including the

Communist Party of Australia (CPA), the Italian Communist Party (PCI) and the Australian Labor Party (ALP).

This study does not analyse the editorial commentary of *Nuovo Paese* nor examine several initiatives undertaken by the newspaper in different fields in the early period, such as the debate and campaign for the teaching of Italian (and by and large community languages) in Australian schools.[5] However, by historicising the experience of *Nuovo Paese*'s editorial board and committee members in particular, this study seeks to fill some gaps in the historiography of Italian press abroad during the Cold War. If during the Cold War (1947–1991) "global superpower rivalry saw an intense politicization of journalism", Italian left-leaning party organisations and press—as far as Italian migrant communities in France, Belgium and Switzerland were concerned—suffered restrictions and suppressions for political reasons.[6] More broadly, the different roles the migrant press played in well over a century have offered a springboard for considerations on a range of themes, according to Lorenzo Prencipe: cultural brokering, maintenance of migrant and minority culture, identity making, language transmission and education, political propaganda, religious proselytism and transnational linkages.[7]

Newspapers and periodicals are a valuable source of data that document the political and socio-economic experience of migrant groups and their different stages of assimilation and integration in the host societies.[8] Indeed, print-based newspapers and other forms of media by, and for, Italian diasporic communities around the world have been a stimulating field of research for migrant historians in recent years.[9]

Yet, the second half of the twentieth century remains an area less studied, when compared with the first half.[10] Studies like Pietro Pinna's on the leftist Italian press in Europe, which challenges the thesis of a substantial absence of Italian-language left-wing periodicals among Italian migrants after the Second World War, are encouraging but still rare.[11] In addition, little attention has been given to the lived experiences of editors, editorial board members and journalists and their historical presence within a post-1945 migration context. The recalling of their lived experiences allows us to appreciate the transformative power of political mixing and interacting but equally the imbalanced power relationships between political cultures.

The case study of *Nuovo Paese* aims to provide new understandings, for instance, into one particular category of migrant activist, the so-called "*impegnati*" (literally, those actively involved in a cause), to borrow Lidio

Bertelli's term, that is, politically active and better-educated migrants who arrived from Italy in the late 1960s and in the course of the 1970s, and brought with them the political and social experiences of contemporary Italy.[12]

Initially, at least, the presence of the "*impegnati*" in *Nuovo Paese* was substantial as many served in the editorial board and/or in one of the four editorial committees (Melbourne, Sydney, Adelaide and Brisbane). They "were essential in maintaining and expanding ties with [contemporary] Italian culture", economist Joseph Halevi, who had a long association with FILEF in Sydney, once remarked.[13] Crucially, their oral history testimonies, which form the bulk of those interviewed for this study, tell us about the significance and impact of imported politics, political mixing and political (dis)engagement on a personal and organisational level.

What this chapter seeks to demonstrate is that the vicissitudes of *Nuovo Paese*'s activists did not occur in isolation from the wider political milieu, from the predominance of conservative politics in Australia to Eurocommunism and the emerging role of progressive politics in the Italian society, and to the surrounding presence of globalising forces— Cold War politics, Communism, anti-Communism, migrations and return migrations.[14] A fresh reading of *Nuovo Paese*'s experience begins to emerge when the early history of the newspaper is ultimately framed within the setting of political activism, transculturalism, transnationalism and oral history of former editors, editors-in-chief and editorial committee members, including Joe Caputo, Umberto Martinengo, Ignazio Salemi, Stefano de Pieri, Cira La Gioia, Pierina Pirisi, Cathy Angelone and Franco Lugarini (see Table 8.1).

CONTEXTUALISING THE EARLY PERIOD OF *NUOVO PAESE*

Nuovo Paese claims to be Australia's longest-serving magazine in the Italian community. Although this is not strictly true, it succeeded where other likeminded newspapers had failed. Some saw in *Nuovo Paese* the ideal heir of an earlier newspaper, *Il Risveglio* (1944–1956), of the pro-Labor *Italia Libera*, the movement founded by left-wing anti-Fascist émigrés during the Second World War.[15] In practice, it succeeded the short-lived monthly tabloid *Il Nuovo Paese* (1963–1966) of the left-leaning *Lega Italo-Australiana*. This tabloid enjoyed some financial support from the CPA and aspired to be an independent and inter-class newspaper for the Italian-speaking community.[16]

Table 8.1   *Nuovo Paese's* editors, editors-in-chief and editorial committees, 1974–1984

Editors	Editorial committees		
	Melbourne	*Sydney*	*Adelaide*

Editors

Joe Caputo (May 1974–Aug. 1976)
Umberto Martinengo (Sept. 1976–Jun. 1977)
Igrazio Salemi (Jul.–Oct. 1977)
Umberto Martinengo (Oct. 1977–Jun. 1978)
Stefano de Pieri (Jul. 1978–Aug. 1980)
[Position not listed] (Sept. 1980–Feb. 1981)
Cira La Gioia (Mar. 1981–Aug. 1982)
Pierina Pirisi (Sept. 1982–Apr. 1984)
Brunc Di Biase (from May 1984)

Editor-in-chief
[Position not listed] (May 1974–Aug. 1976)
Joe Caputo (Sept. 1976–Oct. 1979)
Frank Barbaro (from Nov. 1979)

Co-editor-in-chief
Umberto Martinengo (Jul.–Oct. 1977)

Melbourne

Catiny Angelone (May 1974–Aug. 1979)
Eric Austin (Jul. 1977–Aug. 1978)
Flavia Coassin (Apr.–Dec. 1983)
Ariella Crema (Sept. 1978–Nov. 1979)
Carmelo Darmanin (Sept. 1980–Aug. 1982)
Dave Davies (from Apr. 1983)
Tom Diele (from Apr. 1983)
Stefaro de Pieri (Sept. 1976–Jul. 1978; Sept.–Dec. 1980)
Ted Forbes (May 1974–Aug. 1982)
Gaetano Greco (from Sept. 1982)
Ted Innes (Jul. 1977–Nov. 1979)
Cira La Gioia (Sept. 1980–Mar. 1983)
Franco Lovece (Apr. 1983–Feb. 1984)
Franco Lugarini (from Sept. 1982)
Umbero Martinengo (Nov. 1975–Aug. 1976)
Bill O'Erien (May–Oct. 1974)
Stefania Pieri (Mar. 1981–Aug. 1982)
Pierina Pirisi (Sept. 1982–Mar. 1983)
Corrado Porcaro (Apr.–Dec. 1983)
Mirna Risk (Sept.–Nov. 1980)
Ignazio Salemi (May 1974–May 1976)
Carlo Scalvini (Mar.–Jun. 1978; Aug. 1978–Feb. 1981)
Franco Schiavoni (Sept. 1979–Dec. 1980)
Jim Simmonds (from Jul. 1977)
Peter Symonds (Sept. 1982–Mar. 1983)
Giovanni Sgrò (from May 1974)
Gianfranco Spinoso (Mar.–Jun. 1978; Aug. 1978–Aug. 1980)
Marisa Stirpe (Apr. 1983–Feb. 1984)
Dick Wootton (Jul. 1977–Aug. 1982)

Sydney

Edoardo Burani (Sept. 1982–Apr. 1983)
Chiara Caglieris (from Apr. 1983)
Claudio Crollini (from Apr. 1983)
Bruno Di Biase (from Sept. 1979)
Nino Ghiotto (Apr. 1983–Feb. 1984)
Francesco Giacobbe (from Sept. 1982)
Elizabeth Glasson (from Apr. 1983)
Joseph Halevi (Sept. 1980)
Claudio Marcello (Sept. 1979–Aug. 1982; from Dec. 1982)
Helen Moody (Apr.–Dec. 1983)
Brian Paltridge (from May 1984)
Marco Pettini (from Sept. 1984)
Pierina Pirisi (Jul. 1978–Aug. 1982; from Apr. 1983)
David Robinson (Sept. 1980–Aug. 1982)
Nina Rubino (from Apr. 1983)
Pino Scuro (from May 1984)
Vera Zaccari (from May 1984)

Adelaide

Frank Barbaro (from Sept. 1980)
Ted Gnatenko (from Sept. 1978)
Enzo Soderini (from Jul. 1978)

Brisbane
Dan O'Neil (Sept. 1979–Aug. 1982)
Gaetano Rando (Sept.–Oct. 1979)

With an identical-sounding name to its predecessor but without the *"Il"* (The), *Nuovo Paese* was purposely launched on 1 May 1974, international workers' day, which in Australia falls on other days according to states and territories. It was one of the first major initiatives of the recently founded Melbourne branch of FILEF. Established in Rome in 1967 and inspired by democratic and anti-Fascist principles, FILEF is a voluntary-based organisation still in operation today in Italy and with branches abroad that engages in welfare, education, culture and lobby activity for Italian migrants and their families. It aims to speak to and for the working class and progressive elements of the Italian communities abroad in matters that include worker, welfare and pension rights, language education and teaching, and production of contemporary Italian culture. Nominally apolitical, FILEF enjoys the support of the left. From 1967 until 1991, it entertained a close relationship with the PCI.

The launch and initial period of activity of *Nuovo Paese* occurred against the backdrop of events that allowed the FILEF Melbourne branch, which was set up in 1972, to become the most active in Australia for a number of years. Less than two years from its foundation, FILEF was one of the recipients of the Welfare Rights Officers Program, funded by the Whitlam Labor government.[17] The programme allowed activist Cathy Angelone to be employed as FILEF welfare migrant officer in 1974. Thanks to the financial and organisational support provided by the Fitzroy Ecumenical Centre (FEC), FILEF was able to carry out a survey among Italians in the blue-collar Melbourne suburb of Coburg. Part of the FEC funding was subsequently diverted to cover expenses for the opening of a FILEF welfare office, which also became the first premises of *Nuovo Paese*. In April and September of that year, FILEF participated to two ABC Access TV Programs, granting the organisation public exposure and contacts with mainstream media.

Nuovo Paese charged itself with the task to keep the local Italian-speaking proletariat informed. As stated in its masthead, it claimed to be "The democratic fortnightly in Italian of the workers in Australia". Simultaneously, it sought to educate its readership by making them aware of their rights. The newspaper bore the attention-grabbing bilingual sub-heading, *"Impara a riconoscere i tuoi diritti"* (Learn to recognise your rights). It kept its readers abreast of events by publishing articles of workers' struggles and workers' successes in Australia, Italy and elsewhere. It republished news items from *L'Unità, The Guardian, The Tribune* and other left-wing newspapers.

Over half of the newspaper's coverage was dedicated to Australian and international news and approximately one-fifth of the content was published in English, which constituted a higher percentage than any other Italian-language print media outlets.[18] The goal of publishing some content in English was to appeal to a broader audience, including second-generation Italian-Australians who were keen to be informed about Italian events locally and internationally but lacked the necessary language skills.

Nuovo Paese never sought to compete with the more successful commercial newspapers *La Fiamma* (1947–present) and *Il Globo* (1959–present) or seriously challenge their established community roles. *La Fiamma* and *Il Globo*, in terms of circulation and readership, reached a wider cohort of the population than *Nuovo Paese*. By the early 1980s, Il Globo had a circulation of over 26,000, *Nuovo Paese* of around 6000–7000.[19] They also played a multifaceted and influential role in the life of thousands of post-war Italian migrants.[20] Instead, *Nuovo Paese* found in the working class, and in the progressive sections of the community, its ideal reader. In order to be known and read, *Nuovo Paese* replicated a well-tested formula for financial support and distribution: it struck a deal with sponsoring unions that agreed to purchase copies of the newspaper and distribute them free of charge to their Italian-language members (see Table 8.2).[21] As far as copies purchased by the unions were concerned, an undated document from the FILEF Melbourne Archive, but presumably from the 1980s, sets the number at 1395. A note from July 1987 put the number of union-purchased copies at a slightly higher level, 1646. Other notes, but again without date, give a figure of around 1400 copies.[22] *Il Progresso Italo-Australiano* (1956–present) successfully endeavoured something similar almost two decades before.

The unions were not solely involved in the financing and delivery of print runs. They constituted an important component of the editorial board of *Nuovo Paese* as well. The founding editor of the fortnightly, Joe Caputo, was a full-time union official of the Clothing and Allied Trade Unions (CATU) of Australia. Eric Austin, the CATU Secretary, served in the editorial board of Melbourne. So did Edward "Ted" Forbes and Bill O'Brien, also trade union officials. The former was assistant secretary of the Victorian branch of the Federated Miscellaneous Workers' Union (FMWU), and the latter also assistant secretary but of the Victorian branch of the Australian Railways Union (ARU).

Table 8.2   *Nuovo Paese*, selected data

Administration premises (1974–present)	Frequency and format (1974–present)	Number[a] of sponsoring trade unions (1974–1984)	Number of print runs (1974–1984)
Victoria	Biweekly (Tabloid, 8	1974: Not listed.	1974: 8500
34–36 Munro St, Coburg	pages, May 1974–	1975: 14	approx.[b]
(May–Nov. 1974)	Feb. 1977)	1976: 17	1975: –
18 Munro St, Coburg	Biweekly (Tabloid,	1977: 23	1976: –
(Dec. 1974–Jul. 1976)	12 pages, Mar.	1978: 23	1977: 6000
2 Myrtle St, Coburg (Jul.	1977–Dec. 1983)	1979: 25	approx.[c]
1976–Feb. 1977)	Monthly (Tabloid,	1980: 25	1978: –
7 Myrtle St, Coburg (Mar.	12 pages, Jan.	1981: Not listed	1979: –
1977–Mar. 1981)	1984–Dec. 1985)	1982: 27	1980: –
276a Sydney Rd, Coburg	Monthly (Magazine,	1983: 29	1981: 6–7000
(Apr. 1981–Jun. 1984)	35–54 pages, Jan.	1984: 29	approx.[d]
New South Wales	1986–present)		1982: 6000
423 Paramatta Rd,			approx.[d]
Leichhardt (Jul. 1984–Apr.			1983: 6000
1989)			approx.[d]
South Australia			1984: 6000
15 Lowe St, Adelaide (May			approx.[d]
1989–present)			

Source: *Nuovo Paese*

[a]Highest number of sponsoring trade unions in any given calendar year

[b]Gianfranco Cresciani, *No Country for Revolutionaries. Italian Communists in Sydney 1971–1991: Their Activities, Policies and Liaison with the Italian and Australian Communist Parties* (North Melbourne: Australian Scholarly Publishing, 2018), 71

[c]Simone Battiston, "How the Italian-Australian Left and its Press viewed *Il Globo*", in *Il Globo: Fifty Years of an Italian Newspaper in Australia*, ed. Bruno Mascitelli and Simone Battiston (Ballan, Vic: Connor Court Publishing, 2009), 87

[d]FILEF Melbourne Archive, "Advertising Agencies" folder, (uncatalogued)

In Melbourne *Nuovo Paese* forged a solid link with the ALP. Jim Simmonds, the Labor State Member for Reservoir in the Victorian Legislative Assembly (1969–1992) and State Minister for Employment and Training (1982–1985), and Ted Innes, the Labor Federal Member for Melbourne (1972–1983), were editorial board members and both broadly involved in FILEF activities. The late Giovanni Sgrò, member of the Melbourne newspaper's editorial committee and FILEF Secretary, was the figure that more than any other personified the involvement of Italian migrants in local left politics.

Sgrò (Seminara, 1931–Melbourne, 2019) emigrated from Calabria in 1952 and within a short time of his arrival he led protests against the poor conditions at the Bonegilla Migrant Centre.[23] He worked as a painter and decorator and joined the ALP in 1958. By the early 1970s, he was president of the Coburg party branch and one of Labor's State conference branch delegates. In 1976, he and June Enigsh, the Brunswick Girls High School principal, disrupted the opening of the Victorian Parliament by unfurling a banner protesting against the lack of adequate facilities in areas with high levels of migrant-background students. They narrowly avoided being arrested, although Sgrò was temporarily locked up in a rarely used cell in the parliament building.[24]

This incident strengthened Sgrò's credentials as Labor activist, and his political ascendency accelerated when he secured the preselection for the safe Labor seat of the Melbourne North province in the Victorian Legislative Council in 1977. He served as electoral secretary to Jim Simmonds in 1978–1979 before being himself elected in the 1979 Victorian Parliament (the first Italian-born to do so). In order to highlight the progressively multicultural fabric of Australia's contemporary society, he delivered his maiden speech partly in Italian. He held the seat until 1992.

Rev. Dick Wootton of the Uniting Church was a member of the Melbourne editorial board whilst *Tribune* reporter Dave Davies was contributor of articles. Moreover, an increasing number of Italian migrants, some of whom had recently immigrated to Australia, committed to the board; among them were Pierina Pirisi (arrived 1970), Carlo Scalvini (1971), Stefano de Pieri (1974), Stefania Pieri (1974), Umberto Martinengo (1975), Edoardo Burani (1975), Cira La Gioia (1979) and Mirna Risk (Cicioni) (1979). Other members immigrated before 1970, including Giovanni Sgrò (arrived 1952), Franco Schiavoni (1957), Franco Lugarini (1961), Joe Caputo (1966) and Tom Diele (1969). Others still immigrated with their families as children and belong to the so-called 1.5 generation: Cathy Angelone (arrived 1954), Franco Lovece (1958), Gianfranco Spinoso (1960) and Marisa Stirpe (1964). A handful were born in Australia to Italian migrant families; this latter category comprises figures like Gaetano Greco (born 1959).

Although different cohorts of activists revolved around FILEF and *Nuovo Paese*, their activism in Cold War times was invariability marked by transnationalism and transculturalism, and it was kept under the watch of the Australian intelligence and law enforcement agencies.

Transnational, Transcultural and Under Surveillance: *Nuovo Paese*'s Activism in Cold War Times

Thanks to the transnational nature of their activism, migrant members of the *Nuovo Paese* editorial office and of the editorial committees were capable of (re)connecting and maintaining their political identity. For example, they were able to enrol into party schools, attend party congresses and celebrate anti-Fascist and communist traditions, often through the *Feste de L'Unità* (PCI festivals), in both Italy and Australia. They were also exposed to other political traditions nurturing the transculturality of the newspaper and of the FILEF organisation. Transculturality took form in different ways: editorial members enrolling in Australian left political parties; joining trade unions; attending local party functions; and inviting state and federal politicians to speak to FILEF public debates. *Nuovo Paese* allocated ample coverage to all these activities.

By reaching out to the Australian trade union movement and the Australian left, without severing the links with progressive contemporary Italy and its main political referent, the PCI, *Nuovo Paese*/FILEF looked to both Canberra and Rome. In a nutshell, they demonstrated how to transcend ethnic community boundaries whilst simultaneously affirming within them a transnational dimension. In such a position, a process of transculturation and political cross-fertilisation took place which, in turn, encouraged interactions of different left political cultures. The diverse composition of the editorial committees, the newspaper's efforts to support Labor in electoral times[25] and the Labor Party's endeavour to reach out and support FILEF initiatives were all examples of interactions that were regarded to be mutually beneficial.

But if Italian migrants in Australia ought to be viewed transculturally, as well as transnationally, as Francesco Ricatti recently advocated,[26] a fresh perspective may aid to analyse critically the dynamics and complexities of imported politics. Seminal studies on transculturalism posit that contact and mixing between cultures is not always "an equal process" and that transculturalism generates enabling as well as destructive forces due to the "unequal power relationships between cultures",[27] including, I would add, political cultures.

Political mixing allowed FILEF activists to access the Labor political elite and be viewed as the linchpin with the local Italian proletariat. Yet, in a period still marked by anti-Communism, interactions with FILEF—which was perceived by some as a front organisation of the PCI—could prove to be potentially perilous politically. Equally, the electoral ambitions of some in the younger cohort of Italian activists, most of whom had joined the PCI and supported radical agendas, at least initially, could present an opportunity but also a challenge for the ALP. The Labor Party favoured figures like Giovanni Sgrò instead who championed an integrationalist approach and embodied the Labor hopes of tapping into the ethnic vote. The benefits and drawbacks of transcultural activism and political mixing were fully exposed during, and in the wake of, the legal and political case linked to Ignazio Salemi, a central figure of *Nuovo Paese* and FILEF in the 1970s.

A journalist and migrant rights campaigner, Salemi, moved from Italy to Australia in 1974 to help coordinate the activities of FILEF, including the launch and running of a newspaper. He was a PCI official and a point of reference for the local network of Italian communists too. With the exception of *The Tribune* reporter Dave Davies, who had a minor role as editorial committee member, Salemi was the only professional journalist of *Nuovo Paese*. He came with a wealth of journalistic knowledge and experience. He had worked as *L'Unità* correspondent in Budapest and Prague in the 1960s and served as editor of FILEF's Rome monthly *Emigrazione* in the early 1970s. He was also known for his excellent organisational skills and for galvanising activism.

In 1976, Salemi found himself at the centre of a controversial dispute over his amnesty application which led to a prolonged court action—he had overstayed his temporary entry permit the year before and sought to regularise his residence status. The Fraser conservative government rejected his amnesty application and sought to deport him. For the conservative press he was simply a "red" troublemaker and an importer of unwanted foreign politics Australia should rid of. The "Salemi case" saw FILEF being directly involved through a plethora of initiatives, including fundraising, circulation of petitions, promotion of public debates and issuing of bilingual bulletins, not only in Melbourne but also in Sydney, Adelaide and beyond, initiatives to which different ethnic communities participated. *Nuovo Paese* kept readers abreast of events and urged them to participate in FILEF-led initiatives.[28] Letters to the editor expressing readers' prevalent feelings of anger and complaint towards the government and its immigration minister Michael MacKellar in particular were frequently published.[29]

The case generated political solidarity within the left, and a passionate campaign seeking to prevent the government to deport Salemi. Labor entities who also served in the *Nuovo Paese* editorial committee, like Ted

Innes, then Shadow Minister for Immigration and Ethnic Affairs, threw their political weight behind the campaign. Labor Federal MPs Gordon Bryant, Bill Brown and Tom Roper provided political backing too. Support for Salemi came from the opposition leader Gough Whitlam as well as the Australian Council of Trade Unions president Bob Hawke, who threatened to undertake walk-offs and bans to prevent the Italian journalist's forced departure.

The case came to an abrupt end when Salemi, who had spent months in hiding and exhausted every legal avenue available, was arrested by the Australian Federal Police and deported to Italy in October 1977. The "Salemi case" had produced an ambivalent result: FILEF enjoyed a great deal of solidarity, locally and internationally, but this also made it a target even before the case came to the fore. What became known as the 1975 "Italian communists move in" incident, followed by an arson attempt on the FILEF premises in Coburg that partly damaged the editorial office of *Nuovo Paese*, demonstrated that anti-Communism in Australia was still alive and kicking.[30] In the wake of these incidents the solidarity within and outside the organisation intensified. Long-time FILEF activist, PCI entity and editorial committee member Franco Lugarini once summarised it as follows:

> Who knows. They saw that [FILEF] had been growing too much, and as a result they started to harass us. First of all, they burned down the FILEF office. […] So for several nights we slept outside; a friend of mine, Bruno Pace, and I slept in the car […]. They realised that we did not bother anyone—it was just propaganda—and that we carried no weapons, bombs and stuff like that. […] It strengthened us. We stuck together even more because we had the unions behind.[31]

The strengthening of the camaraderie in the organisation due to external pressures had the side effect, however, of instilling a climate of suspicion internally, especially towards newcomers. It was in part fuelled by the broader Cold War climate and in part by the widespread knowledge that the Australian Security Intelligence Organisation (ASIO), and the police were monitoring closely the Salemi's movements and those of other activists. Illuminating is the one episode evoked by Cathy Angelone and Ignazio Salemi about a young researcher, who was invited to attend the FILEF meetings, but due to bias towards her nationality she was falsely rumoured to be an intelligence officer:

Angelone: D*, my American friend, [was] the one who they considered to be a Central Intelligence Agency (CIA) agent, but she was not.

Salemi: I found it all over the world that when there was an American, [people would say]: "They are from the CIA".

Angelone: Two episodes. I remember D* coming to a women's meeting. […] And I remember that after the meeting ended we were all there in the parking lot, [ready to] leave. D* was already gone. First A*, then another: "But you know you have to be careful, certain things do not have to be said because you know that one … and then, who is she, she is American". […] No one said that she was CIA, but more or less. And that was one episode. I hardly knew her then. […] Then after a while, […] there was a meeting at the Albion Hall of a group of comrades. Something had happened in Italy, […] a carnage [due to a terrorist attack] […]. We were all there talking and so on. Then D* came in and all hell broke loose!

Salemi: But this thing was quite widespread.

Angelone: In her presence [people said]: "But who told you to come here? Who are you? What do I know that you are not from the CIA?" At some point I lost it. I had just returned from the Philippines—I went to a conference, always with this Uniting Church, where […] I learned that [the Marcos regime] had arrested, tortured and killed one of the girls I had met there, a Filipino union organiser. And [people attending that meeting] were making those scenes for D*. And I said: "What are you saying? […] You are making up all these stories for an American girl who comes here and in the world this is happening …". Then, in the end I said: "Among other things, she is not from the CIA. She is my friend. I told her that there was a meeting tonight." At that point no one said a thing.

Salemi: But the [rumour] was widespread, because once the son of I* [said]: "Everybody says that she is from the CIA …".[32]

Reservations about the loyalty of the newcomer were impulsive but not wholly unjustified if one considers that FILEF and the Italian communist network in Australia were thoroughly infiltrated by ASIO agents and informers.[33]

Alleged police and intelligence community operations against the FILEF activists did not dispel the fog of suspicion that the Italian left organisation was a target by the authorities as much as anti-Communist forces. Lugarini used to volunteer for *Nuovo Paese* by distributing print runs in the Melbourne area and stressed that:For five years in a row the police seized my car. I used to distribute four hundred print runs [of *Nuovo Paese*] a week. I would take them to all the bars, kiosks, and piz-zerias in Melbourne. I would drop a bundle of them and leave. [...] Once I had a briefcase and put it under these print runs in the back seat. [...] I went to dinner. [I then returned to my car], and the car is gone. [...] I went to the police and reported the theft. After two or three days they called me [...]: "Is this your car?". "Yes." "See if something is missing." I said: "There was a briefcase. It is gone." They took it. "You can take your car home."[34]

According to Lugarini, the police later returned his briefcase, minus the notebook that contained the contact details of local PCI members.

Even after Salemi's deportation, FILEF and its activists continued to be a target. In January 1978, the Coburg office was broken into after a failed attempt in December of the year before. Although nothing of value was stolen, the office was turned upside down. FILEF immediately blamed "certain press" (conservative press) for instigating a "hate campaign" towards the Italian organisation.[35] For some oral sources, the blame was to be found elsewhere:

Once they stole my car. I went to the police to report the theft. After three or four days, at midnight, two policemen came to my home. I opened the door [and they said]: "Look, if you want your car, come to Flemington Police Station". I took a cab and found my car at the police station. I always found my car at the police station. They never found anything, and they never did anything to us. But only to me [it happened] because they knew that I was the organiser of everything [PCI-related]. Then, once they broke into the FILEF office from the roof. They went inside. They did not steal anything, but you could tell they had been there. Then, Giovanni Sgrò called the Coburg police. The police came and they told him that it was the forensic team. They did photocopies but they never told us anything. They always kept an eye on us.[36]

The Salemi case generated signs of tensions. The reasons were manifold: the case could have potentially jeopardised the granting of future entry permits to PCI officials; it sensationally exposed the presence of the PCI (and FILEF's association to it) in Australia; it caused embarrassment for the PCI in Rome; and critically, it could have derailed the chance for Sgrò, who had won preselection for a safe Labor seat just months before Salemi's deportation, to be elected to the Victorian Parliament.[37]

Unlike Sgrò, Salemi did not fit any particular migrant category. His internationalist yet ethnocentric approach was ill-suited for the integrationalist one brought forward by Sgrò. This tension was reflected in *Nuovo Paese*, which experienced a rapid turnover of editors and various resignations. An oral history of *Nuovo Paese* offers a new understanding of the transnational and transcultural effects on migrant activism and the meaning of key events and people in the memory of the early history of the newspaper.

LOOKING BACK: FOR AN ORAL HISTORY OF *NUOVO PAESE*

The recollections of editors, editors-in-chief and editorial committee members who served during the first decade were initially gathered for a study on FILEF Melbourne and Italian migrant activism of the 1970s. The semi-structured interviews were part of a PhD project that sought to investigate the reasons that lay behind the rise, success and decline of the Melbourne branch of FILEF. Recollections of *Nuovo Paese* are thus situated against the broad picture of political activism and migrant mobility.

Interviewees had to make sense of the past and reflect on their own political activism, life trajectory and overall migrant experience. They often talked in collective terms when referring to FILEF, the network of Italian communists in Australia or the newspaper, but in the first person when self-assessing their role as single agents of change or placing themselves in the historic map of migrant activism.

Joe Caputo (editor, 1974–1976; editor-in-chief, 1976–1979) offers one good example. He stressed the collective effort of establishing FILEF in Melbourne and launching *Nuovo Paese* under Salemi's stewardship whilst reflecting about his role in the migrant rights movement and own political peregrination from radical to reformist politics:

> [...] the Labor victory of December 1972 [...] gave us the opportunity to emerge from underground.

> Salemi had what we were lacking. [...] he was dynamic.

[But] I think organising ourselves like the PCI was a mistake on our part. [...] A few years after Salemi was expelled, I started to reflect [...][And eventually] I joined the Labor Party.[38]

Another example can be found in the testimony of Salemi, whose recalling interspersed with familiar narratives of left-wing political activism:

[We] had two parallel organisations. One [was that of the PCI]—because I could not let the PCI tradition be lost; I needed it, didn't it?—and [the other was] FILEF, which was the official organisation in Australia. We already had four, five bases in Australia [...] We awakened a political debate that had workers on one side, although we obviously also had to talk to others who were not workers; because not all immigrants are workers. We think that in all the communities, in all groups, in all societies there are the rich, the poor, the workers, the exploiters, and so on.[39]

Conversely, he talked in the first person when claiming merit for the newspaper's initiative: "The newspaper was the tool I wanted. So, I sought an agreement with various unions suggesting them the need for us to correctly guide the Italian workers, because the firms were full of Italian labor."[40]

Oral historians Alessandro Portelli and Luisa Passerini encourage us, however, to go through and beyond the recollecting of mere facts and memories.[41] Testimonies of the infamous 1975 "Italian communist move in" incident, and ensuing arson attempt, added little to what was already known factually. Yet, they told us a great deal more about the meaning of that single event for the activists interviewed (the beginning of the end for Salemi in Australia and the long-term consequences of his deportation) which still stirred up mixed emotions decades later.

The recalling of influential figures in the Italian-Australian left such as Giovanni Sgrò, Giuliano Pajetta (the Emigration Office head of the PCI) and Salemi himself to give another example offers the opportunity to reflect upon the implications of imported politics, political ambitions and party hierarchies in migrant communities.

The centrality of the figure of Ignazio Salemi, whose journalistic expertise and media experiences were critical for launching and editing *Nuovo Paese*, was a common thread in the testimonies. Umberto Martinengo (editor, 1976–1978), who was put in charge of the biweekly soon after joining FILEF and learned editorial skills from Salemi, drew a sketch of him that echoes the beliefs shared by many:[42]

For me he was a bit of a political master. [...] And in my opinion Salemi brought this great breath of enthusiasm, because he had just come from Italy, [and] he already had multiple experiences abroad. [...] He was versatile. He had great journalistic, organisational, and apparatus experiences. [...] So when Salemi arrived—he was also dynamic as a person—[he brought] the latest developments here in Australia in an environment that was a bit rusty, let's say. [...] And so it brought this wave of excitement, because in Italy there was this wave of enthusiasm with the newspapers, *L'Unità*, radio broadcasts, continuous contacts with Italy, the *Botteghe Oscure*, with the union Italian General Confederation of Labour. And this enthusiasm was created here. [...] So, Salemi had this great merit of getting at least one section of the Italians of Australia, always a minority but perhaps less minority than before, in the orbit of the contemporary world.[43]

In 1978, following Salemi's deportation and disagreements with Rome, in particular with Giuliano Pajetta, Martinengo parted company with *Nuovo Paese*, finding employment with the moderate Sydney-based newspaper La Fiamma.[44] He became an "outsider" quite early on and offered an anti-rhetorical picture of the Italian-Australian left and its then state of play:Now, looking at it in hindsight, it can also be admitted that [as far as FILEF was concerned] there was much more propaganda than a particularly large numerical presence. [...] The Gramsci Club, the Di Vittorio Club, the National Association of Italian Partisans. ... There were a lot of subsections, but at the end of the day, numerically, there were few of them. More than we were at the beginning, but we could not say that [...] suddenly the Italians of Victoria had all become communists. [...] After a few years the whole thing got a little deflated. Meaning, Giovanni Sgrò went to Parliament, Salemi had returned to whence he had come from. Some others, including myself, went missing, so to speak; life takes you in different directions, perhaps unexpected. The glue that held everything together, the political organisation, the newspaper, the unions, the Labor party, came off. [...] Within the microcosm of FILEF, the propulsive push ended, precisely due to the absence of people who had contributed in these years.[45]

The overlapping of the end of an exciting, initial period for Martinengo, who had just a few years before moved to Australia, with the end of his activism in the FILEF, the PCI and *Nuovo Paese*, meant that for him the "wave of excitement" was short-lived, although its impact and memory endured.

Retaining young and dynamic activists was a major issue for organisations like FILEF due to the constant lack of adequate funding, which affected *Nuovo Paese* too. Dealing with external political agendas was perhaps a higher hurdle to overcome. The testimonies of Martinengo and Stefano de Pieri (editor, 1978–1980) illustrated more than others this point:

> [...] If we had to survive on advertising money, like a commercial newspaper, with publicity and sales, [*Nuovo Paese*] would have folded on the spot because there was zero advertising [and] sales. There were some unions that bought hundreds of copies in bulk that they were supposed to distribute to their Italian-speaking members—for heaven's sake, let's not investigate what happened to those newspaper bundles or at least to some of them. The income was scarce, certainly not enough; perhaps [enough] to pay the printing costs. But if then you calculate the labour costs and so on. ... The funds came from the FILEF, let's say from Rome, and from the [Italian Communist] Party. [...] And I remember, in fact, that this speech was made, "where are we going?". At one point I hoped to do something more and better. Instead the indication from Rome was to not proceed towards a strengthening of the newspaper but rather to its downsizing.[46]

The precarious financial standing of the newspaper, which chiefly relied on the work of volunteers and personnel meagrely paid, was indeed a thorny question for de Pieri who took the opportunity to elaborate on this point in a way that provides insights into unbending political agendas and heavy-handed party interventions:

> The hours spent in those booths writing the newspaper on my own, because the others did not come. The anxieties to close the issue, to find the money, to write. Pajetta on the phone to give us a hard time; he who wrote to you on flimsy paper. [...] Without money. Where do you think the money came from to pay my rent? Those years that I gave, from mid-1974 to 1978/79. Then Martinengo arrived and he was given a salary and I became Martinengo's assistant. Then Martinengo left and passed the job to me, on a cheap wage. The money came from the unions, and then some government grants that we were able to get, from donations. ... Look, from the party [*PCI*] directly I believe that we received very little. The money that came from the Italian fund for Italian-language newspapers and periodicals printed abroad. I think a good deal of funding came from that for a few years. [...] The newspapers went to the unions that covered the production costs, and some pocket money for me. But there was never humanity in there. Yes, there were always comrades who singu-

larly took me home for a meal [...], but it is a question of dignity. [...] I remember that I met Pajetta in Rome and told him that I did not like the fact that FILEF was infiltrated by the communist party and that for me the political relationship was to be established with the Labor party. We did not part in good terms.[47]

Along with Pajetta, Sgrò was another figure called into question by a young and ambitious de Pieri who suffered top-down party directives as much as rigid hierarchy within the Italian-Australian left. Sgrò, who was preselected for a safe Labor seat, embodied the link between the local Italian community and the ALP and for the PCI the go-between in Australia, even though he was a Labor, and not a Communist, entity.This thing [to drop the CPA and embrace the ALP] did not come spontane-ously [to Pajetta], or perhaps they did not want to touch the trusted man, Giovanni Sgrò, or perhaps for the time being one Italian emblem in the ALP was enough. Or maybe they thought it was a too delicate matter that was not to be compromised in any way. "Leave him [Sgrò] alone and let him act." "We have our man in there, and that's enough for the moment, and no adventurism." ... These expressions, adventurisms. There were all these phrases ... "everyone in their place, all still!", "We don't do things for adventurism". This thought within the PCI that the adventurism was not to be done. One does not operate outside the party lines. There was a discipline and one must follow the line. The rest was adventurism.[48]

By around 1980, de Pieri left *Nuovo Paese* and FILEF. He became a mul-ticultural advisor to the Victorian state minister Peter Spyker before becoming a celebrity chef and a passionate campaigner on environmental and regional issues. Tensions with Sgrò came to the surface a decade later, when de Pieri unsuccessfully ran for preselection against him, the memory of which was still fresh more than a decade on.[49]

For Cira La Gioia (editor, 1981–1982), Sgrò guaranteed legitimacy and freedom of movement for FILEF. He was the ethnic broker. He had the role of bringing forward this uneven yet complementary relationship between the left element of the Italian community and the Labor party. Cira evoked one significant episode in order to better explain Sgrò's role and her own trajectory in *Nuovo Paese*. When she criticised the Vehicle Builders Union of racism through the columns of the newspaper, she experienced first-hand how easy local politics could be upset and unforgiv-ing. She was rumoured to have been "paid by the capitalists" and of being "a spy". The fellowship she found when she first entered the organisation paved way to a crude awakening: "I felt that some of these comrades had suddenly turned into people with whom there was no comradery at all. It was tough, very harsh."[50] Fearing a backlash against the union-sponsored newspaper, an *ad hoc* FILEF committee put Cira "on trial". She was asked to publish an apology in the biweekly. She did but simultaneously quit *Nuovo Paese* and FILEF.[51] She later regretted to having published it.

Joe Caputo was another one who felt the pressures of local politics when directing *Nuovo Paese*. He was founding editor, and later editor-in-chief, from 1974 until 1979.[52] His political activism began with the participation in the Vietnam War Moratorium Campaigns. He later joined the CPA and eventually the PCI. In his workplace, he was appointed union official for the CATU. In 1972, he became a member of FILEF and two years later began his role as *Nuovo Paese* editor under Salemi. In 1976 he was appointed editor-in-chief, a position he held until 1979. Around this time, the FILEF management accused Caputo of making unauthorised contacts with the Melbourne daily *The Age*. He was suddenly expelled from the organisation. Caputo claimed to be the victim of political "purges" and internal political tensions. He eventually quit FILEF and *Nuovo Paese*, but also the communist parties he had been an active member of, and joined the ALP, later becoming mayor of Brunswick and later of Moreland.

CONCLUSION

In its initial period, *Nuovo Paese*, an alternative outlet in the migrant and minority press in Australia targeting Italophone readers, was political and politicised in different ways. It accommodated different left political cultures, for example, Communist and Labor, different cohorts of migrants and activists and different personalities with their agendas. It was also a site where transnationalism and transculturality thrived. During and after the so-called Salemi case, the transnational and transcultural dimensions of *Nuovo Paese* (and FILEF) showed their potentials as well as their limitations. For example, the friction between Salemi's internationalist yet ethnocentric approach, on the one hand, and Sgrò's integrationalist approach, on the other hand, created tensions and fractures within the organisation and the newspapers. The impact of security intelligence activities and Cold War-era anti-Communism applied further strains to the organisation which suffered a few setbacks and struggled financially, despite the solid link with the trade unions and the ALP. Once Salemi was deported back to Italy, several editorial board members left.

By historicising the early period of *Nuovo Paese*, this chapter delved into the history and memory of the early editorial board and committee members during one of its most politically charged and controversial phases of the newspaper. By drawing on oral history, this chapter also focused less on familiar narratives of left-wing political activism, often expressed in collective terms and placing emphasis on formative moments, and turned its attention on how and why some interviewees disengaged from the newspaper and in some instances from being actively involved in the left. Ultimately, *Nuovo Paese* represents a stimulating case study for examining voices of challenge in the field of migrant and minority press in the later part of Australia's twentieth century.

Acknowledgement I wish to thank the interviewees who generously shared with me the memories of their activism; sadly some of them have passed away since the interviews were carried out. I am also in debt to the anonymous reviewers and the book editors for their valuable and constructive feedback, as well as those who read and commented on earlier drafts of this chapter: Edoardo Burani, Joe Caputo, Mirna Cicioni, Dave Davies, Bruno Di Biase, Julie Kimber, Pierina Pirisi, Anne Sgrò, Gianfranco Spinoso and Marisa Stirpe.

NOTES

1. In 1982, the geographical distribution of *Nuovo Paese*, for instance, was as follows: 4090 (Victoria), 1000 (New South Wales & Australian Capital Territory), 800 (South Australia), 95 (Queensland), 75 (Western Australia) and 20 (overseas). See FILEF Melbourne Archive, "Advertising Agencies" folder (uncatalogued). See also Caroline Alcorso, Cesare Giulio Popoli and Gaetano Rando, "Community networks and institutions", in *Australia's Italians: Culture and Community in a Changing Society*, ed. Stephen Castles, Caroline Alcorso, Gaetano Rando and Ellie Vasta (St. Leonards, NSW: Allen & Unwin, 1992), 118; Gaetano Rando, "I giornali di lingua italiana in Australia", *Studi Emigrazione* 46, no. 175 (2009): 621.
2. News items are now sourced by the main Italian media agencies. See: http://filefaustralia.org/nuovo-paese-2/
3. Mariella Totaro-Genevois, *Cultural and Linguistic Policy Abroad: The Italian Experience* (Clevedon, UK: Multilingual Matters, 2005), 197; Val Colic-Peisker, "A New Era in Australian Multiculturalism? From Working-class 'Ethnics' to a 'Multicultural Middle-class'", *International Migration Review* 45, no. 3 (2011): 562–587; Luca Marin, "La Federazione Italiana Lavoratori Emigrati e Famiglie (FILEF): un esempio di attivismo tra gli

emigranti in Australia dal 1972", in *Per una storia della popolazione italiana nel Novecento*, ed. Alessio Fornasin and Claudio Lorenzini (Udine: Forum, 2016), 81.

4. For recent studies on ethnic media becoming source of activism for transnational migrants, see, for instance, Syeda Nayab Bukhari, "Ethnic Media as Alternative Media for South Asians in Metro Vancouver, Canada: Creating Knowledge, Engagement, Civic and Political Awareness", *Journal of Alternative and Community Media* 4, no. 3 (2019): 86–98.

5. On the teaching of Italian in Australian schools, see the published collection of *Nuovo Paese* articles and interviews in Bruno Di Biase and Brian Paltridge, eds., *Italian in Australia: Language or Dialect in Schools? Sull'italiano in Australia: Lingua o dialetto nelle scuole?* (Sydney: FILEF Italo-Australian Publications, 1985).

6. Sune Bechmann Pedersen and Marie Cronqvist, "Foreign Correspondents in the Cold War: The Politics and Practices of East German Television Journalists in the West", *Media History* 26, no. 1 (2020): 75; Pietro Pinna, "La stampa di emigrazione di 'sinistra' in Europa", *Studi Emigrazione* 46, no. 175 (2009): 653–670.

7. Lorenzo Prencipe, "Stampa 'in e di' emigrazione. Informazione nell'ottica della 'formazione'", *Studi Emigrazione* 46, no. 175 (2009): 515–524.

8. Bénédicte Deschamps, "Echi d'Italia. La stampa dell'emigrazione", in *Storia dell'emigrazione italiana. Arrivi*, ed. Piero Bevilacqua, Andreina De Clementi, and Emilio Franzina (Roma: Donzelli Editore, 2002), 313–334.

9. Matteo Sanfilippo, *Nuovi problemi di storia delle migrazioni italiane* (Viterbo: Sette Città, 2015), 95–120.

10. Matteo Sanfilippo, "Araldi d'Italia? Un quadro degli studi sulla stampa italiana d'emigrazione", *Studi Emigrazione* 46, no. 175 (2009): 678–695.

11. Pietro Pinna, "La stampa di emigrazione di 'sinistra' in Europa", *Studi Emigrazione* 46, no. 175 (2009): 653–670.

12. Lidio Bertelli, *A Socio-cultural Profile of the Italian Community in Australia* (Melbourne: Catholic Intercultural Resource Centre, 1986), 4.

13. Totaro-Genevois, *Cultural and Linguistic Policy Abroad*, 196.

14. Methodologically, the research has delved into archival material, past issues of *Nuovo Paese* and fourteen oral history interviews. Nearly all editors and editors-in-chief, and about a quarter of editorial committee members, of the 1974–1984 period were interviewed (see Table 8.1).

15. See the list of periodicals and magazines in Pantaleone Sergi, *Stampa migrante: Giornali della diaspora italiana e dell'immigrazione in Italia* (Soveria Mannelli: Rubettino, 2010), 125–126; Caroline Alcorso, Cesare Giulio Popoli and Gaetano Rando, "Community networks and institutions", in *Australia's Italians: Culture and Community in a Changing Society*, ed. Stephen Castles, Caroline Alcorso, Gaetano Rando

and Ellie Vasta (St. Leonards, NSW: Allen & Unwin, 1992), 118; Gaetano Rando, "I giornali di lingua italiana in Australia", *Studi Emigrazione* 46, no. 175 (2009): 621; Gianfranco Cresciani, *No Country for Revolutionaries. Italian Communists in Sydney 1971–1991: Their Activities, Policies and Liaison with the Italian and Australian Communist Parties* (North Melbourne: Australian Scholarly Publishing, 2018), 10–12.

16. Simone Battiston, "How the Italian-Australian Left and its Press Viewed *Il Globo*", in *Il Globo: Fifty Years of an Italian Newspaper in Australia*, ed. by Bruno Mascitelli and Simone Battiston (Ballarat, Vic: Connor Court Publishing, 2009), 75–79; Cresciani, *No Country for Revolutionaries*, 39.

17. Mark Lopez, *The Origins of Multiculturalism in Australian Politics 1945–75* (Melbourne: The University of Melbourne Press, 2000), 268.

18. Brennan Wales, "La stampa italiana nell'Australia multiculturale", *Il Veltro* 32, no. 1/2 (1988): 133–136.

19. For *Il Globo* figures see, Mike Zafiropoulos, "The Ethnic Media in Australia", *BIPR Bulletin* 12 (1994): 28–34. See also more recent figures of *Il Globo* (35,000 readers) and *La Fiamma* (18,000–23,000 readers) in Mariella Totaro-Genevois, *Cultural and Linguistic Policy Abroad: The Italian Experience* (Clevedon, UK: Multilingual Matters, 2005), 200.

20. Francesco Ricatti, *Italians in Australia: History, Memory, Identity* (Cham, Switzerland: Palgrave, 2018), 122–130.

21. The raising number of subsidising unions over time proved the accord a success: from a handful of unions in 1974 to 14 the following year to almost 30 in 1984. The increased subscriptions by participating unions expanded the distribution geographically too: from a dozen members in Victoria and two in New South Wales in 1975 to 14 members in Victoria, eight in South Australia, five in New South Wales and two in Western Australia in 1984 (see Table 8.2).

22. FILEF Melbourne Archive, '*Nuovo Paese*' folder (uncatalogued).

23. The Bonegilla Migrant Reception and Training Centre was Australia's largest camp set up to receiving and training newly arrived migrants to Australia. It operated between 1947 and 1971 and processed some 300,000 migrants. For recent scholarship on migrants and refugees in Australian history, including the Bonegilla Migrant Centre, see: Ruth Balint and Zora Simic, "Histories of Migrants and Refugees in Australia", *Australian Historical Studies* 49, no. 3 (2018): 397–398.

24. Kristina Kukolja and Lindsey Arkley, "Unwanted Australians: Giovanni Sgrò", *SBS News*, July 11, 2016, https://www.sbs.com.au/news/unwanted-australians-giovanni-sgro.

25. See: *Nuovo Paese*, "Don't rubbish Australia. Spazza via agrari e liberali", May 15, 1974, p. 6; *Nuovo Paese*, "Return democracy. Come si vota per l'Australian Labor Party", December 9, 1975, p. 3; *Nuovo Paese*, "Il 5

maggio vota ALP", April 28, 1979, p. 1; *Nuovo Paese*, "I Laburisti propongono investimenti pubblici", February 26, 1982, p. 1; *Nuovo Paese*, "Elezioni nel Victoria. Come votare", March 26, 1982, p. 1.

26. Francesco Ricatti, *Italians in Australia: History, Memory, Identity* (Cham, Switzerland: Palgrave, 2018). See chapter one in particular.

27. Vince Marotta, "The Multicultural, Intercultural and the Transcultural Subject", in *Global Perspectives on the Politics of Multiculturalism in the 21st Century*, ed. Fethi Mansouri and Boulou Ebanda de B'béri (New York: Routledge, 2014), 90–102.

28. See: *Nuovo Paese*, "Nuovo attacco ai lavoratori", August 17, 1976, pp. 1, 2; *Nuovo Paese*, "Valanga di proteste al ministro McKellar [*sic*]", August 17, 1976, p. 3; *Nuovo Paese*, "Continua la lotta per la democrazia", September 4, 1976, pp. 1, 2; *Nuovo Paese*, "Iniziative e proteste per il 'caso Salemi'", September 4, 1976, p. 6; *Nuovo Paese*, "Un ambiguo silenzio durato già troppo", September 18, 1976, p. 1; *Nuovo Paese*, "Solidarietà alla FILEF", October 30, 1976, p. 2; *Nuovo Paese*, "Il dibattito in Parlamento su Salemi e sulla FILEF", October 30, 1976, p. 3; *Nuovo Paese*, "Ondata di solidarietà per il caso Salemi", May 26, 1977, pp. 1, 2; *Nuovo Paese*, "Importante presa di posizione delle Unioni e dell'A.L.P.", July 9, 1977, p. 1; *Nuovo Paese*, "MacKellar ammette: deportazione 'politica'", September 17, 1977, pp. 1, 2; *Nuovo Paese*, "Espulso Salemi, la lotta continua", October 29, 1977, p. 1; *Nuovo Paese*, "I commenti della stampa italiana alla deportazione di Salemi", November 12, 1977, p. 3.

29. See: *Nuovo Paese*, "I nostri lettori sul caso Salemi", August 17, 1976, p. 2; *Nuovo Paese*, "Gli amici della classe operaia", September 4, 1976, p. 2; *Nuovo Paese*, "Preoccupazione per il futuro di Salemi", May 26, 1977, p. 2; *Nuovo Paese*, "Una strategia antioperaia", July 9, 1977, p. 2; *Nuovo Paese*, "Coraggio Salemi", October 15, 1977, p. 2; *Nuovo Paese*, "Le proteste per l'espulsione di Salemi", November 12, 1977, p. 2; *Nuovo Paese*, "L'arroganza del potere liberale", November 26, 1977, p. 2.

30. *The Age*'s Saturday edition had published a front-page article with an attention-grabbing title sensationally linking FILEF with the communist party. See Simone Battiston, *Immigrants Turned Activists: Italians in 1970s Melbourne* (Leicester: Troubador Publishing, 2012), 55, 68–73.

31. Interview of Franco Lugarini with the author, April 9, 2003.

32. Interview of Cathy Angelone and Ignazio Salemi with the author, April 5, 2003.

33. Gianfranco Cresciani, *No Country for Revolutionaries. Italian Communists in Sydney 1971–1991: Their Activities, Policies and Liaison with the Italian and Australian Communist Parties* (North Melbourne: Australian Scholarly Publishing, 2018), 53.

34. Interview of Franco Lugarini with the author, April 9, 2003.
35. *Nuovo Paese*, "Nuova provocazione contro la FILEF", January 21, 1978, pp. 1, 2.
36. Interview of Franco Lugarini with the author, April 9, 2003.
37. Simone Battiston, *Immigrants Turned Activists: Italians in 1970s Melbourne* (Leicester: Troubador Publishing, 2012), 55, 85–86.
38. Extracts of the interview were published in *Simone* Battiston, *Immigrants Turned Activists*, 52, 55, 91–92. See also, interview of Joe Caputo with the author, January 14, 2003.
39. Interview of Ignazio Salemi and Cathy Angelone with the author, April 3, 2003.
40. Interview of Ignazio Salemi and Cathy Angelone with the author, April 3, 2003.
41. Alessandro Portelli, "What Makes Oral History Different", in *The Oral history reader*, ed. Robert Perks and Alistair Thomson (London: Routledge, 1998), 67; Luisa Passerini, *Autobiography of a Generation: Italy, 1968* (Hanover: Wesleyan University Press, 1996).
42. A student of classics at the University of Milan, Martinengo was politically active with communist groups and took part in the student protests of 1968. He arrived in Melbourne in 1973. Before finding employment with FILEF in 1975, he completed a Diploma of Education at La Trobe University and had a stint as secondary school teacher.
43. Interview of Umberto Martinengo with the author, December 24, 2002.
44. James Panichi and Maurizio Pascucci, "A Passionate, Stimulating Broadcaster", *The Sydney Morning Herald*, June 28, 2010, https://www.smh.com.au/world/a-passionate-stimulating-broadcaster-20100627-zc1j.html
45. Interview of Umberto Martinengo with the author, December 24, 2002.
46. Interview of Umberto Martinengo with the author, December 24, 2002.
47. Interview of Stefano de Pieri with the author, January 22, 2004.
48. Interview of Stefano de Pieri with the author, January 22, 2004.
49. *The Age*, "Eat, Drink and Be Murray", June 28, 2002, https://www.theage.com.au/entertainment/eat-drink-and-be-murray-20020916-gdulbm.html
50. Interview of Cira La Gioia with the author, May 19, 2004.
51. Simone Battiston and Sabina Sestigiani, "Percorsi d'emigrazione e di militanza politica: donne italiane in Australia tra gli anni settanta e ottanta del Novecento", in *Lontane da casa. Donne italiane e diaspora globale dall'inizio del Novecento a oggi*, ed. Stefano Luconi and Mario Varricchio (Torino: Accademia University Press, 2015), 201–203.
52. He was born in Italy but emigrated to Brazil as a child before resettling with his family in Australia in 1966.

CHAPTER 9

Painting Queensland Red: Hugo Kunze, Transnational Print Culture and Propaganda for Socialism

Andrew G. Bonnell

In recent years, historians of nation-states such as Germany have paid increasing attention to the transnational dimensions of history. In the case of Germany, this has involved paying closer attention to transnational links and entanglements both within Europe and globally, looking at the ties between Germans in the homeland and German-speaking communities abroad. The greater attention to transnational and diasporic histories promises to improve communications between those engaged in "national" histories and migration historians as a specialised branch of historiography.[1] As Stefan Berger has recently noted, the transnational turn has also affected the writing of German labour history.[2] This chapter can be seen as a case study in the ways in which transnational labour movement history and migration history can mutually inform each other.

A. G. Bonnell (✉)
School of Historical and Philosophical Inquiry, University of Queensland, St Lucia, QLD, Australia
e-mail: a.bonnell@uq.edu.au

© The Author(s), under exclusive license to Springer Nature Switzerland AG 2021
C. Dewhirst, R. Scully (eds.), *Voices of Challenge in Australia's Migrant and Minority Press*, Palgrave Studies in the History of the Media, https://doi.org/10.1007/978-3-030-67330-7_9

173

The socialist labour movement in the age of the Second International (1889–1914), centred mainly in Europe, consisted of parties which were the representatives of the working class of industrial and industrialising nations. To no small degree, these parties, and the dissemination of their programmes and ideologies, were also a product of a particular stage of development of what Benedict Anderson famously called "print capitalism": the confluence of the development of print technology and a capitalist market which promoted the diffusion of its products. In the late nineteenth century, the development of advances in paper-making technology and printing (rotary presses) enabled the rise of the "penny press", and the possibility of cheap mass circulation of print media enabled socialist parties to spread their ideas among urban workers in countries where economic development had been accompanied by growth in literacy rates.[3]

In a way of which Karl Marx himself would have approved, Marxist ideas and terminology were able to reach a mass base, in some form at least, thanks to these economic and technological advances. This was particularly evident in Germany, where the German Social Democratic Party, which became the world's first million-strong mass party by 1914, came to maintain a press network consisting of some 90 newspapers, with combined circulation of hundreds of thousands.[4]

In Anderson's argument, early "print capitalism" helped the middle classes of scattered provinces imagine themselves as members of one nation, potentially able to read the same newspapers and books as citizens in relatively distant cities. By the late nineteenth century, cheap socialist newspapers helped to foster a consciousness of belonging to a single working class. If language barriers and national political barriers sometimes coincided, the socialist press could also cross national borders: by post, smuggling and migrating workers taking papers with them. Where communities of migrant workers were large enough, as in the United States, they might try to start their own newspapers to substitute for the ones they had known in their homeland, where newspapers were becoming increasingly indispensable as vehicles for the expression of political parties' programmes and worldviews.[5] Where that was not the case, as in the Australian colonies in the late nineteenth and early twentieth centuries, where groups of German immigrants were even more widely dispersed than in North America, socialist workers still sought to participate in transnational networks of communication in print.[6] The career of Ernst Hugo Kunze (1867–1934), a Dresden-born master painter and socialist activist and propagandist active in Queensland in the early 1900s, illustrates the ways in which this could be done.

GERMAN SOCIAL DEMOCRATIC NEWSPAPERS AND AUSTRALIA

When Hugo Kunze (as he was usually known) set sail for Australia in late 1887, arriving in Brisbane in February 1888,[7] he left behind him a German Empire in which the German Social Democratic Party had already been outlawed by Chancellor Otto von Bismarck for nearly a decade (the anti-socialist law was in force from 1878 to 1890).[8] There is no evidence that Kunze was personally driven to emigrate by the repressive laws which enabled the authorities to exile activists from their place of residence within Germany—his name does not appear on any of the lists of banned persons in the Kingdom of Saxony (where the authorities were particularly alarmed by the rise of socialism in Saxony's cities and its rapidly industri-alising landscape). But Kunze's subsequent recollections of life in Germany under the anti-socialist law suggest that the 19-year-old emigrant had already been taking an active interest in Social Democratic politics.

With the Social Democratic Party banned from all activities (except for standing candidates for parliament), socialist activists exiled from their homes and hundreds of socialist publications banned during the party's years of illegality, the clandestine circulation of the party's newspaper, *Der Sozialdemokrat* (The Social Democrat), played a crucial role in keeping the party in being, keeping its communications networks alive and in spreading the ideas of the exiled socialist theorists Karl Marx and Friedrich Engels within Germany. *Der Sozialdemokrat* was first published in Zurich in September 1879. When the German authorities cracked down on the newspaper being sent to subscribers through the mail, the party resorted to organised smuggling to ensure continued distribution in Germany. The "Red Field Post", as the smuggling network came to be known, was run by socialist activist (and so-called Red Postmaster) Julius Motteler.[9] From October 1888, the newspaper was published in London, following pres-sure on Switzerland from Germany to deport *Der Sozialdemokrat*'s editors.

Hugo Kunze, who grew up in Dresden, the capital of the Kingdom of Saxony, during the period of the anti-socialist law, later retold anecdotes in the Queensland labour movement newspaper, *The Worker*, of how German Social Democrats outwitted Bismarck's police spies to get the contraband copies of *Der Sozialdemokrat* into Germany: concealing papers in milk-cans, for example. (Other ruses included false mastheads with innocuous titles, or labelling consignments as "Swiss cheese".) One member of the party volunteered to be a police informer and alerted the police to small decoy consignments of newspapers in order to distract them from the main supply, at the same time as he funnelled his pay from Bismarck into the party coffers.[10] By whatever means, the smuggling was successful: in Kunze's Dresden, on the other side of Germany from the Swiss border, some 400 subscribers to *Der Sozialdemokrat* received their copies regularly in 1887.[11] Kunze wrote: "Literature obtained under conditions such as these was highly treasured at the hearths of the people, where privilege and the oppressor with all his serfs are powerless to confiscate". He continued, writing that the dedication to their own cause that German working people had developed under such conditions had led to "the most united and best organised Socialist party in the world". Kunze drew a parallel between the German socialists' "Red Field Post" and the propaganda work which he was then undertaking as part of Brisbane's socialist group, the Social Democratic Vanguard:

> The Vanguard, by its persistent devotion to propaganda work, will, under the reign of the new Imperialism into which Australia has just entered, make itself worthy of similar persecution, [...] persecution will help the spread of Socialism which alone can permanently and finally can [*sic*] conquer Capitalism. [12]

In another issue of *The Worker*, Kunze told of his own experience of a police raid in a Dresden pub, when he was not yet 18 years old, when the police came in search of socialist propaganda and forbidden literature. Kunze feigned innocence, claiming to be there just for a card game. The party *Vertrauensmann* (organiser)—a man called Fechner—managed to swallow an incriminating piece of paper before the police got around to questioning him. Despite their failure to find forbidden literature, the police searched the homes of the 11 men questioned in the pub, and the latter were subsequently denounced to their employers as socialists, with some being sacked as a result. But the story had a satisfying dénouement:

> the next night an election leaflet was distributed in that town from end to end, proclaiming the Socialists' aims and hopes to the down-trodden toilers. A police proclamation in the capitalist press against its circulation as soon as discovered ensured it being read.[13]

Copies of *Der Sozialdemokrat* even made it as far as Australia. Members of the South Australian Allgemeiner Deutscher Verein (General German Association, ADV) wrote to Julius Motteler in 1889–1890 to acquire copies for their library, along with other Social Democratic literature.[14] The

ADV had been founded in 1886: in contrast to the conservative Deutscher Club in South Australia, which was dominated by landowners, the ADV was run by workers sympathetic to Social Democracy. The ADV's library contained a collection of Social Democratic literature that resembled a party library in a German city, with socialist books, pamphlets and a range of periodicals. These included a good run of the Social Democratic Party's theoretical journal, *Die Neue Zeit* (The New Age), the party's illustrated humorous and satirical papers, *Der wahre Jakob* (The True Jacob) and the *Süddeutscher Postillon* (The South German Postilion), and *Die Neue Welt* (The New World), the literary supplement for the party's main daily newspaper *Vorwärts* (Forward).[15] Individual German emigrants to Australia wrote to Motteler as well, like Adolf Bröse, barber and tobacconist in Rundle Street, Adelaide. Bröse wrote to Motteler in January 1890, stating that he had been a subscriber to *Der Sozialdemokrat* when he lived in Hamburg, until August the previous year, and he now wished "to step into the ranks once again"—subscribing to the paper was tantamount to membership of the outlawed party.[16] Interestingly, in addition to ordering copies of *Der Sozialdemokrat* and the best-selling work by August Bebel, *Woman in Socialism*, the ADV also sought Motteler's assistance in getting a subscription to the German socialist newspaper *Vorwärts*, published in Buenos Aires, suggesting a sense of shared identity with the wider German socialist diaspora.[17]

A similar association of German socialists, which functioned primarily as a reading group, was formed in Melbourne in 1886 under the name Verein Vorwaerts (The Forward Association). (*Vorwärts* was a name frequently adopted by Social Democratic associations in Germany and was taken as the name of the party's main daily newspaper in 1891.) The association's secretary, Louis Gross, seems to have kept up with *Der Sozialdemokrat*, writing to the paper in 1890 to congratulate the German Social Democratic Party on its success in the elections of February 1890. Gross reported on the state of opinion in Melbourne, where the election had aroused significant attention, even if accurate details had been hard to glean from the capitalist press there: "The press in Melbourne is without exception hostile to socialism", Gross wrote.[18]

Sadly, few records survive of the activities of the Verein Vorwaerts, nor have records of its library, which is said to have been substantial, been preserved. It may be reasonable to assume that the Verein Vorwaerts library was similar to the collection of the ADV.[19] However, historians of the socialist left wing of the Australian labour movement such as Bertha

Walker (whose grandfather, Louis Gross, was at one time a leading figure in the Verein Vorwaerts) and Verity Burgmann have pointed to the association as an example of the influence which foreign-born socialists, particularly those of a German background, exercised on left-wing and internationalist politics in the 1890s and early 1900s.[20]

HUGO KUNZE AND THE QUEENSLAND LABOUR MOVEMENT PRESS

After arriving in Brisbane in early 1888 and becoming naturalised in 1891, Hugo Kunze became involved in the emergent politics of the labour movement in Brisbane during the course of the 1890s. Labour movement politics in Australia differed markedly from the situation in Germany: trade unionism and practical industrial work was at the forefront in Australia, tending to eclipse explicitly socialist ideas. However, there was a small but very active socialist wing of the Australian labour movement in the 1890s and early 1900s, and activists from Europe, especially Germany, played a significant role on that socialist left flank. These immigrant socialists contributed to a more internationalist outlook on the left wing of the labour movement, both in terms of theory and also in terms of their own experience and political formation (see Fig. 9.1).[21]

In Brisbane, the key socialist organisation in the first few years of the twentieth century was the Social Democratic Vanguard (SDV), which was formed in 1900 by Ernest (Ernie) Lane (brother of the socialist writer and Paraguay colonist, William Lane) and a small group of like-minded activists, including Kunze. The Manifesto of the Social Democratic Vanguard proclaimed it part of the "great international Labour Movement". Its objective was to urge "a revival of Socialist activities". After the industrial conflicts of the early 1890s in Queensland, the "capitalistic oligarchy" were reasserting themselves, and Labour leaders were starting to show themselves wanting in their commitment to "the basic principles of social regeneration".[22] The SDV saw its role as to act as a "Socialist propagandist organisation",[23] and its work consisted largely in publishing and disseminating socialist tracts and leaflets. The SDV's members also regularly furnished the labour press, including *The Worker*, with articles.

Supported by subscriptions and donations from across Queensland, the SDV concentrated "on the free distribution of socialist literature, principally pamphlets obtained through various sources, supplemented

Fig. 9.1 Hugo Kunze and wife Elizabeth Ralston Kunze, c. 1890. Photographer unknown. (Photograph courtesy of Ms Lexie Smiles)

occasionally by original productions of members", as Ernie Lane recalled in his autobiography: "we scattered broadcast the Socialist Doctrine".[24] Lane singled out the role of Kunze in this work for special praise: "Hugo Kunze was one of the immortals with regard to his devotion to the working class and his fidelity to the highest ideals of the movement. He undertook the onerous duty of dispatching all the literature and it was indeed a labour of love."[25] Kunze himself described the need to spread the socialist message as requiring active work of persuasion: "The arrival of socialism is not only dependent upon social evolution, but upon the work and guidance of the men and women of today".[26]

The SDV wrote and produced some 17 tracts and leaflets of its own between 1901 and 1903, including a short brochure on "Woman and the Social Problem" written by "Eznuk" (a transparent pseudonym for Hugo Kunze, which he also regularly used in his newspaper articles for the labour press). Kunze's pamphlet drew on the American socialist press for its material, but he may also have been influenced by the German Social Democrat leader August Bebel's best-selling *Woman and Socialism*, first published in 1879 and frequently reprinted.[27] By the time Kunze's pamphlet appeared, the SDV was claiming to have over 500 members, and it maintained a club-room in Queen Street, Brisbane, along with a library and book depot.[28]

The original tracts of the SDV only accounted for a small part of the total propaganda effort of the group. In January 1903, the third annual general meeting of the SDV reported on the work of Kunze, the "Literature Distributor":

> The Literature Distributor's report showed that this most important part of Vanguard work had been faithfully attended to. Comrade Kunze is always very much in earnest, and this propaganda work for Socialism is to him truly a labour of love. During 1902 he has despatched 749 parcels of literature to different parts of our State, making no less than 19,222 messengers of the Gospel of Justice and Happiness sent on their errand of mercy within the last twelve months. In the three years the Vanguard has been engaged in this work 1501 parcels containing altogether 70,870 pieces of reform literature have been distributed gratis. Surely a noble effort, and one which must some day, let us hope in the not too distant future, yield a rich harvest of converts for Socialism. This work will be vigorously continued; already, during January, nearly another thousand leaflets have been sent out and, if possible, Distributor Kunze intends to beat all his previous records during this year.[29]

The same report also mentioned another SDV project—the "Van", a "Socialist travelling Van", which would act as a mobile library travelling around Queensland. Kunze was identified as one of the colleagues responsible for this project. (This project was not ultimately realised in practice.) At the same time, it was reported that the SDV's "book depot" was maintaining a "steady sale of first-class Socialist literature". The book depot made a small profit, but its object was primarily "to get Socialistic works into the hands of the people, at the lowest possible prices consistent with making the depot self-supporting".[30] One of Kunze's SDV comrades once described him as keeping a "map whereon is shown in red the localities which the literature [mailed out by the SDV] covers".[31] The object of the master painter Hugo Kunze was to paint Queensland red, in order to prepare Queensland for the advent of a genuinely socialist political party.

Another way in which the SDV sought to spread socialist ideas in Queensland, apart from disseminating flyers and pamphlets, was through newspapers. In addition to running a regular "Vanguard" column in the pages of the Brisbane *Worker*, the SDV also made use of other regional labour movement newspapers in Queensland. By October 1900, the SDV could announce that: "Two more papers—Mount Morgan *Truth* and Bundaberg *Patriot*—have granted space for a column of Vanguard notes and Socialistic writings, making eight now in full swing".[32]

Kunze was not able to harness the German-language immigrant press to his propaganda campaigns: these were either politically conservative or ostensibly apolitical commercial enterprises. In neither case were they hospitable to articles promoting socialist ideas.[33] The longest running German-language newspaper in Australia was the South Australian *Australische Zeitung*. Increasingly, it was aligned with the state's conservative, landowning, monarchist and Lutheran elite and upper-middle class who gathered in Adelaide's Deutscher Club. A social and political gulf separated the Deutscher Club from the left-leaning workers and artisans who congregated in the Allgemeiner Deutscher Verein (ADV).[34] The *Australische Zeitung* reported only sparingly on the ADV's activities, and, when it did so, did not conceal its hostility towards Social Democracy: thus, the newspaper recorded the fact that the ADV marked the 1892 May Day festivities with "a concert, a theatre performance, and *without bombs*".[35] A few years later, in 1896, Carl Wiese, the secretary of the ADV, felt the need to complain that the *Australische Zeitung* had misrepresented the association's May Day activities.[36] In New South Wales, the *Deutsch-Australische Post* was actually run by the Sydney chapter of the right-wing nationalist, pro-imperialist Pan German League. Its political stance was therefore militantly anti-socialist.[37] The early Victorian German-language press began promisingly, but failed to take root. Victoria saw a number of short-lived attempts at founding newspapers (between 1859 and 1863) by the Rhineland radical democrat Hermann Püttmann, an author and experienced journalist and "Forty-Eighter" (i.e. a veteran of the revolution of 1848–1849), who had been an associate of Karl Marx and the radical poet Georg Weerth. Unfortunately, Püttmann's ventures failed to strike a chord in Victoria's German-speaking community, partly due to what Volkhard

Wehner calls Victorian Germans' "political inertia" in this period, the aftermath of the Gold Rush.[38] Consequently, in Wehner's words, "by 1873 Victoria's German-language press was dead".[39] In Hugo Kunze's own Queensland, the German-language press oscillated between conservatism and pragmatic pursuit of the farming and commercial interests of German settlers, and at times these papers seem to have been shoestring operations chasing limited supplies of advertising revenue.[40]

The SDV went into a decline following Ernie Lane's departure for his brother's Cosme colony in Paraguay, split after the ambitious Queensland Labor politician Joe Collings sought to drag the group to the Right (which led to the departure of both Kunze and another Marxian socialist, Andy Anderson) and ceased to exist altogether in 1909. Kunze continued to write occasionally for the labour movement press. In September 1905, he wrote to *The Worker* to defend German Social Democracy against a casual slur in the paper. *The Worker* had written:

> It is wonderful that a brainy people like the Germans, and the preachers of the revolutionary class war, should submit so patiently to the iron-heel methods of their rulers. It is enough to make the soul of a blackfellow revolt, yet nothing deadlier than a sausage is ever thrown at a tyrant in Germany.

Kunze took the (casually racist) editorialist of *The Worker* to task, arguing that German Social Democracy had to deal with the "remnants of feudalism" which a "cowardly and spineless middle class" had completely failed to get rid of.[41]

Drawing again on his knowledge of German conditions, Kunze wrote on the German "Hottentot elections" of 1907 and on "Liberalism the Betrayer" in 1908, and he engaged in a polemical debate with *The Worker* about revolutionary socialism and his opposition to the White Australia policy.[42] At the same time, Kunze continued to be a successful master painter, being elected to the council of the Master Painters' Association in 1914. As an employer, he was said to employ only staunch union members, and he spoke out publicly in support of minimum wages (Fig. 9.2).[43]

KUNZE AND TRANSNATIONAL SOCIALIST PRINT CULTURE

In October 1902, the regular Vanguard column in the Brisbane *Worker* announced to its readers that:

Fig. 9.2 Kunze's painting business cart and workers, Brisbane, c. 1900–1910. (Photographer unknown. Photograph courtesy of Ms Lexie Smiles)

Fifty sample copies of the 'International Socialist Review', published monthly at Chicago, U.S.A., are to hand, and can be obtained through the Vanguard. Single copies 6d, or 4s 6d per annum: postage to be added. The "Review" enables comrades to keep in touch with the Labour-Socialist movement of the whole world, which is of particular importance at the present juncture. The number on hand contains an article on 'Socialism in Australia', with special reference to Labour-in-politics in Queensland.[44]

The article on socialism in Australia, with special reference to Queensland, was by Hugo Kunze himself.[45] His article on the state of socialism in Australia from the vantage point of Queensland emphasised the role of the printed word: "The one great influence in directing the labor forces here into the right channels undoubtedly has been the institution of labor journalism, in conjunction with trades federation".[46] Kunze also described the propaganda work of the SDV in this article, which he explained as necessary to guard against the "danger of principles being sacrificed to expediency". The SDV's "free and plentiful circulation of Socialist literature" was intended to "maintain and spread the spirit of class-consciousness".[47]

Kunze's comrade in the SDV, Andrew (Andy) Anderson, also contributed to *The International Socialist Review* from 1903 to 1905. The connections between the SDV and *The International Socialist Review* highlight the role of the Chicago publisher Charles H. Kerr in aiding the dissemination of socialist literature in the English-speaking world, including cheap but durable editions of works by Marx and Engels (including the Communist Manifesto), Wilhelm Liebknecht and Karl Kautsky (along with other socialist writers, including of course the Americans Eugene Debs and Daniel de Leon). Frank Farrell's history of the left in Australia refers to a "virtual cascade of books from the Kerr & Co. press of Chicago" and highlights the influence of this literature on groups such as the Australian Socialist League and the Victorian Socialist League (which was to become linked to the Verein Vorwaerts in Melbourne).[48] Kunze was still in correspondence with the publishing house of Charles H. Kerr in the early 1920s, a fact that was noted by an ever-suspicious Commonwealth Investigation Branch in 1922 in a report: "Communicates with Kerr, Printer of Chicago, who circulates militant literature".[49]

Kunze's international links were not confined to Charles Kerr & Co. He continued to follow events in Germany and interpret German socialist politics for an Australian readership. For example, Kunze contributed a detailed account of William Liebknecht's funeral for the SDV's columns in

The Worker in October 1900.[50] The fact of Liebknecht's death had been widely reported in August, including in such regional Queensland papers as *The Gympie Times and Mary River Mining Gazette*,[51] the *Maryborough Chronicle, Wide Bay and Burnett Advertiser*, and the *Toowoomba Chronicle and Darling Downs General Advertiser*,[52] among others. The two-month delay before Kunze published his much more detailed and atmospheric account of Liebknecht's funeral in Berlin reflects the time it would have taken him to receive a copy of *Vorwärts* or other German Social Democratic papers which enabled him to go beyond the brief telegraphic announcements of the rest of the Australian press. The same delay occurred with the publication by *Vorwärts* of the SDV's message of condolences to the German party on Liebknecht's death, which the German paper reported on 1 November 1900.[53] Around the time of Liebknecht's funeral, the SDV announced that Kunze had been corresponding with J. A. Verhoef, the editor of the Dutch socialist newspaper, *Het Volk* (The People), which was cited as an example of the fact that socialists around the world were interested in maintaining contact with their comrades in Australia.[54] Further evidence of this last connection is missing, but the reference to the recently founded Dutch paper is another indication of Kunze's keen interest in maintaining international links.

In addition to drawing on the German Social Democratic press, Kunze used his own knowledge of German conditions to correct what he saw as distortions in the Australian non-socialist press. After the Social Democratic gains in the June 1903 elections in Germany (polling over three million votes), Kunze took the Brisbane *Courier* to task for trying to suggest that the party was equivalent to the Liberals in the British Empire. On the contrary, Kunze stressed, German Social Democracy "is an avowedly revolutionary movement, having for its fundamental aim the 'abolition of private property and the collective use of capital for the development and improvement of mankind, in order to give all a life worthy of men'. German Social Democracy is engaged in a fight to the finish with all sections of the capitalistic forces."[55]

In May 1904, *Vorwärts* ran a front-page story on the formation of a labour government in Queensland, including a large part of an article translated from the Brisbane *Worker*. No correspondent or translator is named but it is not far-fetched to speculate that Kunze may have had a hand in the article's appearance in Germany one way or the other.[56] Kunze would not have been the only German Social Democrat in Australia to write to *Vorwärts*, or get published in the German paper's columns: Carl

Mitscherlich, secretary of the Verein Vorwaerts in Melbourne, succeeded in getting *Vorwärts* to publish his summary of Australian conditions in August 1908.[57] This underlines the fact that members of these groups of German Social Democrats sought to stay informed of events in Germany through subscribing to the Social Democratic press, even if it took several weeks for the newspapers to reach Australian cities. No doubt these newspapers were highly valued and shared in the reading rooms of the ADV and the Verein Vorwaerts whenever they arrived. There is even evidence of two Australian subscribers to the radical syndicalist newspaper, *Der Freie Arbeiter* (The Free Worker), as of 1914: one Hans Voit, of Adelaide, and E.P. Hönicke, in Carlton, Victoria, who also subscribed to the German-language anarchist newspaper from New York, *Die Freiheit* (Freedom).[58]

Adelaide and Melbourne were the only Australian cities that gave rise to stable organisations of German Social Democratic workers, although there is some evidence of Social Democratic gatherings in Sydney. Elsewhere, individual Germans could be found in the small socialist groups which sought to influence the early Australian labour movement. Hugo Kunze was one of these. Unlike their counterparts in the United States and parts of South America, German socialists in Australian cities lacked the critical mass to produce their own newspapers, and the conservative or apolitical German-language press in Australia was largely closed to them, or even actively hostile. Under these conditions, Kunze, for one, made what use he could of the Australian labour movement press. These German Social Democrats in Australia sought to keep in contact with the German and international socialist movement as much as they could through newspaper subscriptions and through the dissemination of socialist literature sourced from Charles Kerr of Chicago and other sources. If the sea routes were slow by today's standards of instantaneous communication, and the supply lines could be tenuous, German socialists in Australia in the era of the Second International still worked to maintain a transnational socialist print-culture network, which carried news and ideas, as well as sustaining a sense of international socialist identity despite the vast distances. Not only did these transnational print-culture networks serve to transmit socialist ideas, participation in them also enabled members of socialist diasporas to practice their internationalism.

From a contemporary perspective, the life of Hugo Kunze reflects the age in which the organised labour movement was characterised by the figure from Bertolt Brecht's celebrated poem: "Questions of a Worker Who Reads". The movement drew its strength from the new working-class socio-cultural milieus created by industrialisation, and communicated through the medium of cheap printing. If today's instantaneous global electronic communication enables news and information to travel without delays around the world, it remains to be seen what forms of social solidarity the new media will be able to sustain in the future to replace the older forms that have largely been dissolved.

NOTES

1. Sebastian Conrad, *Globalisation and the Nation in Imperial Germany*, trans. Sorcha O'Hagan (Cambridge: Cambridge University Press, 2010); Krista O'Donnell, Renate Bridenthal and Nancy Reagin, eds, *The Heimat Abroad. The Boundaries of Germanness* (Ann Arbor: University of Michigan Press, 2005); Stefan Manz, *Constructing a German Diaspora. The "Greater German Empire", 1871–1914* (London and New York: Routledge, 2014); Alexander Maxwell and Sacha Davis, "Germanness beyond Germany: Collective Identity in German Diasporic Communities", *German Studies Review* 39, no. 1 (February 2016): 1–15.

2. Stefan Berger, "Introduction: The Revival of German Labour History", *German History* 37, no. 3 (September 2019): 283–284.

3. Benedict Anderson, *Imagined Communities* (London: Verso, 1983); Régis Debray, "Socialism and Print", *New Left Review* 46 (N.S.) (July/August 2007): 5–28.

4. See Dieter Fricke, *Handbuch zur Geschichte der deutschen Arbeiterbewegung 1869 bis 1917* (Berlin: Dietz, 1987), Bd.1, 495–560; Kurt Koszyk, *Die Presse der deutschen Sozialdemokratie. Eine Bibliographie* (Hannover: Verlag für Literatur und Zeitgeschehen, 1966). On the diffusion of Marxian ideas through the Social Democratic press and "grey literature" (pamphlets and brochures), see Andrew G. Bonnell, "Did They Read Marx? Marx Reception and Social Democratic Party Members in Imperial Germany, 1890–1914", *Australian Journal of Politics & History* 48, no. 1 (2002): 4–15.

5. Renate Kiesewetter, "German-American Labor Press. The *Vorbote* and the *Chicagoer Arbeiter-Zeitung*", in Hartmut Keil, ed., *German Workers' Culture in the United States, 1850 to 1920* (Washington DC and London: Smithsonian Institution, 1988), 137–155; Elliott Shore, Ken Fones-Wolf, James Philip Danky, James P. Danky, eds, *The German-American Radical Press: The Shaping of a Left Political Culture, 1850–1940* (Urbana and Chicago: University of Illinois Press, 1992).

6. For context, and separate discussion of the German communities in the major states, see Andrew G. Bonnell, "Transnational Socialists? German Social Democrats in Australia before 1914", *Itinerario* 37, no. 1 (April 2013): 101–113.

7. For biographical details on Kunze, see Andrew G. Bonnell, "From Saxony to South Brisbane: the German-Australian socialist Hugo Kunze", in *Labour History and its People*, ed. Melanie Nolan (The 12th Biennial National Labour History Conference, Australian National University 15–17 September 2011) (Australian Society for the Study of Labour History, Canberra Region Branch and National Centre of Biography, Australian National University, Canberra, 2011), 299–309.

8. Vernon L. Lidtke, *The Outlawed Party: Social Democracy in Germany, 1878–1890* (Princeton NJ: Princeton University Press, 1966). In this period, the party was named the Socialist Workers Party of Germany.

9. See Ernst Engelberg, *Revolutionäre Politik und rote Feldpost 1878–1890* (Berlin: Akademie-Verlag, 1959); Joseph Belli, *Die Rote Feldpost unterm Sozialistengesetz* (Bonn: J.H.W. Dietz Nachf., 1978 [1912]); Friedrich Pospiech, *Julius Motteler, der "rote Feldpostmeister", Kampfgefährte von Bebel und W. Liebknecht* (Esslingen am Neckar: no publisher, 1977).

10. "The Vanguard Round Table", *The Worker*, April 13, 1901 (Kunze writing under the pseudonym "Eznuk").

11. Engelberg, *Revolutionäre Politik*, 284–285.

12. "The Vanguard Round Table", *The Worker*, April 13, 1901.

13. "Eznuk" in "The Vanguard Round Table", *The Worker*, September 22, 1900. Kunze refers to the town simply as D___, but the anecdote is plainly autobiographical. Dresden was blanketed with illegal Social Democratic election flyers on the eve of the 1881 Reichstag elections, and again in 1884. On efforts by the authorities and non-socialist parties to combat the rise of Social Democracy in Saxony, see the outstanding study by James Retallack, *Red Saxony: Election Battles and the Spectre of Democracy in Germany, 1860–1918* (Oxford: Oxford University Press, 2017) (See 161–166 for a discussion of Social Democratic pre-election agitation in Dresden, including the use of *Der Der Sozialdemokrat* and flyers).

14. International Institute for Social History (IISH), Amsterdam, Julius Motteler Papers, nos. 372, 377, 898, 1033, 1148, 1156, 1226, 1327 (the last of these being Motteler's very extensive international mailing list). I am indebted to Samuel Finch for bringing these references to my attention.

15. Katalog der Bibliothek des Süd-Australischen Allgemeinen Deutschen Vereins (printed catalogue), Adelaide, 1909, State Library of South Australia.

16. IISH, Motteler Papers, 377/2, Bröse to Motteler, January 3, 1890.

17. IISH, Motteler Papers, 1226/1, Carl Wiese to E. Bernstein & Co., August 20, 1890. Wiese was secretary of the ADV.

18. "Korrespondenzen. Melbourne", *Der Sozialdemokrat*, no. 22, May 31, 1890.

19. On the Verein Vorwaerts, see the (slim) file, National Archives of Australia (NAA) dating from the time of the First World War, 'Socialischer Verein Vorvarts [*sic*], Trusties Carl Mitscherlich, F W & We, Emil Flues, 1917–1918'; NAA, MP16/1 1918/21. The fullest account to date is by the historian of Victoria's German population, Volkhard Wehner, "The Verein Vorwaerts", unpublished MS [2018]. I am grateful to Dr Wehner for allowing me to read a copy of this work.

20. Bertha Walker, *Solidarity Forever!* (Melbourne: The National Press, 1972); Verity Burgmann, '*In Our Time'. Socialism and the Rise of Labor, 1885–1905* (Sydney, London, Boston: George Allen & Unwin, 1985).

21. Burgmann, '*In Our Time'*; Frank Farrell, *International Socialism and Australian Labour* (Sydney: Hale & Iremonger, 1981), Ch.1; Walker, *Solidarity Forever!*

22. *The Red Light. Manifesto of the Social-Democratic Vanguard*, Brisbane, 1901, 1, accessible online at www.reasoninrevolt.net.au/biogs/E000311b. htm; see also *The Worker* (Brisbane), May 5, 1900, for the inaugural version of the Manifesto (with Kunze named as one of the members of the executive). On the SDV, see Burgmann, '*In Our Time'*, 186–192; Jeff Rickertt, "Organising the Revolution by Ballot: Queensland's State Socialists, 1889–1905", *Queensland Journal of Labour History* no. 11 (September 2010): 9–23. See also Rickertt's biography of Ernie Lane: Jeff Rickertt, *The Conscientious Communist. Ernie Lane and the Rise of Australian Socialism* (North Melbourne: Australian Scholarly Publishers, 2016), 72–79.

23. *The Red Light*, 2.

24. E.H. Lane, *Dawn to Dusk. Reminiscences of a Rebel* (Brisbane: William Brooks, 1939), 78.

25. Lane, *Dawn to Dusk. Reminiscences of a Rebel*, 79.

26. Eznuk [pseudonym for Kunze], "The Trust Problem", *The Worker*, October 25, 1902; also cited by Rickertt, *The Conscientious Communist*, 77.

27. "Eznuk", *Woman and the Social Problem* (Vanguard Tract No.14), Brisbane, n.d. [1902].

28. "Comrade Mary", *An Appeal to Women* (Vanguard Tract No.13), Brisbane, n.d., 1. More details can be found in Rickertt, "Organising the Revolution by Ballot".

29. "Social Democratic Vanguard", *The Worker*, February 28, 1903.

30. "Social Democratic Vanguard".

31. "Comrade Sam", "Social-Democratic Vanguard", *The Worker*, June 30, 1900.

32. "Social Democratic Vanguard", *The Worker*, October 13, 1900.

33. The best reference on the German-language press in Australia in this period is Rebecca Vonhoff, *Spoken through the Press: German-Australian*

identity and influence during the Kaiserreich, Doctor of Philosophy thesis, University of Queensland, 2011.

34. Vonhoff, Spoken through the Press, Ch.6. See also the research of Samuel Finch on the Germans in South Australia (in progress).

35. "Kolonielle Angelegenheiten", *Australische Zeitung*, May 4, 1892.

36. "Kolonielle Angelegenheiten", *Australische Zeitung*, May 13, 1896.

37. Vonhoff, Spoken through the Press, Ch. 4.

38. Volkhard Wehner, *The German-speaking community of Victoria between 1850 and 1930* (Münster: LIT-Verlag, 2018), 106–110, quotation 110. On Püttmann, see also Leslie Bodi, "Püttmann, Hermann (1811–1874)", in *Australian Dictionary of Biography*, Volume 5 (Melbourne: Melbourne University Press, 1974), online at http://adb.anu.edu.au/biography/puttmann-hermann-4421. Bodi states that Püttmann learned typesetting, which enabled him to type-set his own papers in the absence of type-setters proficient in German in Melbourne.

39. Wehner, *The German-speaking community*. 107.

40. See Vonhoff, Spoken through the Press, Ch. 5; Alan Corkhill, *Queensland and Germany* (Melbourne: Academia Press, 1992), 185–189. For an anecdotal account of how precarious the existence of the *Nordaustralische Zeitung* was, see: Emil Hansel, "Six months in Brisbane", in Jürgen Tampke, ed., *Wunderbar Country. Germans Look at Australia, 1850–1914* (Sydney: Hale & Iremonger, 1982), 101–105. Hansel was hired for a job on the paper only to find that it went broke and was sold to another proprietor three weeks later.

41. E. H. Kunze, "German Social-Democracy", *The Worker*, September 16, 1905.

42. E. H. Kunze, "The German Elections. An Interesting Glimpse", *The Worker*, February 16, 1907; "Liberalism the Betrayer. History Repeats Itself", *The Worker*, April 25, 1908; "Jack London on the Labour Party", *The Worker* (Brisbane), February 20, 1909; "Revolutionary Socialism and the Labour Party" [by Kunze], and "The Discussion is Resumed", *The Worker*, 27 February 1909 (editorial disagreeing with Kunze); Andrew M. Anderson, "Revolutionary Socialism v. Labour Party" and "Qui vive" [pseud.], "Marx and Some Marxians" (rejoinder to Anderson), *The Worker*, March 13, 1909.

43. "Master Painters", The Brisbane *Courier*, January 30, 1914; 'Inspector D.A. Mackiehen to Investigation Branch, Attorney-General's Department, March 27, 1922', NAA, Canberra, A402/W248; "World of Labour", *The Worker*, February 6, 1913.

44. Eznuk, "The Trust Problem".

45. E. H. Kunze, "Socialism in Australia. With Special Reference to Labor in Politics in Queensland", *International Socialist Review*, III, no. 3 (September 1902): 161–164.
46. Kunze, "Socialism in Australia", 162.
47. Kunze, "Socialism in Australia", 164.
48. Farrell, *International Socialism and Australian Labour*, 10.
49. 'Inspector D.A. Mackiehen to Investigation Branch, Attorney-General's Department, March 27, 1922', NAA, Canberra, A402/W248 German Revolutionaries allied to Communists (1922–1924).
50. "The Vanguard Round Table", *The Worker*, 20 October 1900.
51. On 6 August 1900, with a very brief mention of the funeral on 14 August.
52. Both on 8 August, 1900.
53. *Vorwärts*, no.255, 1 November 1900, under the rubric "Partei-Nachrichten".
54. T. L. J., "Social-Democratic Vanguard". *The Worker*, October 13, 1900. The chief editor of *Het Volk* was actually the Dutch socialist leader Pieter Jelles Troelstra but there was a Dutch socialist writer called J. A. Verhoef who may also have worked on *Het Volk*.
55. Eznuk, "The German Elections", *The Worker*, June 27, 1903.
56. "Die Arbeiterpolitik in Australien", *Vorwärts*, no.125, May 31, 1904. Another article from Australia appeared a few months later, but this one was credited to G. Hutchinson, "Die australische Arbeiter-Regierung", *Vorwärts*, no.174, July 27, 1904.
57. "Vermischtes. Aus Australien", *Vorwärts*, no.179, August 2, 1908.
58. Landesarchiv Berlin, A. Pr. Br. Rep 30 Berlin C, Polizei-Präsidium, Nr.15642. Akten der Abteilung des Kgl. Polizei-Präsidiums zu Berlin, betreffend Australien, 1912–1914, Bl.8–10. See Hönicke's article, "Brief aus Australien", *Der freie Arbeiter*, no.24, June 13, 1914, clipping in Akten der Abteilung des Kgl. Polizei-Präsidiums zu Berlin, Bl.8.

CHAPTER 10

"Virtually a Victory": *The Australian Woman's Sphere* and the Mainstream Press During Vida Goldstein's 1903 Federal Candidature

Natasha Walker and Catherine Dewhirst

On 16 December 1903, non-Indigenous British subjects lined up at polling booths across Australia to vote in the first Federal election with white women sharing equal franchise.[1] Signifying a landmark political event in Australia's history since Federation in 1901, the day was doubly momentous for women who were entitled to cast their votes as well as stand for election. Although the colony of South Australia had already legislated women's equal rights on both grounds in 1894, female candidates could be listed on the Federal polling tickets in all states, which occurred for the first time in Victoria and New South Wales, representing the "New Woman".[2] House of Representatives candidate Selina Anderson polled 17.74 per cent for Dalley (an inner-Sydney suburb of the time) and Senate

N. Walker • C. Dewhirst (✉)
University of Southern Queensland, Toowoomba, QLD, Australia
e-mail: natasha.walker@usq.edu.au; catherine.dewhirst@usq.edu.au

© The Author(s), under exclusive license to Springer Nature
Switzerland AG 2021
C. Dewhirst, R. Scully (eds.), *Voices of Challenge in Australia's Migrant and Minority Press*, Palgrave Studies in the History of the Media, https://doi.org/10.1007/978-3-030-67330-7_10

candidates Ellen (Nellie) Martel and Mary Ann Moore Bentley, also from New South Wales, polled 18,502 and 18,942, respectively.[3] It was, however, Vida Goldstein's (1869–1949) results that dwarfed those of her fellow suffragists. She had initially been reluctant to stand for election, but in campaigning for the Senate in Victoria she polled 51,497 votes, just over half the votes of the winning candidate.[4] As she commented in her post-election analysis: "The successful candidates were either ex-Ministers of the Crown or had the support of the press or wealthy organisations behind them".[5] In her brief conciliatory speech of 7 January 1904—a letter read out in the Oxford Chambers of Bourke Street, Melbourne, after the votes were announced, and later printed in *The Australian Woman's Sphere* to inform women and men across the nation—she wrote:

> I very much regret that I am unable to be present at the declaration of the poll to day. May I therefore ask you to express my gratitude to the 51,497 electors of Victoria who supported my candidature—the first attempt of a woman in British dominions to enter Parliament. I stood as the representative of the best interest in the nation—the home. I stood as a protest against press domination and the creation of the vicious system of machine politics. I had the prejudices of ages to fight, and yet I secured more than half the votes of the candidate heading the poll. The result is virtually a victory, and I thank my supporters most cordially.[6]

Goldstein's candidature in 1903 had never been solely about winning. Rather, she had clearly interpreted her role from the much broader challenge of changing perceptions about women in politics. To focus on representing women's interests in Federal Parliament she stood as an Independent. This enabled her to protect her social and domestic policies for women from erosion and to safeguard their concerns against party politics, while also aiming to ensure that women recognised and embraced their democratic responsibilities. Although it meant that she was thus without the backing of a major political party, she also lacked the support of the many women's organisations, which had originally rallied for woman suffrage.[7] This reluctance from members within and official decisions by these organisations to back her candidature, particularly in Victoria, was caused by the belief that to stand for the Federal Senate before the state vote had been achieved would jeopardise any chances of the law coming to pass.[8] However, one major advantage that Goldstein had was her position in the monthly newspaper, *The Australian Woman's*

Sphere (1900–1905). As its founding director and chief editor, she was not only able to take advantage of the print medium to disseminate news of her campaign, but also to dispel misconceptions at a public level about what she stood for, particularly in light of the provocative and misleading publicity from the dominant periodical press. *The Australian Woman's Sphere* effectively supported the dual aims of Goldstein's political candidature and changing perceptions about women in politics.

Australian women represented approximately 45 per cent of a population of 3,774,072 in 1901.[9] Yet, as funding and the figures on subscription rates suggest, Goldstein's newspaper catered to a minute sector within Australian society; those interested in radical political change through gender equality. Officially launched in September 1900 with the aid of an anonymous benefactor and kept afloat with the assistance from Henry Hyde Champion (Goldstein's brother-in-law), *The Australian Woman's Sphere* relied on income from advertisers, continued subscriptions and additional donations until 1905, when it folded.[10] It published a dedicated "Received Subscriptions" column each month, with the exception of four months, from September 1900 until September 1902 only, which totalled 1069 subscriptions—297 (1900); 394 (1901); and 378 (1902)—with an additional 524 people and organisations recorded as providing donations between 1900 and 1903.[11] Presumably many would have been repeat subscriptions, but the majority came from Victoria and included smaller numbers from all of the other states, as well as a handful from the United Kingdom and New Zealand. There was also an increase in international subscriptions from April 1902 during Goldstein's tour of the United States of America. The breadth of the newspaper's circulation remained small as well, but it was publicly visible, selling through newsagents and bookstalls, post offices, women's organisations and book arcades. *The Australian Woman's Sphere* became the political organ of the Women's Federal Political Association (WPA). This was a non-party organisation, founded by Goldstein on 10 June 1903 and dedicated to educating women on their new political responsibilities and to pushing political reform for the protection of women and children, until its dissolution in 1919.

That Goldstein was one of the most significant women attempting to enter a national political arena dominated by men as a representative of women's concerns for the first time in the history of Australia, the British Empire and the world is largely known today.[12] Yet, her point that she stood partly to oppose "press domination" suggests she was fighting another battle—one against the mainstream press. In the early 1900s, two of the most established Victorian newspapers dominated political and social debates, and attempted to sabotage her candidature: *The Age* (1854–), under proprietor and chief editor David Syme (1827–1908), and *The Argus* (1846–1957), under British proprietors, Lauchlan Mackinnon, Godfrey Spowers and Edward Wilson, who appointed David Watterston (1845–1941) as editor in 1903.

Although historians have acknowledged the significance of Goldstein's campaign for Australian feminist history, as well as the role of both feminist and general presses in transmitting information throughout the campaign,[13] the relationship between *The Australian Woman's Sphere* and *The Age* and *The Argus* has received only a smattering of attention. Audrey Oldfield explains the importance of the political endorsements of *The Age* and *The Argus* during the 1903 elections: while initially reporting well enough on Goldstein's movements, with a limited four seats only possible in the Victorian Senate and the threat an Independent posed to their conservative or worker-oriented favourites, the mainstream press became increasingly negative.[14] Indeed, Oldfield highlights the "Labour, not Sex" slogan having been used against Goldstein specifically by such newspapers in order to direct their readership to their own preferred candidates. Similarly, Farley Kelly notes how *The Age* was at first welcoming, then turned to patronising statements, while *The Argus* happily printed dissenting women's voices about the vote.[15] Likewise, Jeanette Bomford mentions the chauvinistic and patronising reactions of a few mainstream and popular newspapers—*Punch*, *The Argus*, *Truth* and *The Bulletin*—to the news that Goldstein was standing for election, and later *The Age* on her political programme.[16] In the earliest works on Goldstein's campaign, Norman MacKenzie and Jenni Mulraney use newspaper sources specifically to outline the developments, highlighting the demeaning and patronising comments from the press, including those within *The Age*, *The Argus* and *Punch*, and—of note—the more supportive coverage from the provincial press.[17] Mulraney also illustrates the tactics of the same mainstream and popular newspapers to smear her candidature, including the descent of some papers to stereotyping her appearance, and suggests how Goldstein's decision to stand for Parliament was interpreted as "revolutionary" in a confronting way.[18] However, MacKenzie mentions Goldstein's assertion that the "opposition of the press" contributed to the failure of her candidature.[19] He argues instead that the newspapers were mostly "favourable". "Even those papers which opposed Miss Goldstein's candidature gave her a good deal of space and normally reported on her fairly", with the only concession being "the increasingly sharp opposition of the *Age* [which] was a severe handicap".[20]

MacKenzie's suggestion that any press is good press speaks to the longer trajectory of women's historical presence in the public sphere. Women were neither new to journalism, nor to establishing newspapers at this time. This history dates back to the seventeenth century with the first daily newspaper (at least known by 1889) appearing in London in 1702 and launched by Elizabeth Mallet for "spar[ing] the public at least half the impertinences which the ordinary papers contain".[21] Feminist historians have today uncovered a consistent interaction with the general periodical press during the suffrage era. From the 1850s, the coverage of the suffrage movement by mainstream newspapers evolved into dedicated women's pages.[22] The theme was one of domesticity through articles and advertising, which exploited the rising consumerism and commodification of female readers.[23] Yet British suffragists and suffragettes deliberately exploited new technological advances in the printing press, with an increased use of photography, to stage public protests for their propaganda efforts.[24] In fact, John Mercer points out that the development of visual media within the mainstream press "evolved alongside the development of the militant suffragette campaign".[25] Jane Chapman observes that when the suffrage movement was covered in the mainstream press, it had a palpable impact on "laws, policies, and in symbolic representations of women as subjects".[26] Katherine Kelly notes that these feminists used the spectacle of public protest to increase the visibility of their cause and, although by itself this did not result in political change, it integrated the image of "marching women as citizens of the nation".[27] Feminists therefore took advantage of the wider periodical press to promote awareness of their cause and to insert themselves into the changing social and political landscape of the early twentieth-century public gaze.

Sarah Pedersen indicates that the Scottish mainstream press responded to the suffrage movement with vigorous public debate representing all sides of the struggle, particularly within correspondence pages, as reflections of the individual concerns of the women who wrote them.[28] Such columns could be influential factors within the wider movement, seen in Almoth Wright's "letter to the editor" published in *The Times*. He declared women to be mentally unfit for the vote on the same day the Conciliation Bill (1912) was being debated, and his contribution to *The Times* was referenced throughout the debate, with the result that the Bill was once again defeated.[29] Mainstream press coverage of the suffrage movement was often dependent on the bias of the editors and reporters, as Elizabeth Burt notes.[30] She argues that regardless of their view on suffrage, editors who had strong opinions on the movement published more articles covering it than editors who did not.[31] This history disrupts Jürgen Habermas' public-private sphere model, contested as gender-blind by a number of feminist scholars, through the neglected recognition of a "gender subtext" within the roles of worker, consumer and citizen, assumed to be reserved for men.[32] The gender subtext identifies political, economic and sexist *subtexts*, which second-wave feminists confronted en masse from the 1960s, but challenged much earlier by Goldstein.

It is against this backdrop that a similar interplay was occurring between *The Australian Woman's Sphere*, *The Age* and *The Argus* over the "woman question" during the Federal election of 1903. This chapter explores the pressures Goldstein faced in representing women in a political and social sphere dominated by men. Although *The Age* and *The Argus* were, on limited occasions, impartial, they questioned Goldstein's eligibility and parodied the divisions within and between women's suffrage organisations, as well as her political policies, and ignored her efforts to educate women on their rights and how to prepare for election day. By focusing on the editorials, articles and letters to the editor through the lens of a gender subtext within the three newspapers, and other sources by Goldstein, the separate political interests and wider social influence of the press reveal the initial reactions to Goldstein's candidature, the misrepresentation and controversies surrounding her campaign, and what she called the "political machine". Exploring the commentary between these three newspapers over the months leading up to the federal election on 16 December 1903, and the months thereafter, identifies the media campaign against her and reveals her unyielding retaliation as an outspoken feminist and aspiring female politician against a series of intimidating tactics. We argue that an analysis of the debates amplifies the complex relationship of how the *virtual victory* emerges from the sudden shared space of the first Federal election with equal suffrage, and the often-overlooked exchange between minority and mainstream newspapers. In taking up the challenge to represent women's concerns for the duration of her candidature, Goldstein stepped down from the editorship of *The Australian Woman's Sphere* and local suffragist Mary Malcolm, who was affiliated with the Women's Progressive League, Carlton, stepped in.

THE FEDERAL WOMAN CANDIDATE

The Federal election of 1903 was preceded by the Federal Electoral and Franchise Bill of 1902, deciding who to include in and exclude from the Commonwealth franchise. Despite opposition from conservative forces, the Bill was passed and ensured that white women could vote for the first time. Their decades-long struggle of suffrage activism for equal enfranchisement had finally been achieved, on the Federal level at least. Western Australia (1899), New South Wales (1902), Tasmania (1903), Queensland (1905) and Victoria (1908) passed legislation for the vote only and, with the exception of South Australia (1894), legislation for women to stand for state parliament took considerably longer in all states.[33] At the crucial point of the legislation of women's Federal franchise being announced, Goldstein was in Washington, DC, in order to represent Australia at the International Woman's Suffrage Alliance Conference.[34] The connections she made at the conference connected Australia to the international women's suffrage movement, and Goldstein's observations of the United States' political system influenced her decision to form the WPA as an organisation independent of political allegiances.[35] The American political system left much to be desired in Goldstein's opinion: "The people of England under a monarchical form of government enjoy more real political freedom than do the people of the great American Republic."[36] This was due to the "political machine", she wrote, which caused the American people to be "bound hand and foot, forced, if they vote at all, to vote according to the dictation of the party bosses".[37] Goldstein's position on the "political machine" left her vulnerable to the organised attacks of the Australian Conservative and Labor parties, supported by *The Age* and *The Argus*.[38]

David Syme brought strong business skills in transforming *The Age* from a family-run colonial-city newspaper to a press empire of international esteem, and he was politically aligned with the conservative Protectionist Party.[39] Editor for *The Argus*, David Watterston, no doubt continued the trend of his predecessors, Frederick Haddon and Howard Willoughby, under his penmanship when he was appointed as editor in the year of the election: the conservative Free Trade Party.[40] David Dunstan suggests that *The Age* became "a doctrinaire instrument and aspired to become a maker and breaker of ministries" under Syme's control, whereas *The Argus*, "not a provocative political engine of the same sort", was potentially reactionary, taking "more extreme stances than it might otherwise have adopted".[41] Both would have been preoccupied with competing against each other for readership and political influence during the election campaign, with very little concern for the "woman question", the new "experiment" of women's participation in Federal politics and the minor status of *The Australian Woman's Sphere* until the likes of Goldstein increased the stakes by delivering a not inconsequential campaign. *The Australian Woman's Sphere* provided an essential defence against their attacks and a means for making their tactics transparent. As Goldstein summed up after the election:

> All through the campaign it was amusing to see how persistently the rabid anti-suffragists wooed the political affections of the women. Before the suffrage was granted to the women these gentlemen said that women could not fail to be degraded by taking part in politics. Now they talk grandiloquently about the refining, elevating influence of women in the political arena, and urge them to perform the sacred duty of voting—"for us".[42]

The primary purpose of *The Australian Woman's Sphere* was to connect the various women's organisations across Australia and internationally, creating a network to fight for women's rights across the world. Most subscriptions, though small, came from Australia, with the largest monthly total of 119 for September 1902: 64 from Victoria; 21 from Queensland; 9 from New South Wales; 4 from South Australia; 1 each from Western Australia and Tasmania; and 17 from the United States and 2 from New Zealand.[43] Although there were a few male subscribers, the newspaper was mostly circulated amongst women, with *The Australian Woman's Sphere* promoting the sharing of the newspaper amongst friends in order to spread the message of political equality and the social support of women and children.[44] Yet, as noted above, the newspaper remained restricted to a comparatively small readership, unable to compete with the circulation of the daily press. It also faced greater scrutiny from opponents of female suffrage, and from those who felt threatened by the encroachment of women into the public sphere of politics, dominated by men, and the newspaper business, dominated by male editors.[45]

During one of the WPA's meetings, in August 1903, it was unanimously proposed that Goldstein stand as a candidate for the Federal Senate.[46] She agreed only on the condition that this was the official position of the organisation, and within four days, on 14 August 1903, the Association voted 29 to 8 in favour of her candidature.[47] The small number of members who held back on endorsing Goldstein did so because they did not wish for a woman candidate so soon after the national franchise and before state suffrage had been won in Victoria.[48] To prevent the fracturing of the organisation, it was decided that funds raised by the Association would go towards educating women on their political responsibilities—one of the Association's main goals—and not Goldstein's candidature.[49] This lack of financial support and her late start to the campaign left Goldstein at a disadvantage amongst her opponents. Despite her stepping down as editor during the electoral campaign, her role as a prominent feminist and the newspaper's focus on the woman vote nevertheless meant considerable coverage within its pages, even if it did not aid in courting financial support. As president of the WPA, Goldstein and the members had established very clear goals regarding the education of women for the Federal election, including "the circulation of leaflets on political subjects, the delivering of educative and organising lectures in every important centre ... and the subsequent forming of local branches to carry on its work in every district".[50]

Individual responses to Goldstein's candidature were published in *The Australian Woman's Sphere*, detailing the divided support of women's organisations across individual, state, national and international levels. Each month the newspaper published a segment on the campaign, "Miss Goldstein's Candidature: Various Views", in order to share responses sent into their offices as well as extracts of the coverage from other newspapers, thus assembling and disseminating a significant account of the debates by readers and organisations. Letters of support from prominent Australian feminists included Rose Scott and Henrietta Augusta Johnson, from New South Wales and Victoria, respectively.[51] International newspapers, such as the Boston *Woman's Journal* and *The New York Sun*, also reported their interest in Goldstein's candidature, which *The Australian Woman's Sphere* printed, the latter stating: "Miss Goldstein possesses the highest character and ability, and at least will have a great opportunity to conduct a splendid campaign of education towards higher ideals in public life."[52] Back in Australia, *The Queensland Worker* remarked on the unstable support of women's organisations and questioned the vocal opposition of the Victorian Women's Franchise League to woman candidates: "Are the Victorian women ashamed of their sex or their Senate?"[53]

The response of women's organisations to Goldstein's candidature was not unanimously supportive, particularly in Victoria. Even the Women's Christian Temperance Union (WCTU), as one of the largest women's organisations with branches across the world,[54] was divided. The Victorian executive of the WCTU declared its opposition to woman candidates for state election, arguing that it would "prejudice the interest of the women's cause at the present juncture",[55] again the belief that this would jeopardise the battle for the state franchise. However, the national executive of the WCTU disagreed, arguing in its national organ, *Our Federation*: "women have never won any improvement in the condition of their sex by sitting down to wait." Various letters of support from other WCTU branches were published in *The Australian Woman's Sphere*—from Elizabeth Nicholls, ex-president of the WCTU's National executive, Miss Lodge from the Hobart branch and Mrs Trundle from the Brisbane branch— indicating wider agreement.[56] Overseas branches of the WCTU also sent in their support for Goldstein. In New Zealand, for example, Miss L. M. Smith, editor of *The White Ribbon*, from the New Zealand branch, encouraged her: "I have taken the liberty of publishing your portrait in our little paper. I need scarcely say that I view your candidature with much interest."[57] In addition, she forwarded a copy of their current issue, which included comments disagreeing with the actions of the Victorian executive of the WCTU. Margaret McLean of the Victorian branch executive maintained its position against supporting woman candidates, arguing that the decision was made with the support of the constituents. Mary Malcolm, as acting editor of *The Australian Woman's Sphere*, printed her letter in full along with the newspaper's response, supporting the good work done by the WCTU: "But as to that particular resolution, we think the executive went out of its way to commit a blunder in making a declaration which is in direct opposition to one of their own principles—'no sex in citizenship'."[58]

In contrast, what emerges from a number of issues of *The Age* and *The Argus* leading up to the Federal election is a strong sense of social anxiety around the practical reality of woman entering politics. *The Australian Woman's Sphere* regarded reports of Goldstein's candidature from within the mainstream press as positive exposure of the woman's cause: "The Conservative 'Argus', that has never before treated the subject but with sneer and ridicule, came out at once with a serious leader on the subject. The 'Age', too, has given prominence to the matter, and the country press has also given it extensive notice."[59] At the beginning of the campaign in August 1903, *The Argus* published a letter to the editor which recognised the significance of a woman candidate and the unfairness of the response that Goldstein's candidature had received, an excerpt of which later appeared in *The Australian Woman's Sphere*: "'Why, you are forgetting that you are a woman. You may vote for men, but surely you do not desire to assert an equality with them in the political sphere. It is really most impertinent of you to do so.' I confess this seems to me, as a disinterested onlooker, to be unfair to women."[60] Significantly, an editorial from *The Age* offered Goldstein some advice, quoted within *The Australian Woman's Sphere*: "That Miss Goldstein is a protectionist on principle and that she will always vote straight with the [protectionist] party goes without saying ... she may be expected to have very strong feelings, and to express them in the strongest language that Parliamentary etiquette will sanction."[61] However, *The Australian Woman's Sphere* did not print the more unflattering and biased pieces from this article, such as: "Woman is an emotional being"; and "If Miss Goldstein succeeds in forcing her way into Parliament in spite of the lawyers we do not see what would remain to be achieved by woman to make her transformation complete".[62] Doing so would have cast doubt on the lawfulness of Goldstein's candidature to the newspaper's readership and, in fact, misinforming potential voters of her eligibility. Analysis of the coverage within the mainstream press reveals how the immediate negative response to Goldstein's candidature was quickly followed by a more explicit misinformation campaign.

Misrepresentation: Eligibility and the "Fiscal Question"

From the start of Goldstein's campaign, *The Age* and *The Argus* targeted her political eligibility and social and domestic policies, distorting her stance on fiscal responsibility, free trade and protectionism. In fact, both newspapers pounced on the question of her eligibility to qualify for election. This campaign was quickly apparent within *The Age* and obvious enough that London's *The Reformer* remarked on it:

> The British public will watch with keen interest the candidature of Miss Vida Goldstein for a seat in the Federal Parliament of Australasia. The Melbourne "Age" devotes a long header to the situation, which it tries to treat lightly and as without serious import; at the same time, however, we note an undercurrent of editorial alarm at the prospect which Miss Goldstein's candidature crops up.[63]

Even before Goldstein's candidature had been announced, *The Argus* ran an article questioning women's eligibility in the Federal election and, with

The Age, directed this attention to her after she had been nominated.[64] *The Australian Woman's Sphere* alleged that the political parties had spread rumours and "false reports" regarding her qualifying to stand for the Senate.[65] In an article explicitly titled, "Women Candidates for Parliament: Are they eligible?", *The Argus* questioned the Minister for Home Affair Sir William Lyne, who had said: "I am certain that women can become members of the Senate if they can command a sufficient number of votes".[66] And, *The Argus* went further to infer that Lyne had misinterpreted the law:

> Sir William Lyne, however, has made the mistake of applying the Federal Acts Interpretation Act to the constitution. ... Legal members of the Federal Parliament state there is room for much argument as to whether women are eligible to become federal legislators, and the constitutional and legal issues involved are so subtle and delicate that they will not give a final opinion without looking up the whole question.

This, of course, was not true, but the more serious criticism of both newspapers can be discerned from articles reporting on Goldstein's Town Hall meetings in Prahran in their 14 November issues, where they turned attention to the fiscal question and where a gender subtext aligns with discrediting her as a serious politician.

There are two key, yet subtle, differences in the articles printed by *The Age* and *The Argus*. Firstly, Goldstein charged a fee for the general public to attend all of her meetings because the venues needed to be hired. Someone from the audience at Prahran must have questioned this. Both newspapers then attempted to suggest she had elevated herself to the standard of one of her more experienced male competitors. From *The Age*: "Miss Goldstein, who was received with loud applause, prefaced her address by an explanation that she had to charge 'a silver coin' for admittance because she was only a 'poor woman who has to work hard for her living'. Besides, did not Mr G. H. Reid do much the same thing?"[67] *The Argus*, noting the hall to be very crowded, phrases it slightly differently: "It was all very well, she said, for a great luminary like Mr G. H. Reid to charge for admission. Nothing was said about that. But when a lesser fight, like herself, ventured to do the same it was received with severe comment."[68] Secondly, they continued with the theme of her fitness for election, reporting on one of Goldstein's more significant political aims about the failure of the Legislative Council of Victoria to pass the Reform Bill for women's enfranchisement, but both portrayed her position as a radical, with *The Age* stating: "Miss Goldstein blamed the Legislative Council for blocking the vote of the women as far as the State Parliament was concerned, and later on she frankly admitted she thought State Parliaments were now totally unnecessary, and ought to be abolished."[69] This kind of reportage deflected the goal of her Town Hall meeting. According to *The Argus*, Goldstein had remarked: "The Legislative Council had grossly abused the power it was supposed to wield when it made itself a House of direct veto. The people should see that such a state of things either ended or mended."[70] Then, in referring to the closing of the meeting, *The Age* represented Goldstein as someone who did not understand politics and suggested that she was incompetent in answering questions:

> At the close of the meeting Miss Goldstein answered a number of questions, but candidly admitted that some of them touched upon what she termed 'obscure political problems', were rather puzzling, and again reminded her audience that she intended specially to devote herself to the elucidation of social and domestic problems.[71]

The Argus made a similar allusion:

> Miss Goldstein then answered a number of questions, including one from a lady in the scullery, and the replies were loudly applauded. The candidate confessed to one elector, who endeavoured to cross-examine her, that she had not studied the justice of certain duties, and refused to manufacture answers to please her audience. The elector thereupon presented her with a copy of the tariff.[72]

Such coverage could be extremely damaging and might only have been counteracted by Goldstein continuing to meet with the public, but it suggested that her campaign's emphasis on social and domestic policies relative to women, children and the family was insignificant when compared with the economic issues of protectionism and free trade. Where we may glean her response to such questions can be clarified from one of her articles at the start of her campaign, stating that "[i]t is suicidal to divorce the home and the State":

> I have always maintained that wherever there are women's and children's interests to be considered, women should be there to consider them. [...] When any measure dealing with social and domestic affairs is under consideration, it is pathetic—when it is not amusing—to see men foundering

along, where women, from their personal experience and intimate knowledge of what touches their lives at a hundred points, could steer a straight course. [...] As introduced in the House of Representatives, the discrepancies in the salaries to be paid to men and women for doing exactly the same work ... were all in favour of the men! In order to get the principle of equal pay for equal work embodied in the Bill ... some of us were compelled to spend days lobbying members ... showing them the many injustices in the Bill, from the woman's point of view.[73]

Goldstein was not the only Australian feminist to fall victim to the political machinations of these newspapers' own party politics through selective paraphrasing from events, which questioned women's capacity to deal with economic policies. At an event organised by the WPA with 200 attendees and presided over by Sir William Lyne, where Rose Scott addressed the crowd, *The Argus* noted some comments that Scott made regarding free-trade and the franchise: "She believed in free trade because she regarded it as the cause of freedom. (Applause.) But it had been left to protectionists to enfranchise women, and the vote was of more importance than the fiscal question. It was better for women to have the active support of a protectionist like Sir William Lyne than to support some other man, because he happened to be a consistent champion of free trade."[74] *The Age* phrased it differently: "Women wanted to have a vote because they wanted to have a voice in the national housekeeping, but representation was of infinitely more importance than the mere vote. Franchise meant freedom, and not to have the franchise meant not to be free."[75]

Closer to the election date, *The Australian Woman's Sphere* published Goldstein's campaign manifesto under its regular column, "Opinions of Federal Candidates on Federal Politics", which clarified her position on fiscal responsibility, protectionism and free trade: "I am a protectionist. I believe in free trade absolutely—as a theory. As a working principle I believe it to be impracticable in a young country, especially when we have the majority of the world's workshops forging ahead with high protectionist tariffs."[76] In the month before the election, *The Age* ignored her stance and returned to the report on the Prahran Town Hall meeting of 14 November to repeat "Too much, she thought, was made of the fiscal question. Free-trade was not free, and protection did not protect; still her sympathies were with the protectionists",[77] implying that she had no economic policy. Only a few days after this article *The Age* further attacked

Goldstein's patriotism and loyalty to the Crown, accusing her of "not [being] in favour of paying immense subsidies to England to protect us".[78]

There were further daily articles in November on Goldstein's "fiscal question". *The Age* had been contacted by her committee in order to clarify her position and the newspaper wrote: "The member of the committee says Miss Goldstein 'is quite outspoken in her advocacy of protection'". But the article follows up with its original interpretation of Goldstein's words: "Free-trade was not free, and protection did not protect. Too much was made of the fiscal question."[79] Goldstein responded to *The Age* the next day to clarify her position which again was reinterpreted in a polemical manner:

Miss Vida Goldstein writes under date 23rd November from Korumburra, protesting against being classed as an "opportunist" on the fiscal issue. Speaking at Prahran on the 14th inst. Miss Goldstein had not trimmed her sails so neatly, for she was then reported as saying, "Too much was made of the fiscal question". Too much, forsooth, and this from a protectionist! The lady doth protest too much. We are quite prepared, however, to concede Miss Goldstein the privilege of her sex—of changing her mind; and if her latest utterance is that she is a protectionist, we hope she will hold to her fiscal faith consistently, intelligently, and not talk about fiscal unbeliefs, and "that free-trade was not free, and protection did not protect".[80]

The Age then doubled down on its representation of Goldstein's views, reducing her to an opportunist:

[Goldstein] resents being classed as an "opportunist", but her remarks at Maryborough recently are sufficient to show what her fiscal belief then was. She then said, "Free-trade was to her mind the ideal trade, and protection was a necessary evil in a young country. She did not take a keen interest in the fiscal question for this reason." After an utterance of this nature Miss Goldstein can scarcely wonder that she has been classed as an "opportunist".[81]

The Australian Woman's Sphere refuted these claims and called *The Age* out for its misrepresentation, but, as a monthly newspaper, its reach was significantly shorter than the arm of a national daily newspaper. They also connected such opposition to *The Age*'s ticket for the election: "It is evident that the 'Age' is seriously afraid that Miss Goldstein will attract a large number of votes away from its own selected four for the Senate. Nothing could be more unfair than the way in which it has tried to discredit Miss Goldstein by distorting and actually misrepresenting her views as to protection."[82] *The Argus* did not follow suit. It recognised Goldstein's position on free-trade and protectionism: "She stood as a thorough-going democrat and protectionist, though the great social problems were of more importance than the fiscal issue. She was against a hush capital, and favoured a system of sound finance, which was badly needed in Australia."[83] For Goldstein and *The Australian Woman's Sphere* this was what they meant by the "party machine" politics.

The "Political Machine" and the "Ticket"

While *The Age* and *The Argus* fought against Goldstein's candidature through selective and deliberately misconstrued reportage and did not report honestly on her policies, *The Australian Woman's Sphere* hit back with attacks on their preferential voting system: the "ticket" problem. It began by guiding its readers not to support existing political parties as they were "controlled and directed by men" and would "simply help per-petuating the old order of things".[84] The newspaper argued that the wom-an's vote should be based on social and moral questions, more than political ones, and that women "should not be misled by the various organisations touting for certain 'tickets', nor by the partisan lists of the daily press. Let them exercise their own judgement and boldly follow it".[85] In an article, "The Tyranny of the Ticket", published after the election, *The Australian Woman's Sphere* argued that the insidious nature of the "ticket" was an American invention:

> The promoters of great companies, the founders of 'trusts', all who were anxious to build up gigantic fortunes by the unscrupulous exploitation of their fellow countrymen, soon recognised the power that lay in the 'ticket' system. They saw that, if they could capture the caucuses of the parties, they would have the whole country in their toils, whenever their own party was successful. They had no desire to enter the State Legislature or Congress themselves, but they planned that the men who were put on the 'tickets' should be their delegates, their creatures, who would do what they were told, and they planned successfully. Millions of dollars are subscribed to the party funds, newspapers are bought, bribes are scattered with lavish hands, for these men know that they will get it all back, with compound interest, when they can manipulate the Legislature at their will.[86]

The "political machine" was opposed within the pages of the minority presses, with one such newspaper, the *Avoca Free Press* commenting: "Is not Miss Vida Goldstein vastly superior to many of the old women masquerading in male attire in the Legislative Council, and the brainless fossils attempted to be thrust down the public throat by the 'Age' and the 'Argus'?"[87]

Mirroring the American invention, *The Age* and *The Argus* both published "tickets" within the columns of their papers in the lead up to both the Senate and House of Representatives elections to advise their readership on who to vote for. *The Age* "ticket" supported the protectionist candidates—the "Liberal Four"—for the Federal Senate and included a mock election ticket of all candidates, with Robert W. Best, J. L. Dow, William McCulloch and James Styles as those to select.[88] *The Argus* "ticket" for the Federal Senate supported the free-trade "Victorian Four", providing another sample for Frederick Thomas Derham, John McIntyre, Edmund Edmonds Smith and John Montgomery Templeton.[89] As *The Australian Woman's Sphere* explained to its readers, *The Age*'s selections were based on personal friendships: "Now 'The Age' includes on its recommended list Mr Dow and Mr Wm. McCulloch. The former is one of the staff of the 'Age', and the latter is a personal friend of Mr. Syme's. ... The influence of a great newspaper may be a power for good, but it may also be, and sometimes is, a power for evil. We advise women voters to exercise their own judgement, and certainly not to be influenced by so manifestly unfair a papers as the 'Age' has proved itself to be."[90] The newspaper also mentioned how influential but unpredictable this system had proven to be in the past, using the example of Senator Fraser: "Senator Fraser was returned at the head of the poll at the last election for the Senate. This was undoubtedly due to the fact that he was nominated on the tickets of both of our daily contemporaries. That he was on the 'Argus' ticket occasioned no surprise, for he is, and always has been, as conservative as the 'Argus' itself. That he also appeared on the 'Age' list of candidates recommended to the electors did occasion surprise, for the 'Age' is supposed to be the organ of advanced Liberalism."[91] After the 1903 election, *The Australian Woman's Sphere* also explained that only two of *The Age*'s preferences were elected in the Senate election of 1903, and "they were certain of a very large vote whether the 'Age' has supported them or not", and that not one of *The Argus*' selections was elected.[92] *The Australian Woman's Sphere* concluded—somewhat optimistically—that "When the press descends to support the 'ticket' system, and gives itself over to 'machine' politics, its influence on the voters sooner or later wanes and loses all power".[93]

In contrast with the "ticket" system, *The Australian Woman's Sphere* published advice for educating women on what to expect on the day, noting tips for voting, starting with checking whether they were on the electoral roll and giving the address to write to if needed. It described how to cast the vote on polling day:

> Go to the polling booth of your district, and give your name to the returning officer; he will supply you with a ballot paper on which will be printed a list of candidates in alphabetical order. ... In the Senate election you must place crosses against the names of four candidates, and *four only*, or your vote will be invalid.[94]

The newspaper also advertised a "Mock Election", run by the Women's Federal Political Association, to offer practical experience for women on how the day would unfold and women's new place in the event.[95] The "Opinions of Federal Candidates on Federal Politics" column also enabled candidates to share their political views as they pertained to women, a column that was "open to all shades of opinion".[96] By ensuring that women knew how to use their votes—and in one case assuring their Queensland readers that they could vote—*The Australian Woman's Sphere* supported women's engagement with their new political citizenship responsibilities, providing practical advice and highlighting which candidates supported woman's issues.[97] Goldstein's campaign had not been focused on personal power but on women's rights and education. As she later explained: "Voting means responsibility, responsibility means power, and power always commands respect."[98]

The Age and *The Argus* were not blind to *The Australian Woman's Sphere*'s criticism of their "tickets", and argued that Goldstein's Women's Political Association had a "ticket" of its own. In 1904, the organisation established its objection to "ticket"-voting within the charter of the organisation and also created Article 8, "a list of approved candidates for recommendations to the electors".[99] *The Age* gave an account of the meeting: "Miss Goldstein, the president, laid emphasis on the statement that a 'recommendation' was not a 'ticket', and the meeting, meekly accepting her dictum unanimously carried the clause."[100] Goldstein refuted their implication of hypocrisy by writing to the editor:

You imply that "a list of approved candidates" is the same thing as a "ticket". It can easily be seen that the two are entirely dissimilar, since a "ticket" nominates exactly the number of candidates to be elected, thus preventing any choice on the part of the electors, while our list will contain the names of all the candidates, however many, who are in sympathy with the vital points of our programme, and will leave the electors free to exercise their own judgement in deciding for whom they will vote.[101]

That *The Age* provided space for Goldstein to defend herself and her organisation, as it had done during the senate campaign, was probably due to a mellowing in the post-election phase and the fact that two of the "Liberal four" had won seats. *The Age* also recognised women's responses on election day in comparison to men: "the women of Melbourne seemed to exercise their privileges with good sense and intelligence, and to take a far keener interest in the polling than the thousands of male electors who stood gazing at and cheering the scores of the cricket match."[102] As Goldstein commented on *The Argus'* post-election criticism: "*The Argus* maintained that, having had all the advantages of being 'a pioneer', my failure to secure a bigger vote does not augur well for the future of lady candidates."[103] This was curious, according to Goldstein, because "a pioneer of a movement labours under overwhelming disadvantages, and I was no exception to the rule. I had against me the combined power of the morning and labour papers, deliberate misrepresentation by two of them, a considerable lack of the sinews of war, and the prejudice of sex." And, she explained further:

I stood for the sake of a cause, the cause of women and children; I stood as a protest against the dictation of the Press, against the creation of the ticket system of voting, and I am proud to think that over fifty thousand people in Victoria supported me in what seemed at the outset a most unpopular crusade... I had the majority of the people who heard what I had to say with me, in regard to the desirability of women entering Parliament. I think they agreed with me on the other two points also, but I am convinced as to the first. The women especially made no secret of the fact that they had come to my meetings believing women "had no business in Parliament", but having heard the arguments as to why the interests of the home should be as directly represented as are the manufacturing, farming, mining and labouring interests, they had quite changed their minds.

The political fallout of the final results showed less than 50 per cent of the population had voted, with the exception of the states of Queensland

(55 per cent) and Victoria (51 per cent).[104] More women voted in Victoria (46 per cent) than in any other state and Goldstein's efforts are strongly suggested here. Certainly, the campaign she ran through *The Australian Woman's Sphere* and in public meetings allowed her to reach a great number of women and men, with the result of 51,497 votes representing "virtually a victory". Her message that the "home" was central to Australian politics and economics not only challenged beliefs about women's place and role in politics but also exposed gender inequality and discrimination. The interplay between *The Australian Woman's Sphere* and *The Age* and *The Argus* revealed the influence of the mainstream press' "political machine" and strategies to discredit a competitor. This reflected wider anxieties as the changing social and political landscape shifted towards an uncertain future with women entering the debates. That Goldstein continued to lobby government and run for election another three times to change beliefs and legislation about women's capabilities and contributions, is largely a forgotten history. The approach of contesting two of the most respected Melbourne newspapers, and even the conservatism of women at the time, was as significant back then as it remains a challenge today, and as much in the press as in the Federal Parliament. In an era where the voices and experiences of all women, men and children are meant to count—irrespective of racial, ethnic and/or cultural background, sexual orientation and other perceived differences—Goldstein's story is central. As Prime Minister Julia Gillard put it, there is no place for sexism and misogyny, and politicians "should think seriously about the role of women in public life and in Australian society because we are entitled to a better standard than this".[105]

Acknowledgement The authors of this chapter would like to thank the University of Southern Queensland's Office of Research for a Summer Scholarship awarded to Natasha Walker in support of writing the early stages of this chapter.

NOTES

1. The Commonwealth Franchise Act of 1902 passed the right to vote and stand for election to white women at the same time as legislating against Indigenous Australians. Aboriginal women were originally included in the 1895 franchise in the colony of South Australia where Aboriginal men already had voting rights, "by default" from manhood suffrage, from 1856 as they did also in Victoria in 1857 and New South Wales in 1858

(and later in Tasmania in 1896): Julie Evans, Patricia Grimshaw, David Phillips and Shurlee Swain, *Equal Subjects, Unequal Rights: Indigenous People in British Settler Colonies*, 1830s–1910 (Manchester and New York: Manchester University Press, 2003), 69–70.

2. On the respective parliamentary debates and passing of legislation in Adelaide in 1894 and Melbourne in 1903, see Audrey Oldfield, *Woman Suffrage in Australia: A Gift or a Struggle?* (Cambridge: Cambridge University Press, 1992), 38–39, 63–66. The "New Woman" emerged as a term from Britain in Australia and suggested a new generation of women confronting gender relations and the stereotypes of nurturers and carers. It came to represent a "new" woman emerging in the "New Nation". See: Susan Magarey, "History, cultural studies, and another look at first-wave feminism in Australia", *Australian Historical Studies* 27, no. 106 (1996): 96–110 [online]; Clare Wright, *You Daughters of Freedom* (Melbourne: Text Publishing Company, 2018), 133; Marilyn Lake, *Progressive New World: How Settler Colonialism and Transpacific Exchange Shaped American Reform* (Cambridge, MA, & London, 2019), 149.

3. Sue Tracey, "Anderson, Selina Sarah (Senie) (1878–1964)", *Australian Dictionary of Biography* (Canberra: National Centre of Biography, Australian National University, 2005) http://adb.anu.edu.au/biography/anderson-selina-sarah-senie-12773/text23043 (accessed January 25, 2019); Margaret Bettison, "Martel, Ellen Alma (Nellie) (1865–1940)", *Australian Dictionary of Biography* (Canberra: National Centre of Biography, Australian National University, 2005) http://adb.anu.edu.au/biography/martel-ellen-alma-nellie-13081 (accessed January 25, 2019); Margaret Bettison, "Ling, Mary (1865–1943)", *Australian Dictionary of Biography* (Canberra: National Centre of Biography, Australian National University, 2005) http://adb.anu.edu.au/biography/ling-mary-13048 (accessed January 25, 2019).

4. Vida Goldstein, "The Senate Election" *The Australian Woman's Sphere*, January 15, 1904, p. 392. The four candidates who won the seats were William Trenwith (102,384), Robert Best (97,693), Edward Findley (88,614) and James Styles (85,382). Those who polled less than Goldstein were Sir B. O'Loghlen (27,170), G. H. Wise (21,056) and H. R. Williams (19,061).

5. Vida Goldstein, "The Australian Woman in Politics", *Review of Reviews*, January 20, 1904, p. 49.

6. Vida Goldstein, "The Senate Election", *The Australian Woman's Sphere*, January 15, 1904, p. 392. There were earlier cases of women being elected into political roles, but as Norman MacKenzie notes, Goldstein was virtually the first to do so in a "constituted national legislature":

Norman MacKenzie, 'Vida Goldstein: The Australian Suffragette', *Australian Journal of Politics and History* 6, no. 2 (1960): 190.

7. "Women in Parliament", *The Australian Woman's Sphere*, September 10, 1903, p. 347. Women's organisations at this time include the Women's Federal Political Association, the United Council for Women's Suffrage, Women's Christian Temperance Union (Victoria) and the Political Labour Council (Women's branch).

8. Wright, *You Daughters of Freedom*, 141.

9. 'Australian Historical Population Statistics', Historical Population, *Australian Bureau of Statistics*, https://www.abs.gov.au/statistics/people/population/historical-population/latest-release (accessed April 1, 2021).

10. James Keating, *Distant Sisters: Australasian Women and the International Struggle for the Vote, 1880–1914* (Manchester: Manchester University Press, 2020), 142.

11. The four months that did not publish a "Received Subscriptions" column include the January 1901 issue, as well as the January, June and August issues in 1902. Columns and articles published between March 1901 and 10 June 1903 were dedicated to cataloguing those who donated to the "War Chest", which supported the various causes of the newspaper, including financial support of the newspapers, the campaign to spread information on women's voting rights and Goldstein's tour of the United States. For example, see: "The War Chest", *The Australian Woman's Sphere*, March, 1901, p. 55; "International Woman Suffrage Conference", *The Australian Woman's Sphere*, January, 1902, p. 136; "Subscriptions to the American Delegates Fund", *The Australian Woman's Sphere*, February 10, 1902, pp. 144–145; "Subscriptions and Donations to the Funds of the United Council for Women's Suffrage for 1901", *The Australian Woman's Sphere*, March 10, 1902, pp. 152–153; and "Women's Sphere Fund to June 5", *The Australian Woman's Sphere*, June 10, 1903, p. 316. On the selling of the newspaper through third parties, see: *The Australian Woman's Sphere*, November, 1900, p. 24; "Business Notice", *The Australian Woman's Sphere*, May 10, 1902, p. 168.

12. On Goldstein's campaigns in 1903 but also 1910 and 1917 for the Senate, and 1913 and 1914 for the Victorian House of Representatives, see Janette M. Bomford, *That Dangerous and Persuasive Woman* (Carlton, Vic.: Melbourne Press, 1993), chapters 4, 6, 8 and 11.

13. See: Wright, *You Daughters of Freedom*, 134–160; Joy Damousi, "An absence of anything masculine: Vida Goldstein and women's public speech", *Victorian Historical Journal* 79, no. 1 (2008): 253; Marilyn Lake, *Getting Equal: The History of Australian Feminism* (Sydney: Allen and Unwin, 1999).

14. Oldfield, *Woman Suffrage in Australia*, 153–154.

15. Farley Kelly, "Vida Goldstein: Political Woman", in *Double Time: Women in Victoria—150 Years*, ed. Marilyn Lake and Farley Kelly (Ringwood, Vic.: Penguin Books, 1985), 168–169, 173.
16. Bomford, *That Dangerous and Persuasive Woman*, 55–56, 63.
17. MacKenzie, "Vida Goldstein": 192–193, 195, 200–201; Jenni Mulraney, "When Lovely Woman Stoops to Lobby", *Australian Feminist Studies* 3, no. 7–8 (1988), 101–103.
18. Mulraney, "When Lovely Woman Stoops to Lobby", 103–109.
19. MacKenzie, "Vida Goldstein": 192–193.
20. MacKenzie, "Vida Goldstein": 199.
21. Nina Rattner Gelbart, "Female Journalists", in *A History of Women in the West: III Renaissance and Enlightenment Paradoxes*, ed. Natalie Zemon Davis and Arlette Farge (Cambridge, MA, and London, 1993), 420–435; Elizabeth Mallet, cited in Elizabeth Cady Stanton, Susan B. Anthony and Matilda Joslyn Gage, ed., *History of Woman Suffrage, Vol. I. 1848–1861* (2nd edn, Rochester, NY: Charles Mann, 1889), 43.
22. Keating, *Distant Sisters*, 136.
23. Jane Chapman, *Gender, Citizenship and Newspapers: Historical and Transnational Perspectives* (London: Palgrave Macmillan, 2013), 64.
24. Chapman, *Gender, Citizenship and Newspapers*: 135–136.
25. John Mercer, "Making the News: Votes for Women and the Mainstream Press", *Media History* 10, no. 3 (2004): 190.
26. Chapman, *Gender, Citizenship and Newspapers*, 16–17.
27. Katherine E. Kelly, "Seeing Through Spectacles: The Woman Suffrage Movement and London Newspapers, 1906–13", *European Journal of Women's Studies* 11, no. 3 (2004): 329.
28. Sarah Pedersen, *The Scottish Suffragettes and the Press* (London: Palgrave Macmillan, 2017), 192.
29. Pedersen, *The Scottish Suffragettes and the Press*, 12.
30. Elizabeth V. Burt, "The Wisconsin Press and Woman Suffrage, 1911–1919: An Analysis of Factors Affecting Coverage by Ten Diverse Newspapers", *Journalism & Mass Communication Quarterly* 73, no. 3 (1996), 620.
31. Burt, "The Wisconsin Press and Woman Suffrage": 629.
32. Nancy Fraser, *Unruly Practices: Power, Discourse, and Gender in Contemporary Social Theory* (Minneapolis, MN: University of Minnesota Press, 1989), 122–137. Refer also to the arguments of Marilyn Waring on gender analysis: Marilyn Waring, *If Women Counted: A New Feminist Economics* (San Francisco Harper & Row, 1988).
33. New South Wales (1918), Queensland (1918), Western Australia (1920), Tasmania (1921) and Victoria (1923): see Oldfield, *Woman Suffrage in Australia*, 15, 222–223.

34. Goldstein was commissioned by the Victorian Government, the Criminology Society and the Trades Hall Council to enquire into child neglect, the penal system, and the trade unions, respectively, during her trip: Bomford, *That Dangerous and Persuasive Woman*, 33; Wright, *You Daughters of Freedom*, 100.
35. Bomford, *That Dangerous and Persuasive Woman*, 52.
36. Vida Goldstein, *To America and Back: A lecture by Vida Goldstein*, prepared by Jill Roe (Sydney: Australian History Museum, 2002), 25.
37. Goldstein, *To America and Back*: 25–26.
38. Wright, *You Daughters of Freedom*, 160.
39. Elizabeth Morrison, "David Syme's role in the rise of the Age", *Victorian Historical Journal* 84, no. 1 (2013): 27–30.
40. David Dunstan, "*The Argus*: The life, death and remembering of a great Australian newspaper", in *The Argus: The Life and Death of a Great Melbourne Newspaper (1846–1957)*, ed. Muriel Porter, 3–15 (Melbourne, Vic.: RMIT Publishing, 2003), 7.
41. Dunstan, "*The Argus*", 9.
42. Vida Goldstein, "The Australian Woman in Politics", *Review of Reviews*, January 20, 1904, p. 48.
43. "Subscriptions Received Up To September 5th 1902", *The Australian Woman's Sphere*, September 10, 1902, p. 207. Subscription numbers ceased to be published from 1903.
44. "Woman's Sphere", *The Australian Woman's Sphere*, September 10, 1903, p. 342.
45. For more on women's negotiation in the newsroom, see Jean Marie Lutes, *Front Page Girls: Women Journalists in American Culture and Fiction, 1880–1930* (New York: Cornell University Press, 2006).
46. "Woman's Sphere", *The Australian Woman's Sphere*, August 10, 1903, p. 329.
47. "The Women's Federal Political Association", *Australian Woman's Sphere*, September 10, 1903, p. 343.
48. "Women in Parliament", *The Australian Woman's Sphere*, September 10, 1903, pp. 346–347.
49. "The Town Hall Meeting", *The Australian Woman's Sphere*, September 10, 1903, p. 343.
50. "Organisation for the Federal Campaign", *The Australian Woman's Sphere*, June 10, 1903, p. 310.
51. "Miss Goldstein's Candidature: Various Views", *The Australian Woman's Sphere*, September 10 1903, p. 344.
52. *The New York Sun*, cited in "Miss Goldstein's Candidature: Various Views Continued, No. 3", *The Australian Woman's Sphere*, November 10, 1903, p. 369.

53. "Miss Goldstein's Candidature: Various Views", *The Australian Woman's Sphere*, September 10 1903, p. 344.

54. For background on the union's transnational span at this time, see Lake, *Progressive New World*, 140–146.

55. "Miss Goldstein's Candidature: Various Views."

56. "Miss Goldstein's Candidature: Various Views"; "Miss Goldstein's Candidature: Various Views, No. II", *The Australian Woman's Sphere*, October 10, 1903, p. 357.

57. Miss L. M. Smith, cited in "Miss Goldstein's Candidature: Various Views Continued, No. 3", *The Australian Woman's Sphere*, November 10, 1903, p. 369.

58. "The WCTU and Miss Goldstein's Candidature", *The Australian Woman's Sphere*, December 5, 1903, p. 385.

59. "Women in Parliament", *The Australian Woman's Sphere*, September 10, 1903, pp. 346–47.

60. Fair Play, "Miss Goldstein's Candidature: To the Editor of the Argus", *The Argus*, August 8, 1903, p. 16; "Miss Goldstein's Candidature: Various Views", *The Australian Woman's Sphere*, September 10, 1903, p. 344.

61. "The Age", *The Age*, August 22, 1903, p. 10; "Miss Goldstein's Candidature: Various Views", *The Australian Woman's Sphere*, September 10, 1903, p. 344.

62. "The Age", *The Age*, August 22, 1903, p. 10.

63. *The Reformer*, October 15, 1903, cited in "Miss Goldstein's Candidature: Various Views Continued, No. 4", *The Australian Woman's Sphere*, December 5, 1903, p. 381.

64. "Women Candidates for Parliament: Are they eligible?", *The Argus*, August 5, 1903, p. 5; "The Age", *The Age*, August 22, 1903, p. 10. See also Mulraney, "When Lovely Woman Stoops to Lobby", 101–103.

65. "From Some Prominent Women", *The Australian Woman's Sphere*, December 5, 1903, p. 385.

66. "Women Candidates for Parliament: Are they eligible?", *The Argus*, August 5, 1903, p. 5.

67. "A Lady Candidate: Social and Domestic Legislation", *The Age*, November 14, 1903, p. 12.

68. "The Senate: Miss Goldstein at Prahran", *The Argus*, November 14, 1903, p. 16.

69. "A Lady Candidate: Social and Domestic Legislation", *The Age*, November 14, 1903, p. 12.

70. "The Senate: Miss Goldstein at Prahran", *The Argus*, November 14, 1903, p. 16.

71. "A Lady Candidate: Social and Domestic Legislation", *The Age*, November 14, 1903, p. 12.
72. "The Senate: Miss Goldstein at Prahran", *The Argus*, November 14, 1903, p. 16.
73. Vida Goldstein, "Should Woman Enter Politics", *Review of Reviews*, August 20, 1903, p. 135.
74. "Why Women Want the Vote: Address by Rose Scott', *The Argus*, July 10, 1903, p. 3.
75. "Why Women Need to Vote. Paper By Miss Rose Scott', *The Age*, July 4, 1903, p. 12.
76. "Opinions of Federal Candidates on Federal Politics", *The Australian Woman's Sphere*, October 10, 1903, p. 360.
77. "A Lady Candidate: Social and Domestic Legislation", *The Age*, November 14, 1903, p. 12.
78. "The Senate Candidates: Miss Goldstein in Melbourne", *The Age*, November 17, 1903, p. 6.
79. "Miss Goldstein's Fiscal Faith", *The Age*, November 24, 1903, p. 6.
80. "The Senate: Miss Goldstein's Fiscal Faith", *The Age*, November 25, 1903, p. 8.
81. "Miss Goldstein's Fiscal Faith", *The Age*, November 26, 1903, p. 6.
82. *Australian Woman's Sphere*, "Woman's Sphere", *The Australian Woman's Sphere*, December 5, 1903, p. 377.
83. "Miss Goldstein at Leongatha", *The Argus*, November 26, 1903, p. 6.
84. "Women and Party Politics", *The Australian Woman's Sphere*, July 10, 1903, p. 322.
85. "Close Up the Ranks", *The Australian Woman's Sphere*, December 5, 1903, p. 383.
86. "The Tyranny of the Ticket", *The Australian Woman's Sphere*, January 15, 1904, p. 394–95.
87. The *Avoca Free Press*, cited in "Miss Goldstein's Candidature: Various Views, Conclusion", *The Australian Woman's Sphere*, January 15, 1904, p. 393.
88. "Whom to Vote For: Liberal Candidate, The Senate", *The Age*, December 5, 1903, p. 11.
89. "Senate Ballot-Paper: How to Mark It", *The Argus*, December 16, 1903, p. 8.
90. "'The Age' and the Election", *The Australian Woman's Sphere*, December 5, 1903, p. 382.
91. "'The Age' and the Election"; "Woman's Sphere", *The Australian Woman's Sphere*, September 10, 1903, p. 341.
92. "The Tyranny of the Ticket", *The Australian Woman's Sphere*, January 15, 1904, p. 394–395.

93. "Wanted—A New Party!", *The Australian Woman's Sphere*, February 15, 1904, p. 406.
94. "Hints to Women Voters", *The Australian Woman's Sphere*, October 10 1903, p. 355.
95. *The Australian Woman's Sphere*, October 1903, p. 356.
96. "Opinions of Federal Candidates on Federal Politics", *The Australian Woman's Sphere*, August 1903, p. 335.
97. "The World Moves", *The Australian Woman's Sphere*, August 1902, p. 194.
98. Vida Goldstein, "The Political Woman in Australia", *The Nineteenth Century and After: A Monthly Review* 56, no. 329 (1904): 109.
99. "Women's Federal Political Association", *The Australian Woman's Sphere*, March 15, 1904, p. 419.
100. "The State Elections: Women's Vote Organising", *The Age*, March 8, 1904, p. 5.
101. Vida Goldstein, "Women's Political Association: To the Editor of The Age", *The Age*, March 9, 1904, p. 6.
102. "Federal Elections Polling Day: Heavy Women's Vote. Many Seats Still in Doubt. Melbourne Contest Uncertain. Break Down of Counting Arrangements", *The Age*, December 17, 1903, p. 5.
103. Vida Goldstein, "The Australian Woman in Politics", *Review of Reviews*, January 20, 1904, p. 49.
104. Voter percentages were: 47% New South Wales (women 41%, men 53%); 55% Queensland (women 45%, men 62%); 33% South Australia (women 23%, men 42%); 45% Tasmania (women 34%, men 55%); 51% Victoria (women 46%, men 57%); 28% Western Australia (women 15%, men 36%): Department of Social Services, Australian Government, *Our Centenary of Suffrage*, July, 2009. https://www.dss.gov.au/our-responsibilities/women/publications-articles/general/our-centenary-of-womens-suffrage (accessed November 11, 2020).
105. Julia Gillard, Speech, House of Representatives, Australian Parliament, October 10, 2012, https://www.youtube.com/watch?v=fCNuPcf8L00 (accessed July 10, 2020).

CHAPTER 11

An Elite Minority: The *Medical Journal of Australia*'s Place in Australian and Global Publishing

Jeremy Fisher

The study of the history of publishing in Australia has centred largely on what the industry terms "trade" publishing of books, that is, the commercial publishing of works marketed to the general public.[1] Scant attention has been paid to scientific and educational publishing, both of which have been significant segments of the publishing industry in Australia alongside professional and legal publishing, and which produce journals and serials as well as books, profitably so in the twentieth century but with more paltry returns in the twenty-first.[2] While textbooks have underwritten the creation of culture, I have documented how educational publishing provided the financial base for the iconic Australian publisher Angus & Robertson's publication of Australian literature.[3] Scientific, technical and medical (STM) publishing has never been a large segment of Australian publishing and it has had little study perhaps because of this but perhaps also because most students of publishing history come from the

J. Fisher (✉)
School of Humanities, Arts, Social Sciences and Education, University of New England, Armidale, NSW, Australia

© The Author(s), under exclusive license to Springer Nature Switzerland AG 2021
C. Dewhirst, R. Scully (eds.), *Voices of Challenge in Australia's Migrant and Minority Press*, Palgrave Studies in the History of the Media, https://doi.org/10.1007/978-3-030-67330-7_11

humanities. What study there has been of STM publishing in Australia is very sketchy.[4] A feature of the academic study of publishing in Australia is that practitioners from the industry have been involved, sometimes in the provision of case studies, or, as in the case of this writer, because their careers have gravitated to academia. That brings a close involvement with the subject under study, a place where I was trained as an editor and worked as an employee. As a result, the following narrative has some autobiographical elements to it, some brief biographies as well as material from an interview and through this intertwined material it attempts to shed some light on those who are often in the shadows, the editors of journals. In particular, it documents the influence of this privileged minority, the editors of the *Medical Journal of Australia* (*MJA*), on the development of editorial practices and standards in Australia today. However, as a piece of writing it is also an evolution of the practice-led research that is a feature of the creative arts as they are manifested within an interdisciplinary academic framework:

> how individuals and groups are constituted can offer powerful ways of understanding the situation we are in, as artist-academics, and thus provide grounds for developing a way through what is, for many of us, a wicked problem: how to be both artist and academic; how to produce both art and knowledge products.[5]

The role of the editor, and the work of individual editors, has not been studied much in Australia. The work of Clem Cristesen, founding editor of the literary journal *Meanjin*, has been examined as has the life and work of Beatrice Davis, but both were working primarily in what may be broadly termed the arts.[6] STM editors, specifically medical editors, and their work have not been studied. This chapter is an attempt to redress the balance as well as give an indication of how their editorial practice and standards have permeated the profession of editing in Australia.

The issue of whether a privileged group of medically trained personnel may be considered a minority is of course debatable, privilege being one of the things minority groups most lack.[7] My own previous studies of minority press have focused on an acknowledged minority, the LGBTQI+ community.[8] However, that community is far more disparate and less cohesive than the medical profession and some members of it are privileged. Many jurisdictions have also removed the legal, religious and moral restrictions that prevented LGBTQI+ people from living lives equitable with their heteronormative identifying fellow citizens. Despite their lack of disadvantage, because their social cohesion and similarities in behaviour and practice gives them a degree of uniformity, it is actually simpler to consider professional groups such as the legal or medical professions as minorities than it is to so categorise the alphabet soup of LGBTQI+ people. I have chosen that approach here. The social homogeneity of the first part of the twentieth century with educated, privileged men in unquestioned positions of power and women in subordinate roles was also reflected in the manner in which the *MJA* was produced and managed.

A further point of consideration is how small a proportion of the population of Australia is composed of medical practitioners. There were 128,003 Australian registered medical practitioners of all types and specialities as of December, 2020.[9] Australia's population was 25,693,059 people as at 30 September, 2020.[10] This means about 0.5 per cent of the Australian population are registered medical practitioners, a substantial numerical minority.

Over 100 Years of Medical Publishing

The *MJA* has existed for over 100 years, first appearing on 4 July 1914. It was established by the state branches of the then British Medical Association to provide a means by which medical research and development in clinical practice in Australia could be communicated to the medical profession. The *MJA* is a leading light within the small Australian STM publishing sector serving a minority group—a privileged and educated group it must be said and also a highly influential one. Today, what was the British Medical Association in Australia has morphed into the politically powerful Australian Medical Association, which publishes the *MJA* through a fully owned company that is still called the Australasian Medical Publishing Company (AMPCo), as it was named in 1913. The company originally operated out of the British Medical Association Building at 30–34 Elizabeth Street, Sydney, but in 1925 it moved to The Printing House in Seamer Street, Glebe. Then as the company expanded so did The Printing House until it was a four-storey building that filled the entire triangular block between Seamer and Arundel Streets (on the Glebe side of the footbridge that now crosses Parramatta Road from the University of Sydney). The building was bought by the University of Sydney in 1989 and the company moved to Kingsgrove; then in 1994 to North Sydney; to Pyrmont in 2002; to Clarence Street, Sydney, in 2008; and to Kent Street,

Sydney, in 2015. As will be shown, these changes reflect what the company has undergone in the latter part of the twentieth and the twenty-first centuries as the print-centred company confronted the digital age.

The *MJA* first appeared as a weekly which compiled into volumes, volume 1 for the first half of the year and volume 2 for the second half. Page numbers continued issue to issue of each volume so that all issues, with the index and any supplements (usually on special topics and sometimes funded by drug companies) could be bound together as a book. It is now published 22 times a year, twice monthly except in January and December. The original page size was the pre-metric quarto (approximately 210 × 280 millimetres) and remains about the same. The first covers were typeset, but illustrations and colour were added as printing technology advanced. As of September 2019, the *MJA* had a print circulation of 28,575, but online readership was increasing with 249,821 website visits per month and 335,240 average page views per month.[11]

As part of Australian Medical Association membership, each member receives a copy of the *MJA* with the association paying the company a subscription fee. This model worked well for the association in the early days. The company prospered in the 1940s and 1950s when it dominated scientific publishing in Australia and returned dividends to the association. AMPCo printed journals, such as *Oceania*, originating from the University of Sydney, as well as ephemeral student publications, books, pamphlets and brochures.[12] While the *MJA* is published for a minority community, with a subscription base of those within that community who chose to join the national association, the company from its early days saw its role as providing a service to the broader academic community. With the money it made from its printing and publications the company could afford to be benevolent and philanthropic. These days though the company is a much-reduced concern and has been a financial drain on the medical association, but the *MJA* remains still influential.

The people who have written for and edited the *MJA* have made it the national institution it is today, acknowledged as "Australia's premier medical journal" and with a history of publishing medical research of more than a century.[13] Some of them may have been Nobel laureates but the vast majority are known only within the medical and scientific communities in Australia. Yet the *MJA*'s editors in particular have proven to be just as knowledgeable and objective, if at times eccentric, and have ensured that editorial excellence is paramount at the *MJA*. Their editorial rigour has had a strong influence on the development of editorial standards in

Australia, something that the natural reticence of the *MJA*'s editors has ensured is little known. In the study of Australian publishing practice, while there has been considerable scrutiny of the history and practice of editing in Australia, and the role Beatrice Davis played, until now little attention has been given to the *MJA* and its role in fostering editorial integrity.[14]

THE *MEDICAL JOURNAL OF AUSTRALIA*'S EDITORS AND THEIR ECCENTRICITIES

In 1977, I was appointed as an *MJA* copy editor, my first full-time job after graduating from university and teachers' college. The *MJA* offices appeared to exist in a time warp. As indicated earlier, the offices were located in Glebe, an inner suburb of Sydney that was administered by the Anglican Church from its establishment through a land grant to the chaplain of the First Fleet, Richard Johnson, in 1790.[15] Under the Church's neglect, the area became a slum, but the Whitlam government (elected in December 1972) bought Glebe from the Church and undertook urban renewal under Minister for Urban and Regional Development Tom Uren. This work was still ongoing in 1977 and today Glebe is a sought-after inner-city location.

Life at the *MJA* in 1977 seemed much the same as it must have been when the editor who would become the legendary Beatrice Davis (1901–1992) worked there for seven years with Mervyn Archdall (1884–1957), who was the *MJA*'s second editor and the one who set the editorial standards. Davis is most renowned for the decades she spent as editor at Angus & Robertson, nurturing the careers of many who were or would become distinguished writers, such as Eve Langley, Thea Astley, Xavier Herbert and Tom Hungerford, and developing a distinctive Australian literature, though one averse to modernist tendencies; "she avoided the contemporary urban themes favoured by writers like Dymphna Cusack, Ruth Park, D'Arcy Niland, and Kylie Tennant".[16] She was still alive in 1977. If she had wandered into the *MJA* offices she might have recognised her old manual typewriter on this writer's desk, the wooden box divided into three sections where the cards for the *MJA*'s index were filed, and many of the books on the library shelves, a wide variety of texts on diverse subjects sent for possible review in the journal and kept for editorial use.

Archdall first worked alongside Henry William Armit (b. 1870), who interviewed and employed Davis (she recalled him as "a fascinating older man"),[17] and who had been appointed first editor in 1913 when he came out to Sydney with his German wife, Maria Josephine, and daughter.[18] Armit was bilingual in English and German. He had studied physics and chemistry in Bonn. After his return from there to Britain, he studied medicine. He was known for attention to detail and grammatical rigour, perhaps influenced by his translation of articles from German medical journals. As well, he had written a work on hypnotism, beginning the informal tradition that the editors of the *MJA* cultivated diverse and wide-ranging interests.[19]

Armit died at the age of 50 from septicaemia associated with tonsillitis. At his funeral at St Thomas' Anglican Church, North Sydney, on 14 March 1930, as an indication of his standing within the medical and scientific community in Australia, he was farewelled by representatives of the British Medical Association, the Linnean Society, Sydney Hospital, Royal North Shore Hospital, the School of Tropical Health and Medicine, the Australian Veterinary Association, pharmaceutical companies and Angus & Robertson.[20] Mervyn Archdall was appointed editor on Armit's death. The editorial standards he instigated at the *MJA* were heavily influenced by his background. Archdall had joined the *MJA* as assistant editor in 1922. He was an accomplished musician appearing as a soloist with the Royal Philharmonic Society and he and his wife were frequently invited to Sydney's society events.[21] In October 1930, *The Sun*'s Social Chatter column reported that "Mrs. Mervyn Archdall has taken a house at Katoomba for a month, where she is spending a holiday, accompanied by her mother (Mrs. Thompson) and her sister (Miss Nellie Thompson). Dr. Archdall goes up for week-ends".[22] Archdall shared the same name as his father, who was born in Ireland and arrived in Sydney with his German wife of two months, Martha, on 27 November 1882. The older Archdall was a fiercely evangelical Anglican who raged against what he perceived as the liturgical failings of Catholicism; he was also a critic of Darwinism. Mervyn, his eldest child, married Mary Thompson, daughter of the rector of Franklin, Tasmania, in Hobart on 30 March 1910. The service was performed by the bridegroom's uncle, the Anglican Bishop of Tasmania.[23] The young Archdall served in the Australian Army Medical Corps in France and Belgium in 1917 and 1918, attaining the rank of Captain.[24] He served at the 2nd Australian General Hospital and found some time for relaxation with other staff after the cessation of hostilities appearing in

Fig. 11.1 Mervyn Archdall (left) at the 2nd Australian General Hospital in France in 1918. (Source: Australian War Memorial, Canberra)

a Pierrot troupe (see Fig. 11.1). He was also the first editor of the *Australian and New Zealand Journal of Surgery*, published by the Royal Australasian College of Surgeons, from 1927.[25]

Archdall was the person who trained Beatrice Davis as an editor. He also had experience working with books, having moonlighted as an editor for Angus & Robertson while he was assistant editor. Angus & Robertson under Walter Cousins successfully published medical textbooks in the 1930s. When Archdall became editor of the *MJA* his workload prevented him from working on them so he passed them over to Davis. She worked freelance on them for some years until she was offered a full-time job. She moved to Angus & Robertson as a full-time editor in 1936.[26]

In 1937, Davis married a doctor, Frederick Bridges, superintendent of Royal Prince Alfred Hospital, whom she had met through her work at the *MJA*. He was some years older than she was, divorced, with two children. Nevertheless, the couple was "not short of a quid", which no doubt helped sustain her in her relatively unremunerative work as a book editor, though the marriage was brief as Bridges died of tuberculosis in 1945. She would not leave Angus & Robertson until March 1973 when she was retrenched, along with most of the existing editorial staff, by the new management of entrepreneur Gordon Barton, who had bought the company in 1970. Barton's management team was led by Richard Walsh, appointed as publisher in 1972 at a time coincident with the move of the Angus & Robertson offices from George Street, Sydney, to Cremorne on the lower North Shore. Davis' days as the most influential editor in Australia, acting as unofficial arbiter of almost all that comprised Australian literature, publishing Ion Idriess, Colin Simpson, Miles Franklin and numerous other famed Australian writers, were close to the end, though she kept working from home for publishing firm Thomas Nelson.

Archdall's role grew beyond being a mere editor. He worked as an advocate for and representative of the British Medical Association in Australia. For instance, he visited Canberra when the High Court ruled for doctors against changes to the Pharmaceutical Benefits Act and he represented the British Medical Association in Australia at international events such as the congress of the World Medical Association and meetings of the British Medical Association in the United Kingdom.[27] He also travelled extensively within Australia to visit British Medical Association state branches and meetings of speciality colleges such as the Royal Australasian College of Surgeons.[28] Davis had first met Archdall through his musical activities. She was a musician too, a pianist and, according to her:

> Strangely enough, it was through playing the piano that I got into publishing. Because in those days there were music clubs in every suburb worth its salt and while I was playing at the music club, a man was singing at the music club. We subsequently said, 'How do you do' on the ferry boat going to town and one day, in great distress, he said, 'I am in great trouble because my secretary is leaving'. I immediately said, 'How much do you pay her?' 'Um', he said, '£3.15 a week'. So with some impertinence I said, 'I'll take the job'.[29]

In Davis' words, the *MJA*:

> was a splendid place to learn the details of the game because the medical publishing company had a beautiful printing works and it was there at the, in very familiar ground for me because the university was opposite and I could spend all the lunchtimes in the Fisher Library, wander round the quadrangle. So with the printing works just below the office of the medical journal, you learned all the practicalities of typesetting and what it meant if you made corrections and how to deal with proofs and so on and so on. This was running the medical journal and helping with the editorial side of it.[30]

I myself had the very same experience nearly 50 years later. The ground floor was taken up by hot metal typesetting machinery and printing presses, many dating back to the foundation of the company. Management and the proofreaders occupied the second floor. The Australian Medical Association's national office was on the third floor and the editorial offices were on the top floor with panoramic views out over the city and to the east. The total staff consisted only of the four medical editors, their secretary, an assistant, the chief sub-editor, Olga Zimoch, myself and another sub-editor, a librarian and the administrator of the *Medical Directory of Australia*. Zimoch (who trained me) had worked in a variety of menial jobs after she first arrived in Australia as a displaced person from Poland where she had attained a medical degree which was not recognised in Australia. She had such an extensive command of written English, however, that she had been a book editor at John Wiley & Sons before she accepted the job at the *MJA*.

The editors began each morning by reading the papers. In addition to the Sydney papers, *The Age* was delivered from Melbourne and *The Times* came in weekly from London. As well, they looked through the *Lancet*, the *New England Journal of Medicine*, the *Journal of the American Medical Association* and the *British Medical Journal* as these came in weekly, as well as all the specialist journals from Australia and overseas such as *The Australian and New Zealand Journal of Psychiatry* and the *Journal of Internal Medicine*. The company also produced some of the specialist journals on behalf of the various speciality Colleges. Reuben Hertzberg, the editor of the ophthalmology journal, would often drop in for morning tea, which was a time when the whole staff gathered together to discuss events relevant to the day's work as well as current events and cricket. A trolley was wheeled out of the tiny kitchen with a teapot, cups and saucers and a plate of biscuits. If it were a staff member's birthday, there would be a cake with plates and cake forks. The editorial team was its own little "family" on the top floor of the Printing House, cut off from the rest of AMPCo. Sometimes Dorothy Tremlett who had recently retired as chief copy editor would join in; she had taken Beatrice Davis' position in 1936 and still felt part of the family. She too had been trained by Archdall.

Tremlett had a long association with the *MJA*. A play she had co-written with the poets John Le Gay Brereton, A. D. Hope and others was printed by AMPCo in 1928.[31] Like Davis, she spoke fluent French. She also acted: she played the part of Lady Chiltern in Oscar Wilde's "An ideal husband" in the Sydney University Dramatic Society's 1931 production.[32] As well, she was a poet, writing poems in French. She was a contemporary of Davis at North Sydney Girls High School and both of them then graduated in Arts from the University of Sydney, both with French as a major. After graduation, Tremlett worked as librarian for the Sydney branch of Alliance Française. Both women shared a passion for music. Dorothy sang while Davis was a pianist. Dorothy lived in Mosman, close to Davis' home at Folly Point, Cammeray. It is possible, probable even, that Davis recommended Dorothy as her replacement. Their very similar Protestant, middle-class habits and values aligned perfectly with those of Archdall. Unlike Davis, Tremlett remained single. She worshipped at St Barnabas' Church, Broadway, colloquially known as Barney's, where Minister Michael Jensen remembered her as "the last of the old ladies".[33] The church, which burned down in 2006 but has been rebuilt, had close associations with Anglican evangelicals at the University of Sydney.

The *MJA*'s editor when I joined the staff was Dr Ronald Winton (1913–2004) (see Fig. 11.2). He had been assistant to Archdall, commencing in 1947. During the Second World War, he served in the medical corps in Palestine and New Guinea, leaving service with the rank of Lieutenant-Colonel. He took over from Archdall in 1957.[34] Winton was a religious man with a humanitarian streak. He had strong views on the sanctity of life; he opposed euthanasia, calling it "murder" at a meeting of the inter-Varsity Fellowship at the University of Sydney.[35] From 1952 to 1972 he was the Honorary Warden of the "International Friendship Centre" (a large old home called "Wingham", a hostel at Drummoyne established in 1952 by Sydney Anglican Archbishop and Mrs Mowll) for overseas students, whose treatment in Australia he was concerned about.[36] Winton was one of the founders of the New University Colleges Council, which was incorporated in 1960, and a signatory to the Council's Articles

Fig. 11.2 This portrait of Dr Ronald Winton hangs in the board room of the Australasian Medical Publishing Company © Australasian Medical Publishing Company. Reproduced with permission

of Association.[37] Under his editorship the *MJA* began to document the health of Australia's Indigenous population. The *MJA* published regular supplements devoted to Aboriginal health issues and these shed light on the appalling conditions Indigenous populations continue to endure. These papers are now published online and made freely available to all interested parties. Examples of the many significant papers the *MJA* has published are a study of variant forms of carbonic anhydrase in the Indigenous population, and treatment advice for lead poisoning in infants whose mothers sniff petrol.[38]

Winton was highly respected in medical circles worldwide, being elected Chairman of the International Congress of Christian Physicians and Chairman of the Council of the World Medical Association at various times. He worked with international colleagues and ensured the *MJA* adopted the Vancouver Convention referencing system; this system is concise and sparse in its use of punctuation. He also oversaw the introduction of the use of Système Internationale (SI) Units (the metric units used in science and medicine) in the *MJA*. In her obituary of Winton, Laurel Thomas wrote: "Outside work, his passions included music, literature, theology and history (he lectured in the history of medicine at the University of Sydney). These topics often flavoured staff morning teas, to everyone's great delight".[39] Winton was awarded a Medal in the Order of Australia in the 1997 Queen's Birthday Honours list "for service to medicine, particularly in the fields of medical publication, history and ethics".[40] He articulated what the *MJA* had come to represent in the 1950s and 1960s: a compassionate conservatism strongly influenced by the evangelism of Sydney Anglicanism. Winton was soon to retire to be replaced by his deputy, Dr Arthur Gwynn.

Dublin-born Arthur Gwynn (1908–2008) was in the Royal Army Medical Corps in Italy during the Second World War where he was wounded and awarded the Military Cross. He came to Australia in 1948 intending to continue to New Zealand to climb mountains but by chance he read an advertisement and so became officer in charge and medical officer to the second Australian National Antarctic Research Expedition to Macquarie Island.[41] Mount Gwynn on the island is named after him. Two months after his return to Australia in 1950, he volunteered to board HMAS *Australia* on an emergency evacuation voyage to Heard Island.[42] With two other expeditioners, he features on an Australian Antarctic Territory postage stamp raising the Australian flag over Antarctica. He returned to Heard Island for the 1953 winter when he was bitten by an elephant seal and stitched himself up; his interest in zoology, however, remained undimmed. He married Pat Howard in 1956, then took up the position of *MJA* deputy editor, where he remained for 20 years. He took over as editor in 1977 and retired in 1978. Gwynn was much more interested in science generally rather than the practice of medicine.

Two other doctors made up the medical editorial staff: Dr Laurel Thomas and Dr Jill Forrest, who was also the University of Sydney carillonist; Forrest would head over to the university at lunch times and the bells would begin ringing from the tower of the Great Hall. This mixture gave the *MJA* editorship a broad spectrum of the arts, science and philosophy.

The Legacy of the *Journal*

The Australasian Medical Publishing Company, however, was not faring well. In 1977, it was haemorrhaging cash from the Australian Medical Association's balance sheet. As a printing company, it was way behind the times, still using hot metal typesetters and old printing machines. The many compositors were all artisans and skilled enough to recognise upside down and back to front any grammatical or measurement errors that might have crept past the proofreaders. The proofreaders, mostly men but a few women, read all the copy for printing to each other in little rooms off long, dim corridors on the first floor, above the clang and rumble of the presses on the ground floor. All were on the payroll.

Inevitably economics ruled. Within six months of my starting work at the *MJA*, the printing presses were gone and the printing outsourced. Two computer keyboards replaced the numerous hot metal typesetting machines. Staff numbers dropped dramatically, except on the editorial floor. It was the beginning of major changes at the *MJA* and the end of an era, with The Printing House disappearing and the digital world emerging. All direct links to Archdall ceased to exist.[43]

However, over at Angus & Robertson, from 1936 Beatrice Davis trained two generations of editors in the manner Archdall had trained her. By 1979 there were sufficient editors working in publishing in Sydney for them to form a society to discuss matters relevant to their profession. I met Davis when she gave an address at the Society of Editors (NSW) where she railed against gender-neutral language (which to its credit the *MJA* had already embraced).[44] During my tenure as president of the Society of Editors (NSW) in 1986 negotiations began to establish an industry-supported Graduate Diploma of Editing and Publishing at Macquarie University, mirroring a similar course at Royal Melbourne Institute of Technology in Melbourne. In 1998, the state societies of editors joined together to form the Council of Australian Societies of Editors which developed the *Australian Standards for Editing Practice*, codifying for the first time what an editor needs to know and how this knowledge should be measured.[45] The state editors' societies united to form the Institute of Professional Editors in 2008.

At the *MJA*, the most climactic event occurred in 2015 when editor Professor Stephen Leeder was removed, and all but two of the editorial advisory board resigned, after a disagreement over a decision by the AMPCo Board to outsource production of the *MJA* to the multinational publisher Elsevier. Jae Redden, with whom I had worked at book publisher McGraw-Hill, was General Manager of AMPCo at the time (she was promoted to Chief Executive Officer in August 2015). As she explained in an interview for this chapter, costs to the AMA for the *MJA* were increasing year by year. AMPCo was not in a good financial state when she arrived in 2013.[46] There were 50 staff members, 25 of whom worked on the *MJA*. Professor Leeder was content with his editorial position and independence, but the AMPCo Board looked to explore alternatives. Redden proposed outsourcing production as a means of trimming costs. She approached publishers for quotes, but Leeder was precluded from initial discussions because outsourcing was still merely a proposal. Elsevier, Wiley and another publisher offered quotes. As Redden had worked previously for Elsevier in Singapore, she excluded herself from the final choice of publisher, and AMPCo chose Elsevier. Leeder felt deceived and that his editorial independence had been infringed.

As of January 2019, the *MJA* has been produced by Wiley for AMPCo. Though now it appears in print fortnightly, its digital platform is increasingly prominent. The research the *MJA* publishes continues to be reported by the general news media and it remains a forum which the medical profession uses for its ongoing education. While not one of the world's leading medical journals, the *MJA* is well regarded; it claims to be among the top 30 general medical journals in the world.[47] It is known for publishing research of special relevance to Australia. As this paragraph is being written, ABC News is reporting that the *MJA*'s most recent issue features a report on bullying amongst healthcare workers.[48] The *MJA* has also published globally significant research such as a paper on the value of lithium in treating psychosis and papers on *Campylobacter* (now *Helicobacter*) *pylori* and its role in causing peptic ulcers.[49] Lead author of these latter articles Barry Marshall was awarded the Nobel Prize in Medicine or Physiology in 2005 as a result of this research. While these are admirable achievements in its key role as a medical journal, its role in the development of professional editing in Australia remains largely unsung. That is likely the way the men and women who worked behind the scenes to produce the journal would prefer it. Shedding some light on their personalities, foibles and personalities shows that overall they reflected what society expects of health professionals—probity, discretion and dedication.

NOTES

1. For example, Martin Lyons and John Arnold, ed., *A History of the Book in Australia 1891–1945: A National Culture in a Colonised Market* (St Lucia, Qld: University of Queensland Press, 2001); Craig Munro and Robyn Sheahan-Bright, eds, *Paper Empires: A History of the Book in Australia 1946–2005* (St Lucia, Qld: University of Queensland Press, 2006); Patrick Buckridge and Belinda McKay, ed., *By the Book: A Literary History of Queensland* (St Lucia, Qld: University of Queensland Press, 2007).
2. Australian Bureau of Statistics, Canberra. *1363.0—Book Publishers, Australia, 2003–04* https://www.abs.gov.au/AUSSTATS/abs@.nsf/Loo kup/1363.0Main+Features12003-04?OpenDocument (the ABS ceased collecting this data in 2004).
3. Jeremy Fisher, "The Neglected Textbook: Placing Educational Publishing in Australia in Context", *Script and Print* 36, no. 4 (2012): 200–212.
4. Rod Home, "Case-study: Science Publishing", in *A History of the Book in Australia 1891–1945: A National Culture in a Colonised Market*, ed. M. Lyons and J. Arnold (St Lucia, Qld: University of Queensland Press, 2001), 292–294.
5. Jen Webb, "The Logic of Practice? Art, the Academy and Fish out of Water", *TEXT*, Special Issue Number 14—Beyond Practice-Led Research, October (2012) 2–3, http://www.textjournal.com.au/speciss/issue14/Webb.pdf.
6. For Cristesen, see Jenny Lee, "Clem Cristesen and his Legacy", *Australian Literary Studies* 21, no. 3 (2004): 410–412; Laurie Hergenhan, "Clem Christesen (1911–2003)", in *Proceedings of The Australian Academy of the Humanities*, ed. B. Bennett (Canberra: The Australian Academy of the Humanities, 2003), 45–46. For Davis, see Jacqueline Kent, *A Certain Style: Beatrice Davis, A Literary Life* (Melbourne: Viking, 2001); Jacqueline Kent, "Case-study: Beatrice Davis", in *Paper Empires: A History of the Book in Australia 1946–2005*, ed. C. Munro and R. Sheahan-Bright (St Lucia, Qld: University of Queensland Press, 2006), 177–182; Anthony Barker, *One of the First and One of the Best: Beatrice Davis, Book Editor* (Melbourne: Society of Editors (Vic), 1991).
7. The medical profession fits four of the five criteria identified for minority group status: physical/cultural traits that set them apart; collective identity; shared social rules; and a tendency to intermarry. However, the profession is rarely discriminated against. Joseph R. Feagin, *Race and Ethnic Relations*, 2nd edn (Englewood Cliffs, NJ: Prentice Hall, 1984), 10.
8. Jeremy Fisher, "Sex, Sleaze and Righteous Anger: The Rise and Fall of Gay Magazines and Newspapers in Australia", *Text*, Special Issue 25: Australasian Magazines: New Perspectives on Writing and Publishing

(2014), 1–12, http://www.textjournal.com.au/speciss/issue25/Fisher. pdf; Jeremy Fisher, "The Writing and Publishing of Australia's First Gay Novel", *Australian Literary Studies* 29 no. 4 (2015), 62–72.

9. 'Registrant Data. Reporting period: 01 October 2020 to 31 December 2020', *Medical Board of Australia*, https://www.medicalboard.gov.au/ news/statistics.aspx (accessed April 5, 2021).

10. 'Population', *Australian Bureau of Statistics*, https://www.abs.gov.au/ statistics/people/population (accessed April 5, 2021).

11. 'Advertise', *Medical Journal of Australia*, https://www.mja.com.au/ advertise (accessed April 5, 2021).

12. Student publications for example, J. Le Gay Brereton, J. E. Burrow, H. M. Green, A. D. Hope, H. G. Howarth, Joan Mackaness, P. E. Smyth, F. A. Todd, Dorothy Tremlett and W. F. Wentworth-Sheilds, *The Temple on the Hill: A Mask, Presented at the University of Sydney, in Lent Term, 1928* (Sydney: Australasian Medical Publishing Co, 1928). Books for example, Ronald Winton, *From the Sidelines of Medicine* (Sydney: Australasian Medical Publishing Co., 1983).

13. Norman Swan, "100th Anniversary of the Medical Journal of Australia", *ABC Radio National Health report*, June 9, 2014, https://www.abc.net. au/radionational/programs/healthreport/100th-anniversary-of-the-medical-journal-of-australia/5505020#transcript.

14. Rowena McDonald, *Between a Work and a Book: Publishers' Editing at Angus & Robertson Publishers in Sydney, Australia in the Mid Twentieth Century* (Armidale: A thesis submitted for the degree of Doctor of Philosophy of the University of New England, 2013); Kent, *A Certain Style*; Kent, "Case-study"; Barker, *One of the First and One of the Best*; Institute for Professional Editors, *Resources for Editors*, http://iped-editors.org/Resources_for_editors.aspx.

15. Frances Pollon (compiler), *The Book of Sydney Suburbs* (Sydney: Angus & Robertson, 1990), 109.

16. Barker, *One of the first and one of the best*; Kent, *A Certain Style*; Kent, "Case-study"; Beverley Kingston, "Davis, Beatrice Deloitte (1909–1992)", *Australian Dictionary of Biography*, http://adb.anu.edu.au/biography/ davis-beatrice-deloitte-17805.

17. Beatrice Davis, Interviewed by Suzanne Lunney, National Library of Australia Oral History project, recorded on 19 May 1977 at Folly Point, NSW, nla.gov.au/nla.obj-215119627.

18. W. L. Calov, "Armit, Henry William (1870–1930)", *Australian Dictionary of Biography* (Canberra: National Centre of Biography, 1979) http://adb. anu.edu.au/biography/armit-henry-william-5051/text8419 (accessed April 3, 2018).

19. Auguste Forel, *Hypnotism or, Suggestion and Psychotherapy: A Study of the Psychological, Psycho-physiological and Therapeutic Aspects of Hypnotism,* trans. H. W. Armit (London: Rebman, 1906).

20. *The Sydney Morning Herald,* "Obituary. Dr Henry William Armit", March 15, 1930, p. 19, http://nla.gov.au/nla.news-article16633689.

21. *Everyones* 4, no. 192, November 23, 1923.

22. *The Sun,* "Social Chatter", October 21, 1930, p. 14. http://nla.gov.au/nla.news-article224232807.

23. *Huon Times,* "Wedding Bells", April 6, 1910, p. 2. http://nla.gov.au/nla.news-article137266327.

24. D. W. A. Baker, "Archdall, Mervyn (1846–1917)", *Australian Dictionary of Biography* (Canberra: National Centre of Biography, 1979) http://adb.anu.edu.au/biography/archdall-mervyn-5044/text8401 (accessed online August 25, 2018).

25. P. F. Burke, "ANZ Journal of Surgery: A Most Hearty Collaboration", *ANZ Journal of Surgery* 77, 12 (2007): 1038–1044.

26. Barker, *One of the First and One of the Best.*

27. On the Pharmaceutical Benefits Act see *The Age,* "Doctors Pleased with Judgment", October 8, 1949, p. 3. On the World Medical Association see *The Advertiser,* "Doctors Against Control", December 11, 1948, p. 2. On meetings of the BMA see *Maryborough Chronicle,* "Empire Doctors in Conference", September 18, 1948, p. 4.

28. *The Age (Melbourne),* "Visitors for Surgeons' Meeting", March 15, 1939, p. 5. http://nla.gov.au/nla.news-article205987792.

29. Davis, Interviewed by Suzanne Lunney.

30. Davis, Interviewed by Suzanne Lunney.

31. Brereton et al., *The Temple on the Hill.*

32. *The Sun,* August 7, 1931, p. 12 (final extra). Web. January 24, 2019, http://nla.gov.au/nla.news-article224715643.

33. Sydney Anglicans, "The Unforgettable Fire: Burning Memories from Barney's", https://sydneyanglicans.net/blogs/insight/the_unforgetable_fire_burning_memories_from_barneys, May 24, 2006 (accessed February 4, 2019).

34. Laurel Thomas, "Ronald Richmond Winton OAM, MB BS, FRACP, FRACMA", *Medical Journal of Australia* 181, no.1 (2004): 26.

35. *The Sydney Morning Herald,* "Euthanasia 'Murder'", says Doctor", November 16, 1950, p. 3. http://nla.gov.au/nla.news-article1818665.1.

36. Ronald Winton, "Asian Students in Australia", *The Sydney Morning Herald,* January 21, 1954, p. 2. http://nla.gov.au/nla.news-article18405783.

37. Ian Walker, "The New Universities Colleges Council", *Lucas* n.s. no.1 Autumn (2009): 139–161.

38. N. M. Blake and R. L. Kirk, "Widespread Distribution of Variant Forms of Carbonic Anhydrase in Australian Aboriginals", *Medical Journal of Australia* 1 (1978): 183–185; S. R. Powell, S. Bolisetty, and G. R. Wheaton, "Succimer Therapy for Congenital Lead Poisoning from Maternal Petrol Sniffing", *Medical Journal of Australia* 184, no. 2 (2006): 84–85.

39. Thomas, "Ronald Richmond Winton OAM, MB BS, FRACP, FRACMA".

40. The Queen's Birthday 1997 Honours (June 9, 1997), *Commonwealth of Australia Gazette. Special*, p. 16, http://nla.gov.au/nla.news-article240725442. Accessed February 5, 2019.

41. Harriet Veitch, "Man of Action had an Inquisitive Mind: Arthur Gwynn, MC, Doctor 5-8-1908–31-1-2008", *The Age*, April 17, 2008, p. 19.

42. *The Daily News* (Perth), "Doctors to the Rescue", July 29, 1950, p. 1, http://nla.gov.au/nla.news-article84469968

43. Laurel Thomas succeeded Gwynn as editor in 1978, with Jill Forrest as her deputy. The economic travails of the publishing company, however, had an impact on the pattern of long-term editorships and the *MJA* began to adapt to the modern world. In a bid to reduce costs, AMPCo switched publication to fortnightly in 1978. Thomas left in 1981 with the Chairman of the AMPCo Board, Sir Keith Jones, acting as editor until the American Dr Alan Blum was appointed in 1982. Blum was replaced by acting editor Dr Kathleen King in 1983. Dr Alistair Brass was editor from 1983 to 1985. Brass had been involved in the campaign to end the war in Vietnam and also involved himself in the development of the Australian medical response to HIV. Kathleen King replaced him from 1985 to 1989 when The Printing House was sold, then Laurel Thomas and Jill Forrest returned as joint editors from 1989 to 1994 with Thomas as sole editor in 1995. Professor Priscilla Kincaid-Smith was briefly acting editor in 1995 before Dr Martin van der Weyden took up the reins from 1996 until 2011. He was succeeded by Dr Annette Katelaris until 2012. In this year the *MJA* began to publish all of its research articles free to access online. Dr Ann Gregory was acting editor until 2013 followed by Professor Stephen Leeder.

44. The meeting took place on 22 October 1986 at the Kirribilli Neighbourhood Centre and featured Davis in conversation with novelist Christopher Koch and poet Thomas Shapcott. Source: *The Society of Editors (NSW) Newsletter*, February 1987.

45. *Australian standards for editing practice*, http://iped-editors.org/About_editing/Editing_standards.aspxe (accessed November 28, 2019).

46. Jae Redden, telephone interview with Jeremy Fisher, March 24, 2019.

47. *Medical Journal of Australia*, https://www.ampco.com.au/medical-journal-of-australia/ (accessed 5 November 2018).

48. Johanna Westbrook, Neroli Sunderland, Victorial Arkinson, Catherine Jones and Jeffrey Braithwaite, "Endemic Unprofessional Behaviour in

Health Care: The Mandate for a Change in Approach", *Medical Journal of Australia* 209, no. 9 (2018): 34–38.

49. John F.J. Cade, "Lithium Salts in the Treatment of Psychotic Excitement", *Medical Journal of Australia* 2, no. 36 (1949): 349–352; B. J. Marshall, David B. McGechie, Peter A. Rogers and Ross J. Glancy, "Pyloric Campylobacter Infection and Gastroduodenal Disease", *Medical Journal of Australia* 142, 8 (1985): 439–444; B. J. Marshall, John A. Armstrong, David B. McGechie and Ross J Glancy, "Attempt to fulfil Koch's Postulates for Pyloric Campylobacter", *Medical Journal of Australia* 142, no. 8 (1985): 436–439.

CHAPTER 12

Counter-Hegemony in Ethnic Media: An Agonistic Pluralism Perspective

John Budarick

Ethnic print, broadcast and digital media have long been involved in debates over issues at the heart of liberal democratic politics. Integration, cultural identity and relationships between diverse social and political groups were discussed in many early ethnic newspapers, and continue to feature in digital and broadcast ethnic media today. The history of ethnic print in Australia, and elsewhere in the world, attests to their complex role in engaging with political and social issues, including integration, identity, language and cultural autonomy. As a rich and diverse field dating back to the middle of the nineteenth century, the migrant press in Australia has played a role, amongst other things, in cultural and linguistic maintenance, the settlement of migrants, local and national politics and labour movements, and relationships with countries of origin. In addition to providing an important resource for migrant identities and cultures in Australia, migrant newspapers have been important players in the politics of migration.[1]

J. Budarick (✉)
University of Adelaide, Adelaide, SA, Australia
e-mail: john.budarick@adelaide.edu.au

C. Dewhirst, R. Scully (eds.), *Voices of Challenge in Australia's Migrant and Minority Press*, Palgrave Studies in the History of the Media, https://doi.org/10.1007/978-3-030-67330-7_12

Elsewhere, dominant political, social and cultural norms have been engaged with, negotiated and challenged. In the United States, the early Black press directly challenged slavery. Other migrant newspapers were published partly in English or ran English editions in an attempt to reach a wider audience and challenge common misconceptions of migrant groups. Furthermore, the Latino and Chinese press have both historically engaged with and challenged policies over employment of migrants, immigration and discrimination.[2]

In their study of the immigrant press in Australia, Miriam Gilson and Jerzy Zubrzycki examine the complex and diverse role of ethnic newspapers. Their work highlights the dual role of ethnic print, which was never simply restricted to a single intended community. Despite long established public and political fears over ethnic ghettoisation, Australia's immigrant press from 1848 to 1964 played a dual role of:

> providing for its readers a stepping stone from an old life to a new. It caters for the desire for news of the homeland and advises retention of some old loyalties. ... At the same time, by instructing its readers in Australian ways, by encouraging them to overcome difficulties, and to co-operate actively with their new countrymen, it leads to an understanding and acceptance of their future in Australia.[3]

Although couched in a somewhat outdated language of linear integration, these practices reflect the inward and outward facing nature of much ethnic media, beginning with early print forms and continuing in the broadcast and digital age.

While certainly not always the case, migrant newspapers—and ethnic media in general today—also focus significantly on the local area of their production. Despite fears of ethnic segregation through these media, they tend to be both inward and outward facing. As Augie Fleras argues, they are both "reactive and proactive" in their social roles.[4] Migrant press and ethnic media more generally can therefore be understood within wider political and social frameworks, as they contribute not only to migrant community maintenance but to the place of migrants and ethnic minorities in wider democratic culture.

While this dual function of ethnic media has been described and analysed in a series of studies,[5] there is as yet little work focusing on the wider theoretical context. This chapter explores the relationship between ethnic media and democracy by analysing ethnic and migrant journalism through the lens of Chantal Mouffe's theory of agonistic pluralism.[6] Mouffe's post-foundational approach rejects the consensus politics associated with the public sphere, and instead argues for the necessary re-articulation of ineradicable differences between political identities. Difference, she argues, cannot be transcended through rational consensus, nor placated through ideas of liberal equality.[7] Instead, it should be embraced and seen as an inevitable part of all politics.

Through agonistic pluralism, the relationship between (ethnic) journalism, news and democracy can be reconsidered. The mainstream journalism industry's response to the so-called crisis of journalism—defined by the polarisation of the body politic and the related fragmentation of media, the rise of far-right politics and the normalisation of the language of extreme racism and nationalism—has predominantly revolved around a reimagining or recapturing of fundamental journalistic values and norms. A reinvestment in professional journalism, a re-emphasis on objectivity, autonomy and truth. The journalist, rather than the advocate, must retake centre stage in public debates that require rational discourse and accurate information. Professional forms of journalism need to reclaim their privileged position in the face of political, social and cultural movements that have challenged their legitimacy in the public sphere.

Remarkably, race and racism are largely absent from these discussions. When racism is broached, it is largely framed in terms of concerns over the normalisation of racism in public discourse as a result of the contravention of long-held norms of politics and journalism. How journalism works—its foundational values and practices—are rarely challenged in this framework. Broad ideals, such as truth, autonomy and neutrality, are seen as appropriate for dealing with racism and extremism. That those very ideals, and the way they have structured journalistic practice, are themselves built upon racial inequality is largely overlooked when racism in the Western world is identified as abnormal and of a bygone era.[8]

My task in this chapter is to think about the relationship between migrant media and democracy in a way that challenges many of the assumptions of mainstream journalism. How might we (re)imagine ethnic media and journalism in a way that disrupts conventional understandings of journalism's relationships to race and democracy, and the latter two's relationships to each other? How do ethnic media challenge and question dominant journalism and politics, calling into question their grand claims to equality, rationality and a disinterested neutrality? The very emergence of the migrant press and later ethnic media in the liberal democratic world is itself, in part, evidence of the failure of the fourth estate and of popular politics to understand and include ethnic and racial minorities in their discourses. [9]

In attempting to achieve this task, this chapter starts from a post-foundational position owing much to the work of post-structuralist theorists.[10] Broadly speaking, the power of employing post-structuralism for understanding ethnic media is that it approaches political norms and social orders as contingent. In applying a post-structuralist discourse approach to journalism, critics argue that key journalistic values, and their relationship to democratic norms, are based on the exclusion of alternatives rather than on their adherence to a foundational and universal set of values.[11] The power of dominant journalistic ideologies and practices is due to the collapse of discourse and objectivity, the naturalisation of one form of journalism as legitimate, as professional and as in need of rescuing in the face of a polarised political community.[12]

Within this terrain of discursive contest, I argue that ethnic and migrant media can and should be allocated a counter-hegemonic position. That is, rather than locate them within a contingent field of journalistic professionalism, in which claims to authority are the outcome of struggles to define the journalistic field, we can articulate ethnic media as challenging many tropes of traditional journalism, and as exposing the political nature of the relationship between journalism, race and democracy. To demonstrate this, the work of African-Australian journalists and media producers will be analysed. Focusing predominantly on broadcast media (but also incorporating some digital and print) data from interviews will be used to show the way in which journalism is imagined differently amongst marginalised migrant communities.

At the time of this research, community radio was one of the most common forms of African media in Australia. Several programmes are broadcast in a specific language, such as the Harari language programme on 3CR in Melbourne or *Voice of Ethiopia* on 3ZZZ. These programmes often have the maintenance of language, tradition and community as at least one of their aims. Others are broadcast in English, such as *African Australian Voice* on 3CR, and have developed a pan-African identity with the aim of providing a voice to African-Australians. Most radio programmes are broadcast weekly. The accessibility of community media and the online environment is vital for these programmes, which often have an associated social media presence and are run on a voluntary, not for profit basis.

There are few African-Australian newspapers in existence. There are, however, some magazines available. Some of these are associated with particular language groups, such as *Negat African Magazine* which is published in Amharic. Others, such as *Change Magazine*, are published in English and are general interest, focusing on culture, fashion, food and notable community figures. The lack of newspapers and the relative scarcity of magazines were explained by one participant in this study as being due to their cost and the amount of work that goes into each publication. Many African countries also have strong oral cultures, making broadcast an easier, cheaper and more effective medium.

Community television programmes such as *Africa Amara* and *Oz Africa* also play an important role in showcasing African-Australian artists, designers, musicians and community leaders. Like radio programmes, these media utilise community television as a way of accessing broadcast without the prohibitive costs associated with commercial media. African-Australian media are also present online. One of the more prominent examples is Africa Media Australia, which has a website and produces articles, video and audio in English with a pan-African focus.

These ventures are largely self-funded. African-Australian radio tends to be based on volunteer staff working through community radio. Some print, online and television content gets advertising payment, including from the government. However, the outlets are also largely voluntary in nature. Audience reach is difficult to ascertain for community media and self-funded online media. Often, impact is measured in more qualitative ways through the amount of phone-ins to radio programmes and the extent to which community members discuss media with producers during informal on-the-street chats.

JOURNALISM, RACE AND DEMOCRACY: DEFINING JOURNALISM IN THE CONTEXT OF ETHNIC DIVERSITY

Both industry and academic approaches to journalism tend to relate it to the tenets of liberal democracy, often understood loosely and as involving a variety of ideals, concepts and practices.[13] The influence of liberal democracy is born out in claims towards individual freedom, autonomy and the rational exchange of information. Expanding on this, the centrality of deliberative democracy and the public sphere in media studies over the past 30 years or more has positioned journalism, the press and media more broadly, as vital to the construction of a space wherein the exchange of views and information can take place free from disruptive influence. Quality journalism, imagined as the provision of factual and truthful information in the public interest by autonomous professionals, is vital to both the free exchange of ideas and the protection of the public sphere from the market and politics.

Both perspectives rest on normative theories of the press and journalism, with an understanding of a universal individualism, or a value-free space for legitimate consensus guiding expectations of the role of media in society. Neither perspective, nor journalism's relationship to them, has taken race sufficiently into account. As Charles W. Mills argues, the notion of the cooperative society of free and equal citizens, upon which liberal democratic theory was built, projected an image of a polity missing people of colour, women and Indigenous peoples.[14] What is more, the active marginalisation, exploitation and displacement of such peoples that made the liberal democratic state possible are rarely taken into consideration.[15] The public sphere as a normative theory has also been critiqued for failing to account for diverse groups excluded from the original bourgeois public sphere—women, migrants, the poor.[16] Some have argued instead for the existence of multiple public spheres, based in part on diverse social concerns and forms of communication.[17]

Both liberal and deliberative norms and ideals align closely with dominant norms of professional journalism. Liberalism's emphasis on individual rationalism, equality and an open marketplace of ideas has guided a journalistic commitment to the provision of factual information and a variety of viewpoints in public debates. It also shaped journalistic ideals of an autonomous journalism that both stands outside and supports this political culture. Ideals of journalistic rationality and independence also slot seamlessly into the language of the public sphere, co-opted in journalistic language as the space of the common-sense centre, the rational middleground constitutive of "society". Journalism's will to consensus is easily justified through the language of deliberation, with emphasis placed on the coming together of divergent views to transcend difference. In articulating a space distinct from private, market and government realms, the public sphere provides the pivot around which journalism positions itself as the fourth estate, the autonomous defender of *the* public.

I argue that both of the approaches discussed above—liberal individualism and the public sphere—pose problems when it comes to race and ethnic media. Liberal democracy tends to see the market as an equal space, wherein the best ideas win. It fails to account for embedded racial inequality in social or media systems, which is reflected in the unequal access to and control over powerful means of communication. The public sphere as a metaphor has also been accused of this same shortcoming, as it posits a space of rational debate transcendent of power in which the strongest arguments ascend over others. Neither approach provides the tools with which to appreciate the racialised hegemonic relations embedded in dominant forms of journalism and debate, nor to deconstruct and challenge these inequalities.

A post-foundational perspective can provide an answer to these shortcomings in two ways. Firstly, it facilitates a view of journalism as based on a discursive struggle to define the field, rather than on a set of objective skills-based criteria.[18] Secondly, Mouffe's work provides a framework through which to see such an approach to journalism as a positive part of an agonistic and pluralist democratic culture, one that lacks a transcendent position free from politics itself. Dissensus and difference are for Mouffe not crises that require the establishment of a space of rational discussion and consensus building. They are, instead, constitutive of the political and thus are only overcome through the hegemonic imposition of one political constellation over others. This has ramifications for journalism as an institution, migrant journalism and the normative ideas of democracy it speaks to.[19]

Several authors have analysed journalism as a sight of discursive struggle, where different constructions of what journalism is, and who a journalist is, meet and compete in an uneven discursive field.[20] Journalistic cultures and values are contextual, rather than universal. They are shaped by myriad social forces, rather than based on a pre-political transcendent foundation. Within particular contexts—for instance, what Jean Chalaby would call the Anglo-American tradition—particular "discursive nodes" take up hegemonic positions, drawing others towards them, or excluding and marginalising difference.[21] These nodes are articulated through concepts and ideals such as professional autonomy, objectivity and neutrality. Their hegemonic position is not based on a foundational set of criteria, separate from its contextual environment and to which all journalists and all forms of journalism aspire and commit. Instead, their positioning is the result of hegemonic and counter-hegemonic battles, that is, exclusions, articulations and disarticulations. Dominant understandings of journalism are thus the result of "struggle over discursive authority in conversations about the meaning and role of journalism in society".[22]

Migrant media have, over the past century and a half, shown a remarkable range of journalistic values, ideals and practices in their work and organisation. Some overarching values are shared with other types of journalism; a commitment to factual accuracy and a general commitment to creating a better society. In addition to these similarities, there are also significant differences that are not necessarily the outcome of deliberate individual strategies, but result from the nature of surrounding and competing discourses. Migrant and ethnic media's relationship with the broader social and political environment may engender alternative approaches to news creation and information dissemination. Thus, normative values, such as autonomy, may be problematic in the migrant and ethnic press.[23] Ethnic and migrant media may embrace overt community involvement and, in doing so, problematise the myth of detachment used by mainstream journalists in claiming some sort of neutrality. The advocacy of ethnic and migrant journalism, with its explicit identification of problems, proposal of solutions and rejection of pretensions of disinterest, contrasts with the dominant media discourse of an objective method, a critical, dispassionate and systematic way of determining facts and (in some more hyperbolic discourses) truth.

The identity of the journalist is also a contested discursive construct, one that involves race, gender and ideologies of professionalism.[24] As Nico Carpentier argues, the professional journalist is articulated as "objective, as a manager of people and (other) resources (based on their responsibility/property), as autonomous and as a member of a professional elite who are semi-professionally linked to a media organization".[25] According to Thomas Hanitzsch and Tim Vos, journalistic roles and identities emerge through interactions with external actors—audiences, other journalists, political actors. Through these interactions, journalism and the journalist become discursively sedimented, as a range of contingent identifications align to give shape to the normalised ideal. This norm then constantly renews itself, in the face of continuous challenge. It does this through communities of practice that rest on what Charles Husband would call ideologies of professionalism. These include forms of discursive and practical consciousness, the former relating to institutionalised training and education, and the latter through more abstract ideals of inherent journalistic qualities, such as "having a nose for a story".[26]

For ethnic minorities and migrants, the discursive construction of journalism involves not only debates and conflicts over defining terms, values and practices but also over racial and ethnic identities and their relationship to journalism and democracy. For Husband, the professional journalist is personified in the white male. The de-racialisation of whiteness means it sits neatly next to claims of neutrality, as a "non-negotiable natural state of being".[27] The migrant journalist is, in this relationship, constructed as the other, what post-structuralists might call the "constitutive outside". They are identified as belonging to a particular group, aligned with certain community and political interests that members of the dominant ethnic group are able to deny at will, allowing the latter to claim to act objectively in the best interests of liberal democratic society. As a result, minorities become fixed in their ethnic groups, and ethnic journalism and journalists are defined as speaking only from, and for, a certain community.[28] There thus emerges a "tension between finding a voice as a minority group and being forced, or allowed, to only speak as a member of that minority group to similar others".[29]

That certain forms of journalism establish a hegemonic position in the field of possibilities is inevitable. For migrant newspapers and journalists, it is important that these discursive journalistic forms are seen as contingent, rather than transcendent, and that other forms are given space to provide counter-hegemonic challenge and disarticulation. The importance of these processes can be better understood through an analysis of the work of African-Australia journalists and media producers.

THE POLITICS OF ETHNIC MEDIA: THE CASE OF AFRICAN MEDIA

The work of African-Australian media producers has taken place in the context of over a decade of moral panics over African migration, integration and crime in Australia. A series of flash-points have emerged, with mainstream media coverage, public and political debate converging into intense, divisive and heavily racialised narratives on the problems of African (read black) migration.[30] In 2007, in the midst of series of racially motivated attacks against people of African descent in Melbourne, then Immigration Minister Kevin Andrews publicly questioned the ability of African refugees to settle in Australian society. A decade later, a series of mediated moral panics emerged over so-called African gangs in Melbourne. The so-called African gangs problem has emerged with almost hysterical media coverage matched only by the histrionics of some of the nation's leading politicians.[31]

African media in Australia are diverse, as would be expected of such a diverse continent. The label of "African-Australian" is not without problems. It is employed in this chapter not only as a useful shorthand designation but also due to a theme of pan-African unity that has been present amongst some African-Australian media producers, without wholly defining them or their work. Thus, African media includes more language-specific media from particular countries (Ethiopia, Sudan), as well as media from particular language and cultural groups within those countries (such as Harari language media from Ethiopian born migrants). It also includes pan-African media, in English, with a wider African imagined audience.

The data discussed below comes from 14 in-depth interviews with African-Australian journalists, media producers and presenters from community radio and television programmes, websites and a magazine. Specifically, interviewees come from a website, *Africa Media Australia*, a community television programme, *Africa Amara TV*, Change Magazine and eight different community radio programmes from 3CR, 3ZZZ, Radio Skid Row and SBS, respectively. Of the radio programmes, four are broadcast in English, with the other four in an African language, sometimes mixed with English.

As is to be expected, African media perform a range of functions and are produced based on different and overlapping motivations. Reflecting other literature on ethnic and migrant media, producers are motivated by both cultural maintenance and challenging mainstream misconceptions about African-Australian people and issues.[32] Cultural maintenance can come in a specific form, as is the case in Harari language broadcasting, or a broader pan-African form, as when African celebration days are celebrated. Challenging mainstream interpretations and discourses can also take the form of direct engagement with media and public, or via producing more positive stories about African-Australians.

In a practice that echoes Susan Forde, Kerrie Foxwell and Michael Meadows' findings that community ethnic media act as a way of encouraging political participation by migrants,[33] several African media producers include guests on their programmes from mainstream institutions such as law enforcement, government and the legal profession. They do this sometimes in order to pass on information to their communities (e.g. about migration law or voter registration), and sometimes in a more agonistic and combative fashion, as a way to challenge dominant discourses around migration and in particular African youth crime.

In performing these various roles, African media producers, writers, broadcasters and journalists take certain positions in relation to overlapping cultural and social groups. Some overtly articulate their role as journalists, but in ways that ground them within an African community for whom they speak. As one interviewee says: "I just think everybody needs to be heard. So, when you're in society and you're a minority. ... [It] doesn't mean you don't have views. So essentially why I became part of [the website] was to help Africans tell their stories" (Amara,[34] female, interviewed 2012).

This explicit identification with a community can also be seen in the overt task of engaging with, informing and challenging wider public perceptions. Here, African-Australians see their role as correcting and re-educating. Public knowledge is here a space of conflict and disagreement, one in which dominant media interpretations are not beyond direct challenge. The founder of a leading African-Australian news website says:

> Every time there is a media publication that I see as negative for the African, I want to organise an interview with the journalist that published that ... as a way to kind of say hey, you know, it's OK you can publish that, you can publish your media, but we would like you to be able to give us a little bit of the understanding why you're reporting in this way rather than the other why. ... I mean it's some sort of soft monitoring. (Lloyd, male, interviewed 2012)

In the context of a pluralist approach to politics and journalism, the above statement contains many elements of agonistic politics. It challenges the neutrality ideal of mainstream journalism, seeing it rather in terms of "negative" or "positive" coverage. The male participant accepts the media's right to publish their work but also insists on his own right to challenge their interpretations. Finally, he sees the media coverage as one of many options, not as an inevitable reflection of a single, underlying truth. To understand ethnic journalism, it is necessary to move away from normative theories around journalism ethics and practice.

The values and practices of several African journalists are misaligned with dominant understandings of modern liberal journalism. Theirs is an explicit advocacy position, one which rejects the image of the autonomous journalist, free from the messy binds of political involvement and able to observe from a detached position. They produce media rather from a particular standpoint, as community members with an interest in the cultural, social and political well-being of that community. Public knowledge is a site of contestation, and mainstream media are directly and indirectly challenged in a way that problematises the dominant interpretation of events and issues.

Again, there is nothing wholly unique about such a situation. Matthew Matsaganis and Viki Katz describe the advocacy position taken by ethnic journalists, and the way they negotiate their specialist identities (those related to their role as ethnic journalists) and their inclusive identities (those attuned to dominant journalistic ethics, values and practices).[35] Although a lack of resources impedes on their ability to enact their inclusive identities as journalists, dominant journalistic norms are not challenged, but rather negotiated, with a recognition that "the 'advocate' label highlights how these [ethnic] producers are different from their mainstream counterparts in ways that mark them as less professional, thereby reinforcing their specialist identities".[36]

It is precisely these markings that *are* challenged through a post-structuralist approach. Under the post-structuralist perspective, the hegemonic norms that marginalise the journalists in Matsaganis and Katz's study, and that tend to push migrant and ethnic media producers towards a specialist position, in which they can only speak on behalf of their communities, would be fundamentally challengeable and challenged.[37] None of this is to say that ethnic journalists, broadcasters and producers necessarily lack or reject dominant norms of professionalism. Rather, it is an approach which denies the naturalisation of dominant journalistic ethics, values and practices.

As several authors have pointed out, the journalistic ideal of objectivity is highly racialised.[38] As Jane Rhodes, a woman of colour, wrote when reflecting on her own experiences in newsrooms:

> As an employee with multiple outsider identities, I was never trusted. My editors assumed that I could never be neutral—that my identification with other aggrieved groups would overwhelm my journalistic skills. The mantra of objectivity was a convenient device through which to enforce a gendered hegemony that would make a feminist of anti-racist position problematic.[39]

This is fundamentally important for ethnic journalists, migrant media and racial minorities. The ethics of objectivity, neutrality and a dispassionate coolness best serve those who require little radical change to social and political systems and structures. As sociologists have been saying for some time, the structures, organisational practices and guiding principles of mainstream journalism tend towards the conservation of the status quo, thus lacking the tools necessary to confront racism directly at its deeply embedded social and political level.[40] For those who face structural forms of racism, relying on traditional forms of journalism guarantees little in terms of change.

CONCLUSION

At the beginning of this chapter, I posed two questions. The first was how ethnic media and journalism might disrupt conventional understandings of the relationship between journalism, race and democracy. The second asked how ethnic media challenge the grand claims of dominant forms of journalism and politics, particularly in regard to equality, rationality and neutrality. In looking at both questions, it is clear that we need to reconsider any simplistic idea that journalism's relationship to democracy transcends race. That a particular form of journalism enjoys a privileged relationship with democracy should not blind us to the plurality of journalisms, including those alternative forms that, in the case of ethnic media, have been marginalised not because of any inherent and self-evident deficiencies, but due to a complex confluence of race, politics and power. Addressing racial inequalities in both society and journalism can never be achieved by longing for a pure past, but must instead involve dismantling hegemonic structures around politics, race and public knowledge.

On this last point, ethnic media and journalism's importance lies, in no small part, in their counter-hegemonic potential, the way in which their presence articulates dominant forms of journalism as contingent rather than inevitable. How we understand ethnic media's position in wider society depends on how we approach the relationship between journalism and democracy. In this chapter I have argued that a post-structuralist approach is better able to explain the historical role of migrant and ethnic media, and to articulate their current position within democratic societies.

In problematising a normative approach to the journalism-democracy nexus, the work of Chantal Mouffe and others challenges and denaturalises journalistic ethics and values that have marginalised migrants and ethnic minorities. There can be no neutral ground—external to that which gives it shape—upon which to base a final, foundational position. Yet this need not mean a slippage into apathetic relativism. Rather, it means the denial of finality and closure for positions of power. It problematises arguments for particular political or social orders that are based on a natural, objective or universal grounding, one that is beyond social context, interpretation or challenge.

For ethnic minorities and migrant media, it is this latter aspect of the theory that is important. Hegemonic journalistic formations, and their relationship to democracy, must be constantly challenged rather than naturalised, and the results of that naturalisation—the marginalisation of alternative forms and the articulation of hegemonic professionalism with racial identity—must be exposed. A post-structuralist approach allows us to see migrant media and ethnic journalism in a different light, to recognise its constitutive power and to look for, and perhaps even argue for, different approaches based within minority ethnic communities.

These possibilities are particularly important for the African-Australian journalists and media producers discussed in this chapter. Facing significant amounts of media racism that have real impacts on their daily lives, it is important not only that African-Australians have a voice but also that these voices are heard amongst the cacophony of more powerful discourses. Agonistic engagements can be seen in the work of African-Australians as they engage with and challenge structural and individual forms of racism. Their media is, therefore, important not simply because it speaks to a community ignored or criminalised in the mainstream media, but because it helps shape the way this community engages with the inequalities and injustices and Australian society.

Mouffe's work has rarely been applied to media. When it has, it has acted as a theoretical framework to explain the importance of agonistic dissensus and counter-hegemonic challenge in digital media spaces.[41] Its decentralisation of power, and its insistence on difference as constitutive, rather than temporary, makes it highly relevant for migrant media studies. In particular it allows one to read the historical and contemporary nature of ethnic print, broadcasting and digital media as about more than ethnic communities, and instead as also relating directly to the nature of multicultural and multi-ethnic democracies. Mouffe's work insists on seeing ethnic media as more than simply alternative or different, but as part of a complex and uneven communicative environment with ramifications for social and political relations.

NOTES

1. Miriam Gilson and Jerzy Zubrzycki, *The Foreign Language Press in Australia 1848–1964* (Canberra: Australian National University Press, 1967).
2. Matthew D. Matsaganis, Viki S. Katz and Sandra J. Ball-Rokeach, *Understanding Ethnic Media: Producers, consumers and society* (Los Angeles: Sage, 2011).
3. Gilson and Zubrzycki, *The Foreign Language Press in Australia*, 160.
4. Augie Fleras, "Multicultural media in a post-multicultural Canada? Rethinking integration", *Global Media Journal—Canadian Edition* 8, no. 2 (2015): 30.
5. Sherry Yu, "The inevitably dialectic nature of ethnic media", *Global Media Journal—Canadian Edition* 8, no. 2 (2015): 133–140. Fleras, "Multicultural Media in Post Multicultural-Canada".
6. See: Chantal Mouffe, *The Democratic Paradox* (London and New York: Verso, 2000); Chantal Mouffe, *Agonistics: Thinking the world politically* (London and New York: Verso, 2013).
7. Mouffe, *Agonistics*, 3–4.
8. Charles W. Mills, *The Racial Contract* (Ithaca and London: Cornell University Press, 1997); Charles Mills, *Black Rights/White Wrongs: The critique of racial liberalism* (Oxford: Oxford University Press, 2017); Christopher P. Campbell, Kim M. LeDuff, Cheryl D. Jenkins and Rockell A. Brown, ed., *Race and News: Critical Perspectives* (New York: Routledge, 2012).
9. Rockell A. Brown, "African-American Newspaper Coverage of the AIDS Crisis", in *Race and News: Critical perspectives*, ed. Christopher P. Campbell, Kim M. LeDuff, Cheryl D, Jenkins, and Rockell A. Brown (New York: Routledge, 2012), 114.
10. Chantal Mouffe, *The Return of the Political* (London and New York: Verso, 1993); Chantal Mouffe, "Deliberative Democracy or Agonistic Pluralism?", *Social Research* 66, no. 3 (1999): 745–758. Chantal Mouffe, *On the Political* (London and New York: Routledge, 2005).
11. Thomas Hanitzsch and Tim Vos, "Journalistic roles and the struggle over institutional identity: The discursive constitution of journalism", *Communication Theory* 27 (2017): 122.
12. Mouffe, "Deliberative Democracy or Agonistic Pluralism?", *Social Research*; Nico Carpentier, "Identity, Contingency and Rigidity: The counter-hegemonic constructions of the identity of the media professional", *Journalism* 6, no. 2 (2005).

13. Hanitzsch and Vos, "Journalistic roles and the struggle over institutional identity", 121.
14. Charles Husband, "Minority Ethnic Media as Communities of Practice: professionalism and identity politics in interaction", *Journal of Ethnic and Migration Studies* 31, no. 3 (2005): 461–479.
15. Mills, *Black Rights/White Wrongs*, 3.
16. Nancy Fraser, "Rethinking the Public Sphere: A contribution to the critique of actually existing democracy", *Social Text* 25, no. 26 (1990): 56–80.
17. See: Husband, "Minority Ethnic Media as Communities of Practice"; Fraser, "Rethinking the Public Sphere".
18. Hanitzsch and Vos, "Journalistic roles and the struggle over institutional identity", 122; Folker Hanusch and Thomas Hanitzsch, "Comparing journalistic Cultures", *Journalism Studies* 18, no. 5: 525–535; Husband, "Minority Ethnic Media as Communities of Practice", 461–479.
19. Mouffe, *Agonistics*.
20. Hanitzsch and Vos, "Journalistic roles and the struggle over institutional identity".
21. Jean Chalaby, "Journalism as an Anglo-American Invention: A comparison of the development of French and Anglo-American journalism, 1830s–1920s", *European Journal of Communication* 11, no. 3 (1996): 303–326; Carpentier, "Identity, Contingency and Rigidity", 199–219.
22. Hanitzsch and Vos, "Journalistic roles and the struggle over institutional identity", 122. Emphasis in original.
23. Hanitzsch and Vos, "Journalistic roles and the struggle over institutional identity".
24. Carpentier, "Identity, Contingency and Rigidity"; Husband, "Minority Ethnic Media as Communities of Practice".
25. Carpentier, "Identity, Contingency and Rigidity", 214.
26. Husband, "Minority Ethnic Media as Communities of Practice", 464.
27. Husband, "Minority Ethnic Media as Communities of Practice", 466
28. Jane Rhodes, "Journalism in the New Millennium: What's a feminist to do?" *Feminist Media Studies* 1, no. 1 (2001): 49–53. Annabelle Sreberny, "'not only, But Also': Mixedness and media", *Journal of Ethnic and Migration Studies* 31, no. 3 (2005): 443–459.
29. Sreberny, "'not only, But Also'", 445.
30. See David Nolan, Karen Farquharson and Tim Marjoribanks, ed., *Australian Media and the Politics of Belonging* (London & New York: Anthem Press, 2018).
31. John Budarick, "Why the media are to blame for racialising Melbourne's 'African gang' problem", *The Conversation*, August 1, 2018, http://theconversation.com/why-the-media-are-to-blame-for-racialising-melbournes-african-gang-problem-100761 (accessed February 7, 2020).

32. John Budarick, "From marginalization to a voice of our own: African media in Australia", in *Minorities and Media: Producers, industries, audiences*, ed. John Budarick and Gil-Soo Han (London: Palgrave Macmillan, 2017), 37–57.
33. Susan Forde, Kerrie Foxwell and Michael Meadows, *Developing Dialogues: Indigenous and ethnic community broadcasting in Australia* (Bristol: Intellect, 2009), 99–123.
34. Names of participants have been changed for anonymity.
35. Matthew D. Matsaganis and Viki S. Katz, "How ethnic media producers constitute their communities of practice: An ecological approach", *Journalism* 15, no. 7 (2014): 926–944.
36. Matsaganis and Katz, "How Ethnic Media Producers Constitute their Communities of Practice", 938.
37. Matsaganis and Katz, "How Ethnic Media Producers Constitute their Communities of Practice".
38. Husband, "Minority Ethnic Media as Communities of Practice", 461–479.
39. Rhodes, "Journalism in the New Millennium": 49.
40. Herbert Gans, "Deciding What's News", in *Key Readings in Journalism*, ed. Elliot King and Jane L. Chapman (New York and London: Routledge, 2012), 95–104.
41. Emma Jane, "'Dude ... stop the spread': Antagonism, agonism, and #manspreading on social media", *International Journal of Cultural Studies* 20, no. 5 (2017): 459–475; Anthony McCosker and Amelia Johns, "Productive Provocations: Vitriolic media, spaces of protest and agonistic outrage in the 2011 England riots", *The Fibreculture Journal* 22 (2013): 171–193.

BIBLIOGRAPHY

PRIMARY

ARCHIVES AND MANUSCRIPTS

FILEF MELBOURNE ARCHIVE

"Advertising Agencies" folder, (uncatalogued).

JOHN CURTIN PRIME MINISTERIAL LIBRARY

Australia Visit of Mr. Curtin to USA & UK in connection with Prime Ministers' Conference London. Bentley: John Curtin Prime Ministerial Library. 1944, JCPML00768/3.

Curtin, John. "The Question of Mr Angwin's Politics." *Westralian Worker.* Bentley: John Curtin Prime Ministerial Library. February 4, 1927.

Index to John Curtin's speeches in the Digest of Decisions and Announcements and Important Speeches by the Prime Minister, 1941–1945. Bentley: John Curtin Prime Ministerial Library, 2007.

LANDESARCHIV BERLIN

Landesarchiv Berlin, A. Pr. Br. Rep 30 Berlin C, Polizei-Präsidium, Nr.15642.

© The Author(s), under exclusive license to Springer Nature
Switzerland AG 2021
C. Dewhirst, R. Scully (eds.), *Voices of Challenge in Australia's Migrant and Minority Press*, Palgrave Studies in the History of the Media, https://doi.org/10.1007/978-3-030-67330-7

Ministère de l'Europe et des Affaires Etrangères

Ministère des Affaires Etrangères, Correspondance Politique et Commerciale, Nouvelle Séries, box 21.

National Archives Australia, Canberra

Attorney-General's Department. *Chinese Newspapers Australia.* National Archives of Australia: Canberra. 1923, A367, 1923/1824.

'Chinese Republican [Republic] News—Exemption for staff', National Archive of Australia, A433 1947/2/6297 PART 1.

Clyne, Thomas Stuart. *Report of Commissioner.* National Archives of Australia: Canberra. 1945, A374.

Commonwealth of Australia. *Arrival of Chinese Minister to Australia.* National Archives of Australia: Canberra. 1941–1942, A2880, 6/19/3.

Commonwealth of Australia. *Chinese World's News.* National Archives of Australia: Canberra. 1922–1955, series A445, file 232/4/18.

Commonwealth of Australia. *Percy Reginald Stephensen.* National Archives of Australia: Canberra. 1943, A373, 4522B.

Commonwealth of Australia. *Thomas Walsh.* National Archives of Australia: Canberra. 1939, A367, C64736.

'George Bew, Leon Bew, Pearl Bew, Percy Bew, Daisy Alma Bew, George Noel Bew, Walter Bew, Elsie Bew, Edith Bew, Darling Bew'. National Archive of Australia, SP244/2, N1950/2/3885.

'Inspector D.A. Mackiehen to Investigation Branch, Attorney-General's Department, March 27, 1922', National Archives of Australia: Canberra, A402/ W248.

National Archives of Australia: Canberra. 1922–1923, A1, 1923/1089.

'Percy Lee [also known as Bert Hee Lowe]', National Archives of Australia, SP42/1, C1941/1585.

'Socialischer Verein Vorvarts [*sic*], Trusties Carl Mitscherlich, F W & We, Emil Flues, 1917-18', National Archives of Australia, MP16/1 1918/21.

National Library of Australia, Canberra

'Papers of the Chau family,' National Library of Australia, MS10030.

William Liu and Hazel de Berg, 'William Liu interviewed by Hazel de Berg, 1978'. National Library of Australia.

National Film and Sound Archives

Cinesound Productions. *First Chinese Minister Arrives* (newsreel). National Film and Sound Archives: Canberra. 1941, f72226.

"Modern Trends in Art", *The Age*, October 14, 1941, p. 6. Movietone. *Names in the News* (newsreel). National Film and Sound Archives: Canberra. 1941, 126160.

Movietone. *Personalities Living at the Federal Capital* (newsreel). National Film and Sound Archives: Canberra. 1941, 89268.

NOEL BUTLIN ARCHIVES CENTRE

Correspondence, NSW Chinese Chamber of Commerce, 1913–1917, ANU, NBAC 111/2/1.

Minutes of NSW Chinese Chamber of Commerce, Noel Butlin Archives Centre, ANU, NBAC 111-4-1

STATE RECORDS AUTHORITY OF NEW SOUTH WALES

Colonial Secretary's correspondence, item 5/6363, State Records Authority of New South Wales (SRNSW).

Bankruptcy files 1888–1929, item 23567, State Records Authority of New South Wales (SRNSW).

Defunct Company packet for Tung Wah News, no. 3/ 5733 in 1723, State Records Authority of New South Wales (SRNSW).

NEWSPAPERS AND PERIODICALS

Army News
Australische Zeitung
Bendigo Advertiser
Chinese Australian Herald, Sydney
Chinese Republic News, Sydney
Der freier Arbeiter
Der Sozialdemokrat
Evening News
Everyones
Examiner
Il Globo
Huon Times
Kalgoorlie Miner
La Fiamma
Le Courrier Australien
Maryborough Chronicle
Medical Journal of Australia
Nambucca and Bellinger News

News
Nuovo Paese
Review of Reviews
Smith's Weekly
Sunday Telegraph
The Advertiser
The Age
The Argus
The Armidale Express and New England General Advertiser
The Australian Woman's Sphere
The Australian Worker
The Bulletin
The Canberra Times
The Courier-Mail
The Daily News
The Daily Telegraph
The Guardian
The Herald
The Mercury
The Newcastle Sun
The Nineteenth Century and After: A Monthly Review
The Sun
The Sunday Telegraph
The Sydney Morning Herald
The Worker
Truth
Tung Wah News, Sydney
Tung Wah Times, Sydney
Vorwärts
West Gippsland Gazette
Westralia Worker

OTHERS

Act no. 23, *Newspaper Act 1898* (NSW), Accessed February 16, 2020: https://jade.io/article/442225.

Andrews, E. M. *Australia and China: The Ambiguous Relationship*. Carlton, Vic.: Melbourne University Press, 1985.

Brereton, Lewis H. *The Brereton Diaries*. New York: William Morrow and Company, 1946.

British Pathé. *Australia 1942* (newsreel). British Pathé: London. 1942.

Brosses, Charles de. *Histoire des navigations aux terres australes*. Paris: Durand, 1756.

Chung Redden, Jae. Telephone interview with Jeremy Fisher, March 24, 2019.

Coghlan, TA. *General Report on the Eleventh Census of New South Wales.* Sydney: Government Printer, 1894.

"Comrade Mary". *An Appeal to Women.* (Vanguard Tract No.13) Brisbane, n.d.

Curtin, John. "Australian Relations." *Digest of Decisions and Announcements and Important Speeches by the Prime Minister* 7 (November 17, 1941): 6.

Curtin, John. "National Day." *Digest of Decisions and Announcements and Important Speeches by the Prime Minister* 45 (8 October 1942a): 7–8.

Curtin, John. "Nationals in Australia." *Digest of Decisions and Announcements and Important Speeches by the Prime Minister* 23 (March 24, 1942b): 11.

Curtin, John. "Prisoners of War." Digest of Decisions and Announcements and Important *Speeches by the Prime Minister* 28 (May 7, 1942c): 14.

Davis, Beatrice, Interviewed by Suzanne Lunney. National Library of Australia Oral History project. Recorded on 19 May 1977 at Folly Point, NSW. nla.gov. au/nla.obj-215119627

Davis, Beatrice. In conversation with novelist Christopher Koch and poet Thomas Shapcott. The Society of Editors (NSW) Newsletter, February 1987.

Department of External Affairs. *William Yinson Lee.* National Archives of Australia: Canberra. 1916, A1, 1916/31599.

Department of Immigration. *Chinese World News.* National Archives of Australia: Canberra. 1933, A2998, 1952/253.

Eggleston, F.W. to Evatt, H.V. *Documents on Australian Foreign Policy* 7 (November 21, 1944).

"Eznuk", *Woman and the Social Problem* (Vanguard Tract No. 14), Brisbane, n.d. [1902].

Forel, Auguste. *Hypnotism or, Suggestion and Psychotherapy: A Study of the Psychological, Psycho-physiological and Therapeutic Aspects of Hypnotism.* Trans. H. W. Armit, London: Rebman, 1906.

Goldstein, Vida. *To America and Back: A lecture by Vida Goldstein.* Prepared by Jill Roe, Sydney: Australian History Museum, [1902] 2002.

Griffith, George. *In an Unknown Prison Land: An Account of Convicts and Colonists in New Caledonia with Jottings out and Home.* London: Hutchinson & Co, 1901.

Home Affairs Department. *Chinese Times Limited.* National Archives of Australia: Canberra. 1924–1933, A1, file 1933/307.

Home and Territories Department. *"The Chinese World's News" Publication in Australia.* National Archives of Australia: Canberra. 1921, A1, 1921/16152.

Home and Territories Department. W Howe: Chinese Newspapers and the 'White Australia Policy'.

Interview with Nino Randazzo, May 6, 1999, Radio National. "Australia's non-English Press", *The Media Report.* Melbourne: ABC Melbourne, 1999.

Jersey, Lady. "A French Colony." In *The Nineteenth Century: A Monthly Review* 22, 524–535. London: Sampson Low, Marston & Co, 1892.

Kunze, E.H. "Socialism in Australia. With Special Reference to Labor in Politics in Queensland". *International Socialist Review* III, 3, September 1902a, 161–164.

Kunze, E.H. ("Eznuk"). "The Trust Problem". *The Worker,* 25 October 1902b.

Kunze, E.H. ("Eznuk"). *Woman and the Social Problem* (Vanguard Tract No.14). Brisbane: n.d. [1902].

La Fiamma. La Fiamma—I primi cinquant'anni. Sydney: Media Communications, 1997.

Lloyd, Clem and Hall, Richard, ed. *Backroom Briefings: John Curtin's War.* Canberra: National Library of Australia, 1997.

Smith, H. A., F.S.S., *The Official Year Book of N.S.W. 1920.* Sydney: W. A. Gullick, Government Printer 1921.

Stanton, Elizabeth Cady, Susan B. Anthony and Matilda Joslyn Gage, ed. *History of Woman Suffrage, Vol. I. 1848–1861.* 2nd edn, Rochester, NY: Charles Mann, 1889.

Swan, Norman. "100th Anniversary of the Medical Journal of Australia." *ABC Radio National Health report,* June 9, 2014 www.abc.net.au/radionational/programs/healthreport/100th-anniversary-of-the-medical-journal-of-australia/5505020#transcript.

Taylor, George A. *Those were the days: being reminiscences of Australian artists and writers.* Sydney: Tyrell's Limited, 1918.

The Red Light. Manifesto of the Social-Democratic Vanguard, Brisbane, 1901 www. reasoninrevolt.net.au/biogs/E000311b.htm.

Therry, Roger. *Reminiscences of thirty years residence in New South Wales and Victoria,* London: Sampson Low, Son & Co, 1863.

Wehner, Volkhard. "The Verein Vorwaerts." Unpublished Manuscript [2018].

SECONDARY

BOOKS

Anderson, Benedict, *Imagined Communities,* London: Verso, 1983.

Anderson, Benedict. *Imagined Communities.* London & New York: Verso, 1991.

Anderson, Benedict. *Imagined Communities: Reflections on the Origin and Spread of Nationalism.* London: Verso, 2006.

Armillei, Riccardo, and Bruno Mascitelli. ed. *From 2004 to 2016: A new Italian 'exodus' to Australia?* Melbourne: COMITES, 2016.

Barker, Anthony. *One of the First and One of the Best: Beatrice Davis, Book Editor,* Melbourne: Society of Editors (Vic), 1991.

Barbançon, Louis-José. *Gomen à l'ombre Du Kaala.* Kaala-Gomen: Mairie de Kaala-Gomen, 1992.

Battiston, Simone. *Immigrants Turned Activists: Italians in 1970s Melbourne.* Leicester: Troubador Publishing, 2012.

Beaumont, Joan. *Broken nation: Australians in the Great War.* Crow Nest: Allen & Unwin, 2013.

Belli, Joseph, *Die Rote Feldpost unterm Sozialistengesetz.* Bonn: J.H.W. Dietz Nachf., [1912] 1978.

Bertelli, Lidio. *A Socio-cultural Profile of the Italian Community in Australia.* Melbourne: Catholic Intercultural Resource Centre, 1986.

Bomford, Janette M. *That Dangerous and Persuasive Woman: Vida Goldstein.* Carlton, Vic.: Melbourne University Press, 1993

Bones, Helen. *The Expatriate Myth: New Zealand Writers and the Colonial World.* Dunedin, NZ: Otago University Press, 2018.

Bonwick, James. *The White Wild Man & the Blacks of Victoria.* 2nd edn, Melbourne: Fergusson & Moore, 1863.

Bowden, Brett. *The Empire of Civilization: The Evolution of an Imperial Idea.* Chicago: University of Chicago Press, 2009.

Brereton, J. Le Gay, Burrows, J.E., Green, H.M, Hope, A.D., Howarth, R.G., Mackaness, J., Smythe, P.E., Todd, F.A., Tremlett, D., and Wentworth-Sheilds, W.F. *The Temple on the hill: a mask, presented at the University of Sydney, in Lent Term, 1928.* Sydney: The Australasian Medical Publishing Co., 1928.

Bridge, Carl, and Kent Fedorowich. *The British World: Diaspora, Culture and Identity.* London: Frank Cass Publishers, 2003.

Buckridge, Patrick and Belinda McKay, ed. *By the Book: A Literary History of Queensland.* St Lucia, Qld: University of Queensland Press, 2007

Burgmann, Verity. *'In Our Time'. Socialism and the Rise of Labor, 1885–1905.* Sydney, London, Boston: George Allen & Unwin, 1985.

Burton, Antoinette. *After the Imperial Turn: Thinking with and through the Nation.* Durham, NC: Duke University Press, 2003.

Campbell, Christopher P., Kim M. LeDuff, Cheryl D. Jenkins and Rockell A. Brown, ed. *Race and News: Critical Perspectives.* New York: Routledge, 2012.

Chapman, Jane. *Gender, Citizenship and Newspapers: Historical and Transnational Perspectives.* London: Palgrave Macmillan, 2013.

Chen, Shenong. *Being Chinese, Becoming Chinese American.* Urbana and Chicago: University of Illinois Press, 2002.

Choi, C. Y. *Chinese Migration and Settlement in Australia.* Sydney: Sydney University Press, 1975.

Christian, Clifford G., Theodore L. Glasser, Denis McQuail, Kaarle Nordenstreng, and Robert A. White. *Normative Theories of the Media: Journalism in democratic societies.* Urbane and Chicago: University of Illinois Press, 2010.

Coble, Parks M. *China's War Reporters: The Legacy of Resistance Against Japan.* Cambridge: Harvard University Press, 2015.

Coghlan, T. A. and T. T. Ewing. *The Progress of Australia in the Century*. London: Chambers, 1903.

Collins, Jock. *Migrant Hands in a Distant Land: Australia's Post-War Immigration*. 2nd edn. Leichardt: Pluto Press, 1988.

Commonwealth Bureau of Census and Statistics, *Part I Analysis of Population in Local Government Areas and non-Municipal Towns of 1,000 Persons or More*. Canberra: Commonwealth Bureau of Census and Statistics, 1963.

Connell, John. *New Caledonia or Kanaky?: The Political History of a French Colony*. Canberra: The Australian National University, 1987.

Conrad, Sebastian. *Globalisation and the Nation in Imperial Germany*, trans. Sorcha O'Hagan. Cambridge: Cambridge University Press, 2010.

Corkhill, Alan, *Queensland and Germany*. Melbourne: Academia Press, 1992.

Corrieri, Michael. *Italians of Port Pirie: A Social History*. Port Pirie: Our Lady of Martyrs—Port Pirie Italian Community, 1992.

Cresciani, Gianfranco. *No Country for Revolutionaries. Italian Communists in Sydney 1971–1991: Their Activities, Policies and Liaison with the Italian and Australian Communist Parties*. North Melbourne: Australian Scholarly Publishing, 2018.

Cresciani, Gianfranco. *The Italians in Australia*. Cambridge, Port Adelaide: Cambridge University Press, 2003.

Darian-Smith, Kate, Patricia Grimshaw and Stuart Macintyre, ed. *Britishness Abroad: Transnational Movements and Imperial Cultures*. Melbourne: Melbourne University Press, 2007.

Da Silva, Denise F. *Toward a Global Idea of Race*. Minneapolis, MN: University of Minnesota Press, 2007.

Davidson, Alistair. *From Subject to Citizen: Australian Citizenship in the Twentieth Century*. Cambridge: Cambridge University Press, 1997.

Davison, Graeme, John Hirst, and Stuart Macintyre, ed. *The Oxford Companion to Australian History*. Oxford University Press, 1999.

Denoon, Donald, and Philippa Mein Smith. *A History of Australia, New Zealand, and the Pacific*. Malden, MA: Blackwell Publishers, 2000.

Dewhirst, Catherine and Richard Scully, ed. *The Transnational Voices of Australia's Migrant and Minority Press*, Palgrave Studies in the History of the Media. Cham, Switzerland: Palgrave Macmillan, 2020.

Di Biase, Bruno and Brian Paltridge, ed. *Italian in Australia: Language of Dialects in Schools? Sull'italiano in Australia: Lingua o dialetto nelle scuole?* Sydney: FILEF Italo-Australian Publications, 1985.

Douglass, William. *From Italy to Ingham: Italians in North Queensland*. St Lucia, Qld: Queensland University Press, 1995.

Duchen, Claire. *Feminism in France: From May '68 to Mitterrand*. 9th edn, Milton Park: Routledge, 2013.

Due Clemence and Damien Riggs. *Representations of Indigenous Australians in the Mainstream News Media.* Teneriffe, Qld: Post Pressed, 2011.

Dutton, David. *One of Us?: A century of Australian citizenship.* Sydney: University of New South Wales Press, 2002.

Duyker, Edward. *Of the Star and the Key: Mauritius, Mauritians and Australia.* Sylvania, NSW: Australian Mauritian Research Group, 1988.

Engelberg, Ernst. *Revolutionäre Politik und rote Feldpost 1878–1890.* Berlin: Akademie-Verlag, 1959.

Evans, Julie, Patricia Grimshaw, David Phillips and Shurlee Swain. *Equal Subjects, Unequal Rights: Indigenous People in British Settler Colonies, 1830s–1910.* Manchester and New York: Manchester University Press, 2003.

Farrell, Frank, *International Socialism and Australian Labour.* Sydney: Hale & Iremonger, 1981.

Feagin, Joseph R. *Race and Ethnic Relations.* 2nd edn., Englewood Cliffs, NJ: Prentice Hall, 1984.

Fenby, Jonathan. *History of Modern China.* 3rd edition, London: Penguin Books, 2019.

Forde, Susan, Kerrie Foxwell and Michael Meadows. *Developing Dialogues: Indigenous and ethnic community broadcasting in Australia.* Bristol: Intellect, 2009.

Fox, Matthew J. *History of Queensland: its people and industries, The history of Queensland: Its people and Industries: An Historical and Commercial Review descriptive and biographical facts, figures and illustrations: an epitome of progress.* Brisbane: States Publishing Company, 1923.

Fraser, Nancy. *Unruly Practices: Power, Discourse, and Gender in Contemporary Social Theory.* Minneapolis, MN: University of Minnesota Press, 1989.

Fricke, Dieter, *Handbuch zur Geschichte der deutschen Arbeiterbewegung 1869 bis 1917.* Berlin: Dietz, 1987, Bd.1.

Gilson, Miriam and Jerzy Zubrzycki, *The Foreign-Language Press in Australia, 1848–1964.* Canberra: ANU Press, 1967.

Goodall, Heather. *Invasion to Embassy: Land in Aboriginal politics in New South Wales, 1770–1972.* Sydney: Allen & Unwin, 1996.

Goodall Heather and Cadzow Allison, *Rivers and Resilience: Aboriginal People of Sydney's Georges River.* Sydney: UNSW Press, 2009.

Gooding, Paul. *Historic Newspapers in the Digital Age: Search All About It!* London: Routledge, 2017.

Griffen-Foley, Bridget, ed. *A Companion to the Australian Media.* North Melbourne: Australian Scholarly Publishing, 2014.

Heiss, Anita. *Dhuuluu-Yala: To Talk Straight—Publishing Indigenous Literature.* Canberra: Aboriginal Studies Press, 2003.

Heiss, Anita and Peter Minter, ed. *Macquarie PEN Anthology of Australian Aboriginal literature.* Crows Nest, NSW: Allen & Unwin, 2008.

Heyd, Uriel. *Reading Newspapers: Press and Public in Eighteenth-century Britain and America.* Oxford University Studies in the Enlightenment Series. Oxford: Voltaire Foundation, 2017.

Horner, Jack. *Seeking Racial Justice.* Canberra: Aboriginal Australian Press, 2004.

Jacobson, Matthew Frye. *Whiteness of a Different Color: European Immigrants and the Alchemy of Race.* Cambridge, MA: Harvard University Press, 1998.

Keating, James. *Distant Sisters: Australasian Women and the International Struggle for the Vote, 1880–1914.* Manchester: Manchester University Press, 2020.

Kent, Jacqueline. *A Certain Style: Beatrice Davis, a Literary Life.* Melbourne: Viking, 2001.

Koszyk, Kurt, *Die Presse der deutschen Sozialdemokratie. Eine Bibliographie.* Hannover: Verlag für Literatur und Zeitgeschehen, 1966.

Kunz, Egon. *Displaced Persons: Calwell's New Australians.* Sydney: Australian National University Press, 1998.

Kuo, Mei-fen and Judith Brett. *Unlocking the History of the Australasian Kuo Min Tang, 1911–2013.* North Melbourne: Australian Scholarly Publishing, 2013.

Kuo, Mei-fen. *Making Chinese Australia: Urban Elites, Newspapers and the Formation of Chinese Australian Identity, 1892–1912.* Melbourne: Monash University Publishing, 2013.

Lane, E. H. *Dawn to Dusk. Reminiscences of a Rebel.* Brisbane: William Brooks, 1939.

Lake, Marilyn. *Progressive New World: How Settler Colonialism and Transpacific Exchange Shaped American Reform.* Cambridge, MA: Harvard University Press, 2019.

———. *Getting Equal: The History of Australian Feminism.* Sydney: Allen and Unwin, 1999.

Lake, Marilyn, and Henry Reynolds. *Drawing the Global Colour Line. White Men's Countries and the International Challenge of Racial Equality.* Cambridge: Cambridge University Press, 2008.

Lidtke, Vernon L. *The Outlawed Party: Social Democracy in Germany, 1878–1890.* Princeton, NJ: Princeton University Press, 1966.

Lone, Stewart. *Japan's First Modern War: Army and Society in the Conflict with China, 1894–95.* Houndmills: The Macmillan Press, 1994.

Lopez, Mark. *The Origins of Multiculturalism in Australian Politics 1945–75.* Melbourne: The University of Melbourne Press, 2000.

Loy-Wilson, Sophie. *Australians in Shanghai: Race, Rights and Nation in Treaty Port China.* London, UK: Routledge, 2017.

Lyons, Martin. *The Totem and the Tricolour.* Kensington, NSW: New South Wales University Press, 1986.

Lyons, Martin and John Arnold, ed. *A History of the Book in Australia 1891–1945: A National Culture in a Colonised Market.* St Lucia, Qld: University of Queensland Press, 2001.

Lutes, Jean Marie. *Front Page Girls: Women Journalists in American Culture and Fiction, 1880–1930*. New York: Cornell University Press, 2006.

Ma, Min. *Shangren jingshen de shanbian: jindai Zhongguo shangren guannian yan-jiu* [Transformation of the Chinese merchant spirit: studies on modern Chinese merchant concepts]. Wuhan: Huazhong shifan dzxue chubanshe, 2001.

Manz, Stefan. *Constructing a German Diaspora. The "Greater German Empire", 1871–1914*. London and New York: Routledge, 2014.

Mar, Tracey Banivanua. *Decolonisation and the Pacific: Indigenous Globalisation and the Ends of Empire*. Cambridge: Cambridge University Press, 2016.

Martinez, Julia, Claire Lowrie, Frances Steel and Victoria Katharine Haskins. *Colonialism and Male Domestic Service across the Asia Pacific*. London: Bloomsbury Academic, 2019.

Mascitelli, Bruno and Riccardo Armillei. *Australia's New Wave of Italian Migration: Paradise or Illusion*. North Melbourne: Australian Scholarly Publishing: 2017.

Mascitelli, Bruno and Simone Battiston, ed. *Il Globo: Fifty Years of an Italian Newspaper in Australia*. Ballan, Vic.: Connor Court Publishing, 2009.

Matsaganis, Matthew D., Viki S. Katz and Sandra J.Ball-Rokeach. *Understanding Ethnic Media: Producers, Consumers and Society*. Los Angeles: Sage, 2011.

Maynard, John. *Fight for Liberty and Freedom*, Canberra: Aboriginal Studies Press, 2000.

McCallum, Kerry and Lisa Waller. *The Dynamics of News and Indigenous Policy in Australia*. Bristol, UK: Intellect Books, 2017.

Mills, Charles W. *Black Rights/White Wrongs: The critique of racial liberalism*. Oxford: Oxford University Press, 2017.

———. *The Racial Contract*. Ithaca and London: Cornell University Press, 1997.

Mitter, Rana. *Forgotten Ally: China's World War II, 1937–1945*. New York: Houghton Mifflin Harcourt Publishing Company, 2013.

Moreton-Robinson, Aileen. *The White Possessiveness, Property, Power and Indigenous Sovereignty*. Minneapolis, MN: Minnesota Press, 2015.

Moseley, Ray. *Reporting War: How Foreign Correspondents Risked Capture, Torture and Death to Cover World War II*. New Haven: Yale University Press, 2017.

Mouffe, Chantal. *The Return of the Political*. London and New York: Verso, 1993.

———. *The Democratic Paradox*. London and New York: Verso, 2000.

———. *On the Political*. London and New York: Routledge, 2005.

———. *Agonistics: Thinking the world politically*. London and New York: Verso, 2013.

Muhlmann, Geraldine. *A Political History of Journalism*. Cambridge: Polity, 2008.

Munro, Craig and Robyn Sheahan-Bright, ed. *Paper Empires: A History of the Book in Australia 1946–2005*. St Lucia, Qld: University of Queensland Press, 2006.

Nolan, David, Karen Farquharson, and Tim Marjoribanks, ed. *Australian Media and the Politics of Belonging*. London and New York: Anthem Press, 2018.

O'Connor, Desmond. *No Need to be Afraid: Italian Settlers in South Australia between 1839 and the Second World War.* Adelaide: Wakefield Press, 1996.

O'Donnell, Krista, Renate Bridenthal and Nancy Reagin, ed., *The Heimat Abroad. The Boundaries of Germanness.* Ann Arbor: University of Michigan Press, 2005.

Oldfield, Audrey. *Woman Suffrage in Australia: A Gift or a Struggle?* Melbourne: Cambridge University Press, 1992.

Pascoe, Robert. *Buongiorno Australia: Our Italian Heritage.* Richard, Victoria: Greenhouse Publications, 1987.

Passerini, Luisa, *Autobiography of a Generation: Italy, 1968.* Hanover: Wesleyan University Press, 1996

Paszkowski, Lech. *Poles in Australia and Oceania 1790–1940.* Canberra: Australian National University Press, 1987.

Pedersen, Sarah. *The Scottish Suffragettes and the Press.* London: Palgrave Macmillan, 2017.

Perera, Suvendrini. *Australia and the Insular Imagination: Beaches, Borders, Boats and Bodies.* New York: Palgrave Macmillan, 2009.

Phelan, Sean. *Media, Neoliberalism and the Political.* Basingstoke, UK: Palgrave, 2014.

Pollon, Frances, com. *The Book of Sydney Suburbs.* Sydney: Angus & Robertson, 1990.

Pospiech, Friedrich. *Julius Motteler, der "rote Feldpostmeister", Kampfgefährte von Bebel und W. Liebknecht.* Esslingen am Neckar: [no publisher], 1977.

Price, Charles. *Southern Europeans in Australia.* Melbourne: Oxford Press, 1963.

Randazzo, Nino and Ciglar, Michael. *The Italians in Australia.* Melbourne: AE Press, 1987.

Reed, Christopher. *Gutenberg in Shanghai: Chinese Print Capitalism, 1876–1937.* Vancouver: UBC Press, 2004.

Retallack, James. *Red Saxony: Election Battles and the Spectre of Democracy in Germany, 1860–1918.* Oxford: Oxford University Press, 2017.

Ricatti, Francesco. *Italians in Australia: History, Memory, Identity.* Palgrave Studies in Migration History. Cham, Switzerland: Palgrave Macmillan, 2018.

Rickertt, Jeff, *The Conscientious Communist. Ernie Lane and the Rise of Australian Socialism,* North Melbourne: Australian Scholarly Publishers, 2016.

Russell, John, Rod Kirkpatrick and Victor Isaacs. *Australian Newspaper History: A Biography.* Andergrove, Qld: Australian Newspaper History Group, 2009.

Sanfilippo, Matteo. *Nuovi problemi di storia delle migrazioni italiane.* Viterbo: Sette Città, 2015.

Sergi, Pantaleone. *Stampa migrante: Giornali della diaspora italiana e dell'immigrazione in Italia.* Soveria Mannelli: Rubbettino, 2010.

Shattock, Joanne, ed. *Journalism and the Periodical Press in Nineteenth-Century Britain.* Cambridge: Cambridge University Press, 2017.

Shore, Elliott, Ken Fones-Wolf, James Philip Danky and James P. Danky, ed. *The German-American Radical Press: The Shaping of a Left Political Culture, 1850–1940*. Urbana and Chicago: University of Illinois Press, 1992.

Sima, William. *China & the ANU: Diplomats, Adventurers, Scholars*. Acton: The Australian National University Press, 2015.

Spillman, Lyn. *Solidarity in Strategy: Making Business Meaningful in American Trade Association*. Chicago: University of Chicago Press, 2012.

Steel, Frances. *Oceania Under Steam: Sea Transport and the Cultures of Colonialism, c. 1870–1914*. Manchester: Manchester University Press, 2011.

Stevens, Leonie. *'Me Write Myself': The Free Aboriginal Inhabitants of Van Diemen's Land at Wybalenna, 1832–47*. Clayton, Vic.: Monash University Press, 2017.

Strahan, Lachlan. *Australia's China: Changing Perceptions from the 1930s to the 1990s*. Cambridge, Cambridge University Press, 1996.

Stuer, Anny. *The French in Australia*. Canberra: Australian National University, 1982.

Sun, Wanning, ed. *Media and the Chinese Diaspora: Community, Communications and Commerce*. London: Routledge, 2006.

Sun, Wanning and John Sinclair. *Media and Communication in the Chinese Diaspora: Rethinking Transnationalism*. London: Routledge, 2006.

Suttor, William H. *Australian Stories Re-told, and Sketches of Country Life, Australian stories retold, and, sketches of country life*. Bathurst, NSW: Glyndwr Whalan, 1877.

Svensson, Marina, Sæther, Elin and Zhang, Zhi'an, eds. *Chinese Investigative Journalists' Dreams: Autonomy, Agency and Voice*. Lanham: Lexington Books, 2014.

Totaro-Genevois, Mariella, *Cultural and Linguistic Policy Abroad: The Italian Experience*. Clevedon, UK: Multilingual Matters, 2005.

Veracini, Lorenzo. *Settler Colonialism: A Theoretical Overview*. Basingstoke: Palgrave Macmillan, 2010.

Walker, Bertha. *Solidarity Forever!* Melbourne: The National Press, 1972.

Wang, Erh Min. *Zhongguo jindai sixiang shiliun* [History of modern Chinese thought]). Taipei: Hua shi chu ban she, 1977.

Waring, Marilyn. *If Women Counted: A New Feminist Economics*. San Francisco Harper & Row, 1988.

Watson, Irene. *Aboriginal Peoples: Colonialism and International Law*. New York: Routledge, 2014.

Wehner, Volkhard. *The German-speaking community of Victoria between 1850 and 1930*. Münster: LIT-Verlag, 2018a.

Wehner, Volkhard. "The Verein Vorwaerts". Unpublished MS [2018b].

Willard, Myra. *History of the White Australia Policy to 1920*. Melbourne: Melbourne University Press, 1978.

Winton, Ronald. *From the Sidelines of Medicine.* Glebe: Australasian Medical Publishing Co., 1983.

Winton, Ronald. *Why the Pomegranate? A History of the Australasian College of Physicians.* Sydney: Royal Australasian College of Physicians, 1988.

Wright, Clare. *You Daughters of Freedom.* Melbourne: Text Publishing Company, 2018.

Wurth, Bob. *Saving Australia: Curtin's Secret Peace with Japan.* South Melbourne: Lothian Books, 2006.

Yong, C.F. *The New Gold Mountain: the Chinese in Australia, 1901–1921.* Adelaide: Raphael Arts, 1997.

Zhongguo you chuan gong si and Zhuojing He, *China Mail Steamship Co. ltd.; report, 1915–1919.* San Francisco: Shi jie ri bao she, 1919.

Zhou, Min Zhou. *Contemporary Chinese America.* Philadelphia, PA: Temple University Press, 2009.

ARTICLES AND CHAPTERS

Alcorso, Caroline, Cesare Giulio Popoli and Gaetano Rando. "Community networks and institutions." In *Australia's Italians: Culture and Community in a Changing Society*, edited by Stephen Castles, Caroline Alcorso, Gaetano Rando and Ellie Vasta, 106–24. St. Leonards, NSW: Allen & Unwin, 1992.

Alicia, Ferrández Ferrer. "Towards a democratization of the public space? Challenges for the 21st century". In *The Handbook on Diasporas, Media, Culture*, edited by J. Retis and R. Tsagarousianou, 255–268. Hoboken, NJ: Wiley, 2019.

Armillei, Riccardo. "A Statistical Analysis of New Italian Migration to Australia: Redressing Recent Overstatements." In *Australia's New Wave of Italian Migration: Paradise or Illusion*, edited by Bruno Mascitelli and Riccardo Armillei, 53–78. North Melbourne, Vic.: Australian Scholarly Publishing, 2017.

Bacon, Wendy. "A case study of ethical failure: twenty years of media coverage of Aboriginal deaths in custody." *Pacific Journalism Review* 11, no. 2 (2005): 17–41.

Bagnall, Kate. "Early Chinese Newspapers." 2015, https://www.nla.gov.au/blogs/trove/2015/02/19/early-chinese-newspapers.

Bai, Hongy. ""Between Advocacy and Objectivity." In *Chinese Investigative Journalists' Dreams: Autonomy, Agency and Voice*. In. *Chinese Investigative Journalists' Dreams: Autonomy, Agency and Voice*, edited by Marina Svensson, Elin Sæther, Elin and Zhang, Zhi'an, 77–91. Lanham: Lexington Books, 2014.

Balint, Ruth and Zora Simic. "Histories of Migrants and Refugees in Australia." *Australian Historical Studies* 49 (2018): 378–409.

Barko, Ivan. "The Courrier Australien and French-Australian Relations during the Biard d'Aunet Years (1892–1905)." In *The Culture of the Book: Essays from Two*

Hemispheres in Honour of Wallace Kirsop, edited by David Garrioch, 430–46. Melbourne: Bibliographical Society of Australia and New Zealand, 1999.

Battiston, Simone, "How the Italian-Australian Left Viewed *Il Globo.*" In *Il Globo: Fifty Years of an Italian Newspaper in Australia*, edited by Bruno Mascitelli and Simone Battiston, 74–93. Ballarat, Vic: Connor Court Publishing, 2009.

Battiston, Simone and Sabina Sestigiani. "Percorsi d'emigrazione e di militanza politica: donne italiane in Australia tra gli anni settanta e ottanta del Novecento." In *Lontane da casa. Donne italiane e diaspora globale dall'inizio del Novecento a oggi*, edited by Stefano Luconi and Mario Varricchio, 175–205. Torino: Accademia University Press, 2015.

Bechmann Pedersen, Sune and Marie Cronqvist, "Foreign Correspondents in the Cold War: The Politics and Practices of East German Television Journalists in the West." *Media History* 26, no. 1 (2020): 75–90.

Benton, Gregor. "Chinese Transnationalism in Britain: A Longer History." *Identities* 10, no. 3 (2003): 347–375.

Bergantz, Alexis. "'The Scum of France': Australian Anxieties towards French Convicts in the Nineteenth Century." *Australian Historical Studies* 49, no. 2 (2018): 150–66.

Berthon, Hilary. "A Treasure Trove of Community Language Newspapers." In *The Transnational Voices of Australia's Migrant and Minority Press*, Palgrave Studies of the Media History, edited by Catherine Dewhirst and Richard Scully, 209–224. Cham, Switzerland: Palgrave Macmillan, 2020.

Birch, Tony. "The invisible fire": sovereignty, history and responsibility." In *Sovereign Subjects: Indigenous Sovereignty Matters*, edited by Aileen Moreton-Robinson, 105–117. Crow Nest: Allen & Unwin, 2007.

Bishop, Catherine. "Women on the Move Gender, Money-Making and Mobility in Mid-Nineteenth-Century Australasia." *History Australia* 11, no. 2 (2014): 38–59.

Blake, N. M. and R. L. Kirk. "Widespread Distribution of Variant Forms of Carbonic Anhydrase in Australian Aboriginals." *Medical Journal of Australia* 1 (1978): 183–185.

Bonnell, Andrew G. "Did They Read Marx? Marx Reception and Social Democratic Party Members in Imperial Germany, 1890-1914." *Australian Journal of Politics & History*, 48, no. 1 (2002): 4–15.

Bonnell, Andrew G. "From Saxony to South Brisbane: the German-Australian socialist Hugo Kunze." In *Labour History and its People*, edited by Melanie Nolan, 299–309. The 12th Biennial National Labour History Conference, Australian National University, 15–17 September 2011, Australian Society for the Study of Labour History, Canberra Region Branch and National Centre of Biography, Australian National University, Canberra, 2011.

Bonnell, Andrew G. "Transnational Socialists? German Social Democrats in Australia before 1914." *Itinerario* 37, no. 1 (April 2013): 101–113.

Browne, Donald. *Ethnic Minorities, Electronic Media and the Public Sphere: A comparative study.* Cresskill, NJ: Hampton Press, 2005.

Browne, D. and E. Uribe-Jongbloed. "Introduction: ethnic/linguistic minority media-what their history reveals, how scholars have studies them and what might ask next." In *Minority Languages and Social Media: Participation, Policy and Perspectives,* edited by E. Haf Jones and E. Urine-Jongbloed, 1–28. Bristol: Multilingual Matters, 2013.

Brown, Rockell A. "African-American Newspaper Coverage of the AIDS Crisis." In *Race and News: Critical Perspectives,* edited by Christopher P. Campbell, Kim M. LeDuff, Cheryl D, Jenkins, and Rockell A. Brown, 111–136. New York: Routledge, 2012.

Budarick, John. "From marginalization to a voice of our own: African media in Australia." In *Minorities and Media: Producers, industries, audiences,* edited by John Budarick and Gil-Soo Han, 37–57. London: Palgrave Macmillan, 2017.

Budarick, John, and Gil-Soo Han. "Towards a Multi-Ethnic Public Sphere? African-Australian media and minority-majority relations." *Media, Culture and Society* 37, no. 8 (2005): 1254–1265.

Bukhari, Syeda Nayab. "Ethnic Media as Alternative Media for South Asians in Metro Vancouver, Canada: Creating Knowledge, Engagement, Civic and Political Awareness." *Journal of Alternative and Communication Media* 4, no. 3 (2019): 86–98.

Burke, P.F. "ANZ Journal of Surgery: a most hearty collaboration." *ANZ Journal of Surgery* 77, no. 12 (2007): 1038–1044.

Burrows, Elizabeth. "Interrogating and interpreting the mediation of an emerging Australian Aboriginal social movement between 1923 and 1940." *Social Movement Studies* 15, no. 5 (2016): 471–483.

Burt, Elizabeth V. "The Wisconsin Press and Woman Suffrage, 1911–1919: An Analysis of Factors Affecting Coverage by Ten Diverse Newspapers." *Journalism & Mass Communication Quarterly* 73, no. 3 (1996): 620–634.

Cade, John F.J. "Lithium Salts in the Treatment of Psychotic Excitement." *Medical Journal of Australia* 2, no. 36 (1949): 349–352.

Carey, Jane, and Frances Steel. "Introduction: On the Critical Importance of Colonial Formations." *History Australia* 15, no. 3 (2018): 399–412.

Carli, Carlo. 2009. "A community paper for a changing community". In *Il Globo: Fifty years of an Italian newspaper in Australia,* edited by Bruno Mascitelli and Simone Battiston, 96–117. Ballan, Vic.: Connor Court Publishers, 2009.

Carlson, Bronwyn Lee, Lani V. Jones, Michelle Harris, Nelia Quezada and Ryan Frazer. "Trauma, Shared Recognition and Indigenous Resistance on Social Media." *Australasian Journal of Information Systems* 21, (2017): 1–18.

Carpentier, Nico. "Identity, Contingency and Rigidity: The counter-hegemonic constructions of the identity of the media professional." *Journalism* 6, no. 2 (2005): 199–219.

Castles, Stephen. "Italian Migration and Settlement since 1945." In *Australia's Italians: Culture and Community in a Changing Society*, edited by Stephen Castles, Caroline Alcorso, Gaetano Rando, Ellie Vasta, 35–55. North Sydney: Allen & Unwin, 1992.

Caryl, Christian. "Unfinished Business." *Foreign Policy* (June 28, 2010). https://foreignpolicy.com/2010/06/28/unfinished-business-2.

Chalaby, Jean. "Journalism as an Anglo-American Invention: A comparison of the development of French and Anglo-American journalism, 1830s–1920s." *European Journal of Communication* 11, no. 3 (1996): 303–326.

Cocchiaro, Antonio. "The History and the Future of Italo-Australian Associations in South Australia." In *Proceedings: the First Conference on the Impact of Italians in South Australia, 16–17 July 1993*, edited by Desmond O'Connor and Antonio Comin, 67–77, Adelaide: Italian Congress, Italian Discipline The Flinders University of South Australia, 1993.

Colic-Peisker, Val. "A New Era in Australian Multiculturalism? From Working-class 'Ethnics' to a 'Multicultural Middle-class." *International Migration Review* 45, no. 3 (2011): 562–587.

Collins, Jock. "Cappuccino Capitalism: Italian immigrants and Australian business." In *Australia's Italians: Culture and Community in a Changing Society*, edited by Stephen Castles, Caroline Alcorso, Gaetano Rando, Ellie Vasta, 73–84. North Sydney: Allen & Unwin, 1992.

Curthoys, Ann. "'Men of all Nations, except Chinamen': Europeans and Chinese on the Goldfields of New South Wales." In *Gold: Forgotten Histories and Lost Objects of Australia*, edited by Ian McCalman, Alexander Cook and Andrew Reeves, 103–123. Cambridge: Cambridge University Press, 2001.

Damousi, Joy. "An absence of anything masculine: Vida Goldstein and women's public speech." *Victorian Historical Journal* 79, no. 1 (2008): 251–64.

Debray, Régis. "Socialism and Print." *New Left Review* 46 (July/August 2007): 5–28.

Dellios, Alexandra and Eureka Henrich. "Migratory Pasts and Heritage-Making Presents." In *Migrant, Multicultural and Diasporic Heritage: Beyond and Between Borders*, edited by Alexandra Dellios and Eureka Henrich, 1–16. London: Routledge, 2020.

Denoon, Donald. "Remembering Australasia: 2002 Eldershaw Memorial Lecture." *Tasmanian Historical Research Association* 49, no. 4 (December 2002): 225–36.

Deschamps, Bénédicte. "Echi d'Italia. La stampa dell'emigrazione." In *Storia dell'emigrazione italiana. Arrivi*, edited by Piero Bevilacqua, Andreina De Clementi and Emilio Franzina, 313–334. Roma: Donzelli Editore, 2002.

Dewhirst, Catherine. "Collaborating on Whiteness: Representing Italians in Early White Australia." *Journal of Australian Studies* 32, no. 1 (2008): 33–49.

Dewhirst, Catherine. "Colonising Italians: Italian Imperialism and Agricultural 'Colonies' in Australia 1881–1914." *The Journal of Imperial and Commonwealth History* 44, no.1 (2016): 23–47.

Dewhirst, Catherine and Richard Scully. "Australia's Minority Community Printed Press History in Global Context: An Introduction." In *The Transnational Voices of Australia's Migrant and Minority Press*, Palgrave Studies in the History of the Media, edited by Catherine Dewhirst and Richard Scully, 1–17. Cham, Switzerland: Palgrave Macmillan, 2020b.

Dunstan, David. "The Argus: The life, death and remembering of a great Australian newspaper." In *The Argus: The Life and Death of a Great Melbourne Newspaper (1846–1957)*, edited by Muriel Porter, 3–15. Melbourne, Vic.: RMIT Publishing, 2003.

Edwards, Brent. "1959–1969: An early voice of Italians in Australia". In *Il Globo: Fifty years of an Italian newspaper in Australia*, edited by Bruno Mascitelli and Simone Battiston, Ballan, Vic.: Connor Court, 2009.

Everyones 4, no. 192 (23 November 1923).

Faber, David. "The Italian Anarchist press in Australia between the wars." *Italian Historical Society Journal* 17 (2009): 5–11.

Fischer, Nick. "Lacking the will to power? Australian anti-communists 1917–1935." *Journal of Australian Studies* 26, no. 72 (2003): 221–233.

Fisher, Jeremy. "The neglected textbook: Placing educational publishing in Australian in the 21st context." *Script and Print* 36, no. 4 (2012): 200–212.

Fisher, Jeremy. "Sex, Sleaze and Righteous Anger: The Rise and Fall of Gay Magazines and Newspapers in Australia." *Text*, Special Issue 25, 'Australasian Magazines: New Perspectives on Writing and Publishing', (2014): 1–12. http://www.textjournal.com.au/speciss/issue25/Fisher.pdf.

Fisher, Jeremy. "The Writing and Publishing of Australia's First Gay Novel." *Australian Literary Studies* 29 no. 4 (2015): 62–72.

Fitzgerald, John. 'Chinese Australians and the public diplomacy challenge for Australia in the 21st century'. In *Chinese Australians: Politics, Engagement and Resistance*, edited by S. Couchman and K. Bagnall, 267–289. Leiden, Netherlands: Brill, 2015.

Fleras, Augie. "Multicultural media in a post-multicultural Canada? Rethinking integration." *Global Media Journal—Canadian Edition* 8, no. 2 (2015): 25–47.

Fraser, Nancy. "Rethinking the Public Sphere: A contribution to the critique of actually existing democracy." *Social Text* 25, no. 26 (1990): 56–80.

Gabaccia, Donna. "Global Geography of 'Little Italy': Italian Neighbourhoods in Comparative Perspective." *Modern Italy* 11, no.1 (2006): 9–24.

Gans, Herbert. "Deciding What's News." In *Key Readings in Journalism*, edited by Elliot King and Jane L. Chapman, 95–104. New York and London: Routledge, 2012.

Gao, Mobo. "Early Chinese migrants to Australia: a Critique of the Sojourner Narrative on Nineteenth-century Chinese Migration to British Colonies." *Asian Studies Review*, 41, no. 3 (2007): 389–404.

Gardiner, Greg. "Running for Country: Australian Print Media Representation of Indigenous Athletes at the 27th Olympiad." *Journal of Sport and Social Issues,*. 27, no. 3 (2003): 233–260.

Gelbart, Nina Rattner. "Female Journalists." In *A History of Women in the West: III Renaissance and Enlightenment Paradoxes*, edited by Natalie Zemon Davis and Arlette Farge, 420–435. Cambridge, MA, and London, 1993.

Goodall, Heather. "Constructing a Riot Television News and Aborigines." *Media International Australia* 68, no. 1 (1993): 70–77.

Hanitzsch, Thomas, and Tim Vos. "Journalistic roles and the struggle over institutional identity: The discursive constitution of journalism." *Communication Theory* 27 (2017): 115–135.

Hansel, Emil. "Six months in Brisbane." In *Wunderbar Country. Germans Look at Australia, 1850–1914*, edited by Jürgen Tampke, 100–122. Sydney: Hale & Iremonger, 1982.

Hanusch, Folker and Thomas Hanitzsch. "Comparing journalistic Cultures across Nations." *Journalism Studies* 18, no. 5 (2017): 525–535.

Harney, Nicholas. "Italian Diasporas Share the Neighbourhood." *Modern Italy* 11, no.1 (2006a): 3–7.

Harney, Nicholas. "The Politics of Urban Space: Modes of Place-making by Italians in Toronto's Neighbourhoods." *Modern Italy* 11, no.1 (2006b): 25–42.

Heath, Deana. "Literary censorship, imperialism and the White Australia Policy'." In *A History of the Book in Australia: A Nationalised Culture in a Colonised Market*, edited by Lyons Martin and John Arnold, 69–82. St Lucia, Qld: University of Queensland Press, 2002.

Hergenhan, Laurie. "Clem Christesen (1911–2003)." In *Proceedings of The Australian Academy of the Humanities*, edited by B. Bennett, 45–46. Canberra: The Australian Academy of the Humanities, 2003.

Hetherington, Les. "The Sydney French Club, 1885–1893." *The French Australian Review*, no. 58 (Australian Winter 2015): 30–46.

Heywood, Colin. "Society". In *The Nineteenth Century*, edited by T. C. W. Blanning, 47–77. Oxford: Oxford University Press, 2000.

Home, Rod. "Case-study: Science publishing." In *A History of the Book in Australia, 1891–1945: A National Culture in a Colonised Market*, edited by Martyn Lyons and John Arnold, 292–294. St Lucia, Qld: University of Queensland Press, 2001.

Hugo, Graeme. "Patterns and Processes of Italian Settlement in South Australia." In *Proceedings: the First Conference on the Impact of Italians in South Australia, 16–17 July 1993*, edited by Desmond O'Connor and Antonio Comin, 33–66.

Adelaide: Italian Congress, Italian Discipline, The Flinders University of South Australia, 1993.

Husband, Charles. "Minority Ethnic Media as Communities of Practice: professionalism and identity politics in interaction." *Journal of Ethnic and Migration Studies* 31, no. 3 (2005): 461–479.

Il Globo, "Il ponte ideale." November 4, 1959, *Il Globo*. Melbourne: Media Communications, 1959.

Il Globo, "Un esempio da seguire." March 13, 2009, *Il Globo*. Melbourne: Media Communications, 2009a.

Il Globo, "Rete Italia si ridimensiona." August 22, 2019, *Il Globo*. Melbourne: Media Communications, 2009b.

Iuliano, Susanna and Loretta Baldassar. "Deprovincialising Italian Migration Studies: An overview of Australian and Canadian research." *Flinders University Languages Group Online Review* 3, no.3 (2008): 1–16.

Jane, Emma. "'Dude…stop the spread': Antagonism, agonism, and #manspreading on social media." *International Journal of Cultural Studies* 20, no. 5 (2017): 459–475.

Jarlbrink, Johan, and Pelle Snickars. "Cultural heritage as digital noise: nineteenth century newspapers in the digital archive." *Journal of Documentation* 73, no. 6 (2017): 1228–1243.

Jones, Paul. ""A Consequent Gain in the Tempo of Effort': Chinese labour and Chinese industrial activism in Australia, 1941–1945." In *The Past is Before Us*, edited by Greg Patmore, John Shields, and Nikola Balnave (The University of Sydney: Australian Society for the Study of Labour History). http://asslh.econ.usyd.edu.au.

Jones, Paul. "The View from the Edge: Chinese Australians and China, 1890 to 1949." In *East by South: China in the Australasian Imagination*, edited by Charles Ferrall, Paul Millar and Keren Smith, 46–69. Wellington: Victoria University Press, 2005.

Jones, Lancaster. "Italians in the Carlton Area: The Growth of an Ethnic Concentration." *Australian Journal of Politics and History* 10, no.1 (1964): 83–95.

Jordan, Kirrily, Branka Krivokapic-Skoko and Jock Collins. "Immigration and Multicultural Place-making in Rural and Regional Australia." In *Demographic Change in Australia's Rural Landscapes* edited by Gary Luck, Rosemary Black and Digby Race, 259–280. Dordrecht; New York: Springer, 2010.

Juliani, Richard N. "The Italian Community Philadelphia." In *Little Italies in North America*, edited by Robert Harney and Vincenza Scarpaci, 85–104. Toronto: Multicultural Society of Ontario, 1981.

Jupp, James. "Foreword." In *Il Globo: Fifty years of an Italian newspaper in Australia*, edited by Bruno Mascitelli and Simone Battiston. Ballan, Vic.: Connor Court Publishing, 2009.

Kelly, Farley. "Vida Goldstein: Political Woman." In *Double Time: Women in Victoria—150 Years*, edited by Marilyn Lake and Farley Kelly, 167–178. Ringwood, Vic.: Penguin Books, 1985.

Kelly, Katherine E. "Seeing Through Spectacles: The Woman Suffrage Movement and London Newspapers, 1906–13." *European Journal of Women's Studies* 11, no. 3 (2004): 327–353.

Kent, Jacqueline. "Case-study: Beatrice Davis." In *Paper Empires: A History of the Book in Australia 1946–2005*, edited by C. Munro and R. Sheahan-Bright, 177–182. St Lucia, Qld: University of Queensland Press, 2006.

Kiesewetter, Renate. "German-American Labor Press. The *Vorbote* and the *Chicagoer Arbeiter-Zeitung*." In *German Workers' Culture in the United States, 1850 to 1920*, edited by Hartmut Keil, 137–155. Washington DC and London: Smithsonian Institution, 1988.

Kramer, Paul A. "Empires, Exceptions, and Anglo-Saxons: Race and Rule between the British and United States Empires, 1880–1910." *The Journal of American History* 88, no. 4 (2002): 1315–1353.

Kuo, Mei-fen. "The making of a diasporic identity: the case of the Sydney Chinese commercial elite, 1890s–1900s." *Journal of Chinese Overseas* 5, no. 2 (2009): 336–363.

Kuo, Mei-fen. "Confucian heritage, public narratives and community politics of Chinese Australians at the beginning of the 20th century". In *Chinese Australians: Politics, Engagement and Resistance*, edited by Sophie Couchman and Kate Bagnall, 137–173. Boston: Brill, 2015.

Kuo, Mei-fen. "Reframing Chinese labour rights: Chinese unionists, pro-labour societies and the nationalist movement in Melbourne, 1900–10." *Labour History* 113 (2017a): 133–155.

Kuo, Mei-fen. "Jinxin: the remittance trade and enterprising Chinese Australians, 1850–1916." In *Qiaopi Trade and Transnational Networks in the Chinese Diaspora*, edited by Gregor Benton, Hong Liu and Huimei Zhang, 160–178. Abingdon, Oxon, UK: Routledge, 2018.

Kuo, Mei-fen and John Fitzgerlad. "Chinese students in White Australia: state, community, and individual responses to the student visa program, 1920–1925." *Australian Historical Studies* 47, no. 2 (2016): 259–277.

Kramer, Jillian. "Legitimating Fictions': The Rule of Law, the Northern Territory Intervention and the War on Terror". *Law Text Culture* 19 (2015): 12–153.

Lake, Marilyn. "British World or New World? Anglo-Saxonism and Australian Engagement with America." *History Australia* 10, no. 3 (2013): 36–50.

Lee, Jenny. "Clem Cristesen and his Legacy." *Australian Literary Studies* 21, no. 3 (2004): 410–412.

Liu, Hong and Gregor Benton. "The Qiaopi Trade and Its Role in Modern China and the Chinese Diaspora: Toward an Alternative Explanation of "Transnational Capitalism"". *Journal of Asian Studies*, Vol. 75: 3 (2016): 575–594.

Macdonald, John and Leatrice Macdonald. "Italian Migration to Australia: Manifest Functions of Bureaucracy Versus Latent Functions of Informal Networks". *Journal of Social History* 3, no.3 (1970): 249–275.

MacKenzie, Norman. "Vida Goldstein: The Australian Suffragette." *Australian Journal of Politics and History* 6, no. 2 (1960): 190–204.

MacKinnon, Stephen R. "Toward a History of the Chinese Press in the Republican Period." *Modern China* 23, no. 1 (1997): 3–32.

Marshall, B. J., David B. McGechie, Peter A. Rogers and Ross J. Glancy. "Pyloric Campylobacter Infection and Gastroduodenal Disease", *Medical Journal of Australia* 142, 8 (1985): 439–444.

Marshall, B. J., John A. Armstrong, David B. McGechie and Ross J Glancy. "Attempt to fulfil Koch's Postulates for Pyloric Campylobacter." *Medical Journal of Australia* 142, no. 8 (1985): 436–439.

McCosker, Anthony and Amelia Johns. "Productive Provocations: Vitriolic media, spaces of protest and agonistic outrage in the 2011 England riots." *The Fibreculture Journal* 22 (2013): 171–193.

Magarey, Susan. "History, cultural studies, and another look at first-wave feminism in Australia." *Australian Historical Studies* 27, no. 106 (1996): 96–110.

Marin, Luca. "La Federazione Italiani Emigrati e Famiglie (FILEF): un esempio di attivismo tra gli emigranti in Australia dal 1972." In *Per una storia della popolazione italiana nel Novecento*, edited by Alessio Fornasin and Claudio Lorenzini, 77–87. Udine: Forum, 2016.

Marotta, Vince. "The Multicultural, Intercultural and the Transcultural Subject." In *Global Perspectives on the Politics of Multiculturalism in the 21ˢᵗ Century*, edited by Fethi Mansouri and Boulou Ebanda de B'béri 90–102. Hoboken: Taylor & Francis, 2009.

Martin, Jean. "Les débuts du protectorat et la révolte servile de 1891 dans l'île d'Anjouan." *Outre-Mers* 60, no. 218 (1973): 45–85.

Mascitelli, Bruno. "The first 50 years". In *Il Globo: Fifty Years of an Italian newspaper in Australia*, edited by Bruno Mascitelli and Simone Battiston. Ballan, Vic.: Connor Court Publishing, 2009.

Mascitelli, Bruno. "A New Exodus of Italians to Australia?". In *Australia's New Wave of Italian Migration: Paradise or Illusion*, edited by Bruno Mascitelli and Riccardo Armillei, 1–13. North Melbourne, Vic.: Australian Scholarly Publishing, 2017.

Matsaganis, Matthew D., and Viki S. Katz. "How ethnic media producers constitute their communities of practice: An ecological approach." *Journalism* 15, no. 7 (2014): 926–944.

McIntyre, Julie. "Trans-'Imperial Eyes' in the Atlantic on the British Imperial Voyage to Australia, 1787–1791." *History Australia* 15, no. 4 (2018): 1–19.

Mein Smith, Philippa, Peter John Hempenstall, Shaun Goldfinch, Stuart McMillan, and Rosemary Baird. *Remaking the Tasman World*. Edited by Tanya Tremewan. Christchurch, NZ.: Canterbury University Press, 2008.

Mercer, John. "Making the News: Votes for Women and the Mainstream Press." *Media History* 10, no. 3 (2004): 187–199.

Morrison, Elizabeth. "David Syme's role in the rise of the Age." *Victorian Historical Journal* 84, no. 1 (2013): 16–33.

Mouffe, Chantal. "An Agonistic Approach to the Future of Europe." *New Literary History* 43, no. 4 (2012): 629–640.

———. "Deliberative Democracy or Agonistic Pluralism?" *Social Research* 66, no. 3 (1999): 745–758.

Mulraney, Jenni. "When Lovely Woman Stoops to Lobby." *Australian Feminist Studies* 3, no. 7–8 (1988): 94–111.

Nicoll, Fiona. "De-facing *Terra Nullius* and Facing the Public Secret of Indigenous Sovereignty in Australia." *Borderlands* 1, no. 2 (2002): par. 3.

Neilson, Briony. "Settling Scores in New Caledonia and Australia: French Convictism and Settler Legitimacy." *Australian Journal of Politics & History* 64, no. 3 (2018): 391–406.

O'Connor, Desmond and Cosmini-Rose, Daniela. "Pugliesi in Australia: the History and Tradition of the Molfettesi in South Australia." In *Italy's Apulian Migrants: A Historical Resource*, edited by Cristian Talesco, 154–169. Lecce, Italy: Associazione Multiculturale Italo-Australiana, 2011.

O'Connor, Desmond. "The post-war settlement of Italians in South Australia." In *Memories and Identities. Proceedings of the Second Conference on the Impact of Italians in South Australia*, edited by Desmond O'Connor, 57–58. Adelaide: Australian Humanities Press, 2004.

Palombo, Lara. "Racial penal governance in Australia and moments of appearance: disrupting disappearance and visibilizing women on the inside", *Globalizations* (December 12, 2019) https://doi.org/10.1080/14747731.2019.1700047.

Pascoe, Robert. "Place and Community: The Construction of an Italo-Australian Space." In *Australia's Italians: Culture and Community in a Changing Society*, edited by Stephen Castles, Caroline Alcorso, Gaetano Rando, Ellie Vasta, 85–97. North Sydney, Allen & Unwin, 1992.

Pascoe, Robert. "The Italian Press in Australia." In *The Ethnic Press in Australia*, edited by Abe Wade Ata and Colin Ryan, 201–206. Melbourne: Academia Press, 1989.

Pinna, Pietro. "La stampa di emigrazione di 'sinistra' in Europa." *Studi Emigrazione* 46, no. 175 (2009): 653–670.

Portelli, Alessandro. "What Makes Oral History Different." In *The Oral history reader*, edited by Robert Perks and Alistair Thomson, 63–74. London: Routledge, 1998.

Powell, S. R., S. Bolisetty and G. R. Wheaton. "Succimer Therapy for Congenital Lead Poisoning from Maternal Petrol Sniffing." *Medical Journal of Australia* 184, no. 2 (2006): 84–85.

Pozzetta, George "The Mulberry District of New York City: The Years before World War One." In *Little Italies in North America*, edited by Robert Harney and Vincenza Scarpaci, 7–40. Toronto: Multicultural Society of Ontario, 1981.

Prencipe, Lorenzo. "Stampa 'in e di' emigrazione. Informazione nell'ottica della 'formazione'." *Studi Emigrazione* 46, no. 175 (2009): 515–24.

Rando, Gaetano, "I giornali di lingua italiana in Australia." *Studi Emigrazione* 46, no. 175 (2009): 613–22.

Rando, Gaetano. "Aspects of the history of the Italian Language press in Australia 1885–1985." In *Italians in Australia Historical and Social Perspectives*, edited by Gaetano Rando and Michele Arrighi, 197–214. Wollongong NSW, Department of Modern Languages University of Wollongong: 1993.

Rees, Anne. "'Treated like Chinamen': United States Immigration Restriction and White British Subjects." *Journal of Global History* 14, no. 2 (2019): 239–60.

Reynolds, Anne. "Italian Language Print Media in Sydney: A short history of *La Fiamma* newspaper." *Italian Historical Society Journal* 9, no.2 (2001a): 10–13.

Rhook, Nadia. "Affective Counter Networks: Healing, Trade, and Indian Strategies of In/Dependence in Early 'White Melbourne.'" *Journal of Colonialism and Colonial History* 19, no. 2 (2018).

Rickertt, Jeff. "Organising the Revolution by Ballot: Queensland's State Socialists, 1889–1905". *Queensland Journal of Labour History*, no. 11 (September 2010): 9–23.

Reynolds, Anne. "Italian Language Print Media in Sydney: A short history of *La Fiamma* newspaper." *Italian Historical Society Journal* 9, no.2 (2001b): 10–13.

Rhodes, Jane. "Journalism in the New Millennium: What's a feminist to do?" *Feminist Media Studies* 1, no. 1 (2001): 49–53.

Rubino, Antonia. "Multilingualism in the Sydney Landscape: The Italian Impact." In *Multicultural Sydney*, edited by Alice Chik, Phil Benson and Robyn Moloney. London; New York, 2019.

Sanfilippo, Matteo. "Araldi d'Italia? Un quadro degli studi sulla stampa italiana d'emigrazione." *Studi Emigrazione* 46, no. 175 (2009): 678–695.

Schudson, Michael. "The Objectivity Norm in American Journalism." *Journalism* 2, no. 2 (2001): 149–170.

———. "Was There Ever a Public Sphere? If So, When? Reflections on the American Case." In *Habermas and the Public Sphere*, edited by Craig J. Calhoun, 143–163. Cambridge, MA, & London: The MIT Press, 1992.

Sreberny, Annabelle. "'not only, But Also': Mixedness and media." *Journal of Ethnic and Migration Studies* 31, no. 3 (2005): 443–459.

Smith, Philippa Mein. "Retracing Australasia: The History of a British Idea." In *Body and Mind: Historical Essays in Honour of F. B. Smith*, 153–72. Melbourne: Melbourne University Press, 2009.

Steel, Frances. "Anglo-Worlds in Transit: Connections and Frictions across the Pacific*." *Journal of Global History* 11, no. 2 (July 2016): 251–70.

————. "Re-Routing Empire? Steam-Age Circulations and the Making of an Anglo Pacific, c.1850–90." *Australian Historical Studies* 46, no. 3 (2015): 356–73.

Stoler, Ann Laura, and Frederick Cooper. "Between Metropole and Colony: Rethinking a Research Agenda." In *Tensions of Empire: Colonial Cultures in a Bourgeois World*, edited by Ann Laura Stoler and Frederick Cooper. Berkeley: University of California Press, 1997.

Sun, Wanning, John Fitzgerald and Jia Gao. "From multicultural ethnic migrants to the new players of China's public diplomacy: The Chinese in Australia". In *China's Rise and the Chinese Overseas*, edited by B. Wong and C. B. Tan, 55–74. New York: Routledge, 2018.

Thomas, Laurel. "Ronald Richmond Winton OAM, MB BS, FRACP, FRACMA." *Medical Journal of Australia* 181, no.1 (2004): 26.

Van Toorn, Penny. "Indigenous Texts and Narratives." In *The Cambridge Companion to Australian literature*, edited by Elizabeth Webby, 19–49. Melbourne: Cambridge University Press, 2000.

Wakeman Jr., Frederic. "*Hanjian* (Traitor)! Collaboration and Retribution in Wartime Shanghai." In *Becoming Chinese: Passages to Modernity and Beyond*, edited by Wen-hsin Yeh, 298–341. Berkeley: University of California Press, 2000.

Wales, Brennan. "La stampa italiana nell'Australia multiculturale." *Il Veltro* 32, no. 1/2 (1988): 133–136.

Walker, Ian. "The New Universities Colleges Council." *Lucas* n.s., no.1 (Autumn, 2009): 139–161.

Ware, Helen. "Origins of Post-War Immigrants." In *The Australian People: An Encyclopaedia of the Nation, its People and their Origins*, edited by James Jupp, 617–624. North Ryde: Angus and Robertson, 1988.

Webb, Jen. "The Logic of Practice? Art, the Academy and Fish out of Water." *TEXT*, Special Issue no. 14 – Beyond Practice-Led Research, October (2012): 2–3 http://www.textjournal.com.au/speciss/issue14/Webb.pdf.

Westbrook, Johanna, Neroli Sunderland, Victorial Arkinson, Catherine Jones and Jeffrey Braithwaite. "Endemic Unprofessional Behaviour in Health Care: The Mandate for a Change in Approach." *Medical Journal of Australia* 209, no. 9 (2018): 34–38.

Wilson, Alex, Bronwyn Carlson and Acushla Sciascia. "Reterritorializing Social Media: Indigenous People Rise Up." *Australasian Journal of Information Systems* 21 (2017): 1–4.

Wilson Michelle and Pamela Wilson. "Introduction: Indigeneity and Indigenous Media on the Global Stage." In *Global Indigenous Media: Cultures, Poetics, and Politics*, edited by Pamela Wilson and Michelle Stewart, 1–37. London: Duke University Press, 2018.

Wolfe, Patrick. "Structure and Event: Settler Colonialism, Time, and the Question of Genocide." In *Empire, Colony, Genocide: Conquest, Occupation, and Subaltern Resistance in World History*, edited by A. Dirk Moses, 102–132. New York: Berghahn Books, 2008.

Wolfgang, Donsbach. "Journalists and their Professional Identities." In *The Routledge Companion to News and Journalism*, edited by Stuart Allan, 38–48. Abingdon. Oxon: Routledge, 2010.

Yu, Sherry. "The inevitably dialectic nature of ethnic media." *Global Media Journal—Canadian Edition* 8, no. 2 (2015): 133–140.

Zafiropoulos, Mike. "The Ethnic Media in Australia." *BIPR Bulletin* 12 (1994): 28–34.

Zhou, Min and Gregor Benton. "Intra-Asian Chinese Migrations: A Historical Overview." In *Contemporary Chinese Diasporas*, edited by Min Zhou, 1–25. Singapore: Palgrave, 2017.

Zucchi, John. "Ethnicity and Neighbourhoods: Looking Backward, Facing Forward." *Urban History Review* 39, no.1 (2010): 73–79.

THESES

Bergantz, Alexis. "French Connection: The Culture and Politics of Frenchness in Australia, 1890–1914". Doctor of Philosophy thesis. The Australian National University, 2016.

Burrows, Elizabeth. "Writing to be Heard: The Indigenous Print Media's Role in Establishing and Developing an Indigenous Public Sphere". Doctor of Philosophy thesis. Griffith University, 2009.

Emmerson, Mark Joseph. "'Vi er alle Australiere': The Migrant Newspaper *Norden* and its Promotion of Pan-Scandinavian Unity within Australia, 1896–1940." Doctor of Philosophy thesis. University of Southern Queensland, 2015.

Forwood, Naomi. "Les Français En Australie à Travers *Le Courrier Australien* 1892–1901. Analyse Sociologique." Bachelor of Arts Honours thesis. University of Sydney, 1983.

Iuliano, Susanna. "Constructing Italian ethnicity: A comparative study of two Italian language newspapers in Australia and Canada, 1947–1957". Master of Arts thesis. McGill University, Montreal, Canada, 1994.

McDonald, Rowena. "Between a work and a book: Publishers' editing at Angus & Robertson Publishers in Sydney, Australia in the mid twentieth century." Doctor of Philosophy thesis. University of New England, 2013.

Palombo, Lara. "The Racial Camp and the Production of the Political Citizen." Doctor of Philosophy thesis. Macquarie University, 2015.

Simington, Margot. "Australia's Political and Economic Relations with New Caledonia, 1853–1945." Doctor of Philosophy thesis. University of New South Wales, 1978.

Tosco, Amedeo. "Features of early ethnic Italo-Australian newspapers: a case study of L'Italo-Australiano (1885)." Doctor of Philosophy thesis, Centre for Public Culture and Ideas, Griffith University, 2005.

Vonhoff, Rebecca. "Spoken through the Press: German-Australian identity and influence during the Kaiserreich". Doctor of Philosophy thesis. University of Queensland, 2011.

Williams, Shayne T. "Indigenous Values Informing Curriculum and Pedagogical Praxis." Doctor of Philosophy thesis. Deakin University, 2007.

WEBSITES

"Advertise." *Medical Journal of Australia*, https://www.mja.com.au/advertise (accessed April 5, 2021).

Baker, D. W. A. "Archdall, Mervyn (1846–1917)." *Australian Dictionary of Biography*, Canberra: National Centre of Biography, Australian National University, 1979. Accessed August 25, 2014: http://adb.anu.edu.au/biography/archdall-mervyn-5044/text8401.

Bettison, Margaret. "Martel, Ellen Alma (Nellie) (1865–1940)." *Australian Dictionary of Biography*. Canberra: National Centre of Biography, Australian National University, 2005a. Accessed January 25, 2019: http://adb.anu.edu.au/biography/martel-ellen-alma-nellie-13081.

Bettison, Margaret. "Ling, Mary (1865–1943)." *Australian Dictionary of Biography*. Canberra: National Centre of Biography, Australian National University, 2005b. Accessed January 25, 2019: http://adb.anu.edu.au/biography/ling-mary-13048.

Bodi, Leslie. "Püttmann, Hermann (1811–1874)". In *Australian Dictionary of Biography*, Volume 5, Melbourne: Melbourne University Press, 1974.

Budarick, John. "Why the media are to blame for racialising Melbourne's 'African gang' problem." *The Conversation*, August 1, 2018. Accessed February 7, 2020: http://theconversation.com/why-the-media-are-to-blame-for-racialising-melbournes-african-gang-problem-100761.

Calov, W. L., "Armit, Henry William (1870–1930)." *Australian Dictionary of Biography*. Canberra: National Centre of Biography, Australian National University, 1979. Accessed April 3, 2018: http://adb.anu.edu.au/biography/armit-henry-william-5051/text8419.

Cresciani, Gianfranco. "The proletarian migrants: Fascism and Italian Anarchists in Australia", *Radical Tradition: An Australasian History Page*. Accessed January 18, 2020: http://www.takver.com/history/italian.htm.

Cromb, Natalie. "How White Privilege Imposes on Sovereignty", *NITV* June 8, 2017. Accessed February 17, 2020: https://www.sbs.com.au/nitv/article/2017/05/18/how-white-privilege-imposes-sovereignty.

Cromb, Natalie. "Was KAK really cleared of racism?", *Indigenous X*, October 9, 2019. Accessed January 20, 2020: https://indigenousx.com.au/was-kak-really-cleared-of-racism/.

Department of Social Services, Australian Government, *Our Centenary of Suffrage*, July, 2009. Accessed November 11, 2020: https://www.dss.gov.au/our-responsibilities/women/publications-articles/general/our-centenary-of-womens-suffrage.

Gillard, Julia. Speech, House of Representatives, Australian Parliament, October 10, 2012. Accessed July 10, 2020: https://www.youtube.com/watch?v=fCNuPcf8L00.

Italian Historical Society. "Italian migration to Australia (landing page)". Melbourne: COASIT, 1988. http://coasit.com.au/dbtw-wpd/exec/dbt-wpub.dll. Accessed 15 June 2016.

Italian Network, 2016. Italiani all'estero—Giornali Italiano all'estero—Dall'Argentina Zembo (Direttore L'Italiano): "I Quotidiani all'estero stanno scomparendo. La strada della comunicazione globale". http://www.italiannet-work.it/news.aspx?id=35888, viewed 9 September 2019.

Johnston, Elliott. *"Royal Commission into Aboriginal Deaths in Custody National Report"*, Volume 2. Accessed February 20, 2020: http://www.austlii.edu.au/au/other/IndigLRes/rciadic/.

Khiabany, Gholam. "Liberalism in neoliberal times: Dimensions, contradictions, limits." *Open Democracy* (2014). https://www.opendemocracy.net/ourking-dom/gholam-khiabany/new-series-liberalism-in-neoliberal-times-dimensions-contradictions-limit.

KooriHistory.com "Jack Patten, Remembering Jack Patten 1905–1957". Accessed January 30, 2020: http://koorihistory.com/jack-patten/.

Kukolja, Kristina and Lindsey Arkley, "Unwanted Australians: Giovanni Sgrò." *SBS News*, 11 July 2016. https://www.sbs.com.au/news/unwanted-australians-giovanni-sgro

"Le Courrier Australien: le plus ancien journal de langue étrangère en Australie!" *Courrier Australien* (blog), October 24, 2016, https://www.lecourrieraus-tralien.com/le-courrier-australien-le-plus-ancien-des-journaux-franco-australien/.

"Registrant Data. Reporting period: 01 October 2020 to 31 December 2020." *Medical Board of Australia*, https://www.medicalboard.gov.au/news/statis-tics.aspx (accessed April 5, 2021).

Ministero Esteri, "Italiani all'estero". https://www.esteri.it/mae/it/servizi/italiani-all-estero. Accessed 6 October 2019.

National Indigenous Television, "History of NITV", 2015, https://www.sbs.com.au/nitv/article/2015/06/25/history-nitv. Accessed January 28, 2020.

Pennay, Bruce. "The Bonegilla Riot, July 1961: Maintaining favourable Impressions of the Postwar Immigration Program". November 13, 2017.

Accessed 3 February 2020: http://aph.org.au/the-bonegilla-riot-july-1961-maintaining-favourable-impressions-of-the-postwar-immigration-program/.

'Population', Australian Bureau of Statistics, https://www.abs.gov.au/statistics/people/population (accessed April 5, 2021).

SBS News, "Dutton threatens councils over Australia Day date change", November 8, 2018. Accessed January 28, 2020: https://www.sbs.com.au/news/dutton-threatens-councils-over-australia-day-date-change.

Sydney Anglicans. "The unforgettable fire: Burning memories from Barney's." (12 May 2006). Accessed February 4, 2019: https://sydneyanglicans.net/blogs/insight/the_unforgetable_fire_burning_memories_from_barneys.

The Queen's Birthday 1997 Honours (1997, June 9). *Commonwealth of Australia Gazette. Special*, p. 16. Accessed February 5, 2019: http://nla.gov.au/nla.news-article240725442

Tracey, Sue. "Anderson, Selina Sarah (Senie) (1878–1964)." *Australian Dictionary of Biography*. Canberra: National Centre of Biography, Australian National University, 2005. Accessed January 25, 2019: http://adb.anu.edu.au/biography/anderson-selina-sarah-senie-12773/text23043.

Virtual tour, Italian Language media in Leichhardt: *La Fiamma* newspaper and *Rete Italia*, n.d. http://www.virtualtour.com.au/melocco/leichhardt%20-201.6htm, Accessed 22 August 2009.

Watson, Irene. "Why celebrate on the day that marks crimes of colonialism and genocide?" *Indigenous X*, 25 January (2018). Accessed January 20, 2020: https://indigenousx.com.au/irene-watson-why-celebrate-on-the-day-that-marks-crimes-of-colonialism-and-genocide/.

Zongollowicz, Bogumila. "Wroblewski, Charles Adam Marie (1855–1936)." In *Australian Dictionary of Biography*. Canberra: National Centre of Biography, Australian National University. Accessed December 6, 2018. http://adb.anu.edu.au/biography/wroblewski-charles-adam-marie-13258.

OTHERS

Kuo, Mei-fen. "Sydney Chinese press, diaspora capitalism and the White Australia Policy: the case of Percy Lee". In Conference of "Voices of the Australian Migrant and Minority Press: Intercultural, Transnational and Diasporic Contexts", University of Southern Queensland, Toowoomba, 22–23 November 2017b.

Index[1]

[1] Note: Page numbers followed by 'n' refer to notes.